The
Fluttering
Veil

LIBERTY FUND STUDIES ON ECONOMIC LIBERTY

H. B. Acton
The Morals of Markets and Related Essays

James M. Buchanan
What Should Economists Do?

W. H. Hutt
The Keynesian Episode:
A Reassessment

Frank H. Knight
Freedom and Reform:
Essays in Economics and Social Philosophy

Ludwig von Mises
The Theory of Money and Credit

G. Warren Nutter
Political Economy and Freedom:
A Collection of Essays

Benjamin A. Rogge
Can Capitalism Survive?

Vera C. Smith
The Rationale of Central Banking
and the Free Banking Alternative

Leland B. Yeager
The Fluttering Veil:
Essays on Monetary Disequilibrium

LELAND B. YEAGER

The Fluttering Veil

Essays on Monetary Disequilibrium

Leland B. Yeager

Edited and with an Introduction by George Selgin

Liberty Fund
INDIANAPOLIS
1997

This book is published by Liberty Fund, Inc., a foundation established to encourage study of the ideal of a society of free and responsible individuals.

The cuneiform inscription that serves as our logo and as the design motif for our endpapers is the earliest-known written appearance of the word "freedom" (*amagi*), or "liberty." It is taken from a clay document written about 2300 B.C. in the Sumerian city-state of Lagash.

Library of Congress Cataloging-in-Publication Data

Yeager, Leland B.
    The fluttering veil : essays on monetary disequilibrium / by
Leland B. Yeager ; edited and with an introduction by George Selgin.
        p. cm.
    Includes bibliographical references and index.
    ISBN 0-86597-145-5. —ISBN 0-86597-146-3 (pbk.)
    1. Monetary policy. 2. Inflation (Finance) 3. Equilibrium
(Economics) I. Selgin, George A., 1957– . II. Title.
HG230.3.Y43   1997
332.4—dc20   96-20654

Liberty Fund, Inc.
8335 Allison Pointe Trail, Suite 300
Indianapolis, Indiana 46250-1687
(317) 842-0880

Contents

Editor's Note

xi

Introduction: The Significance of Leland Yeager's
Monetary Writings

xiii

Note on the Author

xxi

PART ONE

MONETARY DISEQUILIBRIUM
AND ITS CONSEQUENCES

A Cash-Balance Interpretation
of Depression (1956)

3

Monetarism (1971)

19

The Costs, Sources, and Control
of Inflation (1981)

33

PART TWO

MONETARY MISCONCEPTIONS

Essential Properties of the
Medium of Exchange (1968)

87

What Are Banks? (1978)

111

Individual and Overall Viewpoints
in Monetary Theory (1982)

137

Inflation, Output, and Employment:
Some Clarifications (1982)
163

Money and Credit Confused:
An Appraisal of Economic Doctrine
and Federal Reserve Procedure (1986)
179

PART THREE

**KEYNESIANISM
AND OTHER DIVERSIONS**

The Keynesian Diversion (1973)
199

The Significance of
Monetary Disequilibrium (1986)
217

Injection Effects and
Monetary Intermediation (1990)
253

New Keynesians and Old Monetarists (1991)
281

PART FOUR

**AVOIDING MONETARY
DISEQUILIBRIUM**

Monetary Policy:
Before and After the Freeze (1971)
305

Stable Money and
Free-Market Currencies (1983)
337

A Laissez-Faire Approach
to Monetary Stability (1983)
363

Deregulation and Monetary Reform (1985)
383

CONTENTS

A Real-GNP Dollar (1989)

393

Can Monetary Disequilibrium
Be Eliminated? (1989)

407

Index

427

EDITOR'S NOTE

In preparing this collection, I have made a few minor changes to Professor Yeager's previously published writings. Most of the changes, including the relegation of citations in the text to footnotes, were undertaken to satisfy Liberty Fund's style guidelines. Other changes include the addition of first names of authors mentioned in the text, the spelling out of an acronym or two, the deletion of references to conferences, and the correction of various typographical errors that found their way past earlier editors. In a few very rare instances, with Professor Yeager's permission, I have altered a word or phrase for the sake of clarity. Finally, I have included a new introduction to the chapter "The Costs, Sources, and Control of Inflation," prepared especially for this volume by Professor Yeager.

INTRODUCTION

The Significance of
Leland Yeager's Monetary Writings

Does the success of a capitalist economy depend on the nature of its monetary arrangements? It may surprise readers who are not also economists to learn that, at least according to two influential twentieth-century schools of economic thought, it does not.

The two schools of thought are the Keynesian and the New Classical.[1] Despite their generally disparate views on the proper role of government, economists of both schools share the belief that the quantity and quality of *money* in a capitalist economy is relatively unimportant. On one hand, the post–World War II Keynesian orthodoxy insisted that monetary policy is impotent: changes in the money stock would, by inducing opposite movements in interest rates, promote corresponding changes in the demand for money and therefore leave little scope for monetary policy to influence levels of spending, output, or employment. On the other hand, New Classical theorists reject the Keynesian view that changes in the interest rate serve mainly to clear the money market, and believe that changes in the money stock are direct sources of changes in total spending. However, New Classical theorists also believe that changes in total spending will be mirrored almost perfectly in uniform changes in money prices that leave output and employment unaltered except for occasional random effects. In this view, as in Keynesian caricatures of the "old" classical theory, money is merely a "veil" that ob-

---

1. The term "Keynesian" refers to beliefs of certain followers of John Maynard Keynes (1883–1946), whose thinking dominated macroeconomic thought and policy making in the decades following World War II. According to Keynesians, an economy's rate of employment depends primarily on its level of spending, including government spending. In contrast, New Classical theorists argue that increased private or government spending generally leads to higher prices without stimulating employment. New Classical theorists differ from "old" classical theorists in insisting that random (and hence entirely unpredictable) changes in government spending are the only ones that can possibly influence employment, and then only temporarily.

scures but does not otherwise influence the shape of real economic activity. Consequently, monetary policy "matters" only in the relatively unimportant sense that it determines the path of the "price level."

For more than three decades Leland Yeager, who describes himself as an old-fashioned monetarist and an admirer of Clark Warburton and Milton Friedman, has been engaged in a relentless and often lonely battle against these and related doctrines that deny the importance of money. His efforts have helped to preserve a tradition in monetary theory that goes back at least to David Hume but which also goes in and out (and currently is out) of fashion. Beginning in the 1950s, when (old-style) Keynesian thinking dominated the discourse on economics, Yeager held forth on the preeminent importance of money as a source of economic fluctuations—of booms and depressions—whose influence went far beyond mere changes in interest rates (with consequent changes in money demand, investment, or both) or the price level. Contrary views, according to Yeager, were based on the false assumption that the market for money holdings must always be in equilibrium, an assumption that in turn rested on the failure of many theorists to grapple with and understand the painful, roundabout manner by which any monetary imbalance, or "disequilibrium," must be resolved in real economies.

The reality of monetary disequilibrium, which Yeager sees as the root cause of the business cycle, is especially troublesome to those theorists, including the New Classical theorists, who regard any state of disequilibrium (in which the supply of and demand for one or more goods are unequal) as contradicting the voluntary nature of exchange in a free-market economy. Because no one in a free market is ever *forced* to accept money in trade, all units of money in existence at any moment are held voluntarily. How, then, can a discrepancy between money's supply and demand ever occur? The answer, according to Yeager, arises from money's unique and essential role in a free market, namely, its role as a generally accepted medium of exchange. The medium of exchange is accepted routinely not only by those who intend to hold it as an asset but also by those who *do not* wish to augment their average holdings of money but intend, rather, to exchange it almost immediately for other assets and goods.

A case in point is the borrower from a bank. Though the borrower gladly accepts the proceeds of the loan in the form of money, he or she typically pays interest not to have the money itself but to acquire certain real goods—for example, a house, a car, or working capital. Money is routinely accepted by borrowers only because of the ease with which it can be exchanged for other things that are the real objects of the borrowers' desires. In short, the demand for bank loans or credit is *not* a demand for money per se but is primarily a demand for real goods. Nevertheless, changes in the (nominal) supply of bank loans do typically involve changes in the supply of money. It follows that, at least in the bank loan market, changes in the stock of money can occur independently of prior, equal changes in the public's demand for money holdings, and can give rise to monetary disequilibrium.

Of course, the suggestion that changes in the money supply occur independently of changes in the demand for money does not, by itself, imply any *long-lasting* disequilibrium. Can't price adjustments quickly eliminate temporary imbalances of supply and demand in the market for money holdings, as they do in markets for other assets? Yeager's answer again refers to one of money's special attributes, this one deriving from its conventional role as the unit of account in which prices of other goods are expressed. This attribute of money makes it the one good in a free economy that lacks its own (adjustable) price. The absolute price of money being fixed, its price relative to other goods or assets can be adjusted only by means of adjustments in the money prices of all the other goods. Consequently, a shortage of money requires (in the absence of an appropriate change in the nominal quantity of money) a reduction in prices of goods in general; conversely, a surplus of money requires an increase in prices of goods in general. Insofar as *general* price adjustments are harder to achieve than similar adjustments in any single price, a disequilibrium in the market for money balances is much more likely to persist than a disequilibrium in any other single market.

But why should general price adjustments be particularly hard to achieve? Part of the answer, according to Yeager, is a special coordination problem that is implicit in such adjustments —the fact that they involve what theorists today might call a "network externality." This externality exists because the private benefits to be gained by any one seller from adjusting the prices of his or her products in response to a monetary disequilibrium depend positively on the extent to which other sellers have already adjusted their own prices. Each seller therefore has an incentive to wait for others to go first in making desirable adjustments. As a result, the economy must grope its way slowly toward a new price-level equilibrium. In the meantime, both the price level and *relative* prices continue to be displaced from their ideal, full-equilibrium values—the values they must attain if they are to be accurate guides to entrepreneurial activity.

Episodes of monetary disequilibrium, and long-lasting episodes especially, cannot fail to have serious repercussions. According to the elementary logic of the so-called equation of exchange, any change in either the supply of or the demand for money, to the extent that the change is not immediately and fully reflected in an (equilibrating) change in the price level, will imply changed values of real output and employment. To quote economist John Gurley, "Money is a veil, but when the veil flutters, real output sputters."[2] Moreover, because monetary disequilibrium also involves a distortion of relative prices, its real effects are not limited to mere alterations in *total* quantities of output and employment but also involve qualitative changes in the composition of each, to the detriment of all-around well-being.

All of this suggests that well-designed monetary arrangements and policies are important to the success of any free-market economic system.[3] This point is not, of course, unique to Yeager; indeed, it is a crucial component of the Marxian critique of capitalism. Unlike the Marxists, however, Yeager insists that the defects of exist-

2. John G. Gurley, Review of *A Program for Monetary Stability*, by Milton Friedman, *Review of Economics and Statistics* 43 (August 1961): 308.

3. This does not, by the way, mean that a socialist economy could prosper regardless of its monetary system. On the contrary, I would say (and I think Professor Yeager would agree) that a sound monetary system would be wasted on a largely socialized economy.

ing monetary arrangements in "capitalist" nations are not inherent in capitalism but are alterable consequences of the misguided or mischievous interventions of government.

How, then, can the government of a free capitalistic society responsibly discharge its monetary duties? Yeager's answers to this question have changed considerably over the last twenty years. For example, in the early 1970s he rejected the call of certain "extreme libertarians" to abolish "all government responsibility for money," and argued that the avoidance of monetary disequilibrium by means of a wholly free-market monetary system could occur "only by unbelievable good luck." Part of Yeager's pessimism stemmed, no doubt, from his view that a free-market monetary system would perpetuate the "preposterous" linkage of the medium of exchange and unit of account that has characterized both paper- and commodity-based monetary standards. The separation of monetary functions—that is, the establishment of a unit of account defined independently of any particular medium of exchange, so that some media of exchange might have flexible prices in terms of the unit—has long been and still remains, in Yeager's view, an ultimate desideratum of monetary reform. In his more recent writings, however, Yeager has come to conclude that such a separation of monetary functions can most likely be accomplished in a free-market monetary system in which the sole role of government would be to propose and encourage the use of a particular unit of account. Yeager's change of mind undoubtedly reflects in part the influence of F. A. Hayek and other recent proponents of free choice in currency, whose writings have led him to abandon his earlier belief that money is among the small set of things the government can manage "less badly than unregulated private enterprise."

The writings gathered here are a generous sample—but only a sample—of Yeager's contributions to monetary economics. Only the writings that deal with matters of domestic monetary theory and policy are included. Readers interested in Yeager's views on international monetary affairs will find most of them already gathered in two of his earlier books.[4]

4. See *The International Monetary Mechanism* (New York: Holt, Rinehart & Winston, 1968) and *International Monetary Relations: Theory, History, and Policy*, 2d ed.

The writings are arranged in four parts. Part 1 presents Yeager's "positive" elaborations of the monetary disequilibrium hypothesis in which the real (detrimental) consequences of both deficient and excessive money growth are described. "A Cash-Balance Interpretation of Depression" offers an early monetarist analysis of the consequences of inadequate money growth in an environment of "sticky" prices. The article therefore makes for an interesting comparison with later developments in "disequilibrium" macroeconomics, including recent contributions by self-styled "New Keynesians." "Monetarism" surveys empirical evidence supporting this analysis. Finally, "The Costs, Sources, and Control of Inflation," excerpted from the American Enterprise Institute book *Experiences With Stopping Inflation*, demonstrates Yeager's appreciation of the distorting consequences of *excessive* monetary growth. Yeager's two-sided awareness of the dangers of monetary disequilibrium stands in refreshing contrast to the one-sided awareness of earlier Keynesians (who worried only about deflation) and Austrians (who worried only about inflation).

Part 2 is devoted to what Yeager regards as fundamental misconceptions in modern monetary writings. For example, in "Essential Properties of the Medium of Exchange" Yeager responds to the British Radcliffe Committee Report of 1959, which denied the relevance of conventional monetary aggregates as objects of monetary policy. (Ironically, by the 1980s Yeager felt compelled to admit that "recent and ongoing financial innovations [might have rendered] the very concept of money hopelessly fuzzy," and to confess grave doubts about the practicability of "the familiar monetarist quantity rule" as a basis for monetary policy. He hastened to add, though, that the financial innovations themselves were a response to controls interacting with high and variable rates of inflation that could have been avoided had a money growth rate rule been adopted in the late 1960s.) "What Are Banks?" criticizes the "New View" of James Tobin and others who see banks as pure intermediaries that are

(New York: Harper & Row, 1976). Some of Yeager's additional thoughts on the proper relation between domestic and international monetary policy are offered in "Domestic Stability Versus Exchange-Rate Stability," *Cato Journal* 8 (Fall 1988): 261–77.

incapable of lending to borrowers more than what savers lend to them, and hence incapable of being a source of excessive money in the economy. The remaining essays in part 2 confront errors ranging from monetary fallacies of composition, to the confusion of the "demand for money" with the demand for credit, to the view (attributed to Austrian school economists) that *any* increase in the quantity of money involves distorting "injection effects" and should therefore be avoided.

Part 3 is devoted to Yeager's critical writings on nonmonetarist monetary theories, including Keynesian, New Classical ("Rational Expectations"), and Austrian. What usually is called the Keynesian "revolution" was in Yeager's judgment only a diversion from other, more fruitful avenues of monetary thought. Moreover, the New Classical response to Keynesianism is described as a poor substitute for "old-fashioned" monetarism: the New Classical theorists, unlike the earlier generation of Chicago school writers, rely on the unrealistic Walrasian *tatonnement* view of how prices are determined and thereby rule out the very possibility of monetary disequilibrium. In consequence, they are forced to turn a blind eye to overwhelming evidence of money's role in the business cycle, and instead offer alternative "real" business cycle theories. As for writers of the Austrian school, most, Yeager suggests, have been too quick to downplay the harmful side effects of deflation by focusing almost exclusively on the dangers of excessive money creation, which they exaggerate. Next, Yeager insists that the currently fashionable ideas of so-called New Keynesian economics are neither new nor Keynesian but have been the stock-in-trade of many an old-fashioned monetarist.

Part 4 presents Yeager's still-developing observations on how monetary disequilibrium might be avoided. "Monetary Policy: Before and After the Freeze" spells out Yeager's circa 1971 views on how monetary policy ought to be conducted. In contrast to these early views are Yeager's later, much more radical recommendations calling for a complete withdrawal of government from money and banking. These later recommendations appear in essays, including several written with Robert Greenfield, that have provoked many a critical response, not only from critics of laissez-faire but also from writers who, while agreeing with the desirability of getting government out of the money business, doubt that doing so would lead to the sort of "separated" monetary system envisioned by Yeager and Greenfield.[5] The debate these essays precipitated is still in progress, and its outcome is uncertain. What is certain, though, is that the debate will enhance our understanding of the monetary foundations of a free society—an understanding that already owes a great deal to the writings of Leland Yeager.

GEORGE SELGIN
University of Georgia

5. See George Selgin and Lawrence H. White, "How Would the Invisible Hand Handle Money?" *Journal of Economic Literature* 32 (December 1994): 1718–49; and Selgin and White, "Money and the Invisible Hand: A Correction," *Journal of Economic Literature* 34 (March 1996): 124–25.

NOTE ON THE AUTHOR

Leland Yeager was born on 4 October 1924, in Oak Park, Illinois. He received his A.B. (graduating Phi Beta Kappa) from Oberlin College in 1948, his M.A. from Columbia University in 1949, and his Ph.D. from that same institution in 1952. During World War II Yeager translated Japanese codes for the United States Army. He has since taught at numerous universities, including the University of Virginia, where he is presently Paul Goodloe McIntire Professor of Economics Emeritus, and Auburn University, where he has held the title of Ludwig von Mises Distinguished Professor of Economics since 1985.

PART ONE

MONETARY

DISEQUILIBRIUM

AND ITS

CONSEQUENCES

A Cash-Balance Interpretation of Depression

I
THE CASH-BALANCE APPROACH

The usual account of inflation or depression stresses too much or too little demand for goods and services. It is enlightening to reverse this emphasis by focusing on the demand for and supply of money. The present paper views depression as an excess demand for money, in the sense that people want to hold more money than exists. It views an inflationary boom as an excess supply of money, in the sense that more money exists than people want to hold.

This interpretation has advantages:

1. It provides a unifying framework into which various strands of theory—the saving-investment relation, the alleged Keynesian underemployment equilibrium, the Pigou effect, an interpretation of Say's law, a clarification of the terms "inflation" and "deflation," and the relation between price levels and production-and-employment levels—fit neatly as special aspects. It avoids some pitfalls of partial-equilibrium analysis of individual markets by focusing on the one thing—money—exchanged on all markets.

2. The cash-balance approach achieves this unity by tying macro- and micro-economics together, by handling depression and inflation with the familiar concepts of supply of and demand for a particular thing. In focusing on the cash-balance decisions of individual firms and households, it draws on a leading source of empirical gen-

Reprinted from the *Southern Economic Journal* 22 (April 1956): 438–47, with permission of the University of North Carolina, Chapel Hill, North Carolina 27599.

The author thanks Mr. Norman Lombard and Professor Dudley Dillard for helpful comments on a much earlier and longer draft.

eralizations in economics—economists' "inside" knowledge of human motives and decision making.

3. Viewed as dealing with imbalance between the demand for and supply of money, business-cycle theory sheds some ambitions tending to lead it astray. Actually, there is no more reason to search for one universally valid explanation of such imbalance than there is to search for one universally valid explanation of an excess demand for or excess supply of any ordinary commodity—or for a one-and-only cause of broken legs.

4. An account of the relation between the total money stock and people's efforts to build up, cut, or maintain their cash balances can be presented as a logical translation of the more familiar effective-demand and saving-and-investment theories. Thus nonmonetary theorists will have a hard time showing that the cash-balance approach is wrong, even though they may object to its dragging hidden assumptions about money out into the open.[1]

5. The cash-balance approach helps distinguish between treatment of unemployment due to general deficiency of effective demand and treatment of unemployment due to other troubles. It shows how a policy of price-level stabilization through monetary and fiscal action would coincide with preventing unemployment of the first type while not misusing expansion of demand as an inappropriate weapon against unemployment of the second type.

6. The cash-balance approach need not, surprisingly, presuppose any precise dividing line between money and near-moneys.

II

SAY'S LAW AND MONEY

Say's law, or a crude version of it, rules out general overproduction: an excess supply of some things in relation to the demand for them necessarily constitutes an excess demand for some other things in

---

1. Even ostensibly "nonmonetary" business-cycle theories must, at least tacitly, allow changes in the flow of money. Cf. D. Hamberg, *Business Cycles* (New York: Macmillan, 1951), 193, 216, 217, 220, 372. As Hamberg says on pp. 113–14, and as Gottfried Haberler says in *Prosperity and Depression*, 3d ed. (Geneva: League of Nations, 1941), 101, the acceleration principle cannot dominate the whole economic system rather than just particular sectors unless the money or credit supply is elastic.

4

relation to their supply.[2] This seems an unassailable truism. Apparent overproduction in some industries shows not general overproduction but only disharmony between the relative outputs of various industries and the pattern of consumers' and investors' preferences. Subnormal profit opportunities in some industries must be matched by above-normal profit opportunities elsewhere. *General* depression is impossible.

The catch is this: While an excess supply of some things does necessarily mean an excess demand for others, those other things may, unhappily, be money. If so, depression in some industries no longer entails boom in others. Say's law assumes a peculiar kind of demand for money: people, taken together, are always satisfied with the existing quantity of money and never want to change their total cash balances except to adapt them passively to changes in the total quantity of money available.[3]

Actually, the quantity of money people desire to hold does not always just equal the quantity they possess. Equality of the two is an equilibrium condition, not an identity. Only in what Oscar Lange calls *monetary equilibrium* are they equal.[4] Only then are the total values of goods and labor supplied and demanded equal, so that a deficient demand for some kinds entails an excess demand for others.

Say's law overlooks monetary disequilibrium. If people on the whole are trying to add more money to their total cash balances than is being added to the total money stock (or are trying to maintain their cash balances when the money stock is shrinking), they are trying to sell more goods and labor than are being bought. If people on the whole are unwilling to add as much money to their total cash balances as is being added to the total money stock (or are trying to reduce their cash balances when the money stock is not shrinking), they are trying to buy more goods and labor than are being offered.

The most striking characteristic of depression is not overproduction of some things and underproduction of others but, rather, a

2. Oscar Lange, "Say's Law: A Restatement and Criticism," in *Studies in Mathematical Economics and Econometrics* (In Memory of Henry Schultz), ed. O. Lange and others (Chicago: University of Chicago Press, 1942), 49, 53, 57–58.

3. *Ibid.*, 53.

4. *Ibid.*, 52.

general "buyers' market," in which sellers have special trouble finding people willing to pay money for goods and labor. Even a slight depression shows itself in the price and output statistics of a wide range of consumer-goods and investment-goods industries. Clearly some very general imbalance must exist, involving the one thing—money—traded on *all* markets. In inflation, an opposite kind of monetary imbalance is even more obvious.

III
DEMAND FOR AND SUPPLY OF MONEY

Whether we regard the quantities of money supplied and demanded as stocks or as flows is a matter of convenience rather than of principle.[5] Equilibrium in the stock sense coincides with equilibrium in the flow sense. When people on the whole want to hold exactly the quantity of money in existence, they cannot be wanting to change their cash balances at a rate different from the rate at which this quantity is changing. Similarly, disequilibria in the stock and flow senses coincide. People on the whole cannot keep on trying to adjust their cash balances to equal more or less than the total money supply unless they are at the same time trying to change their cash balances at a rate different from the actual rate of change in the money supply. That is, if people demand cash balances totaling more or less at some particular instant than the existing money supply, then the demanded rate of change in cash balances is infinite (a finite change in zero time). The demanded infinite rate of change in cash balances cannot be equal to any actual rate of change in the money supply.[6]

Households and businesses demand cash balances for what are usually classified as transactions, precautionary, speculative, and in-

5. Edwin Cannan, "The Application of the Theoretical Apparatus of Supply and Demand to Units of Currency," *Economic Journal* 31 (December 1921): 453–54.

6. For another demonstration that excess demand for and excess supply of money in the flow sense coincide, respectively, with excess demand and excess supply in the stock sense, see Don Patinkin, "The Indeterminacy of Absolute Prices in Classical Economic Theory," *Econometrica* 17 (January 1949): 5, 7–9.

vestment motives.[7] Consideration of these motives shows that the total of cash balances demanded tends to be positively associated with the physical volume of transactions paid for in money (which depends in turn on payment practices and other institutional conditions, on the human and business population, and on the level of production or real income) and with the level of prices and wages. Interest rates and expectations of future price levels and business conditions also presumably have some effect on the demand for money. The supply of money can conveniently be regarded at any one moment as a definite quantity, which government and banking operations change over time.

As just implied, the number of money units that people demand to hold in their cash balances varies inversely with the purchasing power, or value, of the unit. (A person wants to hold fewer dollars in America than francs in France.) The similarity between the demands for money and for any ordinary commodity is clear.

For any ordinary commodity, there is some price at which the amounts demanded and supplied would be equal. And so with money: there is some value of the money unit that would equate the amounts demanded and supplied. But—again as is true of any ordinary commodity—the equilibrium value at one particular time might be a *dis*equilibrium value later. Supply and demand schedules are always shifting.

Since the prices of many goods and services are notoriously "sticky," the value of money does not adjust readily enough to keep the amounts of money supplied and demanded always equal as schedules shift. The value of money is often "wrong." Depression is such a disequilibrium: given the existing levels of prices, wages, and interest rates, people are on balance more eager to get money by selling goods and labor than to give up money in buying goods and labor.

This interpretation harmonizes with the Keynesian theory, which attributes a cyclical fall in income to an excess of intended saving over intended investment. The very fact of oversaving implies the existence of some form other than goods in which people can accumu-

7. Albert Gailord Hart, *Money, Debt and Economic Activity* (New York: Prentice-Hall, 1948), 195–208, 523–25.

late savings: if people are trying to save more money than they or others are willing to spend on "real" investment, people on the whole must be trying to acquire larger cash balances than are available in the aggregate. Conversely, if people are trying to spend more money on "real" investment than they or others are willing to save, then people on the whole are trying in vain to reduce their cash balances. (Or, if the money supply is growing, people are demanding additions to their cash balances that are smaller than the additions to the money supply.) It follows that an excess of intended saving over intended investment *is* an excess demand for money and that an excess of intended investment over intended saving *is* an excess supply of money.

Decisions about saving and investment are largely decisions about the holding of cash balances. Some factors affecting businessmen's willingness to make investments—price expectations and the state of business "confidence," for example—coincide with factors affecting the amounts of money that businessmen wish to hold. Keynes himself devotes chapter 17 of his *General Theory* to an analysis of the "essential properties" of money which at times make people prefer so strongly to hold money rather than capital goods that investment is insufficient. He explains that the liquidity premium and low carrying cost of money may keep the demand for it from being readily choked off, that the money supply is inexpansible in a depression (apart from official action), and that the elasticity of substitution of other assets for money is slight. Keynes continues:

> The first condition means that demand may be predominantly directed to money, the second that when this occurs labour cannot be employed in producing more money, and the third that there is no mitigation at any point through some other factor being capable, if it is sufficiently cheap, of doing money's duty equally well. The only relief—apart from changes in the marginal efficiency of capital—can come (so long as the propensity towards liquidity is unchanged) from an increase in the quantity of money, or—which is formally the same thing—a rise in the value of money which enables a given quantity to provide increased money-services. . . .
>
> Unemployment develops, that is to say, because people want the moon;—men cannot be employed when the object of desire

(*i.e.* money) is something which cannot be produced and the demand for which cannot be readily choked off. There is no remedy but to persuade the public that green cheese is practically the same thing and to have a green cheese factory (*i.e.* a central bank) under public control.[8]

In the Keynesian theory, intended saving and intended investment are made equal by fluctuations not so much in interest rates as in income. Excess intended saving cuts income until intended saving falls to the level of intended investment. The cash-balance theory accounts for something equivalent. Excess demand for money means deficient demand for goods and labor, which brings on cutbacks in production and employment. The resulting drop in income reduces the demand for cash balances on account of the transactions motive and probably on account of other motives also.[9] When poverty had cut the total quantity of money demanded down to the quantity in existence, it would no longer be strictly correct, I suppose, to speak of an excess demand for money. The excess demand would be virtual, not actual. Poverty would be suppressing it. The situation would correspond to the somewhat misnamed Keynesian "underemployment equilibrium," in which excess intended saving is being suppressed by the low level of income.

In this situation, any monetary expansion would begin to replace poverty as the means of working off an actual excess demand for money. So would any fall or further fall in prices and wages—at least, so says the theory of the Pigou effect.[10] While stickily *falling* prices and wages are a symptom of an excess demand for money, a suffi-

8. John Maynard Keynes, *The General Theory of Employment, Interest and Money* (New York: Harcourt Brace Jovanovich, 1936), 234–35. For an enlightening interpretation of Keynes's chapter 17, see Abba P. Lerner, "The Essential Properties of Interest and Money," *Quarterly Journal of Economics* 66 (May 1952): 172–93.

9. Emil Küng, *Die Selbstregulierung der Zahlungsbilanz* (St. Gallen: Fehr, 1948), 50–51. J. M. Keynes also recognized that a drop in income would lessen the quantity of money demanded on account of the transactions motive. However, his main emphasis (which to my mind is mistaken) was on how this effect lowers the interest rate and so stimulates investment. "The General Theory of Employment," *Quarterly Journal of Economics* 51 (February 1937): 218.

10. See, for example, A. C. Pigou, "Economic Progress in a Stable Environment," *Economica*, n.s. 14 (August 1947): 180–88. Surprisingly, Keynes himself hints at the Pigou effect in his passages quoted above.

cient *fall* in prices and wages would be a cure. Homeopathy could conceivably work. A rise in the value of money would tend to cut the number of money units demanded and so stimulate spending. Whether reliance on the Pigou effect is a *practical* road out of depression, however, requires some comment later.

The concept of stickiness in the value of money as an obstacle to restoring monetary equilibrium brings out a direct contrast between depression and suppressed inflation. A. P. Lerner has emphasized this contrast by renaming suppressed inflation "suppression."[11] Suppression is the condition of a "sellers' market," general shortages, and impairment of allocation by prices that develops when prices are kept from fully adjusting to monetary inflation. Depression is the opposite condition that develops when prices are kept from fully adjusting to monetary deflation. As Lerner shrewdly remarks, depression is the name for (monetary) deflation with prices kept from falling.

Now we can understand the paradox that either "deflation" or "inflation" would cure depression, and that either "inflation" or "deflation" would cure suppression. The kind of deflation that would cure depression is *price-and-wage* deflation—a big enough rise in the value of money to cut the quantity of money demanded down to the quantity in existence. The kind of inflation that would cure depression is *monetary* inflation—a big enough increase in the money supply (or fall in the demand schedule for cash balances) to relieve the excess demand.

The kind of inflation that would cure suppression is price-and-wage inflation—a big enough fall in the value of money to raise the quantity of money demanded up to the quantity in existence. Here is the sense in the quip that the best cure for (suppressed) inflation is inflation. The kind of deflation that would cure suppression is monetary deflation—a big enough cut in the money supply (or rise in the demand schedule for cash balances) to wipe out the excess supply. (Confusion between price-and-wage and monetary "inflation" and "deflation" has sometimes bedeviled theory and policy. The National Recovery Administration, with its price-raising codes

11. "The Inflationary Process: Some Theoretical Aspects," *Review of Economic Statistics* 31 (August 1949): 195.

of "fair competition," seems to have been an example. In the absence of sufficient monetary inflation, price-and-wage *de*flation is a better treatment for depression than price-and-wage *in*flation.)

One more paradox is now understandable. Depression could conceivably be prevented either by maintaining wages and prices or—barring transitional difficulties—by cutting wages and prices. Wage-price maintenance would be salutary only if accomplished by just enough monetary expansion to avoid an excess demand for money and the symptomatic sticky sag in wages and prices. But barring monetary action, swift reduction of wages and prices to a new equilibrium level would be needed to forestall the excess demand for money that, as we are supposing, would otherwise persist.

Returning to the question whether the Pigou effect is a practical depression cure, we must first note the problem posed by a money supply made up mainly of private debt. Encouragement to money holders through a rise in the real value of their cash balances would be largely offset by discouragement to private money issuers, even though the existence of some commodity money or government-issued money suffices, in principle, for the Pigou effect to work.[12] A second difficulty stems from perverse shrinkage of the money supply, so well emphasized by advocates of 100 percent reserve banking. Third, prices and wages will not in practice go down readily enough for a prompt Pigou effect; and besides, since prices and wages are not all equally flexible or inflexible, a major change in their general level would distort the structure of *relative* prices and so transitionally worsen maladjustments in production and trade. Fourth, a sticky downward sag of prices and wages would cause expectations that worsened the excess demand for money in the meanwhile. Fifth, even if prices and wages could somehow fall suddenly and completely enough to forestall such expectations, the increased real burden of carrying and repaying outstanding debt would discourage business and consumer debtors. (Defaults and so forth would rule out offsetting benefits to creditors, as distinct from holders of actual money.) Sixth, such a rapid change in the purchasing power of

12. Don Patinkin, "Price Flexibility and Full Employment," *American Economic Review* 38 (September 1948): 547–52. Patinkin stresses also the rise in the real value of government securities.

money would subvert money's usefulness as a standard of value. Seventh, inertia would add to transitional difficulties. A person's cash balance is partly a matter of habit and is not adjusted fully and promptly to changes in the value of the money unit. When prices are falling rapidly, people may for a while thus unintentionally hold more purchasing power than usual in money.[13] Finally, fears of default by customers and of demands for early repayment of borrowings, together with worsened chances of borrowing in case of need, tend to increase businessmen's precautionary demands for cash balances when prices are falling. Banks, also, take customers' defaults, bankruptcies, and cash withdrawals as warnings to build up their own liquidity by reducing loans and investments.[14] Even households have reasons for trying to strengthen their cash positions.

Despite all these obstacles, monetary equilibrium would theoretically be restored in the long run at a new and higher value of the money unit; but "in the long run . . ."

The impracticality of waiting for a rise in the value of money to cure an excess demand for it in no way impairs our interpretation of depression as just such an excess demand. Certainly it does not discredit the idea of deliberately managing money to keep its supply and demand always in equilibrium.

IV

NEAR MONEYS

One worry about the cash-balance interpretation of depression arises at first sight. Demand for current output might conceivably be slack in a depression because people preferred to hold liquid assets in general rather than actual money in particular. For instance, could not depression consist in an excess demand for bonds rather than for actual money? No: an excess demand for bonds (or for short-term bills, savings accounts, savings and loan shares, and other interest-

13. In times of inflation, a comparable inertia may worsen the excess supply of money by delaying one's decision to increase one's cash balance. James Harvey Rogers, *The Process of Inflation in France, 1914–1927* (New York: Columbia University Press, 1929), 132, 134, 318–20.

14. Hamberg, *Business Cycles*, 140, 183, 389.

12

bearing obligations to pay money) cannot persist unaccompanied by an excess demand for money itself. Given the prevailing prices, wages, and interest rates, the total value of goods and services that people want to exchange for bonds, directly or indirectly, will not exceed the total value of bonds that people want to exchange for goods and services—that is, people will not want to hold more bonds than exist—unless they also want to hold more money than exists.

The reason can be made clear by supposing, for the sake of argument, that people's preferences do shift away from goods and services and in favor of bonds without also shifting away from goods and services in favor of money. That would mean a shift toward bonds in people's preferences as between bonds and money, which would tend to raise the money prices of outstanding bonds. Bond prices—that is, interest rates—would adjust so as to maintain equilibrium between the desire to hold bonds and the desire to hold money and so prevent an excess demand for bonds relative to goods and services from existing in the absence of a similar excess demand for money. (Bond prices would so rise unless official intervention prevented it. If transactions at prices above the legal maximum were simply forbidden, this very prevention of equilibrium bond prices would be the straightforward explanation of any excess demand for bonds. Such a case would not show that business depressions are typified by an excess demand for bonds but not for money. If, on the other hand, the government used open-market sales to keep bond prices from rising, that very addition to the bond supply and subtraction from the money supply would prevent an excess demand for bonds relative to money and so prevent an excess demand for bonds relative to goods and services in the absence of an excess demand for money relative to goods and services.)

Furthermore, as Hicks's theory of the cost, bother, and risk of security transactions[15] and Keynes's liquidity-preference theory explain, there is some floor below which the interest rate on any particular kind of debt will not go. At this floor rate, the reward for holding bonds is so small that people no longer prefer to hold additional wealth as bonds rather than as cash. Any further strengthening of

15. J. R. Hicks, *Value and Capital*, 2d ed. (Oxford: Oxford University Press, 1946), 163–67.

desires to refrain from buying current output and instead to hold liquid assets must increase the excess demand for actual money along with—or even instead of—the excess demand for bonds.

A rephrasing of this complicated argument is in order. Even if the deficient spending on current output that constitutes a depression is due to an excess demand relative to goods and services for money-plus-bonds rather than for money alone, we may properly focus attention on the excess demand for money. Whatever else may characterize it, a depression must involve an excess demand for money; an excess demand for bonds could not exist alone. People could not behave in a way that would tend (barring price stickiness) to raise the purchasing power of the dollars in which bonds are expressed and yet not also tend to raise the purchasing power of the dollars in which checking accounts and currency are expressed. Furthermore, money is a very good substitute for bonds in satisfying the demand for liquid assets. When bond prices have been bid up to where bonds yield no more interest than the floor rate explained by Keynes and Hicks, then money proper is a perfect substitute for bonds. Anything that would tend to relieve the excess demand for money proper would also tend to relieve the excess demand for liquid assets in general and so would tend to relieve the deficiency in spending on current output.

Even more obviously, depression is not an excess demand for shares of stock in preference to both bonds and money as well as to current output. Actually, the demand for stocks depends on profit or dividend prospects, which are poorer than usual in depression. If depression were an excess demand for stocks and not for money, then the money prices of stocks would tend to rise. This, of course, is the reverse of what actually happens in depressions.

Depression certainly cannot be explained as an excess demand for nonreproducible assets in preference to current output. We know that depressions are not characterized by special eagerness to acquire Old Masters and the like.

In summary, the argument still stands that depression is an excess demand for *money* in preference to current output. The cash-balance interpretation does not depend on any clear dividing line between money and near moneys. If there is an excess demand for money as broadly defined, there must also be an excess demand for money as narrowly defined.

V

POLICY

We have interpreted changes in the general price level as symptoms of the excess demand for money that constitutes a depression and of the excess supply of money that constitutes an inflationary sellers' market. The symptom tends in the long run to be a cure, but only imperfectly. Money management to prevent the symptom would co-incide with management to prevent the disease.

To clinch our understanding of this point, let us visualize a graph measuring the volume of cash balances demanded and supplied along the x-axis and an index of the purchasing power of money along the y-axis. For familiar reasons, the curve showing the demand for money slopes downward from left to right. The supply curve can be regarded as a vertical line. Now, if either schedule shifted in such a way as to cause an excess supply of money at the old level of money's purchasing power, there would be a tendency for the purchasing power to fall. An opposite shift would tend to make the purchasing power rise. Such changes in the value of money would work toward a new equilibrium, but, as explained near the end of section III, only after delay and transitional troubles. If, however, monetary policy always kept adjusting the money supply so as to keep the supply-and-demand intersection at the same level, the value of money would not tend to change. Clearly, then, stability in the value of money is a criterion for continued equality between the quantities of money supplied and demanded. A policy of stabilizing the value of money apparently coincides pretty well with avoiding depressions and inflationary booms.

It does not coincide, however, with a guarantee of permanent full employment. Not all unemployment is due to a general deficiency of effective demand. Some "frictional" unemployment is normal. "Structural" unemployment might prevail if technology and the pattern of consumer demand required use of various factors of produc-

15

tion in fairly rigid proportions: if the factors were in fact available in *other* proportions, some would unavoidably be in excess supply.[16] More plausibly, perhaps, price and wage rigidities might block attainment of the relative price structure needed to make businessmen and consumers choose the production techniques and consumption patterns compatible with full employment. A related difficulty could arise if an autonomous upward push on wages and prices (by union pressure, for instance) kept tending to make the existing money supply inadequate for a full-employment level of business activity. The question would arise whether to "support" a creeping inflation of wages and prices by continually expanding the money supply.

The cash-balance approach, with its emphasis on price-level movements as symptoms of excess demand for or supply of money, makes it clear why money management aimed at price-level stability coincides with preventing unemployment due to general lack of effective demand while not overdoing monetary expansion in a futile attempt to cure the kinds of unemployment that require other treatment.

A possible objection to monetary stabilization is that price-level changes could be measured in many different ways; nobody could say just how much the value of money had changed over a certain period, or even, perhaps, whether the value had gone up or down or held steady. Granting all this, there is still a great difference between a clear change in the value of money as shown by *any* reasonable indicator and, on the other hand, real doubt whether the value had risen or fallen. Maintenance of such doubt would be consistent with successful stabilization and would coincide with avoiding any considerable disequilibrium.

One qualification should be made. Constancy in the value of money indicates continued equilibrium only if individual prices and wages are flexible enough so that disequilibrium *would* show itself in a price-level movement. If incipient price-level changes are to give signals for necessary adjustments in a tentatively chosen rate of

16. Masao Fukuoka, "Full Employment and Constant Coefficients of Production," *Quarterly Journal of Economics* 69 (February 1955): 23–44. For a broader discussion of nonmonetary unemployment, see Lloyd W. Mints, *Monetary Policy for a Competitive Society* (New York: McGraw-Hill, 1950), 15–28.

money-supply growth, then individual prices and wages must be free. Ceilings and floors on individual prices and wages bring to mind Wilhelm Röpke's aphorism, "The more stabilization, the less stability."[17] Röpke's wise insight calls for overall stabilization measures rather than for myriad special interventions.

In short, it is more appropriate for the value of money to be stable than sticky.[18] Stickiness in the value of money is poor responsiveness to forces trying to change it; stability is steadiness through avoidance of forces trying to change it.[19]

This paper says nothing about *how* the quantity of money might best be regulated. Nothing said here necessarily provides a case for (or against) traditional monetary policy proper in preference to regulating the money supply through government budget surpluses and deficits. The cash-balance approach does, however, clarify the case for deliberately regulating the money supply somehow. An understanding of this case should help overcome superstitious qualms about creating money outright to pay for deliberate anti-depression open-market operations or government budget deficits.

17. *Die Lehre von der Wirtschaft*, 4th ed. (Erlenbach-Zürich: Eugen Rentsch, 1946), 268.

18. A. P. Lerner makes a suggestive distinction between stickiness and stability of an ordinary price; see "Essential Properties of Interest and Money," 186.

19. George L. Bach has argued that stabilization of a flexible price level coincides with antidepression and anti-inflation policy: "Monetary-Fiscal Policy, Debt Policy, and the Price Level," *American Economic Review* 37 (May 1947): 232, 236.

Monetarism

A monetarist is an economist convinced by the evidence that the quantity of money and changes in it dominate the total flow of spending in an economy. The government budget and so-called real factors in the economy, including investment incentives, are distinctly subordinate influences when not paralleled by behavior of the money supply. The budget and the real factors are very important, to be sure, in affecting how resources are allocated to the production of various kinds of public and private goods and services; but they are unimportant, in comparison with money, in determining total spending. The monetarist position does recognize that things besides money can have some influence on spending. The view attributed to monetarists that "only money matters" is a straw man invented by critics. The monetarist view of what determines total spending is, rather, that "money matters most."

SUPPORTING EVIDENCE

One kind of monetarist evidence is the fact that throughout recorded history no substantial price inflations have occurred without substantial increases in the money supply in relation to physical output. As for changes in the opposite direction, all depressions and most recessions in United States history have been preceded or accompanied by slowdowns or reversals of money-supply growth. Furthermore, the severity of recession or depression matches the degree of monetary slowdown or shrinkage.

Clark Warburton, joined later by Milton Friedman and Anna J. Schwartz, has compiled abundant evidence. Warburton traces the

Reprinted from the 1971 pamphlet *Monetary Policy and Economic Performance: Views Before and After the Freeze,* with permission of The American Enterprise Institute for Public Policy Research, Washington, D.C. 20036.

evidence back even to the period before American independence. Widespread depression in the American colonies in the late 1760s and early 1770s had been preceded by an act of Parliament in 1764 that prohibited new issues of legal-tender paper money and required the gradual withdrawal of outstanding issues. The business downswing of 1796–97 had been preceded by interruption in the growth of paper-money circulation and bank deposits. In the summer of 1818 the second Bank of the United States, threatened by inability to maintain specie payments, began a severe contraction that brought on a depression lasting about two years. The long depression beginning in 1837 was preceded by monetary disturbances. After several years of great economic expansion fueled by increased gold production, monetary contraction forced by drains of coin from the banks brought on the severe crisis of 1857.[1] Friedman and Schwartz give detailed attention to the period since 1867.[2] They agree with Warburton in attributing the depressions beginning in 1920 and 1929 and the severe recession of 1937 to definite deflationary shifts in policy. Since World War II, the recessions of 1948–49, 1953–54, 1957–58, and 1960–61 are all readily understandable in monetarist terms.

The generally inflationary period since about 1965 offers instructive tests of the monetarist doctrine. A "minirecession" occurred in early 1967, when industrial production sagged and price increases slowed down. Although fiscal policy, as measured by the "full employment deficit" in the government budget, had turned expansionary, money-supply growth had been halted almost completely from May to November 1966. A second test came when the income-tax increase enacted in June 1968 helped swing the full employment budget from a deficit at the annual rate of $15 billion in the second

1. Clark Warburton, "Monetary Disturbances and Business Fluctuations in Two Centuries of American History," in *In Search of a Monetary Constitution*, ed. Leland B. Yeager (Cambridge: Harvard University Press, 1962), 61–93. Besides summarizing his own work, carried out during the years when he almost alone was maintaining and developing the then unfashionable monetarist tradition, Dr. Warburton cites numerous other sources of historical and statistical evidence.

2. Milton Friedman and Anna Jacobson Schwartz, *A Monetary History of the United States, 1867–1960* (Princeton: Princeton University Press, for the National Bureau of Economic Research, 1963).

quarter of 1968 to a surplus of $10.7 billion one year later. Yet the widely expected economic slowdown did not occur, for inflationary money-supply growth had persisted. A third test came in 1969, when forecasters relying on a changed monetary trend were more success-ful than those relying on budget developments. A monetary slow-down beginning early that year produced signs of incipient reces-sion in the second half of the year. This test extended into 1970, when the recession predicted by the monetarists became unmistak-able, even though analysts stressing scheduled tax cuts and a sharp projected rise in business investment spending had looked for a strong economy.[3]

Statistical studies, as well as narrative history, provide evidence for monetarism. Friedman and David Meiselman used United States data for 1897 to 1958 to investigate which is more closely associated with the level of consumption and its changes—the quantity of money or "autonomous expenditures."[4] Autonomous expenditures are those that are supposedly multiplied into total income by the Keynesian "multiplier," that is, investment spending and such ele-ments of "honorary investment" as the government budget deficit and the foreign-trade surplus. Friedman and Meiselman took con-sumption rather than total income as the variable to be explained in order to avoid the mistake of correlating income with a large part of itself, as autonomous expenditures (along with consumption) are. They fitted several different single equations, each using as explana-tory variables one or more of the following: autonomous expendi-tures, the money supply, and a price index. For the period as a whole and for all subperiods except the decade of the Great Depression (when Keynes worked out his theory), consumption proved to be much more closely associated with the quantity of money than with autonomous expenditures. Furthermore, coefficients of partial cor-relation suggested that even the slight relation found between con-

3. Beryl W. Sprinkel surveys these tests of recent experience in *Money and Mar-kets* (Homewood, Ill.: Irwin, 1971). His book also summarizes most of the statistical studies mentioned in this chapter.

4. Milton Friedman and David Meiselman, "The Relative Stability of Monetary Velocity and the Investment Multiplier in the United States, 1897–1958," in *Stabili-zation Policies* (Englewood Cliffs, N.J.: Prentice-Hall, for the Commission on Money and Credit, 1963), 165–268.

sumption and autonomous expenditures reflected the influence of money in disguise.

This result, so unexpectedly favorable to the quantity theory and adverse to Keynesianism and its "multiplier" concept, spawned a vast critical literature.[5] Perhaps the most prominent strand of criticism centered on the concept of autonomous expenditures employed (which, to repeat, includes not only investment but other types of spending that resemble investment in supposedly being more the determinants than the resultants of income and consumption). Some other definition of autonomous expenditures might have yielded results more favorable to Keynesianism. Friedman and Meiselman could reply that they had honestly tried to choose a concept of autonomous expenditures promising on both theoretical and statistical grounds to correspond well with the Keynesian multiplicand and that any blame for the uncertainty of its definition should fall on the Keynesian writers, anyway, rather than on themselves. Another strand of criticism urged that to fit single equations and compare correlation and regression coefficients was an illegitimate oversimplification; tests of more elaborate theoretical formulations might turn out relatively less favorable to the quantity theory. Admittedly, if calculations like those of Friedman and Meiselman were the only kind of evidence supporting monetarism, they would not carry much conviction. They are meaningful, though, in the context of all the other evidence, historical and statistical.

One further comment about this approach seems warranted. Even if consumption should have proved to be more closely associated with autonomous expenditures than with money, contrary to what Friedman and Meiselman in fact found, it is far from obvious that Keynesianism would have been vindicated and the quantity theory discredited. Since autonomous expenditures and consumption are both components of total income, it should not have been surprising if their levels should have been closely associated with each other as the level of their approximate total fluctuated over time. Such an association would not necessarily have proved that one

5. This literature is conveniently cited and sympathetically summarized in Stephanie K. Edge, "The Relative Stability of Monetary Velocity and the Investment Multiplier," *Australian Economic Papers* 6 (December 1967): 192–207.

of them was a strategically important determinant of the other or of their total. It would be less interesting than even a somewhat weaker association between one variable and another of which the first is neither a component nor a fellow-component; and the money stock is not, of course, a component of the flow of income.

More generally, it is not obvious why the magnitude most closely associated with some other magnitude deserves overriding attention; it might be neither the most interesting nor the most controllable one. The number of bathers at a beach may correlate more closely with the number of cars parked there than with either the temperature or the price of admission; yet the former correlation might be less interesting or useful than either of the latter. The correlation between either income or consumption and autonomous expenditures might be closer than the correlation between any of them and the quantity of money; yet the one involving the quantity of money, which is the most controllable of the variables mentioned, could be the correlation of most relevance to policy makers.

Leonall C. Andersen and Jerry L. Jordan fitted equations intended to explain quarter-to-quarter changes in gross national product to United States data for the period 1952–68.[6] The coefficients for variables indicative of government budget changes turned out to be less significant than the coefficients for monetary indicators. The authors found no support for the idea that changes in tax receipts due to changes in tax rates exert any influence on aggregate economic activity. An increase in government spending did appear mildly stimulative in the current and the following quarter, but this stimulus was offset in the two following quarters. On the other hand, the expected influences of changes in the money supply and in "high-powered money" were clearly apparent.

Michael W. Keran extended this approach to the longer period 1919–69.[7] For the whole period and for each of several subperiods (except the war years 1939–46), changes in the money stock had larger and quicker impacts on economic activity than did changes in

6. Leonall C. Andersen and Jerry L. Jordan, "Monetary and Fiscal Actions: A Test of Their Relative Importance in Economic Stabilization," Federal Reserve Bank of St. Louis, *Review* (November 1968): 11–24.

7. "Monetary and Fiscal Influences on Economic Activity—The Historical Evidence," Federal Reserve Bank of St. Louis, *Review* (November 1969): 5–24.

federal government spending. Whenever the monetary and fiscal indicators moved in opposite directions, economic activity moved with the former and counter to the latter.

Julius Shiskin integrated the monetarist and leading-indicator analyses of United States business fluctuations.[8] During the period 1920–67 the rate of change in the money supply reached its turn earlier than the index of leading business indicators on all but two occasions (both minor exceptions occurring in the 1920s). The series for government budget surpluses and deficits, on the other hand, did not meet the conditions required to qualify as a leading, coincident, or lagging indicator. It matched only about one-half and led only about one-third of the turning dates in the index of leading business indicators.

Foreign experiences parallel United States experience. Beryl Sprinkel found a close correlation between money-supply growth and growth of gross national product or spending in seven major capitalist countries.[9] Michael Keran looked for monetary and fiscal influences on economic activity since World War II in eight industrial countries besides the United States. For each country the monetary variable appeared, to a statistically significant degree, to have the expected influence. Among countries for which suitable fiscal indicators were available, only for Japan did the indicator show a significant influence of the kind postulated by Keynesian theory; and even for Japan, this fiscal influence appeared weaker than the monetary influence. Each of Japan's postwar business-cycle troughs came after a slowdown of money-supply growth, and each of the recoveries after monetary acceleration.[10]

8. "Economic Policy Indicators and Cyclical Turning Points," *Business Economics* (Long Island University) (September 1970); this article is summarized at length in Sprinkel, *Money and Markets*, 139–41.

9. "Relative Economic Growth Rates and Fiscal-Monetary Policies," *Journal of Political Economy* 71 (April 1963): 154–59.

10. "Monetary and Fiscal Influences on Economic Activity: The Foreign Experience," Federal Reserve Bank of St. Louis, *Review* (February 1970): 16–28. Even experiences of Austria and Russia during the second half of the nineteenth century support the monetarist argument. From 1863 through 1865 efforts to deflate the Austrian paper gulden back to its metallic parity produced a severe depression that lasted until the war of 1866. In the judgment of two modern Austrian economists, the war-related paper-money issues served as a "deliverance for the entire economy"

OPPOSITION TO MONETARISM

As already mentioned in connection with the study by Friedman and Meiselman, the monetarist position and evidence run into strong criticism. Monetarists are sometimes accused of operating with a "black box."[11] They allegedly purport to demonstrate the influence of money almost entirely by statistical manipulations, giving no adequate theoretical explanation of how this influence is supposed to work. It is true, of course, that several prominent monetarist articles rely almost entirely on statistical associations. One can hardly expect the whole monetarist theory to be repeated even in each primarily statistical article.

The monetarist position is basically an extension of classical and neoclassical theories of money and monetary disequilibrium.[12] The

from the preceding deflation and contributed to the "greatest boom in Austrian history." "The experience gained from the severe economic depression in the wake of [Finance Minister] *Plener's* contractionary measures and from the economic upswing after the expansion of the circulation in the year 1866 confirmed in increasing degree, even if at first without adequate scientific basis, the recognition of a farreaching connection between the monetary system and the development of business conditions." Quotations from Alois Gratz, p. 254, and Reinhard Kamitz, p. 147, in their articles in *Hundert Jahre Österreichischer Wirtschaftsentwicklung, 1848–1948*, ed. Hans Mayer (Vienna: Springer, 1949).

The association between monetary and business conditions in Russia is recognized in P. A. Khromov, *.Ekonomicheskoe Razvitie Rossii v XIX–XX Vekakh* (Moscow: Gospolitizdat, 1950), 293–94; A. F. Jakovlev, *.Ekonomicheskie Krizisy v Rossii* (Moscow: Gospolitizdat, 1955), 388–89; A. Shipov, "Kuda i otchego ischezli u nas denigi?" *Vestnik Promyshlennosti* 9, no. 7 (1860) 33–34, quoted in S. G. Strumilin, *Ocherki .Ekonomicheskoj Istorii Rossii* (Moscow: Sots'ekiz, 1960), 479; and Haim Barkai, *Industrialization and Deflation: The Monetary Experience of Tsarist Russia in the Industrialization Era* (Jerusalem: Hebrew University, 1969), 27–28, 44–45. Statistical analysis of relations between money-supply changes and manufacturing production and other indicators of Russian business conditions gives further support to these generalizations.

11. See, for example, "The Keynesian Revolution and the Monetarist Counter-Revolution," a lecture given by Harry Johnson in December 1970 and printed in *American Economic Review* (May 1971): 1–14. Though Johnson does not actually use the term "black box," a newspaper report (Leonard Silk in the *New York Times*, 30 December 1970, 22) does correctly identify his theme with this line of criticism. For a similar criticism of the monetarists' supposed lack of an adequately worked-out theory, see F. H. Hahn, "Professor Friedman's Views on Money," *Economica* (February 1971): 61–80.

12. See Clark Warburton, *Depression, Inflation, and Monetary Policy* (Baltimore: Johns Hopkins University Press, 1966), especially the papers in part 1.

theory explains what happens if people find themselves holding more or less money than they in the aggregate desire to hold at currently prevailing levels of incomes, prices, and asset yields (including interest rates). People behave in the markets for loans, securities, and goods and services in such ways that they become, in the aggregate, more nearly content with the stock of money in existence. Changes in the nominal money values of income and wealth alter desired money holdings until their total amount no longer clearly exceeds or falls short of the money stock. The nominal changes reflect changes in both prices and physical activity, with the physical changes tending to occur sooner. The process of removing a monetary disequilibrium takes time, operating as it does through both direct channels and indirect channels involving interest rates and the relations between the yields and prices of financial and physical assets. Details are different under different institutional arrangements and otherwise different circumstances, but the general nature of the process is far from mysterious.

More specific criticisms assert that observed relations between money and spending are misleading, since monetary changes may merely accompany or even largely *result from* changes in business conditions. During a business boom, strong demands for credit and rising interest rates prod the banks to use their reserves more fully than usual and to pare down any excess of reserves in relation to loans and investments and demand-deposit liabilities. Even the total quantity of bank reserves may respond to business conditions. Booming credit demands and high interest rates, for example, make the banks more eager to borrow reserve funds from the Federal Reserve. During business recessions, conversely, the supply of bank-deposit money tends to shrink almost automatically. This line of criticism blends into the argument (considered more fully later) that various slippages may make it impossible for the Federal Reserve to control the money supply precisely enough. Furthermore, even precise control over the money supply would not mean control over total spending, since velocity varies partly in a random way, partly so as actually to offset money-supply changes. In other words, all sorts of "real" disturbances in the economy cause the aggregate of money balances demanded in relation to income and expenditure to vary in such a way that monetary control is a rubbery lever indeed for controlling total spending. A corollary of this view rejects the prescription of steady moderate growth in the money supply and calls, instead, for an active policy of continually combating the destabilizing influences supposedly inherent in the private sector of the economy. Such a policy of "fine tuning" supposedly requires a variety of fiscal, monetary, and other weapons.[13]

In reply to critics' skepticism about the observed association between changes in money and business conditions, monetarists can point to numerous occasions when monetary changes were clearly

13. Some of these lines of criticism are well illustrated in James Tobin, "Tobin Attacks Friedman's Theories of Money Supply," *Washington Post,* 16 April 1967, G1, G3. The appearance of this criticism in the popular press is characteristic of its nature and of its intended influence on policy. "The notion that the velocity of money is a constant, independent of economic events but related to slowly changing social institutions and habits, is an old one in monetary economics," says Tobin. "It has survived many previous refutations by the facts." Only later does Tobin admit that the monetarists "do not rely on constant velocity." Actually, they merely deny, after careful study, that velocity behaves in the random or offsetting ways mentioned in the text above. Tobin adopts the

> eclectic view . . . that interest rates, credit and equity market conditions, the activities of financial institutions other than commercial banks, etc., are also important. . . . Changes in the private economy itself—in technology, tastes, population, expectations, etc.—are important sources of instability. Blind steadiness in monetary and other Government policies will not stabilize the economy, any more than a fixed rudder setting will hold a ship on a steady course through changing winds and currents. Like a good helmsman, the Government policy-maker must actively try to anticipate and offset the forces pushing him off course.

The monetarist position is not as simple-minded as Tobin portrays it. Of course all sorts of nonmonetary influences affect aggregate demand and economic activity. But recognizing them in principle is not the same thing as knowing how to use them as signals or handles for countercyclical fine tuning of the economy. Recognizing that the world is complicated is not the same as knowing how to succeed with complicated manipulations. Such knowledge would be a great intellectual achievement and probably useful also. The monetarists say, in effect, "Let's not kid ourselves that we have such knowledge when we don't—at least not yet." As Tobin himself concedes, "a poor helmsman can make things worse." Furthermore, Tobin's belief that the factors he mentions are important does not clash with the view that the best way to keep them from behaving in a destabilizing manner is to preserve a stable monetary environment. Velocity, for example, admittedly is likely to move in the short run counter to a sudden speedup or slowdown in money-supply growth. As with certain other consequences of money-supply change, the immediate or impact effect is likely to be the opposite of the longer-run effect. In fact, as theory and experience both testify, a *sustained* change in the money-supply growth rate is likely to entail a change in velocity that reinforces the effect on spending.

caused by outside changes (such as balance-of-payments or policy developments) other than business prosperity or depression. Phillip Cagan has investigated to what extent monetary changes in the United States have resulted from changes in output or prices. Since long-run changes in the stock of ordinary money trace mainly to changes in "high-powered money," causation running from prices to money should work through the stock of high-powered money. Yet price changes have little scope for affecting the latter's nongold components, and in fact they should affect the Federal Reserve components inversely if stabilization is the goal of policy. As for gold-based additions to high-powered money, any influence of prices works inversely and with a lag, since price inflation tends to discourage gold production and price deflation to encourage it. As for the shorter-run association observed between money and business fluctuations, Cagan stressed how this association has persisted despite far-reaching changes occurring since 1875 in United States financial institutions and markets; this persistence squares poorly with the idea of money as the passive partner in the relation.[14]

Nonmonetarists exaggerate the difficulties that monetary authorities would run into if control of the money supply were made their explicit duty.[15] One set of reasons is easy to conjecture. Most people, or at least most bureaucrats, hardly want their duties and their performance made susceptible of precise specification and measurement. East Europeans should be able to appreciate why the managers of organizations not primarily oriented to profit should prefer to have vague or easy assignments, or plans, and why they should value flexibility in what success indicators to emphasize as they strive to seem to be doing a good job. In comparison with the tasks assigned to Federal Reserve officials and to socialist managers

14. *Determinants and Effects of Changes in the Stock of Money, 1875–1960* (New York: National Bureau of Economic Research, 1965). Michael Keran, in "Monetary and Fiscal Influences on Economic Activity," 19–22, reached similar conclusions on the basis of data for 1919–69: movements in the money stock have been dominated by the behavior of the monetary authorities and not by the behavior of the public.

15. On the feasibility of money-supply control, see, *inter alia*, Allan H. Meltzer, "Controlling Money," Federal Reserve Bank of St. Louis, *Review* (May 1969): 16–24.

and planners alike, the task of managers in capitalist business firms—to earn profits—is a clear-cut assignment indeed.

Understandably, then, it is more comforting to central bankers to think of their work as an art rather than as a science or technology. They can find support in the fact that most or many academic economists have not (or not yet) become converts to monetarism. They watch many indicators concerning not only bank reserves and money but also credit conditions and general economic conditions. They prefer to formulate goals and make judgments based on their own expert feel for the meaning and relative significance of all relevant information. By not pursuing specific targets for anything and by being free to choose among a variety of policy targets and instruments and indicators, they can seem to take account of everything. They have maximum opportunity to shift their emphasis from one variable to another as insight or hindsight recommends.[16] Federal Reserve officials naturally cherish the view that their decisions integrate a vast body of information and judgments continually being obtained from hundreds and thousands of experts in all parts of the United States. But if their assigned task were simplified and were specified more narrowly, their existing large organization and staff might seem superfluous. Furthermore, acceptance of monetarist doctrine would entail recognition of several major blunders in the past. Understandably, they welcome agreement with their own suggestions that their tasks are terribly complicated and require ineffable expertise. Not surprisingly, several prominent antimonetarist articles, including ones suggesting why close control over the money supply might be an impossible assignment, have appeared under official inspiration or auspices.[17]

16. For this view of bureaucratic motives, see Milton Friedman, "Should There Be an Independent Monetary Authority?" in *In Search of a Monetary Constitution*, ed. Yeager, esp. 233–34; and, in particular, John M. Culbertson, *Macroeconomic Theory and Stabilization Policy* (New York: McGraw-Hill, 1968), esp. 431–60. Significantly, Culbertson served seven years as a Federal Reserve economist before returning to academic work. His insights have influenced several of my remarks in the present paper.

17. Some key difficulties supposedly hinge on interaction between the money-supply function and the public's demand for cash balances and on instability of bank reserves available to support demand deposits because of shifts by the public between demand and time deposits. See, for example, Lyle E. Gramley and Samuel

TIGHTENING LOOSE LINKS

The looseness of the links between Federal Reserve actions and money-supply behavior is not only exaggerated but also largely remediable. By giving predominant attention to the money supply and its underlying determinants (high-powered money or bank reserves) and aiming at their steady moderate growth, the Federal Reserve could do much to avoid shaking the links loose. Two of the most-mentioned loose links are changes over the business cycle (in response to interest rate and other changes) in the banks' holdings of so-called excess reserves in relation to deposits and in the public's holdings of currency in relation to deposits. Since business spurts and slumps themselves largely trace to monetary instability, greater steadiness of monetary policy would also improve its precision.

Certain easy institutional reforms would also help. Abolishing time-deposit interest-rate ceilings would go far toward eliminating major shifts in the public's holdings of time deposits relative to demand deposits and currency. Reserve requirements might well be applied uniformly to all commercial banks in the United States and not just to members of the Federal Reserve system. Closing the "discount window" would deprive banks of the opportunity to borrow and repay loans there, actions that make reserve funds come into and go out of existence at the initiative of the banks rather than of the Federal Reserve.

Greater steadiness and greater precision in monetary policy would not only reinforce each other but would also go far toward reducing the fluctuations in velocity of which antimonetarists make

B. Chase, Jr., "Time Deposits in Monetary Analysis," and John H. Kareken, "Commercial Banks and the Supply of Money: A Market-Determined Demand Deposit Rate," in *Federal Reserve Bulletin* (October 1965): 1380–1406, and (October 1967): 1699–1712, respectively. Both these articles reflect the vaunted "New View" in monetary economics presented by James Tobin in "Commercial Banks as Creators of 'Money,' " in *Banking and Monetary Studies*, ed. D. Carson (Homewood, Ill.: Irwin, 1963), 408–19.

Karl Brunner aptly criticizes these and related antimonetarist articles in "The Role of Money and Monetary Policy," Federal Reserve Bank of St. Louis, *Review* (July 1968): 9–24. It should be explained that the St. Louis bank is a maverick—a subversive cell—within the Federal Reserve system.

so much. These fluctuations, especially as they occur over the business cycle, trace largely to unstable money growth.

Greater monetary stability would also ease the unemployment-or-inflation (Phillips curve) dilemma: it would help avoid "demand-shift inflation" so far as this results from cyclical shifts in demand between the consumer-goods and capital-goods industries and between storable goods and nonstorable goods and services; it would avoid the rise in overhead costs per unit of output that occurs when production falls off in recessions; by promoting price-level stability, it would facilitate relative price comparisons and thus favor price competition; it would favor the mutual adaptation of jobs and labor skills; it would favor the mobility of labor and the willingness of business firms to bear the risks of competition, innovation, and capital investment; and it would avoid wasting the willingness to bear risks on the risks of shifts in monetary policy. Economic performance would clearly improve.

The Costs, Sources, and Control of Inflation

INTRODUCTION

In 1984 I had to decide whether to remain at the University of Virginia or move to Auburn University. Considerations of different kinds were pulling in each direction with apparently almost equal total weights. One further consideration favoring the move was the prospect of rising inflation in the United States as chronic government budget deficits kept increasing the government debt and threatening eventual debt monetization. Incurring a large dollar-denominated debt seemed to be wise portfolio diversification as an inflation hedge. The move to Auburn, where I would buy a bigger house than I would otherwise want, would provide the opportunity to incur a large mortgage debt.

The house in Auburn has proved more expensive and caused worse headaches even than I had expected, and second thoughts about a major career move are bound to surface occasionally. The threatened great speedup of inflation has not yet occurred, although its prospect remains. As a monetarist rather than a Keynesian, I never supposed that government deficits are inflationary in themselves; I understood all along that deficit-related inflation hinges on debt monetization. The timing of debt monetization (or conceivably, on the other hand, even an end to the government deficits themselves) depends largely on political considerations, in assessing and predicting which an economist has no special skill.

Admittedly, then, I have guessed wrong about just when inflation would speed up. Now that I am approaching retirement and an age

Reprinted from the 1981 pamphlet *Experiences With Stopping Inflation*, 2–44, with permission of The American Enterprise Institute for Public Policy Research, Washington, D.C. 20036.

at which the burdens of a large house are intolerable, I still must try to plan with a view to future inflation. Portfolio diversification through mortgage debt will not remain a feasible part of my plans much longer. Protecting one's savings against inflation is no simple matter.

Experiences like this contradict complacency about the costs of inflation. Theories about how people can make suitable allowances for inflation illegitimately assume that people know its future rate or at least the probability distribution of its future rates. Theories about the small costs of inflation rely on *assuming away* its costliest aspects. Such theories are empty, for anything at all has only slight costs if its really costly aspects are assumed away. As Arthur Okun used to emphasize, steady and easily allowed for inflation is a myth. Inflation and the policies that breed or threaten it add grievously to the inherent unpredictability of the future. An environment of actual or potential inflation contrasts sharply with an environment of dependably stable money.

Yet cut-and-dried measures of the costs of inflation are almost bound to miss costs like the burdens of an inappropriate house and occasional regrets about a possibly mistaken move. After all, construction and repair services, household and yard services, financial services, transportation and communication services, and other goods continue being produced, and without obvious inefficiency. Lost satisfactions and personal anguish—subjective inefficiencies of various kinds—escape the attention of econometricians. Writers who trivialize the costs of inflation into only the most readily measurable ones are deserving targets of indignation.

THE COSTS OF INFLATION

The costs of inflation include those of otherwise unnecessary efforts to economize on holding cash balances. If one takes seriously the idea that business cash balances are a factor of production, then one should be concerned that their holders' reactions to inflation reduce the amount of this factor in real terms. Both capital and labor

are deprived of part of this complementary factor and suffer productivity losses.[1]

Similar points hold for trade credit. A business firm typically is
holding some non-interest-bearing claims on its customers as part of
a regular customer-supplier relation that both find advantageous.
When money rates of interest come to reflect substantial rates of inflation, the loss of interest involved in holding trade debt, as in holding money, becomes more serious. It becomes worthwhile to take
more trouble in collecting debts promptly, exerting otherwise unad-
visable pressure on debtors. Such efforts consume labor and other
resources. Since debtors have similar incentives to delay payment,
the loss can be considerable.[2]

Several other costs of inflations, although almost impossible to
quantify, are nevertheless real. Business and personal habits (like the
allocation of a family's housekeeping money) have been based on
the assumption of stable prices and are not easily broken; yet leaving
them unbroken in the face of severe inflation creates obvious distortions. Accounting and tax systems, and even the general legal system, have also been based on the assumption of stable money. Rapid
change in money's value twists them out of shape. Legislation may
put these things right again (for a time) but only by reopening closed
issues and consuming time and energy in political discussions. Notions of fairness are also involved. Prices and wages are "made" in
most markets, not just impersonally "determined" by supply and demand. It helps set prices and wages in a way that seems fair to the
parties concerned if one can appeal to precedent, presuming that
what was acceptable before will be acceptable again. A rapidly changing price level invalidates this approach.

It is sometimes said that mild inflation may facilitate changing
relative wage rates as efficiency may require. This advantage, if real

1. Robert Mundell, "Comment," in *Stabilization Policies in Interdependent Economies,* ed. Emil Claassen and Pascal Salin (New York: American Elsevier, 1972), 62.
On the notion of cash balances as a factor of production, also see Reuben Kessel
and Armen A. Alchian, "Effects of Inflation," *Journal of Political Economy* 70 (December 1962): 521–37.

2. John Hicks, "Expected Inflation," in his *Economic Perspective: Further Essays on
Money and Growth* (Oxford: Clarendon Press, 1977), 116–17 (an extract from an article in *Three Banks Review,* September 1970).

at all, can be significant only at low rates of inflation, for it itself depends on some confidence in the value of money. Inflation at a substantial rate entails loss of time and temper in continually revising institutional and quasi-institutional arrangements, as well as in labor unrest. Such considerations are important not only in the labor market. Any system of prices (say, a system of railway fares) should satisfy hard-to-reconcile canons of both economic efficiency and fairness. A system works more easily if it is allowed to acquire some sanction by custom—if it is not frequently being torn up by the roots. Considerations like these form the principal reason why, in the judgment of J. R. Hicks, any inflation should be held to a modest rate.[3]

Inflation at an extreme rate, although not at a merely intermediate rate, significantly increases the costs of transactions as people try to get rid of money soon after receiving it. An observer of the Austrian scene in the early 1920s noted the costs of constant shopping and queuing and the sacrifice of family time together because of frenetic shopping expeditions. Such costs fell mainly on the humbler elements of society, since servants could be assigned the task of shopping in upper-class households.[4]

Inflation sabotages the transmission of information by prices. Ideally, each price conveys information to the prospective buyer of a good about how much sacrifice of other goods its purchase would entail, as well as information about how attractive an offer each prospective seller is making in comparison with his rivals' offers. Inflation renders such information obsolete or unreliable more quickly. Prices and interest rates are also distorted by the particular ways or channels in which inflationary amounts of new money are injected into the economy. For institutional reasons, some prices are less

3. Ibid., 114–16. On the role of notions of equity in setting prices and especially wages, also see Arthur M. Okun, "An Efficient Strategy to Combat Inflation," *Brookings Bulletin* 15 (Spring 1979): 1–5.

4. Charles S. Maier, "The Politics of Inflation in the Twentieth Century," in *The Political Economy of Inflation*, ed. Fred Hirsch and John H. Goldthorpe (Cambridge: Harvard University Press, 1978), 71 n, citing Ilse Arlt, "Der Einzelhaushalt," in *Geldentwertung und Stabilisierung in ihren Einflüssen auf die soziale Entwicklung in Österreich*, ed. Julius Bunzel, *Schriften des Vereins für Sozialpolitik* 169 (1925). Twenty years later, Maier notes, Michael Kalecki would emphasize this aspect of inequality as an argument for rationing in wartime Britain (Kalecki, "Three Ways to Full Employment," in *Studies in War Economics*, Oxford University Institute of Statistics [Oxford: Blackwell, 1947]).

promptly flexible than others, so that inflation further distorts relative prices. Inflation simply cannot be uniform and predictable. Incorrect price signals and incentives lead to patterns of resource allocation different from those that would otherwise occur. The price system becomes less efficient in responding to consumers' tastes and to objective circumstances and in coordinating economic activity. Even if inflation does not shrink the overall real volume of economic activity, however supposedly measured, it may well reduce the ultimate human satisfactions derived from that total because of changes in its composition.

To mention one obvious, though presumably unimportant, example, resources are diverted into books and periodicals on financial survival in inflation and into expensive investment consultations and seminars. More generally, inflation alters the mix of real economic activity. It reduces the relative rewards of sober activity devoted to improving products or cutting the costs of producing or distributing them; it increases the relative rewards of being a crafty operator—of predicting prices and policies, of cleverly wheeling and dealing, of sizing up the intellects and moral characters of potential trading partners and associates. It also puts a relative premium on trying to protect oneself through political activities, broadly conceived, in contrast with more market-oriented activities.[5]

We have already noted that inflation hampers comparing the offers being made by rival potential trading partners. The German inflation of the 1920s, according to a keen observer, suspended the process of selection of the fittest firms.[6] When people are so anxious to part with their melting money that they do not shop around as carefully as they otherwise would, even sellers of shoddy and overpriced goods will find some customers. Although this erosion of the competitive process of rewarding efficiency and punishing in-

5. Some of these points are developed in Axel Leijonhufvud, "Costs and Consequences of Inflation," in *The Microfoundations of Macroeconomics,* ed. G. C. Harcourt (Boulder: Westview Press, 1977), 265–312. As Milton Friedman says, prudent behavior becomes reckless and reckless behavior, prudent. "Inflation and Unemployment" (Nobel lecture, 29 November 1976), p. 20 of typescript.

6. Costantino Bresciani-Turroni, *The Economics of Inflation* (London: Allen & Unwin, 1937), 391–92.

efficiency is most clearly evident in hyperinflations, it presumably occurs in more moderate degree in more moderate inflations.

Another cost that becomes more evident in extreme inflations, when financial assets have ceased to serve as stores of wealth, involves a resort to commodities, foreign exchange, and real estate instead. The unloading of commodity inventories and foreign-exchange holdings when stabilization comes is evidence of the hoarding during the inflation. An example appeared during the credit squeeze imposed in Germany in the spring of 1924 by way of consolidating the recently achieved stabilization. (The period shortly after stabilization provides relevant evidence because the inventory holdings were a hangover from the inflation period and, furthermore, were being maintained partly from fear that the stabilization might come undone.)

The time and effort devoted to coping with inflation, as well as the uncertainty and sheer anxiety it causes, should count negatively in a comprehensive assessment. Seeking to protect their savings, savers must look beyond the familiar financial intermediaries and beyond the stock market. Wise stock-market investment, never easy, becomes all the harder when inflation interacts with conventional accounting and with the tax laws to erode profitability or at least to make it more difficult to assess. Alternatives, including real estate, art objects, and all sorts of "collectibles," are touted as inflation hedges. Placement of savings becomes a less impersonal matter than it is when money is stable. Wise investment in nonstandard assets requires detailed knowledge, including, for some of them, personal contacts and personal knowledge of the abilities and moral characters of specific persons. Savers themselves must grope amateurishly for the expertise that they could leave to financial intermediaries in calmer times. The relevant information, being more specific and heterogenous than information about the conventional outlets for savings, is more subject to obsolescence.

The diversion of savings into unconventional forms presumably interferes with the process of conveying command over real resources not devoted to current consumption into the hands of those who will use those resources for real capital formation (or for its likewise productive counterparts, such as research and training).[7] People's propensity to accumulate wealth, which in more stable times is satisfied by accumulation of real capital goods or of financial assets corresponding to real capital formation, is now satisfied partly by accumulation of assets whose rising values constitute rising wealth more from the narrow personal point of view than from the social point of view. (In technical terms, the rising values of such assets exert a Pigou or wealth effect that makes the economywide propensity to save lower than it would otherwise be and so restricts the allocation of resources into real capital formation.) Economic growth suffers.

The older textbooks of money and banking emphasize the many ways in which the use of money helps make production efficient and responsive to people's wants. It does so by facilitating all of the following: exchange and the fine-grained division of labor, credit operations, financial markets, and real capital formation, and economic calculation and informed choice through comparisons of revenues and costs, of prospective profits in different lines of production, of satisfactions prospectively obtained and forgone, and of the offers of rival potential trading partners. If we take these services seriously, then we should recognize how erosion and instability of money's purchasing power impair the smooth performance of its functions.

Some observers make a still more general argument. Inflation frustrates much personal planning, whether for retirement, travel, or education of one's children. By causing disillusionment and breeding discontent, it excites doubts among people about themselves, about the competence of government, and about the free-enterprise system. Those who have lived through severe inflations have noted the erosion of the work ethic and of other established values, and not merely of the value of money, as the hard-working and thrifty middle class suffers undeserved impoverishment and as

7. For eloquent remarks about the sidetracking of savings from capital formation into gold, jewels, foreign money and foreign securities, luxury cars, furniture, real estate, and so forth; about the appearance of easy gains; about the separation created between activities that are privately and those that are socially most profitable; and about social tensions bred by inflation, see G. A. Costanzo, *Programas de estabilización económica en América Latina* (Mexico City: Centro de Estudios Monetarios Latinoamericanos, 1961), 130–35.

inflation profiteers flaunt their conspicuous consumption. Attitudes toward crime change as people find themselves driven, for self-preservation, to evading various economic controls.[8]

SOURCES OF INFLATION

Understanding the cause of a disorder is likely to be helpful in its treatment. Some persons would have us believe that inflation is a kind of plague or invasion striking from outside and that the role of government is to fight it. Arthur Burns, for example, says that

> there are many causes of inflation. Some arise from within a country, as when demands for goods and services exceed the available supply, or when workers press for increases in wages that exceed improvements in productivity, or when businessmen seek to enlarge their profit margins through higher prices. International factors play a role, as when oil-exporting countries raise the price of oil. It is nevertheless the duty of our federal government under existing law to serve as the balance wheel of the economy, and that involves an obligation to restrain or to offset upward pressures on the general price level that arise in the private economy. Our government has performed this function badly in recent times; and it is therefore basically responsible for the persistent and unprecedentedly rapid inflation that has occurred in our country since the mid-1960s.[9]

Harry Johnson comments on an economist friend working for an international organization:

> One of the responsibilities of a job like that is to claim that inflation is something that happens and no one is really to blame. An irresistible political and social set of forces obliges the politicians to abandon their responsibilities of serving the social good, and along with that goes the idea that somehow the public should be

8. Arthur F. Burns, *Inflation Must Be Stopped,* Reprint no. 99 (Washington, D.C.: American Enterprise Institute, June 1979), 1–2. Professor Leo Grebler has emphasized (in a personal letter) the sorts of cost that amount to abrasion of the entire fabric of society.

9. Ibid., 2–3.

cajoled or persuaded or forced to do the politicians' job for them.
... [S]ervants of governments like to put forward [that interpreta-
tion] to persuade the public that the politicians really are better
than they are in fact. ... [Actually,] it is a politician's job to control
inflation, it is not the responsibility of every individual citizen to
behave in a non-inflationary way, and to ask them to do so is an
abnegation of political responsibility.[10]

Inflations of significant degree and duration always involve monetary expansion. By now, or so one hopes, the reasoning and evidence for this proposition no longer need repeating. Historically,
several kinds of situation have given rise to inflationary money creation. Perhaps the most readily understandable case is creation of
money to cover government deficit spending. The link between deficits and money issue can range from the direct and obvious, as in
rolling the printing presses to pay for a war, to the quite roundabout
and loose, as in the United States nowadays. Creating money to cover
the losses of government-owned enterprises is also a familiar story,
particularly in Latin America. So is creation of money to provide
credit to the private sector.[11]

At least two types of vicious circle have been observed in inflations centering on a government deficit. First, if taxes and the prices
charged by government enterprises are adjusted only with delays or
if income taxes are collected on the basis of incomes earned several
months or a year earlier, then inflation itself tends to increase government expenditures ahead of revenues, widening the deficit and
occasioning still bigger issues of money. (This particular kind of interaction is likely to be absent or outweighed in pay-as-you-go tax systems or in systems in which progressive rates and inflation interact
to raise the effective average tax rate, or both.)[12]

10. Harry Johnson, "Panel Discussion on World Inflation," in *Stabilization Policies in Interdependent Economies*, ed. Emil Claassen and Pascal Salin (New York: American Elsevier, 1972), 312.

11. Early twentieth-century Chile provides an example. A conservative government dominated by a landowner class with heavy mortgage indebtedness pursued
deliberately inflationary policies. See Frank Whitson Fetter, *Monetary Inflation in
Chile* (Princeton: Princeton University Press, 1931).

12. Felipe Pazos, *Chronic Inflation in Latin America* (New York: Praeger, 1972),
97–98.

A second type of vicious circle hinges on the fact that the size of government deficit as a proportion of national income that can be financed by money issue without causing inflation is inversely related to the country's income velocity of money. A rise in the inflation rate not only magnifies money's effect on prices by raising its income velocity but also, once velocity has risen, decreases the relative size of the government deficit that could be financed by money issue without raising prices.[13] In other words, an inflation-motivated rise in velocity increases the inflationary impact of issuing money to finance a government deficit amounting to a given proportion of national income. This is the other side of the coin of the phenomenon sometimes observed at times of successful stabilization, when the decline in velocity due to belief that inflation has stopped facilitates the financing of a temporarily continuing government deficit during the period of transition to a balanced budget.

The early 1970s provide many examples, although hardly history's earliest examples, of imported inflation, including the experiences of Germany and Switzerland (mentioned below). Trying to keep the exchange rate of the home currency fixed in the face of balance-of-payments surpluses expands the home money supply. An intertwining aspect of imported inflation at a fixed exchange rate is that price inflation in the outside world tends to raise prices at home in a direct, mechanical way, particularly prices of import and export goods. Although the local authorities may not think of their choice in just this way, they may act to expand the local money supply so that the rising prices do not erode its total purchasing power in real terms or so that money creation is not left entirely to the process already mentioned, which would leave more of any benefit to foreigners than to the domestic authorities. Massive oil price increases, particularly in countries heavily dependent on imported oil, would spell a mechanical increase of perhaps several percent in the country's price level; and in order not to let this increase erode the purchasing power of the total money supply and exert a contractionary effect on production and employment, the authorities feel some pressure to take steps to expand the money supply. This, in other words,

13. Antonio Gómez Oliver and Valeriano García, "Experiencia inflacionaria reciente en América Latina," *Monetaria* 1 (January–March 1978), 27.

would be monetary ratification of a cost push, with the push happening to come from abroad rather than from labor unions (or from business firms with discretionary pricing power).

Once a momentum of interacting wage and price increases has become established, regardless of just how, the authorities have to face the question whether to "ratify" those increases by money-supply expansion. (Having to make this choice is near the heart of the problem of stopping inflation and will occupy us at length later.) That much can be said in favor of the theory that blames inflation on cost push or a wage-price spiral. But if we recognize that the wage-price momentum got established in the first place by excessive money creation and demand pull rather than by entirely autonomous wage and price increases, we drop any notion that we have found a nonmonetary explanation of inflation.

Monetary inflation originating in a way that combines some features of imported inflation and the financing of government deficits, namely, inflation from foreign-exchange losses, has sometimes been observed in Latin America. Under multiple-exchange-rate systems, political pressures tend toward the central bank's buying foreign exchange at a higher price in local currency, by and large, than its selling price. Its purchases of foreign exchange thus inject more domestic money into circulation than its sales withdraw. In this respect, the process resembles the monetary expansion that occurs when a central bank holds a unitary exchange rate fixed in the face of a balance-of-payments surplus. Insofar as official losses are involved, the process resembles inflationary covering of the deficits of state enterprises. As G. A. Costanzo says, these exchange losses generate a net creation of credit.[14] In other words, the central bank's cheaper sales than purchases of foreign exchange constitute gifts of newly created domestic money to the economy, much as if money were being printed to confer subsidies (as in cases in which food subsidies, in particular, have contributed to government deficits and money creation). (The process also bears an analogy with the way that undervaluation of the home currency on the foreign exchanges can cause imported inflation, even though the inflation is not being exported from anywhere else.) The phenomenon of inflation from

14. Costanzo, *Programas*, 41–42, 48–51.

foreign exchange losses helps explain the logic of movement toward a unified and relatively free exchange-rate system as part of a stabilization program.

Cost push has been mentioned as one potential aspect of the inflationary process. To some extent, but not entirely, the oil price increases since 1973 had an exogenous political cause. F. Leutwiler, president of the Swiss National Bank, is one observer who sees reason to suppose that the inflation already under way in consequence of the last-ditch defense of the Bretton Woods system helped prod the Organization of Petroleum Exporting Countries (OPEC) into action. As he says,

> This particular climate of inflation and exuberant expansion not only prepared the ground, in the autumn of 1973, for the massive increase in the price of petroleum but even made it possible. The sudden rise in price of by far the most important energy product accentuated the upward pressure on the already high rates of inflation in most of the industrialized countries.[15]

Without denying that inflation is a monetary phenomenon, keen observers have also diagnosed it as a political problem. Fritz Machlup mentions episodes when inflation was stopped by strong-willed men with political influence—Monsignor Seipel in Austria in 1922, Dr. Schacht in Germany in 1923–24, and Raymond Poincaré in France in 1926. The fact that inflation can be stopped with a change in the political situation suggests that condoning and making inflation in the first place are also largely political problems.

> We then have to ask what are the motivations of those who control the manufacture of money, the motivations that keep them adding to the stock of money.
> The first and strongest motivation is not to be shot and the second motivation is not to be fired.[16]

15. Remarks at the stockholders' meeting of 24 April 1975, printed at the end of Swiss National Bank, *Bulletin Mensuel* (May 1975), separate pages 1–6, quotation from p. 1.

16. Fritz Machlup, "Panel Discussion," in *Stabilization Policies in Interdependent Economies*, ed. Emil Claassen and Pascal Salin (New York: American Elsevier, 1972), 300.

Broadly speaking, inflation results from preoccupation with the short run and failure to take a long-run view. In episodes of imported inflation, for example, the politicians and central bankers of the victim countries delayed adjusting their exchange rates or floating them upward. Such action would have been unpopular with strong interests, notably import-competing and export producers, and something might have turned up to make such action unnecessary. For another example, consider the United States during and after the Vietnam War. It seemed expedient to delay tax increases or to avoid cuts in nonwar expenditures and to continue running up debt. It seemed convenient for the Federal Reserve system to concern itself with interest rates rather than with the money supply. When inflationary momentum became entrenched, it seemed convenient to the Federal Reserve—as it often seems to national monetary and fiscal authorities generally—to accommodate the rising prices and wages with monetary expansion rather than risk a business slump. If they do happen to blunder into a slump, it seems expedient for the authorities to try to stimulate the economy out of it, even at the risk of reigniting inflation. Briefly, both getting into inflation and then having trouble getting out of it are often political problems associated with the fragmentation of governmental decision making and with the short time-horizons of the decision makers.

Political and what might be called "sociological" impediments to noninflationary monetary policy often intertwine. Richard Cooper aptly says, "I have never been able to understand the impasse between the monetarist and the sociological explanations of inflation. I have always assumed the money supply to be sociologically determined."[17] Erich Streissler may have been right in tracing present-day inflation fundamentally to efforts by economic interest groups to enlist the political process in improving their relative income positions, even if this amounts to trying to divide up total income into shares totaling more than 100 percent.[18] This struggle does or could

17. Quoted in editors' prologue, Hirsch and Goldthorpe, *Political Economy*, 1.

18. "Personal Income Distribution and Inflation," in *Inflation in Small Countries*, ed. Helmut Frisch (Berlin: Springer, 1976), 343–56. What follows in the text is more embroidery on than a summary of what Streissler actually said.

operate in several channels: directly through the government budget and the financing of deficits, through credit allocation and subsidies, and through protectionist, regulatory, and other measures tending to create upward pressures and downward rigidities in wages and prices and appearing to call, in turn, for monetary accommodation. This struggle creates an inflation-prone economy in which "accidents" can play a significant role.

The struggle to divide up a whole into more than 100 percent of itself is self-defeating, of course (especially if we set aside minor and temporary exceptions hinging on capital consumption or deficits in foreign trade), while the very struggle is likely to impair the size of the whole. Even so, no group with meaningful political influence has reason to withdraw from the struggle, for doing so would impair its income share even more. The self-interest of the individual politician likewise requires him to respond to political realities that he might regret but is individually powerless to remedy. Here we have an example of tension between individual or sectional rationality and collective rationality. In other words, a decent restraint in clamoring for government action to redistribute income from others to oneself is a public, not a private, good.

If this diagnosis is correct, then merely to recite the standard monetarist prescription for curing inflation amounts to advocating that the problem be solved, somehow, but without probing deeply enough into the nature of the problem or into what would constitute a solution. The same diagnosis suggests why it is difficult to get a sound anti-inflation program adopted and maintained. Yet the durability and credibility of such a policy have much to do with the expectations of the public and, in turn, with whether its recessionary side effects will be mild or severe.

The sources of inflation have included fallacious ideas. One of them centers on the failure to distinguish firmly enough between the nominal and real quantities of money—numbers of money units and purchasing power of the money supply. In Germany in 1923, for example, eminent financiers and politicians argued that there was neither monetary nor credit inflation: although the nominal value of the paper money supply was enormous, its real value or gold value was much lower than that of the prewar money supply. This doctrine overlooks the obvious reason why the real money stock had become so small: People were economizing drastically on holding wealth in the form of money precisely because inflation was so extreme.

Perhaps the most authoritative supporter of this fallacy in Germany, who expounded it in June 1923 before a committee of inquiry into the causes of the fall in the mark, adding that the gold in the Reichsbank amounted to a considerably higher proportion of the gold value of the paper money in circulation in 1923 than before the war, was Karl Helfferich, celebrated economist and former finance minister.

Rudolf Havenstein, president of the Reichsbank, expounded a related fallacy before the same committee—the doctrine that currency depreciation is due to an unfavorable balance of payments. This fallacy dates at least as far back as discussions of "the high price of bullion" in Great Britain during the Napoleonic wars, when the Bank of England had temporarily been relieved of the restraint on banknote issue posed by the gold redeemability requirement. In Germany, the balance-of-payments theorists commonly pointed to the country's heavy reparations payments. In August 1923, Havenstein denied that credit expansion had been feeding inflation in Germany. He argued that the loan and investment portfolio of the Reichsbank was worth well under half of its prewar value in gold marks.[19]

Variants of the "real-bills doctrine" are sometimes found at work in inflationary processes. Although demolished as long ago as 1802 by Henry Thornton,[20] the doctrine keeps being rediscovered as if it were a profound and original truth. In essence—but variations on this theme do occur—the doctrine holds that new money is not inflationary if issued to finance productive activities, since it will soon be matched by additional goods on which it can be spent. Briefly, the fallacy consists in believing that what happens to the price level depends not so much on the quantity of money as on the particular way in which new money is initially put into circulation. The doc-

19. Bresciani-Turroni, *Economics*, 155–56. Bresciani-Turroni goes on to cite other authorities who held substantially the same fallacious ideas.

20. Henry Thornton, *An Enquiry Into the Nature and Effects of the Paper Credit of Great Britain*, ed. with an introduction by F. A. v. Hayek (New York: Rinehart, 1939). The doctrine was so called because it held that money issues were sound if connected with the banks' discounting of "real bills," that is, lending on bills of exchange associated with the production or marketing of actual goods.

trine fails to realize that creating new money to finance particular activities ordinarily does less to increase total production than to bid productive resources from other activities into the favored ones, while, at the same time, the intensified bidding for productive resources raises costs and prices.[21]

Related to the real-bills fallacy, and in particular to its supposition that the quantity of money is less important than its quality or the nature of its issue, is the notion that money cannot be inflationary if it is solidly backed. Proponents of issuing the assignats during the French Revolution argued, for example, that the issues would be harmless, indeed beneficial, because they were backed by nationalized lands. A preoccupation with backing has sometimes made the authorities passive in the face of imported inflation; creation of money to buy up gold and foreign exchange was supposedly acceptable because, after all, the new money was being backed by the additional reserves acquired in the process.

One last fallacy to mention is the idea often encountered that the monetary authorities are not responsible for what happens to the quantity of money because it is passively responding to developments in income or prices. Indeed it may be, but only if the authorities are subordinating control of the money supply to some other objective, such as low interest rates or a fixed exchange rate. (Having institutions that made the money supply behave passively in some such way would count as an action of the monetary authorities, interpreted broadly to include the legislators or constitution makers.) Or the authorities might be passively creating new money to accommodate an established uptrend in prices and wages as they tried to postpone the painful adjustments expected to accompany an attempt at stabilization.

CLASSIFICATION OF INFLATIONS

Inflations may be classified in several ways besides source or origin: by severity or rate (mild, trotting, or galloping), by how long they

21. For further discussion, see Thornton, *Paper Credit;* or Lloyd W. Mints, *A History of Banking Theory* (Chicago: University of Chicago Press, 1945).

have persisted, by whether they have been continuous or intermittent, by remedial measures taken, if any, and by the results of those measures. An explanation of why these distinctions can be important for the seriousness or the curability of an inflation will take some points for granted that are developed later in the section on momentum of inflation.

Other things being equal, a brief inflation is easier to stop than one of long duration because people have had less time to become accustomed to it, to develop expectations of its continuation, and to make the sorts of arrangements that, though wise from their private points of view, do contribute to its momentum. A wartime inflation is a prime example. The exceptional increases in the money supply have occurred over a few years at most; people recognize the occasion for them as atypical; and the end of wartime money issues signals a return to price stability, if not indeed to price reversals. The wartime inflation, if not actually reversed, can be regarded as a brief transition to a higher price level rather than as a continuing process. From a medium- or long-run perspective, a wartime inflation is a discrete episode of an increase in the money supply bringing a once-and-for-all rise in the price level. Being so recognized, wartime inflations need not go on reinforcing themselves by way of expectations. In earlier times, price levels and not just inflation rates were expected to come down after a war.

For similar reasons, creeping inflation is less serious if intermittent than if continuous. A persistent creeping inflation will tend to worsen if it is not halted, or so Gottfried Haberler has argued.[22] As it continues, more and more people take steps, through labor contracts and otherwise, to protect themselves against expected further

---

22. This is not to say that every creeping inflation inexorably becomes trotting and then galloping. Rather, "an expected and anticipated inflation loses its stimulating power unless it is allowed to accelerate beyond the expected rate and . . . , at a later stage, slowing down the rate of inflation has the same depressing effect on economic activity as stopping it altogether would have had earlier. This is . . . the real meaning of stagflation. . . . If we do not act now to curb inflation we merely postpone the day of reckoning." Gottfried Haberler, "Some Currently Suggested Explanations and Cures for Inflation," in *Institutional Arrangements and the Inflation Problem,* ed. Karl Brunner and Allan Meltzer (Amsterdam: North-Holland, 1976), 150–51.

price increases. Intermissions in inflation, by contrast, provide opportunities for confidence in the value of money to revive.[23]

It would be misleading to say, just because the Civil War and subsequent wars brought successively higher price peaks, that the United States has managed to live comfortably with chronic inflation for well over a century. Deep valleys with long flat bottoms separated those peaks on the long-term price curve, even though each valley was higher than the one before it. Inflations were intermittent—wartime or business-cycle episodes or upward phases of mild long waves. Only from World War II on did the price curve come to look like a flight of stairs, showing no substantial price declines. Not until then did the American people start becoming highly sensitive to inflation.[24]

The most significant change in the climate of expectations may have come even more recently, in the 1960s or 1970s. Several bouts of monetary restraint after World War II, bringing recessions and unemployment, finally (if temporarily) conquered inflation toward the end of the Eisenhower administration. Following the price increases during the Korean War and in the business boom of 1955–56, balance-of-payments deterioration and continuing gold losses after 1957 had argued for returning to price stability. From 1958 through 1964, the wholesale price index remained nearly stable, while consumer price increases averaged only 1.2 percent a year. Then, as another recession was becoming evident during the 1960 presidential campaign, candidate John Kennedy promised "to get this country moving again."[25] The Vietnam War contributed its inflationary pressures a few years later. Haberler, writing in 1966, could say that the United States was then experiencing an inflation unique in its history.[26]

23. Gottfried Haberler, *Inflation, Its Causes and Cures*, rev. ed. (Washington, D.C.: American Enterprise Institute, 1966), 93–94. Haberler was ahead of most economists in rejecting the now discredited notion of a dependable trade-off between unemployment and inflation. After a while, the inflation would be allowed to accelerate as efforts to resist unemployment intensified, or, if inflation were held to a creep, the unemployment would emerge that the creeping inflation was supposed to forestall.

24. Ibid., 56, 94, 97.

25. Philip Cagan, "Monetary Policy," in *Economic Policy and Inflation in the Sixties*, by Cagan et al. (Washington, D.C.: American Enterprise Institute, 1972), 90.

26. Ibid., 97.

In the 1970s, the situation departed still further from earlier American experience. Arthur Okun calls it unprecedented. "[T]he chronic inflation of the seventies is a new and different phenomenon that cannot be diagnosed correctly with old theories or treated effectively with old prescriptions." Before then, inflation rates rarely averaged above 2 percent for any sustained peacetime period. Price and wage decisions relied on the dollar as a basis for planning and budgeting. Labor and management had notions of appropriate wage increases and were willing to sign three-year contracts. Firms set their prices according to actual costs rather than projected replacement costs. Catalog prices were subject to change only infrequently, and salesmen accepted orders for future deliveries at firm prices. Regulatory commissions needed to review utility rates only occasionally. Then, in the mid-1960s, what Okun calls a new era of inflation got under way. Every year since 1968 saw a higher inflation rate than any year between 1952 and 1967. During the 1970s, adjustments to persistent inflation altered wage- and price-setting practices. The notion of appropriate wage increases was revised upward, and escalator clauses spread in labor contracts. Business pricing came to reflect a growing gap between replacement costs and historical costs. Price increases came more often, and many firms stopped taking orders at fixed prices. Such adaptations to chronic inflation speeded up the interaction between prices and wages and other costs.[27]

While unprecedented for the United States, this situation is not wholly unprecedented, nor, despite Okun, does its diagnosis defy old theories. With particular reference to Latin America, Felipe Pazos has explained why wages and prices interact more closely in rapid inflations than in mild ones. He found it not surprising that wages and consumer prices were more tightly correlated over the period 1949–70 in Argentina and Chile than in the United States. Workers are less alert to cost-of-living increases of 1 or 2 percent than to those of 30 percent or more; business firms are less influenced by wage increases of 3 to 5 percent than by increases ten or more times as large. In slow inflations, the increases in the cost of living are a factor of

27. Okun, "An Efficient Strategy," 1–3.

lesser importance in wage negotiations than are the supply and demand for labor, the level of profits, the strength of the labor movement, and the attitude of labor leaders. In intermediate inflations, cost-of-living increases are the major factor in labor negotiations; in hyperinflations, they are essentially the only factor. Rises in the cost of living seem to play an increasingly important role in wage negotiations when inflation rises from 1 or 2 percent a year to 4 or 5 percent or higher. This probably explains, to a large extent, the continuation of wage increases in the United States after 1970 despite the increase in unemployment[28]—but more remains to be said about inflationary momentum.

THE ANALOGY BETWEEN LEVELS AND TRENDS OF PRICES

Brief inflations have been easier to stop than inflations of long duration because they were changes in the level of prices rather than entrenched ongoing processes. This thought brings to mind an analogy between the inertia of an established price and wage *level* and the inertia of an established *trend*. Something like Newton's first law of motion is at work in both cases: Just as a body resists being set in motion or having the speed or direction of its motion changed, so prices on the average resist changes in their level or their trend, particularly cuts in their level or moderation of their uptrend.[29] The analogy suggests that experience with attempts to reverse wartime increases in the price level, as after the Napoleonic wars, the U.S. Civil War, and World War I, may be relevant to today's less ambitious goal of merely leveling off an established uptrend in prices and wages.

The analogy between deflating a price level and bringing down a price trend centers on the concept of stickiness. People tend to think of money as having a fairly definite value or rate of change of value, and they make their price and wage demands and decisions accordingly. But this expectational factor is not the only element of sticki-

28. Pazos, *Chronic Inflation*, 70.
29. Ibid., 88–89.

ness. Cost-price interrelations make it difficult to adjust prices downward without some assurance that costs will adjust downward too.

In an elementary textbook already in its fifth edition fifty years ago, Harry Gunnison Brown considers a case in which restriction of money and credit will cause a business depression unless prices and wages fall sufficiently to maintain the real money stock. In fact, they will not fall steeply and promptly enough.

> There are various customary notions of what are reasonable prices for various goods and reasonable wages for labor of various kinds and, furthermore, each person hopes to be able to get the old price or the old wage for what he has to sell and does not want to reduce until sure that his expenses will also be reduced. And so there is a general hesitancy, a holding off for standard prices, wages, and so on, to the inevitable slowing down of business.[30]

When a change in the volume or growth rate of money and spending has changed what *would be* the equilibrium level or trend of prices, this new equilibrium is not reached immediately. One view of what happens focuses on market conditions determining the millions of distinct prices whose average level or trend happens to be of interest. Another view of the same process is also instructive: The purchasing power of the money unit and its rate of erosion are being determined; but, instead of occurring on one particular market and impinging on one particular price, this process is diffused over millions of individual but interconnecting markets. Precisely because money does not have a specific market and price of its own, adjustment of the level or trend of its value is long drawn out; and the long-drawn-out character of this process contributes to the persistence of price inflation even after its monetary basis may have been stopped. Production and employment suffer because price trends do not fully absorb the impact of the deceleration of money and spending.

This unfavorable split between price and output responses could be avoided or mitigated if people saw truly convincing reasons to be-

30. Harry Gunnison Brown, *Economic Science and the Common Welfare*, 5th ed. (Columbia, Mo.: Lucas Brothers, 1931), 88–89; cf. 84–86, 93, 111–17. Brown goes on to explain in some detail how this difficulty of prompt downward adjustments is largely due to the way that various prices and costs intertwine.

lieve that the inflation was, in fact, being stopped. Unfortunately, no policy maker and no individual seller can confidently guess when prices might decelerate in response to monetary restraint. The individual seller knows only that this does not depend on his own sale and price decisions.[31] The action that would be in the interest of price setters and wage negotiators if they were acting collectively is not necessarily in the interest of each one acting separately. Instead of going first in moderating the rate of rise in the particular price or wage that he sets or negotiates, each one has reason to wait to see whether such restraint on the part of others, intensifying the competition that he faces or moderating the rise in his production costs or cost of living, as the case may be, will make it advantageous for him to *follow* with restraint of his own. This hesitation, though rational for each one, poses what might be called an Alphonse-and-Gaston problem for the collectivity.

Individual price setters and wage negotiators have reason for reluctance to go first in reducing a level of prices and wages that is too high for the nominal quantity of money; they have similar reason for reluctance to go first in breaking an established uptrend. Suppose that policy blunders have made the existing nominal quantity of money too small for the existing price level; money is in full-employment excess demand in the sense that actual cash balances add up to less than would be demanded at full employment, with the result that a depressed level of economic activity is what holds the demand for money down to the existing amount. Barring reversal of the policy blunder, it would be collectively rational for transactors to reduce the general level of prices and wages and other costs enough to make the money stock adequate in real terms for a full-employment volume of transactions. In view of the piecemeal way in which this general level is actually determined and adjusted, however, the individual agent may not find it rational promptly to cut the particular price or wage for which he is responsible, even though it is above the general-equilibrium level. Being first to move would

31. William Fellner, in *Towards a Reconstruction of Macroeconomics,* excerpted in *Solutions to Inflation,* ed. David C. Colander (New York: Harcourt Brace Jovanovich, 1979), 91.

change relative prices, perhaps to his disadvantage. Instead of going first, he may rationally wait to see what others do. Taking the lead in downward price and wage adjustments is more in the nature of public than a private good, and private incentives to supply public goods are notoriously weak. What is individually rational and what is collectively rational may well diverge, as the well-known example of the prisoners' dilemma illustrates. Taking the lead in restraining a price and wage uptrend is a similar case in point.

Noneconomic examples will help make this point still clearer.[32] Most members of a lecture audience might want to avoid sitting in the first few occupied rows, so those arriving early take seats toward the middle or rear. Those arriving later take seats behind the people already seated, leaving the front of the auditorium nearly empty. Most people wind up sitting further back than they really desire. Individually they do not want to move forward, but they wish that the audience as a whole would somehow move forward, leaving its members' relative positions unchanged. Most of the drivers waiting in a gasoline line, for another example, might wish that the line would form later in the morning (or wish that there were no panicky tank topping in the first place); but since each one is powerless to change the behavior of the others, he adjusts to it by joining the line early. Similarly, money-supply contractions or decelerations create situations in which it is nevertheless individually rational for people to persist in setting prices and wages as before, even though a decision to reduce or restrain prices and wages would be rational if it could be made collectively. Individual and collective rationality might be reconciled in this context if everyone came firmly to believe that inflation was being stopped quickly. How such a belief might be created is close to the central question.

The analogy between levels and trends also holds regarding the split of a change in nominal spending between a change in production and employment, on the one hand, and a change in prices, on the other. With the most favorable split conceivable, a deflation or slowdown of money and spending would have its entire impact on

32. See Thomas C. Schelling, *Micro Motives and Macro Behavior* (New York: Norton, 1978).

bringing down the price level or the price trend, as the case might be, with no damage at all to real activity. With the most unfavorable split, deflation of money and spending—either absolute or relative to the existing trend—would exert its entire impact on real activity, with no reduction in the level or uptrend of prices. In reality, of course, the impact falls partly on real activity and partly on the price level or trend. The factors tending to make the split relatively favorable or relatively unfavorable are obviously relevant to the ease or difficulty of stopping an inflation.

The analogy holds between accomplishing mild or extreme price-level reductions and stopping mild or extreme inflations. As Henry Thornton already recognized in 1811, it is a reasonable objective to "restore the standard of the country" after the money has suffered a mild loss of purchasing power and of foreign-exchange value but not to reverse an extreme depreciation.[33] Similarly, stopping a mild inflation does not require as much of a cutback in money-supply growth and as much of a threat to production and employment as trying to stop a more severe inflation. (Some qualifications regarding extreme inflation, however, will be noted later.)

The analogy also holds on several other points. One concerns disappointment of expectations. Just as getting a price level down will disappoint debtors, so will stopping an inflationary trend that they had expected to persist; inflation creates vested interests in its continuation. Another point concerns the Phillips curve, or something like it. In epochs when the price and wage level undergoes discrete changes from time to time but sustained inflations and deflations are unknown, we would find low (that is, reduced but incompletely reduced) price and wage levels associated with relatively heavy unemployment and high levels with slight unemployment. The apparent causation, though, would be spurious. Unemployment would be affected not by the price and wage level as such but by the unexpected monetary change that had also been lowering or raising that level. Something similar holds true of Phillips curves of the more familiar kind, which until recently were interpreted as associating heavy or slight unemployment with low or high wage and price inflation.

33. Speech in Parliament. Thornton, *Paper Credit*, app. 3.

Actually, heavy or slight unemployment was associated instead with decelerations or accelerations of money growth and spending that had not been fully expected and allowed for.

The analogy also holds with regard to policy laxness. If we think that maintaining a particular price level—today's—does not really matter, then we tend to become complacent about changes in it and about inflation. Similarly, if we think that what particular inflation rate we have does not matter much, then we become complacent about accelerating inflation.

Just as we can find analogies between levels and trends of prices, so we could probably find analogies between trends and accelerations. Policy makers could conceivably blunder into a state of affairs in which these more sophisticated analogies became relevant to understanding what is happening. People might become more or less adjusted not merely to continuing inflation but to its continuing acceleration. If so, a monetary change that would tend to reduce—but not stop—the price acceleration might disappoint expectations, transitionally worsen the impairment of economic coordination, and impinge on real activity. (If this remark is not clear, the ensuing discussion of stagflation may help clear it up.)

The analogy between levels and trends does not hold in all respects. (Analogies are, after all, just that, not total correspondences.) The velocity of money is not (permanently) affected by a once-and-for-all change in the price level due to a money-supply change, yet it is affected (once and for all) by a change in the inflation rate. A continuous change in velocity, so far as it depends on the rate of price inflation, presupposes a continuous change in that rate. To put it another way, the particular price level does not, in principle, affect the size of real money balances demanded, but the inflation rate does. Because of general interdependence, affecting real money balances means, in principle, affecting all real magnitudes. Money can be "neutral," then, so far as only its quantity but not its growth rate is concerned. (Money could conceivably be neutral even with regard to changes in its growth rate only if the new money were injected by equiproportionate additions to all individual holdings.)

INFLATIONARY MOMENTUM AND THE SIDE
EFFECTS OF TRYING TO STOP INFLATION

The aspect of the analogy most pertinent to our purposes is that the reasons for sluggishness in reducing a disequilibrium price level carry over to sluggish deceleration of an entrenched price uptrend. Even if a solution to underlying difficulties (such as government deficit spending) does permit stopping the inflationary creation of money, prices and wages will continue rising for months, even years, with a momentum of their own. With nominal money growth slowed, the stock of real money balances shrinks, contributing to monetary disequilibrium and thus to a slowdown in production and employment. Just as a shrinkage that makes the *quantity* of money inadequate to sustain the prevailing *level* of prices contracts real economic activity, so a reduction that makes the money *growth rate* inadequate to sustain an entrenched *uptrend* in prices causes a real contraction or at least restricts real growth. In a sense, stagflation is the consequence of too little current monetary growth against a background of too much growth earlier. The earlier excessive growth established the uptrend still eroding the real purchasing power of the money supply and spending stream. On many such occasions, the unwanted real side effects have apparently made the authorities lose their nerve and switch back to a policy of "growth." (The very prospect of side effects may block a determined anti-inflationary policy in the first place.) Yet from a longer-term perspective than the authorities may feel politically able to adopt, no conclusion follows in favor of accelerating monetary growth again, since doing so would make the stagflation dilemma worse later on.

Reference to the withdrawal pangs of trying to end inflation returns us to our question of how the impact of restraint on money and spending is split between prices and real activity. How unfavorable or favorable the split is depends on the circumstances, considered in this section, that govern how persistent inflationary momentum is. It is a familiar but inexact remark that slow real economic growth or actual recession tends to restrain inflation (and, conversely, that rapid real growth is inflationary). The reverse accords better with the equation of exchange, $MV = PQ$, where Q refers to some measure of real activity or total production. Presumably underlying the common remark is the idea that slowed real growth is one consequence of and serves as a measure or indicator of a slowdown in nominal income and the money supply. If this is what is meant, however, the standard formulation is unfortunate. Imagine—trying to gauge the anti-inflationary intensity of monetary policy by an unwanted side effect of that policy, namely, a real slowdown, especially since, as $MV = PQ$ shows, the side effect competes with the desired price deceleration!

The diagnosis of stagflation that focuses on how the momentum of price and wage increases erodes real money balances and the flow of real spending is, of course, incomplete. Inflation impairs the information-transmitting and coordinating properties of the price mechanism and distorts relative prices, frustrating some exchanges. Just how inflationary quantities of money enter the economy can be relevant, and interest rates may figure among the prices that are distorted. Inflation distorts the pattern of production and resource allocation—in favor, for example, of supposed "inflation hedges." If a policy of trying to reduce inflation seems to be working or to have some chance of success, then people will tend to shift production and resource allocation back toward more normal patterns, giving rise to frictional losses of production and employment.

As an example of distortions during the Brazilian inflation of the 1960s, Alexandre Kafka mentions the hoarding of goods, particularly durable consumer goods. Stabilization would perhaps bring dishoarding of the kinds of durable goods bought by firms and would weaken incentives to accumulate durable consumer goods, so that the industries producing them would suffer recession. Kafka mentions the paradoxical result that at times, in the midst of a stabilization program, the authorities felt obliged to stimulate consumer credit to prevent a real stabilization crisis.[34]

Part of the purpose of ending inflation is to reverse inflationary distortions of resource allocation. Similarly, if stabilization reinstates

34. Alexandre Kafka, "The Brazilian Stabilization Program, 1964–66," *Journal of Political Economy* 75 (August 1967), part 2, 608. The German inflation of 1922–23 likewise caused real distortions of resource allocation that later had to be undone, including impairment of competition and of the selection of the fittest firms.

the competitive process of selecting the fittest firms, then some firms that were being kept afloat by the peculiarities of the inflationary situation will go bankrupt. Their plants and equipment and employees will have to shift into the hands of better management or into more desired lines of production. The shifting will involve frictions, and real activity will suffer for a while.

These considerations reinforce the judgment that stabilization with a pure price impact and no unfavorable real side effects is practically impossible. They also argue that delay makes stopping inflation all the more painful by letting distortions worsen in the meantime.

The distinction between credit-intensive and non-credit-intensive businesses and products is relevant to the side effects of monetary slowdown. In our type of money and banking system, a slowdown in money-supply growth will transitionally tighten credit. This is only a transitional effect, of course, since, in comparison of alternative equilibriums, the real cost or availability of credit does not depend on the quantity of money. But during the transition, the particular burdening of credit-intensive firms can be a further source of resource reallocation and frictions.[35]

Yet these additional characteristics of stagflation should not draw attention away from price and wage momentum. This momentum has two main aspects, "catching up" and "expectations." Both involve complex interrelations and time lags. Prices and wages and other costs are determined in piecemeal and decentralized ways; some firms' selling prices are other firms' costs. Except for coming close to doing so in hyperinflations, not all prices and wage rates rise in step with each other, month by month and week by week. Only the prices of securities and standardized commodities traded on organized exchanges respond to supply and demand from hour to hour and minute to minute. Most individual prices and wages are adjusted only from time to time. As a result, the structure of relative prices is constantly undergoing distortions and corrections. At any time, many prices and wages are temporarily lagging behind others in the inflationary procession. While some workers will have just received wage increases, others will have received their latest increases

35. Cf. Colander, *Solutions*, 105.

perhaps eleven months before and be in line for another increase soon. "A price increase in one sector pushes up costs in others, and each increase then works its way through the price structure. At the stage of final goods and services, price increases add to the cost of living, feeding back on wages and costs in the earlier stages of production, then to work forward again."[36] Not even large nominal gains always "put union wages ahead in *real terms*. Such settlements can represent a catching up with past real losses due to cost-of-living increases." Union power, without being the actual cause of inflation, can contribute to its persistence. "The whipsaw process of each handsome settlement giving rise to militant demands by other unions for equal or better treatment has created the alarming prospect of a very slow cooling of the rampant inflationary psychology."[37]

Revision of expiring contracts is not the only way that catching up, broadly interpreted, works. Some existing contracts, with the parties' intention of keeping abreast of the general trend of money's depreciation, have already scheduled future price or wage increases. If the monetary authority does somehow succeed in getting price inflation down below the rate that had been expected, then nominal wage increases scheduled in view of earlier expectations will result in higher real wage rates than intended, contributing to unemployment.[38]

To notice cost-price interactions is not to adopt a cost-push theory of inflation. In some stages of the inflation process, costs may seem to rise first, with prices following later; yet this sequence can be spurious as evidence of causation. A microview helps show why. A firm's standard response to strengthened demand for its products is to try to increase quantities available for sale. A retailer will order more goods. A manufacturer will order more materials, seek more labor, and perhaps try to expand his plant and equipment. Each individual businessman might think that, given time, he could meet the increased demand for his product without raising prices. Yet as businessmen transmit the increased demands for final products back

36. Cagan, "Monetary Policy," 142.
37. Ibid., 141–42.
38. Herbert Giersch uses this point as an argument for indexing to help avoid unintended spurts in real wage rates when price inflation decelerates. Herbert Giersch, "Index Clauses and the Fight Against Inflation," in *Essays on Inflation and Indexation*, ed. Giersch et al. (Washington, D.C.: American Enterprise Institute, 1974), 6.

to the factors of production, competing for materials, labor, and plants and equipment, they bid up these cost elements. To the individual businessman, then, the chief factor justifying and requiring a rise in his selling prices is the rise in his costs. From his standpoint, the inflation may look like a cost-push process, even though costs are in fact rising as inflationary demands for final products are transmitted back to factors of production.

For these and other reasons, a change in monetary policy and in the flow of spending on final goods and services has its impact spread over many months, even years. If monetary policy were to be tightened and an inflationary expansion of demand checked, much of the adjustment of prices to the earlier demand inflation would remain to be completed. In summary, prices would continue rising for at least three reasons. First, contractual prices and wages would be renegotiated as contracts expired. Second, costs and prices would interact in sequences complicated by the fact that some firms' prices are other firms' costs. Third—a point still to be developed—buyers and sellers would be acting on expectations formed during the period of active monetary inflation.

A study by Joel Popkin sheds light on cost-price interaction and catching up. Popkin distinguishes between primary-goods and finished-goods industries. For the most part, prices respond directly to demand conditions only in the former. Prices of finished goods sold to consumers and other final users, however, are less sensitive to a drop in sales. These prices are based on costs, which include the prices of purchased materials and services. Unresponsive pricing of finished goods means that restraints on total spending can bring inflation down only in a roundabout way. Instead of depressing prices directly, a fall in spending on final goods depresses output. Their producers cut back their orders for raw materials, whose prices do decline in response. Lower costs of materials finally show up in a slowing of price increases for finished goods. Unfortunately, this effect is likely to be minor, since materials figure less heavily than wages in the costs of most finished goods; and wage increases are particularly slow to respond to a slowdown of price inflation. In most industries, Popkin found, unemployment or excess capacity has less influence in wage bargaining than increases in consumer prices and in wages in other industries. The wage-setting process is dominated by past increases in the cost of living and by workers' desire to catch up with wage increases achieved elsewhere. The responsiveness of prices to demand in industries producing basic materials but not in most industries producing finished goods is awkward for macroeconomic policy; yet this differential responsiveness is readily understandable. If the reverse pattern somehow prevailed, stabilization policies would have better prospects of success.[39]

Outside of sectors whose products are traded in organized competitive markets, notions of fairness condition interactions among prices and wages and other costs. Concerned about maintaining their market shares over the long run, sellers try to keep their customers loyal by treating them reasonably in good times and bad, charging prices based on costs and fairly stable percentage markups. Employers and skilled workers, similarly, have a common interest in maintaining their relations over the long run. Employers have invested in a trained and loyal workforce as well as in plant and equipment. They recognize that slashing wages in a slump would make resentful workers quit the next time jobs were abundant. Even during recessions and with plenty of job applicants, firms may have reason to raise wages in step with the wages of other workers in similar situations. Although such price and wage strategies help maintain good relations among customers and suppliers and workers and employers, they do undercut the sensitivity of prices and wages to short-run supply and demand. As a result, prices and wages are slow in responding to an expansion of nominal spending. Similarly, an entrenched inflation is slow to abate when the growth of nominal spending is slowed down. Instead, the early response consists partly of cutbacks in production.[40]

39. Joel Popkin, "Price Behavior in the Manufacturing Sector for Sixteen Industries Classified by Stage-of-Process," National Bureau of Economic Research, Working Paper no. 238 (Washington, D.C., March 1978). Compare a summary and commentary in "Why the Odds Are Against the Inflation Fighters," *Business Week*, 5 June 1978, 83–85. Several discussions of Latin American inflation, as well as Jerome L. Stein, "Inside the Monetarist Black Box," chap. 3 in *Monetarism*, ed. Stein (Amsterdam: North-Holland, 1976), emphasize the catching-up aspects of inflationary momentum.

40. Okun, "An Efficient Strategy," 2.

Because costs and prices interact in complicated patterns and with time lags, many prices and wage rates have catching up to do after monetary expansion is checked. To keep them from catching up somehow would leave them stuck away from market-clearing levels, and the distorted structure of relative prices and costs would interfere with some transactions and so with production and employment. In abstract theory, these distortions could be corrected by declines in some prices and wages that averaged out further increases in others. Actually, the difficulties that obstruct a mere leveling off of upward trends obstruct all the more powerfully any cuts of particular prices and wages. Thus, catching up does obstruct any instant end to inflation.

These considerations, reinforced by historical experience that we shall review, suggest a silver lining to extreme inflation. As inflation persists and becomes faster and more fully expected, people shorten the intervals between price and wage adjustments. The transmission of higher wages and other costs into higher prices and of higher prices into higher wages occurs more rapidly.[41] This shortening of lags means that anti-inflation policy would have less of a problem of prolonged catching up with which to contend. In this respect, it may be easier to stop an extreme inflation than a merely moderate one.

Expectations form the second aspect of inflationary momentum. (Actually, the two aspects overlap and cannot be sharply distinguished, and the interaction of various costs and prices enters into both.) When prices and wages have been rising at a substantial rate for several years, people recognize what is happening, expect it to continue, and make their own pricing decisions and wage demands accordingly. (They do so, anyway, unless some clear-cut change in circumstances provides a reason for doing otherwise. An analysis of the sort presented here, however, even if only rough and intuitive, does support expectations that trends will persist.) With adjustments being made not every day but only from time to time, people will take account of the erosion of the purchasing power of the prices or wages that they receive. In adjusting their own prices or wage demands, they not only will allow for this erosion already experienced since their last adjustment but also may well include an allowance

41. Ibid., 3.

64

for further erosion in the ensuing months. Strong anticipations of inflation can reduce the direct influence of demand on prices (and also of prices on quantities demanded). Cost increases are more readily and fully passed along despite weakness in demand if that weakness is viewed as temporary and prices are expected to continue in an uptrend. Costs and prices push each other up with less friction.[42] As buyers become accustomed to repeatedly paying increased prices and find it increasingly difficult to keep abreast of and compare the prices asked by rival sellers, they become less sensitive to price competition. Sellers become accustomed to passing actual and even expected cost increases on to their customers without meeting too much buyer resistance.

Even a seller of some product or type of labor for which demand is currently deficient—a businessman dissatisfied with his sales or a union leader dissatisfied with his members' employment—may well forgo cutting or may even increase his money price anyway. He can reduce his real or relative price in order to attract buyers simply by keeping its nominal increase smaller than the general inflation rate.[43] When prices and wages are generally rising, to join in the procession is not necessarily to push for an increased price in real terms but simply to avoid an unnecessarily large markdown. Why take less than the market will bear? Why sacrifice to the advantage of others? Even if a seller should experience some drop or lag in sales attributable to an excessive nominal price increase, he could expect the continuing general inflation of costs and prices to make his price soon competitive and acceptable after all. Why reverse a slightly premature price increase that customers will soon be willing to pay?

In a sense, the ordinary nominal money unit loses its character as the unit in which price and wage demands and offers and decisions are formed. Instead, some sort of vaguely conceived purchasing-power unit replaces it. Money illusion of the ordinary sort, predi-

42. Cagan, *Economic Policy*, 143.

43. Axel Leijonhufvud made this point orally in a conference at Rutgers University, Newark, in April 1979, and in "Stagflation" (Lecture at Nihon University, Tokyo, 19 January 1980, mimeographed), 10–11. The point accords well with what Pazos (*Chronic Inflation*, 70 and passim) reports about inflationary Latin America—that the overwhelmingly dominant consideration in wage negotiations is cost-of-living adjustments.

cated on stability of the purchasing power of the nominal unit, breaks down and gives way to an illusion—if indeed it is an illusion—of continuing purchasing-power erosion. Attunement to a perceived trend replaces the presumption of a stable money unit.

Again our levels-and-trends analogy proves helpful. Just as the distinction between individual and collective rationality helps explain the difficulty of reducing a price level, so it helps explain the difficulty of slowing an uptrend. Expectations figure in this difficulty. The less successfully monetary restraint decelerates prices, as we recall, the worse are its recessionary side effects.

Suppose that I, an individual businessman, perceive that a newly introduced policy of monetary restraint ought to stop inflation. (The effect that a policy "ought" to have is the one that it is designed to have in the light of correct economic theory, or the one that it would have if people quite generally understood it and modified their behavior accordingly.) Even so, how can I count on *others* having the same perceptions and modifying their behavior accordingly? How can I be confident that my workers will restrain their wage demands and my suppliers and competitors their prices? I have good reason, as already argued, to postpone changes in my own pricing policy until I get a better reading on what the situation is, including, in particular, on how other people may be modifying their price and wage policies. (My policy, like theirs, had been to keep marking up my selling prices in line with the entrenched general trend unless faced with definite conditions of costs and competition that recommend doing otherwise.) Of course, if I and all other price setters and wage negotiators were to make our decisions collectively and simultaneously, then it would be in our collective interest to avoid the side effects of the new policy of monetary restraint by practicing appropriate price and wage restraint. In fact, though, we make our price and wage decisions piecemeal, opening the way for the previously mentioned divergence between collective and individual rationality.

This divergence is not a defect of the market system but rather the inevitable consequence of the circumstances with which it must cope. One of its great virtues is that it does not require or impose collective decisions. This fact becomes less of a virtue when the problem of stopping inflation arises, but we can hardly expect a world whose features are all desirable in all respects and under all circumstances. The dispersion of knowledge and the fact that it can be effectively used only through decentralized decisions and in a market-coordinated way is one of the hard facts of reality. It forms part of the reason why monetary disturbances can be so pervasively disruptive: They overtax the knowledge-mobilizing and signaling processes of the market. None of this amounts to a recommendation to give up and let an entrenched inflation keep rolling. Far from being a solution, that would make the attempted cure all the more painful when belatedly undertaken.

The expectational aspect of inflationary momentum makes the *credibility* of an anti-inflation policy of great importance to how severe the withdrawal pangs will be.[44] If a program of monetary restraint is not credible—if price setters and wage negotiators think that the authorities will lose their nerve and switch gears at the first sign of recessionary side effects—then those parties will expect the inflation to continue and will make their price and wage decisions accordingly. The unintended consequence will be an unfavorable split between the price and quantity responses to monetary restriction. If, on the contrary, people are convinced that the authorities will persist in monetary restriction indefinitely no matter how bad the side effects, so that the price and wage inflation is bound to abate, then everyone should realize that, if he nevertheless persists in price or wage increases at the same old pace, he will find himself ahead of the stalled inflationary procession and will lose customers or jobs. People will moderate their price and wage demands, making the split less unfavorable to continued production and employment.

It is only superficially paradoxical, then, that in two alternative situations with objectively the same degree of monetary restriction, the recessionary side effects will actually be milder when the authorities are believed ready to tolerate such effects than when the authori-

44. William Fellner has long insisted on points like these. See, for example, his *Towards a Reconstruction*, esp. 2–3, 12–15, 116–18; and "The Core of the Controversy About Reducing Inflation: An Introductory Analysis," in *Contemporary Economic Problems 1978*, William Fellner, project director (Washington, D.C.: American Enterprise Institute, 1978), 1–12.

Carried to an extreme, the view expounded here becomes the currently fashionable doctrine of rational expectations.

ties are suspected of irresoluteness. How, though, could a resolute policy be made convincing from the start? Unfortunately, the required declarations and actions are unlikely under our sort of political system. If, however, the necessary declarations and actions could somehow occur and did succeed in making practically everyone believe that inflation was being stopped quickly, then the monetary slowdown would damage production and employment only mildly.

While a resolute and credible anti-inflation program could thus conceivably turn expectations around almost at once, the catch-up aspect of inflationary momentum appears less tractable. Still, if the turnaround in inflationary expectations were quick and complete enough, relative prices could conceivably be restored to an approximate equilibrium pattern through declines in previously leading prices that averaged out catch-up increases in previously lagging prices. This is just an extreme benchmark case, of course, and not a practical possibility; but it figures in an explanation of why it is important, in comparing historical episodes, to pay attention to how definite and credible the anti-inflation programs were.

Next we note the policy aspect of momentum. Some people do succeed in adjusting to inflation and would suffer if their adjustments were rendered inappropriate. Perhaps the most vivid example concerns young couples who buy more expensive houses than they would otherwise think prudent, incurring almost crushing burdens of mortgage payments in relation to income. They do so because they expect their incomes to rise with inflation, making mortgage payments smaller and smaller relatively. An end to inflation would penalize such people in a double-barreled way. First, the mortgage payments would remain a crushing burden unless they sold the house. Second, prices would probably drop because the exceptional demand for real estate as inflation hedges would have vanished. More generally, taking inflation and the inflation premium out of interest rates would have an impact on property values, benefiting some persons and firms and victimizing others.[45] Still more generally, certain activities—examples have been mentioned—flourish more in an inflationary than in a stable environment. Their shriveling would hurt

45. Clark Warburton, "How to Stop Inflation and Reduce Interest Rates, Now and Permanently" (mimeographed, September 1974), 15.

people who had devoted their money and careers to them. As inflation continues and becomes more deeply ingrained, more and more people get into such a position. Political pressures from them, even if only unorganized pressures, work to keep inflation going.

A probably more important reason for continuing money-supply expansion is that the authorities fear the side effects of discontinuing the monetary accommodation of the entrenched price-and-wage uptrend. (Again the analogy between inflation and an addictive drug comes to mind.) The argument was commonly heard in Germany in the early 1920s that the printing presses had to keep rolling to satisfy the "needs of trade" at constantly rising prices and wages. The same argument has been heeded in the United States in recent years, even though to a less spectacular extent. The Federal Reserve has been expanding the money supply at a rate greater than would be compatible with price stability for fear of the side effects of failing to do so. For some such reason, even a majority of monetarists, apparently, call for stopping inflation only gradually by a merely gradual withdrawal of its monetary accommodation.

CONDITIONS FAVORABLE AND UNFAVORABLE FOR STOPPING INFLATION

Gottfried Haberler has noted "cases where an inflation has been stopped without any prolonged recession," notably those of Germany and France after World Wars I and II. The hyperinflation that climaxed in Germany in 1923 "was an uncontrolled profit inflation, prices running ahead of wages." Germany after World War II had a repressed inflation: Its symptoms were suppressed by tight controls, which also strangled economic activity. Not only was the money overhang removed by currency reform in 1948, but controls were abolished at one stroke, setting the stage for sustained economic expansion. Recent inflation in the United States has been of a different nature and much less amenable to a relatively painless cure.[46]

46. Haberler, in *Institutional Arrangements*, ed. Brunner and Meltzer, 152 n. As the German banker Hermann Abs once said, the German hyperinflation of 1923 was an abscess that could be lanced (whereas the Brazilian inflation of the 1960s

At least two considerations suggest that stopping a hyperinflation should be easier than stopping a moderate inflation. First, monetary disorder has become so extreme that conditions simply cannot be left to continue as they are, and this perception invites a rapid change of expectations. People are so desperate for a usable money that they are ready and eager to believe in a clear break with past policy. A switch in policy can be more credible. (A new money unit, if adopted, contributes to the perception that policy has entirely changed.) A second reason is brought to mind by the observed fact that in extreme inflation, the rate of price increases varies widely from month to month. This free oscillation of price changes reflects the replacement of long-term contracts and price-setting for substantial periods by contracting and wage- and price-setting from day to day. Lumpy adjustments of lagging wages and prices are no longer occurring; inflationary pressures, instead of being partly accumulated and carried over to the following month or year, express themselves as they are generated; the catch-up element of inflationary momentum has disappeared.[47] Furthermore, the disappearance of substantial leads and lags in the inflationary procession means that no important interest group stands to gain or lose according to just when the inflation is stopped; in particular, none has reason to urge delay until after its next round of wage or price adjustments.

Not so paradoxically, then, inflation that practically destroys the old money unit creates a relatively favorable opportunity. Success depends, as ever, on getting money-supply growth under control; but *additional* difficulties—adverse side effects—are relatively slight at the climax of a hyperinflation.

At the other extreme, also, it should be easier to stop a mild inflation than one of an intermediate degree. Mildness keeps inflationary expectations from becoming keen and deeply entrenched. Although prices and wages are adjusted only piecemeal over time, the resulting distortion of relative prices and the catch-up aspect of inflationary momentum are slight. Stopping a mild inflation requires only slight change in money-supply growth and the price-level trend,

---

was a less easily treatable case of blood poisoning). Kafka, "Brazilian Stabilization," 630–31.

47. Pazos, *Chronic Inflation*, esp. 19, 93.

so production and employment are threatened and expectations disappointed only slightly. To invoke our earlier analogy, the difficulty of stopping a merely mild price inflation is slight for the same sort of reason that the difficulty is slight of reversing a merely small wartime increase in the price level.

Intermediate inflation exhibits neither the slightness of the required monetary change and of the associated threat to production and employment required to stop a mild inflation nor the amenability to a quick fix that hyperinflation may offer. An intermediate inflation lacks the opportunities offered by either extreme and combines the catch-up and expectational elements of inflationary momentum at their worst.

The foregoing considerations suggest that, in an inflation such as the United States is experiencing, things may have to get worse before they can get better. We may have to reach a panicky state before taking the cure. This is not to say that it is downright impossible to wind down an inflation of our present type, but extreme practical difficulties do obstruct a direct move back to monetary stability.

The principle that things have to get worse before they can get better was apparently illustrated in France in July 1926, when the danger of degeneration into hyperinflation motivated a dramatic turn in policy. Italy provided another example in the summer of 1947. Even the United States experienced a mild illustration of the principle on November 1, 1978. On October 24, President Carter had announced an anti-inflation program that was regarded as unconvincing, including wage and price controls as it did (so-called voluntary controls). The ensuing deterioration of the price situation and particularly of the dollar's exchange rate prodded the administration to announce further measures on November 1, including gestures of orthodox anti-inflationary monetary policy. These brought recovery of the dollar on the exchanges and a temporary drop in the price of gold. To motivate a resolute and enduring anti-inflation policy, however, the panic over money may have to become worse than in the autumn of 1978.

In some cases, conditions relatively favorable to stopping inflation may hinge on its nature or source. If the process of importing inflation at a fixed exchange rate has been at work, as in Germany

71

and Switzerland in the early 1970s, then floating the exchange rate represents a clear and obvious shift in policy and so should be conducive to turning expectations around. If, furthermore, the monetary authorities responsible for such a currency seize the opportunity provided by floating to pursue a less expansionary policy, a virtuous circle can result. The home currency's upward float on the foreign-exchange market lowers the home-currency prices of imported goods and perhaps of import-competing and export goods also, which is helpful in breaking the momentum of inflation in both its catch-up and expectational aspects. This facilitation of noninflationary money-supply policy further tends to strengthen the currency on the exchanges and so on.

Because its current inflation has for the most part not been imported, the United States lacks the opportunity for a dramatic change of the kind just mentioned. Even so, some aspects of the virtuous circle could operate if the United States could somehow first make progress in winding down its inflation rate. Perception of this progress would help strengthen the dollar on the exchanges. In fact, the historically based greater usefulness of the dollar than of other currencies in international transactions provides plenty of scope for demand to turn in its favor if the inflation cost of holding dollar assets is seen to be abating. On the other hand, the virtuous circle working through import and export prices could not be as important as it was for Switzerland and Germany because of the smaller share of foreign trade in the American economy.

DECONTROL

It could count as a favorable condition for stopping inflation that the inflationary difficulties were being compounded by price and wage and exchange controls, for the increased efficiency resulting from their removal—the increased output or real availability of goods—could help absorb inflationary demands. This remark seems applicable to stabilization programs in Argentina, Bolivia, Paraguay, and possibly Burma and other countries, whether or not the authorities took full advantage of the opportunity mentioned.

Controls have contributed on some occasions to the catch-up aspect of inflationary momentum, reinforcing market practices whereby only some prices rise almost continuously while others climb staircases, as it were, with steps of different lengths and heights. Governments, notably in Latin America, have often delayed adjustments in pegged exchange rates and in public-utility rates and have put price ceilings on foodstuffs, raw materials, and fuel. While temporarily containing cost pressures, the controls have discouraged production of the affected goods and services or have required government spending on subsidies. The economy is exposed, furthermore, to periodic large cost and price readjustments instead of to smaller and more nearly continuous adjustments.[48]

Chile has furnished an apparent example of controls aggravating inflation. Inflation tended to worsen the slow growth of agricultural output because governments tried to repress it with food price ceilings and with exchange-rate policies that also caused agricultural prices to lag behind the rise of other prices. Even after the authorities allowed agricultural prices to catch up, the discouragement to production would sometimes continue because producers expected the catch-up to prove only temporary and the relation between agricultural and industrial prices to keep changing erratically. The resulting deficiency of growth in agricultural output would raise food prices in the long run and so contribute to wage increases or would contribute to foreign-exchange shortages by reducing exports or expanding imports.[49]

CONTROLS

When controls have been working in this way, their removal can understandably assist an anti-inflation program. Just as the removal of controls might be an anti-inflationary factor, so, paradoxically, might their imposition. Their scope and importance as an anti-inflation device, however, are narrowly limited. Perhaps the most nearly economically respectable argument for wage and price controls is that

48. Ibid., 21, 26.
49. Ibid., 40–41.

they can dramatize a policy shift and so help break the expectations that had been contributing to the momentum of inflation.[50] Some such hope underlay the controls instituted by President Nixon in August 1971.[51]

Using temporary controls during a period of economic slack to break the inflationary spiral carried over from earlier conditions must be clearly distinguished from trying permanently to suppress the pressure of excess demand on prices. While the case for temporary controls to hasten the transition warranted by monetary and fiscal restraint is much more nearly respectable than the case for permanent controls, it is far from conclusive. The control policy of 1971 could devise only arbitrary criteria for regulating *relative* wages and prices while the general rate of inflation was being reduced.[52] Because controls lock relative prices into what is or soon becomes a disequilibrium pattern, success with their use probably must come quickly if it is to come at all. Even when adopted as part of a comprehensive program for stopping monetary expansion, controls are less likely to work successfully if recent experience with their inappropriate use has discredited them with the public. The Argentine anti-inflation program that began in 1967 had an apparent brief success with wage and price controls while the exchange rate previously kept fixed at an unrealistic level was adjusted. Monetary expansion resumed, however, and the stabilization collapsed.

Ideally, controls would somehow serve to break the momentum of inflation without being so rigid as to sabotage the price mecha-

50. "Only when the public sees that the inflation has stopped, will it stop expecting the inflation to continue." Abba Lerner and David C. Colander, "MAP: A Cure for Inflation," in *Solutions to Inflation,* ed. David C. Colander (New York: Harcourt Brace Jovanovich, 1979), 212. MAP is the authors' market anti-inflation plan, a variant of tax-based incomes policy. A related argument is that controls could be a synchronizing mechanism and in effect impose a coordinated decision to stop raising prices and wages. The usual piecemeal method of setting prices and wages, under which everyone has reason to wait for everyone else to go first in practicing restraint, would be temporarily set aside. See Robert R. Keller, "Inflation, Monetarism, and Price Controls," *Nebraska Journal of Economics and Business* 19 (Winter 1980): 30–40.

51. William Fellner, "Aiming for a Sustainable Second Best During the Recovery from the 1970 Recession," in *Economic Policy,* ed. Cagan, 256.

52. Ibid.

nism. The search for such an ideal gives rise to proposals for tax-based incomes policies and wage-increase-permit plans.[53]

Exchange Stabilization

Exchange-rate stabilization resembles a wage and price freeze in being an attempt to break into the inflation spiral by fixing *something*. Rapid inflation involves either almost continuous exchange depreciation or at least frequent devaluation of the currency. In such a vicious circle, monetary expansion is not unmistakably the driving force. It is partly the *result* of spiraling prices. The government's expenditures may be rising apace with the price level, while its revenues come from taxes based on the lower prices and nominal incomes of several months before. In a rapid inflation, this lag between the public's incurring taxes and paying them can be a major cause of a government budget deficit covered by the printing press. Some of the extreme European inflations after World War I provide examples. In some episodes, the central bank had been granting commercial credits (and creating money) to satisfy the "needs of trade" at rising prices.

Recognizing these passive aspects of monetary expansion in no way contradicts the quantity theory. Of course, stabilization requires getting monetary expansion under control, but breaking into the vicious circle can be a way of doing just that. The exchange rate may be the point where the break-in can be accomplished with the quickest and most evident results, including a shift of expectations, especially if the exchange rate had come to be regarded as the main indicator of what was happening to the value of money. The Austrian government adopted this approach in 1922. Foreign loan commitments and government pledges of financial probity helped make exchange-rate pegging stick. With confidence returning, the demand to hold purchasing power in the form of Austrian crowns revived. To prevent this slump in velocity from causing severe deflation, the National Bank was able to issue additional crowns while buying foreign exchange. The Bolivian stabilization program of 1956

53. Some of these are reviewed in Colander, *Solutions*.

also focused on exchange-rate stabilization, supported by U.S. aid to cover budget deficits.

The cases mentioned were those of small countries whose domestic currencies were only a minor factor on the world foreign-exchange market and could be pegged to some dominant foreign currency. The United States could hardly do anything similar. The dollar is a bigger factor on foreign-exchange markets than any other single currency. Furthermore, pegging the dollar to one foreign currency would not mean pegging it to foreign currencies in general as long as the foreign currencies were fluctuating among themselves. An attempt by the United States to peg onto some particular foreign currency by borrowing and selling it—and the very mention of borrowing it indicates that the cooperation of the country whose currency was being used would be required—would tend more to depress that particular foreign currency than to stabilize the dollar against foreign currencies in general.

Alternatively, could the United States try to stabilize the dollar against gold? Since gold is not an actual currency in which goods and services are priced, pegging the dollar to it would not do much directly to stabilize prices, not even the prices of imports and exports.

This is not to deny the possibility of a virtuous circle. If the United States could somehow get its inflation under control, then the dollar would tend to strengthen on the foreign exchange market, restraining import and export prices. But this would be the consequence of domestic measures to control the inflation and not a case of exchange-rate stabilization initiating the virtuous circle.

Gradualism or a Quick Fix?

One leading question about historical episodes of ending inflation concerns whether stabilization was sought and achieved gradually or quickly. Almost all of the successes that have come to our attention involved stopping or drastically slowing price inflation within a few months. This fact may have some implications. Anyway, we want to ask what circumstances recommend gradualism and which recommend a quick fix.

The broadest, most intuitive, and least analytical argument for gradualism is that one should tackle a difficult task in small, manageable stages rather than try to accomplish it in one backbreaking effort. One more nearly specific argument is that a stabilization slump results not merely from the erosion of real money and spending by price-and-wage momentum but also from frictions in reversing an inflation-distorted allocation of resources; a gradual reallocation could at least hold down those frictions. Related considerations argue, on the other hand, that gradualness—delay—allows inflation-hedging allocations of resources to become all the more significant, requiring all the larger readjustments later. This consideration is reinforced by the point that a gradual program—that is, an undertaking to get inflation under control eventually—may lack the credibility of a program seen to be vigorous and to have early results.

Alexandre Kafka's preference for gradualism in dealing with Brazilian inflation in the mid-1960s apparently hinged on particular features of the local scene. Government wages and salaries had recently been increased, making government jobs exceptionally attractive, even though government payrolls seemed overloaded already. Furthermore, the minimum wage had recently been increased to a probably excessive level. Since wages and salaries could hardly be reduced in money terms, it was necessary to let inflation continue for a while, Kafka apparently felt, in order to whittle them down in real terms.[54] This condition is really part of the catch-up aspect of inflationary momentum, since to whittle down leading wages or prices relatively is to let the lagging ones catch up.

The Federal Reserve Bank of Minneapolis has argued for a steady and credible but also gradual anti-inflation policy. Its reasons are largely psychological or political. Having observed stop and go and many surprises in macroeconomic policy, many persons would doubt the government's will to reform itself and to persist in a sequence of announced gradual steps toward price stability. To those persons, an actual change of that kind, including, of course, a slowdown in monetary growth, would come as a surprise. This surprise would leave the momentum of prices and wages intact. Recessionary side effects

54. Kafka, "Brazilian Stabilization," 609.

would occur and, as in the past, could lead to abandonment of the anti-inflation program.

Because it would take time for the government to demonstrate its resolve to persist in a program of slowing down the growth of total spending, the initial steps must be small. Once it has demonstrated its determination, however, and as measures of monetary restraint no longer come as surprises, then even large steps would no longer bring severe side effects. (The Bank recognized that if people were not committed by existing contracts and if they somehow did firmly believe that the government would persist in its anti-inflation measures—which, however, is unlikely—then even large initial steps would not cause a recession.)[55]

This argument for gradualness amounts to saying that confidence in a resolute anti-inflation policy simply cannot be achieved quickly; the policy shift is bound to come as a surprise. The strategy, therefore, is to keep the spending restraint mild at first in order to avoid serious side effects but to persist in restraint so that the public comes to perceive the resoluteness of the new policy. As this resoluteness increasingly commands confidence, the policy could even be intensified without severe side effects. The argument does not deny that even a sudden dramatic policy change could bring only mild side effects provided that complete trust in its resoluteness prevailed from the start. Doubt would in fact prevail, however, according to the argument. It takes time to achieve the degree of credibility necessary for avoiding severe side effects.

Juan de Pablo's argument for gradualness likewise hinges on the slowness of any change in perceptions and expectations. Experience with Argentina's stabilization program adopted in 1967 suggested that, when a country has been suffering an inflationary process for a long time, an anti-inflationary strategy based on a sudden reduction in the inflation rate stands at a disadvantage because individuals will not "recognize" that reduction and will continue making their decisions in nominal terms. Around the end of 1967, real rates of interest in Argentina rose considerably as nominal interest rates were reduced less than the rate of inflation. In principle, this rise in real rates should have curtailed the volume of credit demanded, but in

---

55. Federal Reserve Bank of Minneapolis, *1978 Annual Report,* esp. 6–7.

fact an expansion occurred. Another variable affected by money illusion was the real wage rate. Not fully recognizing the slowdown of price inflation, workers tended to demand nominal wages that implied increases in real wages. If businessmen increase their indebtedness despite the rise in the real rate of interest and if workers demand nominal wage increases incompatible with overall productivity growth and price stability, then the only way of "solving" the incompatibilities is to abandon the stabilization program and let prices rise.[56]

In saying that money illusion bars quick success against inflation, Pablo was evidently referring to a distinctive kind of money illusion that develops in inflationary times. Ordinarily, money illusion means persistence in thinking and acting as if the monetary unit were stable even when it is not. Pablo was referring, however, to persistence in a habit of adjusting to a continuous rise in the price level even when that price trend is being broken.

Another argument for only gradual stabilization is that a sudden end to inflation would hurt many people. Assets, such as houses, bought at prices reflecting intensified demand for them as supposed inflation hedges would fall in value if the expected further inflation did not occur. A quick stabilization would be hard on debtors who had borrowed, and at high interest rates, in the expectation of paying off their debts in depreciated dollars. Workers with long-term contracts stipulating periodic future wage increases in line with expected inflation would benefit from rapid stabilization (provided that they kept their jobs), while workers whose contracts came up for revision shortly afterwards would stand at a relative disadvantage. Even if a careful weighing of the economic pros and cons should definitely favor a quick stabilization, a gradual approach might be dictated by the political considerations, including resistance from those who consider all quick measures dangerous.[57]

56. Juan Carlos de Pablo, *Política antiinflacionaria en la Argentina, 1967–1970* (Buenos Aires: Amorrortu Editores, 1970), 112–13. Pablo's points about money illusion and wage rates, phrased differently, enter into Milton Friedman's argument for indexing as a way of helping facilitate an end to inflation.

57. Lerner and Colander, "MAP," 219–20. The authors are reviewing the arguments mentioned in the context of their proposal for a market anti-inflation plan.

The very authors who report these arguments for gradualism recognize that they are not conclusive. One might argue, on the contrary, that a gradual slowing of inflation only spreads the withdrawal pangs over a longer time period, while partially continuing the pains of the inflation itself. Furthermore, gradualism lacks the signs of a dramatic change of course that would be helpful in turning expectations around. The American people would be skeptical after their repeated experience with vague and gradual anti-inflation programs that were abandoned. Furthermore, even if a gradual program really were succeeding, its success could be obscured—and a turnaround in expectations blocked—by upward jumps in the price level due to all sorts of unforeseeable temporary disturbances on the domestic or world scene. The program might be abandoned as a failure before the disturbance ran its course. Gradualism is thus dangerous. A dramatic demonstration may be necessary to break inflationary expectations.[58]

Alexandre Kafka, though judging that gradualism was the only course for Brazil in the mid-1960s, nevertheless recognized some risks. Gradualism dissipates the unique opportunity provided by establishment of a new government, if one has been established. Energetic measures might be acceptable at such a time but be resented later. The task of planning correctly during a period of announced decline in inflation, but decline at an unspecified rate, is almost as hard for businessmen as the task of planning under continuing inflation, and harder than planning under monetary stability.[59] Gradual stabilization perpetuates uncertainty about the purchasing power of the money unit over a long period, whereas quick stabilization cuts short this period of uncertainty.

Kafka distinguished between the speed of stopping inflation and the speed of removing price repressions in the form of controls, subsidies, and the like. It might even help to save some of the decontrol until later, after that step had become less likely to rekindle inflationary expectations.[60]

58. Ibid., 220; and Lerner, "Some Questions and Answers About TIP," in *Solutions*, ed. Colander, 196.

59. Kafka, "Brazilian Stabilization," 610.

60. Ibid., esp. 607.

If controls, and in particular a wage and price freeze, form part of a stabilization program, they are the focus of still another argument for aiming at quick rather than gradual success. A frozen pattern of relative prices and wages will become increasingly wrong and unfair, eroding the acceptability of the controls, as time goes on and as the underlying determinants of supply and demand change. Hence the importance of severe monetary action capable of soon replacing the direct controls.[61]

With regard to political acceptability, Ernest Sturc drew a lesson from the stabilization programs of Austria, Turkey, and Finland in the 1950s: "The period of readjustment and the necessary transfer of resources must not be too long. For the failure to achieve tangible results within a reasonable period is very likely to weaken the political consensus that favors stabilization policies."[62]

The architect of the Bolivian stabilization program of 1956–57, George Jackson Eder, answered the argument for gradualism by quoting Graeme S. Dorrance to the effect that "a gradual approach is fraught with more danger than sudden stabilization." Ending a hyperinflation is bound to produce serious imbalances, tensions, and hardships, which are more pronounced the longer the inflation had lasted and the more exaggerated the distortions it had caused. No nation can be expected to endure a lengthy period of painful readjustment, whereas a sharp break from hyperinflation has an almost anesthetic effect. No nation, so far as Eder recalled, had ever successfully ended a rampant inflation gradually. In Bolivia, such an attempt simply would not have worked.[63]

Irving S. Friedman distinguished between gradualism in the success of a stabilization program and gradualism in taking the necessary measures. Bottlenecks or disturbances that cannot be eliminated at once may make instant price stability impossible. Wishful thinking

---

61. This is one major theme of Pablo, *Política.*

62. Ernest Sturc, "Stabilization Policies: Experience of Some European Countries in the 1950's," *International Monetary Fund Staff Papers* 15 (July 1968): 216.

63. George Jackson Eder, *Inflation and Development in Latin America: A Case History of Inflation and Stabilization in Bolivia* (Ann Arbor: Bureau of Business Research, University of Michigan, 1968), 277. Dorrance's words are quoted from "The Effect of Inflation on Economic Development," *International Monetary Fund Staff Papers* 10 (March 1963): 29.

and promises of quick success may lead to disappointment, with an adverse effect on expectations. Slogans about gradualism, however, may serve as an excuse for inadequate measures, and "gradualism in changing expectations or trends is self-defeating." The public must quickly be given reason to expect ever smaller price increases or even price declines.[64]

The architect of Bolivian stabilization noted the objection that the Bolivian experience might have little relevance for other Latin American countries, where inflation had been less extreme and presumably required less drastic and sudden remedies. His answer was that, wherever inflation has gotten out of control, as in Brazil, Argentina, Chile, and Colombia, a surgical operation and not a palliative was demanded. He could recall no case of uncontrolled inflation that had been cured gradually, as by reducing the annual rate from 100 to 50 to 20 percent and finally to 0. The maladjustments produced during a long inflation and the difficulties and distortions of readjustment are so great that one cannot expect the authorities and the public to suffer patiently for two or three years while the monetary advisor assures them that all will turn out well in the end if they follow his advice. In stabilization above all, "'Twere well it were done quickly."[65]

As implied by some of the points already reviewed, the relative strengths of the arguments for gradual and for quick stabilization depend on the particular circumstances of the case. If all prices, wages, salaries, rents, contractual values, rates, and tariffs are being adjusted at frequent intervals and are being kept nearly in line with each other, that circumstance would argue for quick stabilization. In the opposite case of infrequent adjustments at staggered times, suddenly applying the brakes to both demands and costs would create a pattern that would touch off complaints of injustice. If the brakes were applied to demand only, while costs and prices went on being pushed up as contracts of the lagging groups successively reached their renewal dates, recession would ensue.[66] The distinction between these cases is obviously related to the point made earlier that stopping an

64. "Comment," *Journal of Political Economy* 75 (August 1967), part 2, 651–52.
65. Eder, *Inflation and Development*, xi–xii.
66. Pazos, *Chronic Inflation*, 7.

extreme inflation is in some respects easier than stopping a moderate inflation.

A case relatively amenable to sudden stabilization is one in which a flight from the domestic currency has raised prices, including the price of foreign exchange, to a higher level than the quantity of money, apart from psychological factors, warrants. This was apparently the situation in France in mid-1926. In Germany in November 1923, similarly, the price of foreign exchange and of the new Rentenmark in terms of the old paper marks had been pushed up, in this case by stabilization measures themselves, to above the level previously prevailing on the market. Like devaluing a weak currency with a margin to spare in order to facilitate its subsequent exchange stabilization, this was an example of *reculer pour mieux sauter*.

In an inflationary situation of the current United States type, the processes of cost-price interaction and catch-up prevent an instant stabilization of the price level. Yet this circumstance does not rule out sudden stabilization in the sense of a turnaround of expectations. Two situations are quite different: (1) expecting inflation to continue on its established course, and (2) perceiving a clampdown on money-supply growth and expecting no further price increases except by way of catch-up. If policy makers and the public could understand the catch-up process and why it did not demonstrate a failure of monetary restraint, then a sudden stabilization could be achieved as far as both monetary fundamentals and expectations were concerned.

Alfred Zanker, chief European economic correspondent of *U.S. News and World Report*, recommends some such approach for United States inflation. So far, fears of a bad recession have kept governments in the United States and abroad from acting long and forcefully enough against inflation. At least four times in twenty years, the United States has abandoned the remedy too soon, allowing inflation to resurge from a higher plateau. Policy makers now face a deep credibility gap. Zanker recommends stopping monetary expansion long enough to achieve a basic change in price expectations. A credit crunch and sweeping moves toward a balanced government budget would help restore confidence in the dollar. A publicity campaign would explain why so drastic a cure was needed and how it would succeed.

Historical experience suggests to Zanker that the side effects—layoffs, bankruptcies, and the like—would not be catastrophic and would reach their climax within six to twelve months. Business firms would respond with efforts to hold the line on costs and prices. Soon, with inflation receding fast and government finance looking healthier, interest rates would fall sharply, encouraging capital formation and renewed business expansion. The shock treatment would strengthen the dollar on the exchange markets, would encourage and facilitate anti-inflation programs abroad, and would work toward moderation in the pricing of oil. Such shock treatment is no miracle weapon, no substitute for prudent policies and good management and hard work; but it is more attractive than tolerating a prolonged stagflation.[67]

67. Alfred Zanker, "Shock Treatment for Inflation: Can It Work?" *U.S. News and World Report*, 27 August 1979, 67–68.

PART TWO

MONETARY

MISCONCEPTIONS

Essential Properties of the Medium of Exchange

I

LIQUIDITY AND MONEY

The Radcliffe Report and many writings on nonbank financial inter-mediaries urged more attention to the total liquidity position of a developed economy and less to money in the old narrow sense. This advice met widespread skepticism. Something remains to be said, though, about what facts justify this skepticism and why they are crucial although banally familiar. The actual medium of exchange remains distinctive in ways seldom fully appreciated. The differences between it and other elements of liquidity may be unimportant to the individual; yet they are crucial to the system. An individual holder might consider certain near moneys practically the same as actual money because he could readily exchange them for it whenever he wanted. But microexchangeability need not mean ready exchangeability of aggregates. (Although gold and paper moneys under the gold standard meant practically the same thing to an individual holder, for example, they did not have the same functions and significance in the national economy, especially not at a time of balance-of-payments trouble.) The sound precept of "methodological individualism" prizes information gained by considering the decisions of the individual economic unit, but it does not insist on generalizing from the individual point of view *alone*. The famous fallacy of composition warns against that.

Reprinted from *Kyklos* 21, no. 1 (1968): 45–69, with permission of Redaktion Kyklos, c/o WWZ, Petersgraben 51, CH-4003, Basel.

The author is indebted to Dr. Daniel Edwards and Professors W. H. Hutt, Richard H. Timberlake, Jr., and James M. Waller for many helpful comments. He accepts blame for following not all but only some of their advice.

An excess demand for actual money shows itself to individual economic units less clearly than does an excess demand for any other thing, even the nearest of near moneys. It eliminates itself more indirectly and with more momentous macroeconomic consequences. The present paper, building up to its main conclusion in section V, tries to explain how. It gives new support to the diagnosis of depression as an essentially monetary disorder.

One familiar approach to the definition of money scorns any supposedly *a priori* line between money and near moneys. Instead, it seeks the definition that works best with statistics. One strand of that approach seeks clues to substitutabilities among assets—to how similar or different their holders regard them—by studying how sensitively holdings of currency, demand deposits, and other liquid assets have depended on income, wealth, and interest rates.[1] Another strand seeks the narrowly or broadly defined quantity that correlates most closely with income in equations fitted to historical data. Information obtained from such studies can be important for some purposes. But it would be awkward if the definition of money accordingly had to change from time to time and country to country. Furthermore, even if money defined to include certain near moneys does correlate somewhat more closely with income than money narrowly defined, that fact does not necessarily impose the broad definition. Perhaps the amount of these near moneys depends on the level of money income and in turn on the amount of medium of exchange through the gearing process described in section III below. More generally, it is not obvious why the magnitude with which some other magnitude correlates most closely deserves overriding attention; it might be neither the most interesting nor the most controllable one. The number of bathers at a beach may correlate more closely with the number of cars parked there than with either the temperature or the price of admission, yet the former correlation may be less interesting or useful than either of the latter. The correlation with national income might be closer for either consumption

1. Statistical demand-for-money studies are examples of "individual-experiments," as distinguished from "market-experiments." On that distinction, see Don Patinkin, *Money, Interest, and Prices*, 2d ed. (New York: Harper & Row, 1965), esp. 11–12, 387–94.

or investment than for the quantity of money; yet the latter correlation could be the most interesting one to the monetary authorities.

Of course, a broad definition of money is not downright "wrong" since many definitions can be self-consistent. But no mere definition should deter us, when we are trying to understand the flow of spending in the economy, from focusing attention on the narrow category of assets that actually get spent. It is methodological prejudice to dismiss as irrelevant, without demonstrating their irrelevance, such facts as these: Certain assets do and others do not circulate as media of exchange. No reluctance of sellers to accept the medium of exchange hampers anyone's spending it. The medium of exchange can "burn holes in pockets" in a way that near moneys do not. Supply creates its own demand (in a sense specified later) more truly for the medium of exchange than for other things. These are observed facts, or inferences from facts, not mere *a priori* truths or tautologies.

In comparing the medium of exchange with other financial assets, we must go beyond asking what determines the *amount* of each that people demand to hold. We must also consider the *manner* in which people acquire and dispose of each asset and implement a change in their demand for it. This is presumably what W. T. Newlyn meant in urging a "functional" distinction between money and near money according to "operational effects in the economy rather than [just] according to asset status from the point of view of the owner."[2]

To recognize how nonmonetary liquidity affects total demands for money and for goods and services, we need not blur the definition of money so badly as to subvert measurement and control of its quantity. We need not blur the distinctions between supplies of and demands for assets and between influences on supply and influences on demand. We can define the supply of money narrowly, as a measurable quantity, and see it confronted by a demand for cash balances—a demand influenced, to be sure, by the availability and attractiveness of other assets.

This approach keeps two concepts of "liquidity" distinct. The first, a vague one, corresponds roughly to what Newlyn has called "fi-

2. "The Supply of Money and Its Control," *Economic Journal* 74 (June 1964): 327–46, esp. 335–36.

nancial strength"—the total purchasing power that firms and individuals consider available in their asset holdings and their possibilities of borrowing. This "essentially . . . *ex-ante* concept . . . reflects 'the
amount of money people think they can get hold of.' " What they
could in fact get hold of all at once is something else again. In a second sense, liquidity means the amount of medium of exchange in
existence (or perhaps, as Newlyn implies, the relation between that
amount and the volume of transactions to be performed).[3] Given a
fixed stock of actual medium of exchange, widespread attempts to
sell liquid assets or borrow to mobilize supposed "financial strength"
for spending would partially frustrate each other through declines
in the prices of financial assets, higher interest rates, tighter credit
rationing, and the like.

II
THE EXAMPLE OF CLAIMS ON
NONBANK INTERMEDIARIES

To highlight the properties of the medium of exchange by contrast,
let us focus on the liquid liabilities of nonbank financial intermediaries. (Doing so is an expository device only; most of the disputes
over the intermediaries do not, in their own right, concern us here.)
James Tobin has restated some of the issues raised by Gurley and
Shaw in a helpfully clear and forceful way.[4] He questions the traditional story of how banks create money by expanding credit. If other
intermediaries are mere brokers in loanable funds, then so are the
banks. A savings and loan association is a creditor of the mortgage
borrower and at the same time a debtor to the ultimate saver who
holds its shares; similarly, the commercial bank can be a creditor because it is in debt to its depositors. Only ultimate savers can provide
loanable funds. If in some sense both types of institution do create
credit by issuing their own liquid liabilities, they are alike in that re-

3. *Ibid.* The quotation comes from p. 342, where Newlyn in turn quotes the
Radcliffe Report, para. 390. Newlyn distinguishes still another concept of liquidity,
but it is not directly relevant here.

4. "Commercial Banks as Creators of 'Money,' " in *Banking and Monetary Studies*, ed. Deane Carson (Homewood, Ill.: Irwin, 1963), 408–19.

spect. Bank demand deposits are unique in being actual media of exchange, Tobin concedes; but since each type of claim on a financial intermediary has its own brand of uniqueness, there is nothing unique about being unique. It is "superficial and irrelevant" to insist "that a bank can make a loan by 'writing up' its deposit liabilities, while a savings and loan association . . . cannot satisfy a mortgage borrower by crediting him with a share account." Whether or not money spent by a borrower from a bank stays in the banking system as a whole depends not on how the loan was initially made but on "whether somewhere in the chain of transactions initiated by the borrower's outlays are found depositors who wish to hold new deposits equal in amount to the new loan. Similarly, the outcome for the savings and loan industry depends on whether in the chain of transactions initiated by the mortgage are found individuals who wish to acquire additional savings and loan shares."[5]

Tobin would extend our doubts in this last case to bank deposits also. He envisages "a natural economic limit to the scale of the commercial banking industry." Given their wealth and asset preferences, people will voluntarily hold additional demand deposits only if the yields thereby sacrificed on other assets fall. But beyond some point, lower yields would make further lending and investing unprofitable for the banks. "In this respect the commercial banking industry is not qualitatively different from any other financial intermediary system."[6] Even with no reserve requirements, bank credit and deposits could not expand further when no further loans and investments were available at yields high enough to cover the costs (among others) of attracting and holding deposits.

In so arguing, Tobin slights some familiar contrasts. The banking system as a whole *can* expand credit and deposits so far as reserves permit. There is no problem of lending and spending new demand deposits into existence. No one need be persuaded to invest in them before they can be created.[7] No one will refuse the routine

5. *Ibid.*, 412–13.

6. *Ibid.*, 414.

7. Yet Lyle E. Gramley and Samuel B. Chase, Jr., praise and adopt Tobin's "new view" in their "Time Deposits in Monetary Analysis," *Federal Reserve Bulletin* 51 (October 1965): 1380–1404, see esp. 1381 n, 1385, 1389–90. They work with a model in

medium of exchange for fear of being stuck with too much. Unwanted savings and loan shares, in contrast, would not be accepted and so could not be created in the first place. (And if anyone did find himself somehow holding unwanted shares, he would simply cash them in for money and so make them go out of existence. He would still cash them even if he did not want to *hold* the money instead, since money is the intermediary routinely used in buying all sorts of things.)

A holder of unwanted money exchanges it *directly* for whatever he does want, without first cashing it in for something else.[8] Nothing

which "the quantity of deposits a bank sells depends on the willingness of the public to purchase its deposits. Since this is true for each and every bank in the system, the constraint on bank deposits—and hence on bank asset holdings—is derived from the public's desire to hold bank deposits." They dismiss as "confusion" the view (as they paraphrase it from J. M. Culbertson, "Intermediaries and Monetary Theory: A Criticism of the Gurley-Shaw Theory," *American Economic Review* 48 [March 1958]: 119–31) that "the public has no choice but to acquire" any newly created demand deposits. Apparently they intend more than the old point—see the next footnote—that withdrawal of reserve funds into hand-to-hand circulation can limit bank expansion.

In mentioning possible offsets to expansionary open-market operations by the central bank, Gramley and Chase are in effect merely saying that throwing more logs on the fire could fail to warm a room if at the same time its doors and windows were flung open to the January air.

According to the authors, "open market operations alter the stock of money balances if, and only if, they alter the quantity of money *demanded* by the public." This statement is misleading because it pretends to be more than the near-truism it is. Actually, a change in the stock of money *does* alter the quantity of money demanded—through the familiar process mentioned in the next paragraph of the present text. The quoted statement is analogous to portentously announcing that a price cut intended to expand sales of some commodity will not work unless the quantity of the commodity demanded increases. True enough, but a sufficient price cut *will* increase the quantity demanded.

8. One qualification is minor in this context: When demand deposits are cashed in for currency, the drain on reserves limits banks' assets and deposits. But this limitation works on the supply-of-money side, not the demand side. If the authorities that create "high-powered dollars" and the banks, taken together, want to expand the money supply, they can do so, unhampered by any unwillingness of the public to accept or hold money.

Another minor qualification concerns commercial-bank time deposits. A shift in the public's preferences to them from demand deposits does tend to shrink the latter if the same kind of reserve money, fixed in total amount, is held against both types of deposit. The shrinkage is the smaller, the smaller the reserve ratio for time deposits is in comparison with the ratio for demand deposits. Anyway, the decline in reserves available to support demand deposits is an occurrence affecting the *supply* of demand deposits. By providing enough reserves to support them, the monetary authorities can maintain any desired amount of demand deposits in existence.

is more ultimate than money. Instead of going out of existence, unwanted money gets passed around until it ceases to be unwanted. Supply thus creates its own demand (both expressed as nominal, not real, quantities, of course). To say this is not to assert that there is no such thing as a demand function for money or that the function always shifts to keep the quantities demanded and in existence identical.[9] Rather, an initial excess supply of money touches off a *process* that raises the nominal quantity demanded quite *in accordance with* the demand function. Initially unwanted cash balances "burn holes in pockets," with direct or indirect repercussions on the flow of-spending in the economy, in a way not true of near moneys. Although anyone holding near money has *chosen* to hold it as a store of value at least temporarily and has not just routinely received it in payment for goods or services sold, people do receive money in this way. A person accepts money not necessarily because he chooses to continue holding it but precisely because it is the routine intermediary between his sales and his purchases or investments and because he knows he can get rid of it whenever he wants. People's actions to get rid of unwanted money make it ultimately wanted by changing at least two of the arguments in the demand function for money: the money values of wealth and income rise through higher prices or fuller employment and production, and interest rates may move during the adjustment process.

No such process affects near moneys and other nonmoneys. For an ordinary asset, a discrepancy between actual and desired holdings exerts direct pressure on its price (or on its yield or similar terms on which it is acquired and offered). If the supply and demand for an asset are out of balance, "something has to give." If the something is specific and "gives" readily, the adjustment can occur without widespread and conspicuous repercussions. But the medium of exchange has no single, explicit price of its own in terms of a good

9. J. G. Gurley and E. S. Shaw intimate that J. M. Culbertson harbored some such idea; see their "Reply" to his criticism of their theory in *American Economic Review* 48 (March 1958): 135–36.

The argument about how the supply of money creates its own demand applies to the aggregate of all types of the medium of exchange and not, of course, to dimes alone or currency alone or demand deposits alone. The necessary proviso about suitable proportions of different kinds and denominations of money in their total does not impair the contrast in question between money and near moneys.

other than itself, nor does it have any explicit yield of its own that can "give" readily to remove an imbalance between its supply and demand. Widespread repercussions (described in section V) occur instead.

Like nonmoney assets, borrowing privileges that people do not care to use also fail to touch off any such process. (I refer to the famous idea that unexhausted overdraft privileges are an important type of liquidity.) A magical doubling of all lines of credit, unaccompanied by monetary expansion, would hardly "burn holes in pockets" in the same way a doubled money supply would. And as we have seen, people's initial unwillingness to *hold* all newly created actual money would not keep them from accepting it and would not prevent its creation.

Tobin's idea (already cited) that a decline in interest rates on loans and investments will limit profitable expansion of bank credit and deposits, even if reserves permit, forgets Wicksell's "cumulative process." As money expansion raises prices and incomes, the dollar volume of loans demanded at given interest rates rises also. Yields on bank loans and investments need *not* keep falling. The great inflations of history disprove any "natural limit" posed by falling interest rates.

III
ASYMMETRICAL ASSET PREFERENCES

Let us suppose that the nonbank intermediaries, at their own initiative, somehow issue more claims against themselves to acquire earning assets. (Never mind what makes people acquire these claims in the first place.) As people find themselves holding more and more near moneys relative to both money and nonliquid assets, they exercise what Gurley and Shaw have called a "diversification demand" for actual money.[10] People have some idea of appropriate compositions of their portfolios and will not keep on indefinitely accumulating securities or near moneys unaccompanied by additional money. And

10. "Financial Aspects of Economic Development," *American Economic Review* 45 (September 1955): 515–38, esp. 525–26.

even if, understandably, people did not want additional money as a store of value, they would nevertheless want more of it to lubricate transactions in the other components of their expanded portfolios. Asset preferences thus limit the expansion of near moneys if the money supply is constant; exclusive attention to the low (and voluntary) reserve ratios typical of nonbank intermediaries exaggerates their scope for multiple expansion.[11] Conceivably, though, this limit could be a rubbery one if asset preferences were highly sensitive to interest rates (a question noted again toward the end of section IV).

Besides a portfolio-balancing or "diversification" demand and a portfolio-transactions demand for actual money, a transactions demand connected with ordinary income and expenditure would come into play. It would, anyway, if in some implausible way issuers did expand the stock of near moneys at their own initiative, inflating prices and incomes. People would want larger holdings of the shrunken money units and might cash in some of their near moneys as one way to get money.

Asset preferences work asymmetrically. Because of them, a constant supply of actual money can restrain the expansion of near moneys. But no such restraint works the other way around: not even some sort of ceiling on near moneys could keep the monetary authorities from creating as much money as they wished. In the absence of a ceiling, near moneys tend to gear themselves to the money supply. When monetary expansion has inflated prices or incomes, the desired nominal amounts of borrowing, on the one hand, and of saving and financial investment, on the other hand, will have grown more or less in step and so, therefore, will the amounts of securities and financial intermediation in existence.[12] To dramatize the asym-

11. For a comparison of how the public's asset preferences and their own reserve ratios restrain the nonbank intermediaries, see Donald Shelby, "Some Implications of the Growth of Financial Intermediaries," *Journal of Finance* 13 (December 1958): 527–41.

12. Cf. R. W. Clower and M. L. Burstein, "On the Invariance of Demand for Cash and Other Assets," *Review of Economic Studies* 28 (October 1960): 32–36; and M. L. Burstein, *Money* (Cambridge: Schenkman, 1963), 208, 734–36, 781. With evident approval Roy Harrod describes as a piece of "old orthodoxy" the proposition that bank-credit expansion will promote additional nonbank lending as well. "Is the Money Supply Important?" *Westminister Bank Review* (November 1959): 5.

metry, however, let us suppose that some official ban on the expansion of near moneys thwarts this gearing. As the quantity of money expanded beyond what people initially wanted to hold, competition for the fixed supply of near moneys would drive their yields low enough to keep people indifferent at the margin between them and money. But nothing would keep prices or money incomes from rising until people desired to hold all the new money.

Much of the contrast developed so far boils down to saying that "the most important proposition in monetary theory"[13] holds true of the actual medium of exchange only. Individual economic units are free to hold as much or as little money as they see fit in view of their own circumstances; yet the total of their freely chosen cash balances is identical with the money supply, which the monetary authorities can make as big or small as they see fit. The process that resolves this paradox has no counterpart for claims on nonbank intermediaries; instead, unwanted holdings go out of existence. The proposition also fails for other near moneys, such as securities; but instead of shrinking in actual amount to the desired level, an excessive quantity shrinks in the market appraisal of its total money value.

Expansion of claims on nonbank intermediaries promotes economy in holding cash balances—or so postwar American experience seems to illustrate. Though not entirely wrong, this proposition is loosely phrased. The rise of nonbank intermediaries is not an

---

It follows that given unchanged "wants, resources, and technology," the existence of securities, near moneys, and financial intermediation does not invalidate the comparative-static propositions of the quantity theory. (However, these things presumably do keep a change in the money supply from affecting equilibrium prices in such a direct, quick, and tight way as otherwise.)

Although Burstein and Harrod recognize the gearing stressed in the present paper, their discussions leave doubt whether they recognize the asymmetry also.

Contradicting the principle of gearing, James Tobin and William C. Brainard have envisaged a tendency, operating through asset yields, for the quantity of near moneys to adapt *inversely* to the quantity of money. Their idea apparently is that a change in the quantity of one thing causes opposite changes in the demand for and thus in the equilibrium quantities of its close substitutes. "Financial Intermediaries and the Effectiveness of Monetary Controls," *American Economic Review* 53 (May 1963), esp. 391–92. This article also wins the approval of Gramley and Chase, "Time Deposits in Monetary Analysis," 1381 n.

13. Milton Friedman, in *Employment, Growth, and Price Levels*, part 4 (Hearings before the Joint Economic Committee, United States Congress, May 1959), 609.

autonomous change to which asset holders simply respond. Near-moneys, unlike money, cannot expand unless either monetary expansion or changes in "wants, resources, or technology" make people decide to accumulate more of them. Except as reflected in the yields or other advantages that various assets offer him, the individual does not care about their total amounts in existence. If savings and loan associations, for example, have contributed to the postwar rise in the velocity of actual money, the cause is not the sheer growth in their outstanding shares; instead, it comprises whatever changes have underlain a shift of asset preferences in their favor. These underlying changes presumably include not only the 1950 improvement in insurance features and the postwar uptrend in interest rates, permitting higher rates on savings and loan shares, but also whatever other factors have underlain the opening of new offices in convenient places, paid and word-of-mouth advertising, and a cumulative familiarity. Savings and loan growth has not unambiguously helped *cause* a rise in monetary velocity; both, rather, have *resulted* from more ultimate changes. Much the same is true of expansion in the amounts of other near moneys.

IV

FUNCTIONAL CONTRASTS

An imaginary experiment will further distinguish near moneys from money. Suppose the government gives each citizen a newly printed $1,000 Treasury bill.[14] It resolves not to create money to pay off the bills as they come due; instead, it will sell new ones at whatever interest rate may be necessary. People do not want to continue holding the entire addition to their wealth in the form they receive it in, Treasury bills. They sell some, which raises their yield enough to find voluntary holders for the entire increased amount. Generalized by arbitrage, higher interest rates tend somewhat to restrain the spur that the increased private wealth gives to demands for consumer and investment goods. On the other hand, the higher rates tend to re-

14. We drop savings and loan shares as our standard example of near money because it is hard to suppose that they, being private liabilities as well as private assets, are simply donated into existence.

strain people in demanding larger cash balances to lubricate trans-actions in goods and services at increased prices. Whether prices do rise, however, is not certain; for the new private nominal wealth given out by the government tends to raise the demand for cash balances relative to income and expenditure. The greater the role wealth plays in the demand function for cash balances, the less far-fetched is the possibility that the outcome of the whole experiment might be *de*flation on balance.[15] That possibility would be even less far-fetched if the government had given out long-term bonds rather than short-term bills and would not be far-fetched at all if it had given out con-sumer and investment goods magically conjured into existence. As these examples suggest, the outcome depends on how complemen-tary or substitutable at the margin people regard the new securities given them, other securities, actual money, and commodities. It also depends on how wealth- and interest-elastic the demands for these things are. The actual values of these complementarities, substitut-abilities, and elasticities in particular countries and periods need not concern us here. What highlights the contrast in question is that an increment of near moneys could *conceivably* cause deflation, while the result of expanding the actual money supply could hardly be doubtful.

Newlyn develops his "neutrality" or "functional" distinction be-tween money and nonmoney by inquiring whether a payment fi-nanced from a holding of an asset does or does not tend to change either its total quantity or its price (by changing the relation be-tween supply and demand of loans or securities at the old interest rate). He classifies an asset as money (medium of exchange) if the effect of disposing of some of it to make a payment is "neutral," nei-ther changing the total amount of that sort of asset in existence nor disturbing the loan market. A nonneutral effect occurs when the per-son making a payment either (i) sells some asset or (ii) draws down

15. With similar considerations in mind, Allan Meltzer and Karl Brunner have dropped a thought-provoking hint about how a government budget deficit financed by bond issues rather than by new money could conceivably have an eventually de-flationary influence. "The Place of Financial Intermediaries in the Transmission of Monetary Policy," *American Economic Review* 53 (May 1963): 381. Richard H. Timber-lake, Jr., alludes to a similar possibility, though without necessarily claiming realism for it, in "The Stock of Money and Money Substitutes." *Southern Economic Journal* 30 (January 1964): 255.

his claims on a financial intermediary, causing "a reduction in the aggregate of such claims and a consequential sale of an asset by the intermediary."[16]

Currency changes hands in Newlyn's most obvious example of a "neutral" payment; interest rates feel no *direct* effect. A payment by check, transferring ownership of demand deposits, does cause a fully-loaned-up drawee bank to shrink its loans or sell securities, true enough; but another bank gains reserves and can expand its credit; so this payment is also neutral in Newlyn's sense. (Financing a payment by drawing down a commercial-bank time deposit would be neutral only if reserve ratios were the same against demand and time deposits.) Cashing a savings and loan account wipes it out and is obviously *not* neutral. Similarly, selling a Treasury bill to finance a payment tends to depress the aggregate money value of the bills in existence.

Although Newlyn does not classify a traveler's check, we may gain further insight into his neutrality criterion by trying. When its holder spends a check, he starts it on its way back to the issuer. The issuer obtains funds to honor it by selling securities from his portfolio (assuming, of course, a significant total of check encashments). The resulting upward pressure on interest rates, as well as the shrinkage in the total amount of checks in existence, disqualifies a nonbank traveler's check from counting as a medium of exchange.[17]

16. Newlyn, "The Supply of Money and Its Control," 336. Harold Rose had made some brief remarks anticipating Newlyn's criterion in "Money Still Under Review," *The Banker* 111 (February 1961), esp. 105–6, and in a letter of the same title in the April 1961 issue, 289–90.

In principle, any decision to buy goods or services by parting with money or any other financial asset does have *some* general-interdependence effect on everything in the economy, including the loan market and interest rates. But such effects are more indirect and feeble and even less dependable in direction than the unambiguous direct effects that Newlyn presumably has in mind.

17. But Boris P. Pesek and Thomas R. Saving (*Money, Wealth, and Economic Theory* [New York: Macmillan, 1967], esp. 184, 187, 190, 196–97) assume, with practically no argument, that traveler's checks *are* a medium of exchange, along with currency and demand deposits. In general, however, they insist on the distinctiveness of the medium of exchange even in contrast with close near moneys. The considerations they stress—the net-wealth character of money and its role in the real-balance or wealth effect—are different from but not inconsistent with the argument of the present paper.

As this example reminds us, a seller of goods or services may sometimes accept payment in nonmoney to get his customer's business. In effect he serves as an agent who converts the nonmoney into cash afterward, sparing his customer the trouble of doing so in the first place. Such accommodation does not mean that the asset in question has become a medium of exchange. Things would be different if the custom developed of endorsing traveler's checks in blank and circulating them indefinitely—if each payee accepted them with the intention of passing them along to others and without anyone's asking the issuer to redeem them. (Any reader who thinks that this view of the matter makes the distinction between money and nonmoney ridiculously slight is asked to suspend judgment until the last section of this paper.)

Since payments prepared for by unloading near moneys tend to shrink the amount in existence or raise interest rates in a way not true of payments of actual money, decisions to buy goods and services stimulate total spending less when the purchases are to be financed from holdings of near money than from cash balances. A decision to spend from actual money already held raises velocity directly: instead of merely representing an increase in the desired flow of spending relative to an unchanged cash balance, it represents an autonomous absolute drop in the demand for cash balances. As a matter of arithmetic, an individual's decision to finance expenditure from a holding of near money also implies a rise in velocity—of his unchanged actual cash balance. Of course, he could not succeed in unloading near money unless someone else were induced somehow (perhaps by increased interest rates) to part with cash. Even so, the rise in velocity does not necessarily imply a decline, or even constancy, in the economywide total amount of cash balances eventually desired. On the contrary, the total of cash balances desired for transactions purposes would even increase if spending could rise beyond a certain level. For this reason, any expansion in the total flow of spending on goods and services would meet some restraint, given the actual quantity of money, from the increase that would otherwise occur in the transactions balances desired even by individuals and firms other than those whose decisions had touched off the expansion.

Decisions to spend on goods and services are presumably still less expansionary when the buyers unload holdings of bonds rather than near money. The questions relevant to this comparison concern different effects on the term structure of increased interest rates and the influences of interest rates both on choices between cash and other financial assets and on decisions about saving and investment. Intuitively, also, it makes sense that decisions to spend should be less expansionary when the financing is to come from unloading less moneylike rather than more nearly moneylike assets. The extreme example in this direction would be a desire to finance buying some commodities by unloading an inventory of other commodities. Well, just as it makes a difference whether purchases are financed by unloading commodities or unloading bonds, or by unloading bonds or unloading near moneys, so it makes a difference whether near money or actual money is to be unloaded. Partly for reasons still to be explained, the last distinction is the most noteworthy of all.

Desired shifts from bonds or near moneys into goods and services could raise the velocity of money through raising interest rates. How strongly interest rates influence desired cash balances, on the one hand, and saving and investment, on the other, is too vast an issue for review here. Still, its relation to the main topic of this paper is worth mentioning. Conceivably (as noted in section II), portfolio preferences could shift between actual money and near moneys with extreme sensitivity to interest rates, causing important inflationary or deflationary effects even with the money supply constant. Especially because the available statistical evidence appears contradictory, some general considerations telling against such sensitivity are worth attention. A. J. L. Catt reaches a skeptical conclusion by analyzing the responses of different types of asset holder, particularly the small unsophisticated saver at one extreme, and the large corporation always anxious to keep its funds at work at the other extreme. Similarly, Lawrence Ritter reasons that interest-rate levels and expectations are more relevant to choices between bonds and near moneys, subject to much and little price fluctuation, respectively, than to choices between the medium of exchange and other financial assets.[18] Furthermore, developments that may promote a long-run trend toward greater and greater economy in holding actual cash balances by no means necessarily imply a short-run two-way sensitivity of cash holdings to interest rates.

V

EXCESS DEMAND FOR THE MEDIUM OF EXCHANGE

Some further functional contrasts between the medium of exchange and near moneys bear on the essentially monetary nature of depressions. By Walras's law, any aggregate excess demand for or supply of currently produced goods and services, valued at prevailing prices, must be matched by an aggregate excess supply of or demand for all other things. Demand for current output cannot be excessive or deficient unless, at the same time, the opposite is true of the medium of exchange in particular: at not-yet-changed levels of income and prices, people must be wanting to hold less or more money than exists.[19]

Exceptions hinging on excess demands for non-currently-produced goods other than money are not inconceivable but would be economically unrealistic. In the *General Theory*, Keynes remarks that a deficiency of demand for current output might be matched by an excess demand for assets having three "essential properties": (1) their supply from private producers responds slightly if at all to an increase in demand for them; (2) a tendency to rise in value will only to a slight extent enlist substitutes to help meet a strengthened demand for them; (3) their liquidity advantages are large relative to the costs of holding them. Another point that Keynes notes by implication belongs explicitly on the list: (4) their values are "sticky" and do not adjust readily to remove a disequilibrium.

18. See A. J. L. Catt, "Idle Balances and the Motives for Liquidity," *Oxford Economic Papers*, n.s. 14 (June 1962): 124–37; and L. S. Ritter, "The Structure of Financial Markets, Income Velocity, and the Effectiveness of Monetary Policy," *Schweizerische Zeitschrift für Volkswirtschaft und Statistik*, no. 3 (1962): 276–89.

19. In this context it is unnecessary to dwell on the distinction between flow and stock disequilibriums.

Money is the most obvious asset having these properties. Keynes asks, however, whether a deficiency of demand for current output might be matched by an excess demand for other things instead, perhaps land or mortgages. Other writers have asked, similarly, about other securities, works of art, and jewelry.[20]

My answer is no: Such things might be in excess demand *along with* but not *instead of* money. Money itself would also be in excess demand. One reason is that all other exchangeable things trade against money in markets of their own and at their own prices expressed in money. (This is true even of claims against financial intermediaries if their interest rates count as corresponding, inversely, to prices.) An excess demand for a good or a security tends to remove itself through a change in price or yield. If, however, interest rates should resist declining below the floor level explained by Keynes and Hicks, people would no longer prefer additional interest-bearing assets to additional money, and any further shift of demand from currently produced goods and services to financial assets would be an increase in the excess demand for actual money in particular. (If stickiness or arbitrary controls should keep prices and yields of financial assets from adjusting and clearing the market, the situation would be essentially the same as in the case of price rigidity of other assets, considered in the next and later paragraphs.) The monetary interpretation of deficient demand for current output thus does not depend on any precise dividing line between money and other assets (even though the present paper does draw such a line); if money broadly defined is in excess demand, money narrowly defined must be in excess demand also. Unlike other things, money has no single, definite price of its own that can

20. Keynes, *The General Theory of Employment, Interest, and Money* (New York: Harcourt, Brace, 1936), chap. 17, esp. 230–32. Keynes puts his own emphasis on how an asset with the properties in question might hold the interest rate above the level at which investment would be adequate for full employment; he does not specifically draw the Walras's law implications of an excess demand for money or some such thing. For an illuminating interpretation of Keynes's chapter 17, see Abba P. Lerner, "The Essential Properties of Interest and Money," *Quarterly Journal of Economics* 66 (May 1952): 172–93. For an example of concern with possible excess demand for nonmonetary assets, see Harold Loeb, *Full Production Without War* (Princeton: Princeton University Press, 1946), 93–94.

adjust to clear a market of its own;[21] instead, its market value is a reciprocal average of the prices of all other things. This "price" tends to be sticky for reasons almost inherent in the very concept of money.[22]

Shares of stock and nonreproducible goods like land and Old Masters, even more obviously than bonds and near moneys, do not account for depressions by being in excess demand instead of money. Flexibility in their individual prices would clear their individual markets. But suppose controls or market imperfections hold the price of some such asset down despite a strengthened demand for it. How do its frustrated buyers behave, and with what consequences? They might turn to demanding something else as a second best, leaving the outcome operationally much the same as if they had not wanted the rigidly priced good in the first place. Alternatively, they might continue waiting for an opportunity to buy what they want, meanwhile holding and thus demanding cash balances. While the demand for the medium of exchange would in a sense have strengthened passively or by default, its distinctiveness would still come to the fore.

This point deserves restatement. Demand for an asset other than money, even if one not currently produced, is either equilibrated with its supply (by adjustment in its price if not in its production) or is frustrated. If frustrated, the demand must turn elsewhere. If it turns to other goods, it causes no deficiency of demand for current output. A shift toward leisure, reducing the supply of current goods and services, certainly could not account for an excess supply of these things. A shift toward money could occur, however, with the usual far-reaching consequences.

Not only must the medium of exchange thus be one of the things whose excess demand matches a deficiency of demand for current output, but this excess demand causes more pervasive disruption than excess demand for even the nearest of near moneys. People de-

21. This is true when the same kind of money serves as both unit of account and medium of exchange. The present paper ignores the far-fetched but theoretically challenging concept of a system in which the two functions are split, with the actual medium of exchange fluctuating in price in terms of the separate unit in which ordinary goods and services are also priced.

22. Lerner, "Essential Properties of Interest and Money," esp. 188, 190–93.

mand money to *hold*, true enough, but they are continually adding to and drawing on their holdings and want them of the right size in relation to the flows through them. Because money—unlike even the nearest of near moneys—is the one thing routinely exchanged against all sorts of things, an excess supply of or demand for it does not appear on any particular market or in connection with any particular disequilibrium price. Monetary disequilibrium does not show up as any specific frustration. An individual meets frustration trying to buy or sell various particular goods and services but sees no difficulty attached to money itself. Whatever he might be trying to buy with or sell for money, he does not find money generally unacceptable or generally unobtainable.[23] An unemployed person perceives a deficiency of demand for his labor, not an excess demand for money. He does not want money just to add it permanently to his cash balance, anyway; he wants to earn and spend it.

This divergence between individual and overall viewpoints is crucial to the macroeconomic consequences of monetary disequilibrium. An overall excess demand for money does not manifest itself as such to the individual. Unlike frustrated demand for an ordinary good or service or financial asset, it does not either cause a market-clearing adjustment in one particular price or else force individuals to decide what available things to acquire instead. This peculiarity of monetary disequilibrium is connected with the above-mentioned fundamental proposition: everyone can individually hold as much or as little money as he effectively demands, even though the total supply is fixed. To get it, the individual need only curtail his spending or lending relative to his inflow of income and other receipts, just as someone with more cash than he wants can do the opposite. An economywide excess demand for money shows up not as specific frustration in buying money but as dispersed, generalized frustration in selling things and earning incomes. Furthermore, the per-

23. A qualification about suppressed inflation might seem necessary. The frustration would attach, however, to purchases of the individual goods and services subject to the price controls. Money could still be freely spent on uncontrolled goods. And insofar as practically everything was subject to effective price ceilings, the former money would cease to serve as a general medium of exchange (as in Germany before June 1948). All the analysis here relates to an *actual* medium of exchange.

sons who experience this frustration most keenly are not necessarily those who had wanted to build up their cash balances. Conceivably, the persons who want more money can get it, while those who part with it are those whose reduced incomes keep them from demanding cash balances as large as before.

For the individual, the flow of income and expenditure through his cash balance is less readily adjustable than the balance he holds.[24] But for the economy as a whole (excluding the monetary authorities), the money stock is a datum to which flows adjust. If total cash balances demanded exceed the money stock, the flow of money shrinks in the aggregate and for the typical or average economic unit. This happens as the typical unit shrinks its spending, thereby cutting others' receipts and spurring greater and more widespread efforts to shrink spending into line.[25] Efforts to build up or conserve cash balances make the flow of income and expenditure shrink precisely because money is what routinely flows to accomplish the exchange of goods and services. The shrinkage continues until, from the individual and overall points of view alike, stocks of money no longer are inadequate in relation to the shrunken flows. Eventually, the cash-balance effect stops the decline.

No other excess demand could be as pervasively disruptive as an excess demand for money. The contrast with anything else, ranging from Old Masters to the nearest of near moneys, is instructive. Because a nonmoney does not have a routine *flow* to *be* interrupted or shrunken in the first place, efforts to hold more of the asset than exists cannot cause such pervasive trouble. People cannot try to accumulate Old Masters or Treasury bills or savings and loan shares by

24. His flows are more nearly but not entirely a datum, since adjusting them is, after all, how he adjusts his balance. In a sense, though, he can adjust his balance more sensitively: an adjustment in the sustained level of either his inflow or outflow would mean continuing growth or shrinkage of his balance, while an adjustment of his balance would require only a temporary modification of flows.

25. What difference does it make if some units try to accumulate cash by pushing their own sales harder rather than by cutting their purchases? If their price cuts and intensified sales efforts take customers away from other sellers, but without prices in general being flexible enough to make the real quantity of money meet the demand for it, the incomes that the others have to spend decline; and the analysis continues much the same as in the text. The key point is that people can try to build up or conserve cash balances by cutting purchases of each other's outputs, with a chain of repercussions that hinges on money's role as medium of exchange.

mere passive restraint in spending income, since they do not routinely receive income in any such form. Instead, people must take action to acquire such things on the specific markets where they are sold, and at their own prices (or yields). For a nonmoney, excess demand hits its own market specifically. The frustrated demand either is removed by a rise in the thing's price (or fall in its yield, or increase in its production) or else is diverted onto other things. Its own market, by being disrupted, and its own price, by coming under pressure, serve as buffers limiting the contagion of the imbalance to the rest of the economy—unless the frustrated excess demand for the nonmoney is diverted onto money itself. Because a nonmoney is not a medium of exchange with which other things are routinely bought, no excess demand for it can persist, unaccompanied by an excess demand for money, and yet show up as deficiency of demand for other things in general.

For the medium of exchange, however, excess demand is neither removed directly nor diverted. Because money is traded on all markets and on none specifically its own, and because it has no single price of its own to come under specific pressure, an imbalance between its supply and demand has far-reaching consequences. Its excess demand appears as a deficiency of demand for other things because demand for it can be exercised by mere restraint in spending it. Although money has many close substitutes as a store of value, not even the nearest of near moneys shares with it the simple but momentous characteristic of routine exchange and circulation.

This peculiarity underlines the main theme of this paper: in analyzing the demands for money and other liquid assets, we must go beyond investigating what determines *how much* of each asset people demand to hold. We must also consider *in what way* people go about giving effect to their demands.

An excess demand for money tends to remove itself in a distinctive and unpleasant way. Despite the overall excess demand, anyone can gratify his demand for cash balances simply by keeping part of his income in the form in which he routinely receives it. The routine flow of money income and expenditure shrinks. Anything that shrinks the flow of money interferes—barring complete price flexibility—with the exchange of goods and services. In an advanced economy, people specialize as producers and depend on exchange for the opportunity to do so. Any interference with the process of exchange on the market narrows opportunities for worthwhile production of goods to be exchanged. A fall in the flow of money thus damages production and employment. An inadequate quantity of even the nearest near money could not do the same pervasive damage.[26]

A general deficiency of demand for goods and services must thus be a specifically monetary disorder involving an excess demand for the actual medium of exchange. To emphasize this, let us suppose that all prices are "right" relative to each other but are "too high," in the same proportion, relative to the quantity of money. Everybody is willing to exchange his goods for other people's goods at the ratios implied by their existing money prices. Yet shortage of the medium of exchange interferes. Since people have been trying to build up their cash balances, they initially are failing to spend all the money received by selling their goods and labor. And since others are doing the same, the typical economic unit has trouble earning income. The depression of income is what chokes off the demand for cash balances below what it would be at full employment.[27]

26. Admittedly, an inadequate supply of an important near money—or perhaps, strictly speaking, the resulting unattractiveness of its yield—could make the demand for actual money stronger than otherwise. But the macroeconomic difficulties *would* then involve an excess demand for money, not merely an excess demand for something else *instead*. Furthermore, a sufficient increase in the supply of money could satiate the excess demand for it, even if the quantity of the near money did not increase.

27. Conceivably, an autonomous upward push on wages and prices could be what kept tending to make an existing or even a growing money supply inadequate for a full-employment level of activity. While monetary in nature, the disorder would not be monetary in origin.

A deficiency of money is not the only *conceivable* impediment to the flow of spending and the production and exchange of real income. Relative prices, including wages, could conceivably be wrong. A capricious system of ceilings and floors, for example, could make some prices too low and others too high, yet leave the general purchasing power of money, calculated somehow, correct for the quantity of money in existence. Wrong exchange ratios would hamper production by keeping desires to exchange various goods from meshing. Some goods would be in excess demand and others in excess supply. For each, of course, only the smaller of the desired supply and demand quantities would be the quantity actually exchanged. With exchange impeded, production and real incomes and real purchasing power would suffer also. Like decreed ceilings and floors, mere rigidities in prices and

108

VI

TRANSACTIONS COSTS

Momentous consequences seem to follow from apparently slight differences between close near moneys and actual media of exchange. Whether or not a thing serves as a general medium of exchange might even seem a mere matter of degree, as the example of traveler's checks might suggest. If sellers of goods and services become willing to accommodate buyers by accepting payment in a near money, and if this practice reaches the point where everyone accepts it with no intention of cashing it in because he knows he can simply pass it along to someone else, who in turn will not want to cash it in, then the thing has become an actual medium of exchange.

At some point, apparently, the shading or drift from the properties of close near moneys toward those of money becomes a jump from a difference in degree to a difference in kind. Embarrassingly enough, we seem to have something like the Hegelian-Marxian "jump of quantity into quality." Yet this really may be the way things are with money. Several assets may have low transactions costs, but the asset with the *lowest* costs of all is unique in that respect.[28] Having the lowest transactions costs and being the medium of exchange are properties so related that even a slight disturbance to existing institutions or practices could conceivably be self-reinforcing. Perhaps

wages might similarly block the continuous clearing of markets and choice of production techniques and patterns compatible with full employment after a change in "wants, resources, or technology." The change proving disruptive in the face of price rigidity would not *necessarily* have to be an increase in the propensity to save or in liquidity preference. This point is one of the main themes of W. H. Hutt, *Keynesianism—Retrospect and Prospect* (Chicago: Regnery, 1963).

While "structural" or "frictional" difficulties are thus conceivable, the trouble would not be a *general* deficiency of demand for goods and services. In the real world, such difficulties are less characteristic of depression than is monetary disequilibrium.

28. Transactions costs may take the form of time and trouble, of course. Ambiguity about the lowest transactions costs could explain the coexistence of two or more varieties of medium of exchange. Currency has the lowest transactions costs—loosely speaking, it is the most convenient medium of exchange—in some types of transactions, and demand deposits have the lowest costs in others. But no other asset has lower transactions costs than currency and demand deposits, respectively, in the types of transaction in which each predominates.

the shifting of a ship's cargo offers an analogy. Minor causes can sometimes have major consequences.

If savings and loan shares had transactions costs no higher than those of money, the associations could grant loans in the form of their own shares, confident that the borrowers would be able to spend them directly. The essence of being merely a near money is that people have to be *persuaded* to take it—persuaded by its yield (or by the prospect of losing a sale if the seller did not thus accommodate his customer). For assets on the borderline, what would be adequate persuasion for some takers might not be adequate for others. Hence an asset cannot be a *generally* acceptable means of payment if some inducement is required not merely to persuade people to hold it for some time but even to persuade them to accept payment in that particular form in the first place.

Fortunately, our economy has no assets just on a borderline between serving and not serving as media of exchange. Not even traveler's checks circulate indefinitely without being presented for redemption. So far as this paper has any direct implications at all for policy, and not just for theory—beyond the obvious warning against confusion over a nebulous general liquidity—it warns against blurring the crucial though possibly slight distinctions that keep an awkwardly large variety of assets from coming into routine circulation. Policy should avoid creating incentives to broaden the range of such assets, as it might do if it attached excessive disadvantages to the use of money and to the demand-deposit business. Policy should beware of the institutional instability that could arise from instability in or doubt about the relative lowness of the transactions costs of different assets.

What Are Banks?

I
THE ISSUE OF UNIQUENESS

It is an old but unsettled question whether commercial banks are crucially different from all other financial institutions. Interpretations, not bare facts, are what is at issue. Supposedly refuted doctrines keep surfacing again, while some purported refutations rely on fallacies of their own, or at best on irrelevancies and misplacements of emphasis.

Briefly, banks are a distinctive focus of attention because their demand liabilities form the bulk of the money supply. (Here I am not concerned with their time-deposit operations.) Ordinary supply and demand analysis does not apply to the quantity of demand deposits or of total money. Rather, the demand for money gets adjusted to its supply through a momentous roundabout process.

Current innovations—NOW accounts, third-party payments by thrift institutions, check-writing against money-market mutual funds, and the rest—seem to be blurring the distinctions between demand deposits and other financial assets and between banks and other

Reprinted from the *Atlantic Economic Journal* 6 (December 1978): 1–13, with permission of Southern Illinois University at Edwardsville, Box 1101, Edwardsville, Illinois 62026-1101.

This paper was written largely in reaction to articles by Andrew D. Crockett and Boris P. Pesek, respectively: Crockett's "The Euro-Currency Market: An Attempt to Clarify Some Basic Issues," *International Monetary Fund Staff Papers* 23 (July 1976): 375–86; and Pesek's "Monetary Theory in the Post-Robertson 'Alice in Wonderland' Era," *Journal of Economic Literature* 14 (September 1976): 856–84. The paper was prepared for the October 1977 meetings of the Atlantic Economic Society. Even before the Crockett and Pesek articles appeared, Samuel I. Katz had been urging me to write an article further examining the "New View" of James Tobin and the Yale monetary school, and criticizing the conception of banks as firms engaged in producing the product money that was advocated by Pesek and Thomas Saving. The author is indebted to Professor Katz for discussions and correspondence.

institutions. Still, loss of tidy distinctions from the real world hardly justifies confusion in analysis. We must grasp the distinctiveness of the medium of exchange and its issuers to understand what difference the current changes might make. Perhaps the very concept of the quantity of money is becoming inapplicable, eventually making a quantity-controlled fiat money unworkable. The closing paragraph of the paper returns to this question.

II
THE NEW VIEW

Errors can sometimes be instructive by exposing points requiring clearer or fuller exposition, by sensitizing us to recurrence of old errors in new guises, and by making the correct doctrines stand out in contrast. Andrew Crockett's article of 1976 is an example.[1] Crockett draws a close analogy between banks engaged in the Eurodollar business and domestic nonbank financial intermediaries (NFIs). Then, ironically, he questions the distinction often attempted between credit creation by banks and mere intermediation by other institutions. Of course, he says, if credit is understood as money and money is defined as banknotes and bank deposits, then it is true, tautologically, that banks create money and other institutions do not. "But it could equally well be said that savings and loan institutions create savings and loan deposits, and life insurance companies create life insurance policies." Each institution will competitively acquire both additional liabilities and additional assets if it perceives a profit margin between borrowing costs and investment yields.

But don't banks face fewer constraints than other institutions in creating their liabilities, since only their demand liabilities are means of exchange? Crockett finds this idea misleading "because it concentrates on the immediate consequences of a transaction and not on the subsequent process by which equilibrium in asset portfolios is reestablished." In a closed banking system, true enough, a loan does generate its own deposit. Still, the system cannot expand indefinitely without tending to any stable equilibrium. Its expansion is limited by

1. Crockett, "The Euro-Currency Market."

ordinary cost and demand factors, just as is the market for any other financial asset. . . . Banks can expand their share of total portfolios, therefore, only by increasing their relative attractiveness. This imposes a constraint on the expansion of a bank's business that is exactly analogous to that which applies to nonbank financial intermediaries." If all new bank loans are to be matched by additional deposits, willingly held, the pattern of interest rates must adjust to make deposits more attractive relative to competing financial assets. If the banks are kept from raising their deposit interest rates, the relative adjustment must come through reduced rates at NFIs, which then acquire and relend funds more cheaply. The banks' lending opportunities worsen. While bank deposits cannot disappear through transfer to competing institutions, loss of lending business can curtail them. Crockett finds "no analytical virtue in a distinction between the credit-creating capacities of different institutions."[2]

Several of the points just quoted and paraphrased from Crockett echo Tobin's "New View" of money and banking. These include the points that expansion of bank credit, as of credit from other sources, is limited by cost and revenue factors in an environment of rivalry for customers and that even "in the absence of specific constraints," some equilibrium or limit would exist to the size of the banking system.[3]

All this stands in contrast with a more traditional view, which often employs the money-multiplier formulas of the textbooks: the central bank can control the quantity of money—if it puts its mind

2. Ibid., 376–78.

3. James Tobin, "Commercial Banks as Creators of 'Money,' " in *Banking and Monetary Studies*, ed. Deane Carson (Homewood, Ill.: Irwin, 1963), 408–19. For a sympathetic exposition of the New View, see J. A. Cacy, "Alternative Approaches to the Analysis of the Financial Structure," Federal Reserve Bank of Kansas City, *Monthly Review* (March 1968): 3–9. It is not clear, however, that Cacy actually is a proponent of the New View, as he is castigated for being by Karl Brunner in "The Role of Money and Monetary Policy," Federal Reserve Bank of St. Louis, *Review* (July 1968): 8–24. For samples of work exhibiting important parallels with the New View, see Committee on the Working of the Monetary System, *Report* [Radcliffe Report] (London: Her Majesty's Stationery Office, 1959); Tilford C. Gaines, "Financial Innovations and the Efficiency of Federal Reserve Policy," in *Monetary Process and Policy*, ed. George Horwich (Homewood, Ill.: Irwin, 1967), 99–118; and James S. Earley, Robert J. Parsons, and Fred A. Thompson, *Money, Credit, and Expenditure: A Sources and Uses of Funds Approach*, New York University Bulletin no. 3 (New York: New York University Press, 1976).

to the task—and the public cannot frustrate this control by any un-willingness to hold all the money that the central bank determines maintain in existence.

<h2>III</h2>
<h2>UNSATISFACTORY CRITICISMS</h2>

Not all challenges to the New View and related doctrines show cor-rect understanding of just what is wrong with them and of just how banks are unique. A poorly argued challenge risks reflecting credit on the doctrines attacked. Some defenses of the uniqueness of banks rely on irrelevancies and misplacements of emphasis.[4] Others hinge on downright fallacies. Boris P. Pesek and Thomas R. Saving provide a notable example in their treatise of 1967 and textbook of 1968. On their view, banks, much like manufacturers of refrigerators, are seek-ing profit by producing a particular product, which happens to be money. Banks come close to being updated versions of gold mines.[5] More recently, Pesek has urged a supplementary line of argument. He objects to the money-multiplier analysis of money-supply deter-mination, contending that this approach obscures the roles of costs and revenues and supply and demand in determining the quantity of money. Students risk getting the impression "that the banker has volunteer workers laboring in charity-donated buildings." Pesek wants to analyze the quantity of money with supply-and-demand ap-paratus, with supply schedules reflecting costs of production, much as we would analyze equilibrium quantities of refrigerators and houses.[6] Saving also focuses on how "the supply and demand condi-

4. For an example, see Jack M. Guttentag and Robert Lindsay, "The Unique-ness of Commercial Banks," *Journal of Political Economy* 76 (September–October 1968): 991–1014. The authors consider it crucial that NFIs hold their own reserves in bank deposits rather than base money. Their article draws sympathetic comment from John H. Wood, "Two Notes on the Uniqueness of Commercial Banks," *Journal of Finance* 25 (March 1970): 99–108; and adverse comment from Joseph Aschheim, "Commercial Banks and Financial Intermediaries: Fallacies and Policy Implica-tions," *Journal of Political Economy* 67 (February 1959): 59–71.

5. Boris P. Pesek and Thomas R. Saving, *The Foundations of Money and Banking* (New York: Macmillan, 1968).

6. Pesek, "Monetary Theory," 880.

tions in the money market jointly determine the equilibrium money stock." (In some other respects, though, he appears to be returning to the money-multiplier analysis, or an elaboration of it.)[7]

IV

BANKS AND NONBANKS

In reconciling the individual banker's view with a systemwide view, we must recognize that the banker does not see himself as striving for profits by producing money. If he does grant a loan by creating a deposit with the stroke of his pen, he must be prepared to lose reserves as the borrower writes checks. He must *attract* deposits, persuading depositors to do business with him rather than with his competitors. Banks produce money only as a by-product: total deposits rise and fall with the nominal size of the system as a whole. Pesek and Saving evidently took the idea that the *system* creates money and misapplied it to interpreting the routine business of the individual bank. Failure of that interpretation would be obvious when the size of the banking system and the volume of demand deposits were remaining unchanged. Banks are in the business of producing *services*, not money.[8]

Although bank credit is not distinct in kind from credit from other sources, banks' demand liabilities do remain distinctive. Consequently, when banks in the aggregate expand their lending and investing, they meet with slighter reserve drains than other institutions. To see this difference, let us suppose that members of the public decide to exchange currency (1) for bank demand deposits

7. Thomas R. Saving, "A Theory of the Money Supply With Competitive Banking," *Journal of Monetary Economics* 3 (July 1977): 289–303.

8. Aschheim stresses that although banks are mere brokers in their time-deposit business, they do create loanable funds in their demand-deposit business. See Aschheim, *Techniques of Monetary Control* (Baltimore: Johns Hopkins University Press, 1961), chap. 7. Yet one must be wary of the contention, if Aschheim is indeed making it, that banks are creators *rather than* brokers in their demand-deposit business. Most of the bank's work *is* brokerage, or intermediation, along with provision of related services, including administration of the payments mechanism. In any given period, the volume of a bank's loans and investments maturing and being replaced with new ones is surely larger than any growth of its demand deposits.

and (2), alternatively, for deposits in NFIs. Under alternative 1, most of the funds borrowed and spent by the borrowers remain on deposit in the banking system. (Only "most" remain because the public will take some fraction of its increased total money holdings in currency, even though a smaller fraction than before the hypothesized change in tastes.) Instead of going out of existence, this money is spent around and around until, as a result of what all this spending does to incomes and prices, it is all willingly held after all. (A fuller explanation comes in section 7.) The money supply has expanded by a multiple of the amount of currency initially deposited in the banks.

Under alternative 2, the NFIs receiving the deposited currency exchange it for the bank demand deposits that they find more convenient, thereby providing the banks with more reserve funds, as under the first alternative. The NFIs then relend most of the newly acquired funds, paying out the loans by drawing checks on their bank deposits. Most of those funds leave the reserves of the NFIs, even as a group, since the proceeds of their loans are *not* being paid out and spent and respent while continuing to be held in the form of deposit claims on themselves. The banks, however, having gained reserves, do expand much as under alternative 1. (If, contrary to current practice, the NFIs held their own reserves in currency instead of bank deposits, the expansion of the banking system would be more restrained. As bank deposits expanded, the public would want to hold more NFI deposits also; so the NFIs would regain some of the currency lost in making loans. The consequences of the two alternative NFI reserve practices would differ, however, only in degree. If their liabilities still did not circulate as means of payment—if they had not become banks—the NFIs would still be restricted to an essentially intermediary role.)

Comparing banks with savings and loan associations, Tobin recognizes what he calls the "superficial and irrelevant" fact that

> a bank can make a loan by "writing up" its deposit liabilities, while a savings and loan association, for example, cannot satisfy a mortgage borrower by crediting him with a share account. Whether or not [the money that a bank lends] stays in the banking system as a

whole . . . clearly does not depend on the way the loan was initially made. It depends on whether somewhere in the chain of transactions initiated by the borrower's outlays are found depositors who wish to hold deposits equal in amount to the new loan. Similarly, the outcome for the savings and loan industry depends on whether in the chain of transactions initiated by the mortgage are found individuals who wish to acquire additional savings and loan shares.[9]

Precisely. Yet the difference is far from "superficial and irrelevant." It is far truer of bank loans than of loans from savings and loan associations that when the borrowers spend the proceeds, they touch off a chain of transactions that *does* bring forth willing holders of additional deposits in the lending institutions. People will always accept payment in the medium of exchange; and if they do not want to continue holding it, then, instead of causing it to go out of existence, they will pass it along to someone else. But unwanted savings and loan deposits will not be held—or accepted in the first place.

This contrast between banks and NFIs relates to the two systems as a whole. The individual bank and the individual savings and loans association are in similar positions as they themselves perceive them. Either must indeed reckon on losing most of the funds that it lends. Slighter exposure to reserve leakage characterizes the banking system as a whole; and, as we shall see, the system is distinctive in more ways than that.

V

A NATURAL ECONOMIC LIMIT?

The reason for the banks' relatively slight exposure to reserve leakage runs parallel with the reason why the amount of money is not limited by the demand for it as amounts of other financial instruments are. Yet the New View postulates a "natural economic limit" to the size of the banking system. Given their wealth and their asset preferences, says Tobin, people will voluntarily hold additional demand deposits only if yields fall on alternative assets. But this also means lower yields on loans and investments available to the banks,

9. Tobin, "Commercial Banks," 412–13.

117

making further lending and investing unprofitable for them beyond some point. "In this respect the commercial banking industry is not qualitatively different from any other financial intermediary system." Even without reserve requirements, the banking system's expansion "would be limited by the availability of assets at yields sufficient to compensate banks for the costs of attracting and holding the corresponding deposits."[10] Restating these ideas, Crockett says that banks and NFIs, both as individual institutions and as systems, face similar cost and demand constraints on expansion of their deposits and their portfolios.[11] According to Basil Moore, "Banks like all other business firms make a profit by selling their product above cost, and this necessity of operating at a profit, combined with a downward sloping demand curve for bank loans and deposits, serves to restrict output expansion even in the absence of deposit control through reserve manipulation."[12]

Proponents of this view are evidently not attributing the "natural economic limit" to limitation of base money and to a finite money multiplier, for that would be old stuff and not a *new* view. Those familiar limitations operate on the supply-of-money side, while the New Viewers emphasize limitations on the demand side. They deny crucial differences (to be explained below) between the banking and NFI systems regarding limits to the scales of their operations.[13]

10. Ibid., 414, 416.

11. Crockett, "The Euro-Currency Market."

12. Basil J. Moore, *An Introduction to the Theory of Finance* (New York: Free Press, 1968).

13. Further evidence on the nature of the New View's natural economic limits appears in an article in which Lyle E. Gramley and Samuel B. Chase, Jr., praise and adopt Tobin's approach. See Gramley and Chase, "Time Deposits in Monetary Analysis," *Federal Reserve Bulletin* 51 (October 1965): 1380–1404. My interpretation is pretty much the same as that of a severe critic, Karl Brunner, in "The Role of Money and Monetary Policy," 172–73. In contrast, John H. Wood defends the New View by suggesting that it does not really mean what it says. Instead of clashing with traditional views on matters of substance, it supposedly just recommends a broader methodology, with fuller attention to the circumstances confronting and the responses of banks and other economic actors. See Wood, "Two Notes on the Uniqueness of Commercial Banks," 105–8. Richard T. Coghlan has urged a similar interpretation. See Coghlan, "Analysis Within the 'New View,'" *Journal of Money, Credit, and Banking* 9 (August 1977): 410–27. Yet it simply will not do to interpret writers as saying the opposite of what they avowedly are saying, and to describe the distinction between

VI
DIFFICULTIES FOR
COST-AND-REVENUE ANALYSIS

Tobin and his followers slight some familiar contrasts. No obstacle on the demand-for-money side blocks lending and spending new bank demand deposits into existence. No one need be persuaded to invest in the routine medium of exchange before more of it can be created. The bankers do not need to find someone willing to *hold* it but only someone willing to *accept* it. That person need not even be a borrower or someone selling a security from his portfolio; he might even be an employee whose salary a bank is paying out of excess reserves. Once a person has accepted new money, others from whom he buys goods or services or securities can resist receiving it only by refusing payment of the routine sort for whatever it is they are selling.[14]

It is hard to imagine why a bank might find it more profitable to hold reserves in excess of what the law and prudence call for than to buy riskless short-term securities with them. Despite Tobin's tacit assumption to the contrary, the individual bank is trying to maximize its own profits, not those of the banking system as a whole.[15]

Suppose, then, that a cut in reserve requirements or expansion of the monetary base or shift of the public's preferences from currency to deposits initially gives the banks more excess reserves. The individual bank finds it profitable to invest any it may have. The seller of whatever security it buys deposits the check he receives

---

the New View and the analysis that employs money multipliers as merely one of methodological broadness versus methodological narrowness.

14. Here I am elaborating a bit on Paul F. Smith, "Concepts of Money and Commercial Banks," *Journal of Finance* 21 (December 1966): 648. One might quibble over the fact that some people may either refuse checks and insist on currency or else redeem for currency any checks they do accept. A similar quibble concerns base money sidetracked from serving as reserves against demand deposits into serving as reserves against time deposits. The money-multiplier analysis straightforwardly handles such quibbles as dealing with limitations to the *supply* of money.

15. Cf. ibid., 645–46; and Rainer S. Masera, "Deposit Creation, Multiplication, and the Euro-Dollar Market," Ente per gli Studi Monetari, Bancari e Finanziari Luigi Einaudi (Rome), *Quaderni di Ricerche* 11 (1973), 151.

somewhere, providing his bank with more excess reserves to invest. And so on.

Even applied to the banking system as a whole, something is wrong with the idea that a decline in yields obtainable will check expansion of loans and investments and deposits. That idea overlooks Knut Wicksell's cumulative process.[16] As money expansion raises nominal incomes and prices, the dollar volume of loans demanded rises also, even at given interest rates. The proposition that the supply of money creates its own demand thus applies not only to cash balances (as the following section explains) but also to money being newly supplied and demanded on loan. An unconstrained cumulative process can even lead to embodiment of inflationary expectations in interest rates as described by Irving Fisher. The great inflations of history discredit any notion of expansion being limited as marginal revenues fall in relation to marginal costs. That notion rests not only on an illegitimate imputation of a systemwide viewpoint to the individual banker but also on a more or less tacit assumption of rigid prices.[17]

Cost-and-revenue analysis of the size of the money and banking system runs into a further embarrassment: the real marginal cost of expanding the system's nominal size is essentially zero. And its *nominal* size is what interests us, for some sort of limit to it is necessary for a determinate price level. Since money is a by-product of the banking system's nominal expansion, its costs and revenues are not those of producing nominal money. Banks are in the business of producing *services* instead, including financial intermediation and the services of *real* money balances. In appropriate contexts, as in studies of economies of scale in banking, costs are indeed emphasized. The

16. For lucid discussions of the process, though not specifically of how it bears on the present point, see Don Patinkin, *Money, Interest, and Prices* (New York: Harper & Row, 1965), supplementary note E, esp. 587–97; and Patinkin, *Studies in Monetary Economics* (New York: Harper & Row, 1972), chap. 5.

17. Basil Moore, who wavers between the new and traditional views, recognizes that if all prices were perfectly and instantly flexible, an unregulated banking system could not reach a stable equilibrium. He does not mention the cumulative process, however, and he goes on to argue that since prices are not perfectly flexible in reality, changes in nominal bank credit and deposits would indeed affect earnings relative to costs in such a way as to push the system back toward an equilibrium. See Moore, *An Introduction to the Theory of Finance*, 198.

working of the system as a whole, however, cannot be understood by generalizing from the experience of the individual banker *alone.* The quantity of nominal money cannot be explained by a cost-and-revenue approach that treats its issuers like manufacturers of refrigerators.

VII
HOW SUPPLY OF MONEY CREATES
ITS OWN DEMAND

A further reason why such an analysis does not apply to the quantity of money is that the nominal supply of money creates its own demand. (This proposition applies not to the deposits of any individual bank, of course, but to demand deposits and currency in the aggregate.) People always accept the routine medium of exchange even if they do not want to retain increased holdings of it. An initial excess supply of money touches off a *process* that raises the nominal quantity demanded quite in accordance with the demand function for money holdings as the nominal money values of wealth and income and transactions rise. In the face of an initially deficient money supply, conversely, deflation of prices and real economic activity reduces the nominal quantity demanded. Demand and supply interact, then, not to determine the nominal quantity of money—that is determined on the supply side—but to determine the nominal flow of spending and the purchasing power of the money unit.

This process that reconciles the demand for money with the supply is the theme of what J. M. Keynes called "the fundamental proposition of monetary theory" and Milton Friedman called "the most important proposition in monetary theory."[18] Briefly, everyone can individually hold as much or as little money as he effectively demands, even though the total of all holdings may be exogenously set; for the total flow of spending adjusts in such a way that

18. John Maynard Keynes, *The General Theory of Employment, Interest, and Money* (New York: Harcourt, Brace, 1936), 84–85; and Milton Friedman, statement in *Employment, Growth, and Price Levels*, part 4 (Hearings before the Joint Economic Committee, United States Congress, 1959), 609.

the demand for nominal money becomes equal to the exogenous supply.[19] (This proposition presupposes a closed economy or an economy with a freely floating exchange rate and requires modification for an open economy with a fixed exchange rate; see section 12 below.)

In contrast with what is true of the banking system and money, cost-and-revenue and supply-and-demand analysis *does* apply to the nominal volume of claims on NFIs.[20] In the aggregate as well as individually, NFIs must *induce* depositors to acquire and hold claims against them. Expanding nonbank intermediation in nominal terms means expanding its real scale also as long as exogenous limitation of the nominal size of the monetary and banking system makes the price level determinate. Nominal expansion, together with the required inducements, then does entail additional real costs.

One related difference between money and near moneys concerns how imbalances between supply and demand are adjusted away. If a discrepancy develops between desired and actual holdings of some type of NFI claim, a relatively direct adjustment occurs, through change in its quantity, or in the interest rate paid on it, or both. Unlike money, that claim has a market of its own and a price or yield of its own, and the quantity of it demanded does not have to

19. Tobin evidently overlooked this process in a passage quoted with approval by G. M. Meier. See Tobin, "Asset Holdings and Spending Decisions," *American Economic Review* 42 (May 1952): 115; see also G. M. Meier, "Some Questions About Growth Economics: Comment," *American Economic Review* 44 (December 1954): 936.

Harry Johnson has charged opponents of monetarism with confusion over how nominal and real quantities of money are determined and with "a tendency to discuss monetary problems as if nominal and real money balances are the same thing, and as if ordinary value theory could be applied to the behaviour of money." The Yale theorists "are . . . alert to this confusion but by-pass it either by assuming stable prices and confining their analysis to the financial sector, or by building models based on the fictional construction of a money whose purchasing power is fixed in real terms, thereby avoiding confusion in the analysis at the expense of creating it with respect to the applicability of the results." One may question, however, whether doing as Johnson says the Yale theorists do really shows alertness to confusion. See Johnson, *Inflation and the Monetarist Controversy* (Amsterdam: North-Holland, 1972), 45.

20. As Masera says, Marshall's scissors of supply and demand *do* determine the outputs of domestic financial intermediaries and of banks in their Eurodollar operations. See Masera, "Deposit Creation," 182–83.

be adjusted to the actual quantity in the roundabout way character-istic of the medium of exchange.[21]

VIII
DISTINCTIVENESS FROM REGULATION?

New Viewers sometimes argue that any distinctiveness of banks lies in their being constrained to operate on a scale below the "natural eco-nomic limit." Reserve requirements normally cut short the banking system's expansion, leaving the marginal yield on bank loans and in-vestments in excess of the marginal "costs of attracting and holding the corresponding deposits." This spread explains why "additional loans permitted by new reserves will generate their own deposits." The same would hold true of any other system of similarly con-strained financial institutions. "In this sense it is more accurate to at-tribute the special place of banks among intermediaries to the legal restrictions to which banks alone are subjected than to attribute these restrictions to the special character of bank liabilities."[22]

21. If a determinate nominal size of the money and banking system justifies analyzing the volume of near moneys with cost-and-revenue and supply-and-demand concepts, why can't the process work the other way around? Just as a limited nomi-nal quantity of money enables the demand for near moneys to restrain their quan-tities, couldn't some sort of limitation to those quantities enable the demand for money to restrain its quantity? No. People's notions about appropriate composi-tions of their asset portfolios do work asymmetrically because near moneys are not routinely accepted in payments the way money is. The Keynes-Friedman "fundamen-tal proposition" holds true only of the medium of exchange. See Leland B. Yeager, "Essential Properties of the Medium of Exchange," *Kyklos* 21, no. 1 (1968): 45–69, and esp. 52–55 (reprinted in this volume).

22. Tobin, "Commercial Banks," 416. According to Basil Moore, similarly, "the banking system can best be understood as an industry prevented by quantitative limitation from expanding to its equilibrium size." Although he supposes that the nominal volume of monetary intermediation would be determinate anyway, Moore goes on to suggest reasons for nevertheless singling out commercial banking for quantitative regulation. See Moore, *An Introduction to the Theory of Finance*, 167–69, 195, 197–98, 200–201.

Writers under the Yale influence waver on just what they mean by the "special regulation" characteristic of banking. In some passages they stress reserve require-ments and deposit interest ceilings (see, e.g., Tobin, "Commercial Banks," 414, 416). In other examples they mention the rationing of bank reserves (see Moore, *Intro-duction*, 167–68). In United States actuality, of course, no definite amount of re-serves is "rationed" to the banks. The banks compete for shares of all the funds that

Crockett adds a special twist to the contention that "the existence of reserve requirements . . . makes credit creation conform to the multiplier framework."[23] He suggests that reserve requirements are necessary for a discontinuity in the yield on bank reserves which is crucial to a fairly definite money multiplier. On non-interest-bearing reserves held to avoid a deficiency, the implicit yield is substantial—avoidance of severe legal penalties—but on reserves held in excess of legal requirements plus working balances, the yield is practically zero. Hence the pressure on banks to keep fully loaned up, almost regardless of yields on earning assets.

Actually, setting reserve ratios by law rather than letting banks choose their own makes a difference in degree only rather than in kind. On reserves in excess of prudent working balances, the yield would be negligible, while competition would punish deficiencies that caused defaults or delays in honoring demand obligations. The arithmetic of textbook money-multiplier formulas shows that even with banks holding zero reserves (indeed, even with negative though not too negative reserve ratios, if they could have any economic meaning), the stock of deposit money could be determinate. A minimum acceptable reserve ratio of zero is still a minimum acceptable ratio. Determinacy would follow from the public's desire not to hold too little currency in relation to demand deposits and from the authorities' continued limitation of base money.[24]

can serve as reserves. Central-bank control of that total, the monetary base, hardly counts as distinctive regulation of banks. It is simply one way of exogenously specifying some "critical figure"—some nominal money price or average or total—which, as Schumpeter explains, is necessary for determinacy in any monetary system. See Joseph A. Schumpeter, *Das Wesen des Geldes*, ed. Fritz Karl Mann (Göttingen: Vandenhoeck & Ruprecht, 1970). On the "critical figure," see also section 13, below.

23. Crockett, "The Euro-Currency Market," 380.

24. In this extreme case of currency as the only base money, central-bank control over the monetary base tautologically precludes passiveness in supplying currency. Still, the proposition that the supply of money creates its own demand remains uncontradicted. That proposition refers to the total quantity of medium of exchange and not to particular types separately. The authorities can keep any total nominal stock of money in existence provided that its composition meets the public's preferences. When the controlled monetary base consists of currency only, the restraint on maintaining more than a definite amount of deposit money in circulation resembles the difficulty of getting extreme amounts of $2 bills into circulation in the face of a constant total of other types and denominations of money. Quibbles

An individual bank can expand its operations indefinitely as long as depositors furnish it with the necessary funds at costs it does not find excessive. Even if it had trouble finding qualified borrowers, it could buy securities. In principle, being subject to reserve requirements no more constrains an individual bank than a requirement for additional fire extinguishers would keep a hotel from expanding. The scale of the banking system as a whole is constrained by the determinants of the money multiplier, including reserve requirements, if any, and by a controlled monetary base. Something analogous could be true of any ordinary industry which uses some input in a technologically or legally fixed ratio to some other input or to output and to which that special input is available only in a fixed or highly inelastic supply.

More plausible than focusing on reserve requirements, arguments about specialness through regulation might focus on deposit interest-rate ceilings, perhaps of zero (and in some passages these do seem to be Tobin's and Crockett's focus). Such ceilings presumably restrain banks from competing for depositors and for potential reserve funds that would alternatively remain circulating as currency. Similarly, legal minimum room rates would restrain the expansion of hotels. It is no surprise that legally imposed cartelization can have restrictive effects. Still, competition suppressed in the price dimension can break out in others.

There is a reason for skepticism about the significance and even the existence of the spread that Tobin supposes reserve requirements and deposit interest ceilings to hold open between "the marginal yield of bank loans and investments" and "the marginal cost of deposits to the banking system."[25] Reserve requirements are analogous to a costly technological necessity or, alternatively, to a tax. An individual bank's operations are not limited the way the size of the system is. If, then, any excess of marginal revenue over marginal cost

---

sometimes arise to the effect that $10,000 bills, say, do not circulate as routine media of exchange, are not demanded in whatever amounts are supplied, and so pose an embarrassment to the argument of this paper. See, for example, Milton Friedman and Anna J. Schwartz, *Monetary Statistics of the United States* (New York: National Bureau of Economic Research, 1970), 105. The answer to such quibbles should be obvious by now.

25. Tobin, "Commercial Banks," 416.

persists, it must be due not to reserve requirements but to cartelization imposed by deposit interest ceilings and prohibitions. Even so, as in any cartel, the individual member would like to gain more customers by offering them better terms, perhaps in uncontrolled dimensions; and any failure to do so traces to enforcement measures or to his and other members' wariness about cracking the cartel.

In short, it is far-fetched to trace the difference between banks and other institutions to regulations and an associated unexploitable profit margin.

IX
MACROECONOMIC PROPERTIES OF DEMAND
DEPOSITS AND CURRENCY

Although money is not the main product of banks but rather is a by-product of the system's expansion, this fact in no way forestalls the consequences of its being the medium of exchange. That medium is supplied and demanded in a distinctive way, and imbalances between its desired and actual quantities tend to be adjusted away in a round-about and momentous way.

Generally speaking, markets can react in four alternative ways to excess demand for or supply of something.[26] (1) Excess demand raises and excess supply reduces the thing's price and so too the money value of its total stock. This process can restore equilibrium even if its physical amount, as of Old Masters, cannot adjust. (2) The amount supplied responds to excess or deficiency of demand, as with automobiles, government savings bonds, and deposits in several types of NFI. (3) A frustrated excess demand for something is diverted onto other things. If those other things are ordinary goods and services, rather than money itself, the economic system responds in operationally much the same way as if demands had run in the first place in favor of the goods and services that people wind up buying. (4) Excess demand for a particular thing may reveal itself as an

26. E. Victor Morgan describes the first, second, and fourth ways in "The Essential Qualities of Money," *Manchester School* 37 (September 1969): 237–48. My "Essential Properties of the Medium of Exchange" describes all four and the fourth's relation to money.

excess supply of other things in general; and if their prices are not sufficiently flexible downward, a general excess supply of them would bring curtailment of their outputs and so of real income.

With money, quite distinctively, an excess demand brings the fourth type of response. This happens because its supply and demand do not directly confront each other on a particular market. No actual "money market" exists on which price or quantity adjusts or from which frustrated demanders turn away and move to other markets. The medium of exchange has neither its own specific market nor a specific price of its own that could adjust to correct excess demand or supply. It is "fixed in value in terms of the unit of account"; a $10 bill or $100 demand deposit is worth just 10 or 100 dollars.[27]

For these reasons, an excess demand for money causes more pervasive economic disruption than excess demand for anything else, even the nearest of near moneys. Because money is the one thing routinely exchanged against all sorts of things, an excess demand for it does not appear on any particular market or in connection with any particular disequilibrium price. People meet frustration trying to sell their labor or other goods and services but perceive no difficulty attached to money itself. An economywide excess demand for money shows up not as specific frustration in buying money but as dispersed, generalized frustration in earning incomes.[28]

The momentous consequences of monetary disequilibrium are related to the Keynes-Friedman fundamental proposition mentioned in section 7. Despite an overall excess demand, anyone can satisfy his demand for money balances by simply retaining part of his income in the form in which he routinely receives it. As the typical household or firm shrinks its spending, it cuts the receipts of others and spurs greater and more widespread efforts to shrink spending into line. Barring complete price flexibility, the shrinkage of the flow of money, which routinely changes hands to accomplish the exchange of goods and services, impedes that exchange and so narrows opportunities for profitable production of goods to be ex-

27. Morgan, "The Essential Qualities of Money," 242.

28. It should be obvious how to reword this and the following paragraphs to apply to an excess supply of money, but see my "Essential Properties," 62.

changed. Production and employment suffer. Flows of money and income continue shrinking until holdings of money no longer are inadequate in relation to the shrunken flows.

No other excess demand could be so pervasively disruptive. The contrast between money and anything else, ranging from Old Masters to the nearest of near moneys—even Treasury bills and savings and loan deposits—is instructive. Because nonmoney does not have a routine flow to be interrupted or shrunken in the first place, efforts to hold more of it than exists cannot cause such pervasive trouble. Excess demand for a nonmoney hits its own market specifically. The frustrated demand either is removed by a rise in the thing's price (or fall in its yield) or increase in its quantity or else is diverted onto other things. No excess demand for a nonmoney can persist, unaccompanied by an excess demand for money, and yet show up as deficiency of demand for other things in general. For the medium of exchange in contrast, excess demand is neither removed directly not diverted. Not even the nearest of near moneys shares with money the simple but momentous characteristic of routine exchange and circulation.[29]

One line of argument questions the dire consequences of an excess demand for money and suggests that the demand will tend to adapt itself to the actual quantity in a relatively direct and painless way, so that its quantity need not severely constrain transactions. When faced with a shortage of coins in particular, people will cooperate in various ways to carry out their transactions anyway. (Most obviously, the customer will give the retailer the extra dime or two cents needed to reduce the amount of change due.) Similarly, G. A. Akerlof suggests, people will cooperate to keep their transactions going

---

29. After summarizing the foregoing line of argument, as found at greater length in my "Essential Properties," David G. Pierce and David M. Shaw say— apparently with nothing more specific in mind than the principle of general economic interdependence—that an excess demand even for a nonmoney will have some repercussions in markets beyond its own: "So the difference between mediums of exchange and other assets would appear . . . to be a matter of degree rather than of kind." See Pierce and Shaw, *Monetary Economics: Theories, Evidence, and Policy* (London: Butterworths, 1974), 39–42. Yet the difference *is* one not only of extreme degree but also of kind. In particular, it concerns the different *ways* in which people go about giving effect to their demands for nonmoneys and for money.

when *total* money is in short supply. They may adjust payments schedules appropriately and make increased use of trade credit.[30]

This optimistic argument is mistaken but instructive. If only coins are in short supply, then even though the demand for them presumably is associated with income, income of course does not have to fall to whatever level would choke off the excess demand. (At so fallen a level of income, total money would be in excess supply, exerting upward pressure on income.) A shortage of coins appears as a quite specific difficulty, and ways of coping with it are fairly obvious. In a sense, coins *do* have a market of their own on which they exchange against money of other kinds. Frustrations in obtaining them promote coin-economizing expedients and divert demand away from them, much as frustrated demand for Old Masters tends to be diverted onto other things. The contrast between the ways in which people perceive and respond to a shortage of coins in particular and a shortage of total money lends force to the points already made in this section.[31]

30. George A. Akerlof, "The Questions of Coinage, Trade Credit, Financial Flows, and Peanuts: A Flow-of-Funds Approach to the Demand for Money," Federal Reserve Bank of New York, *Research Paper* no. 7520 (September 1975).

31. This section had to precede our tackling a question related to the "asymmetry" argument of footnote 21. With the quantity of money limited, according to that argument, demand for near moneys limits their amount that can be gotten into existence; yet the converse does not hold: a limited quantity of near moneys does not enable the demand for money to limit its actual quantity. Similarly, doesn't a limitation on currency restrain the demanded and actual quantity of demand deposits, while no such limitation runs from demand deposits to currency? (One might think so from remarks in section 8. There, however, I was considering an extreme case in which base money consisted of currency only; here I am supposing that the central bank furnishes enough noncurrency base money to provide bank reserves for whatever supply of deposit money it desires to maintain in existence.)

Well, the distinction between near moneys, on the one hand, and demand deposits plus currency, on the other hand, is sharper and more significant than the distinction between demand deposits and currency. A limit on either demand deposits or currency cannot block injection of the other type of money into circulation. True, if the creation of deposit money went far enough to inflate prices and nominal incomes, people would experience a shortage of currency, whose quantity is by hypothesis fixed. But this would be a readily identifiable shortage, like a shortage of coins; and people would have similar incentives to cooperate to keep transactions going.

This denial of asymmetry presupposes that demand deposits remain a routine medium of exchange. To the extent that demand deposits lost that role because a currency shortage was forcing banks to default on their commitment to redeem them in currency on demand, propositions about the medium of exchange would cease fully applying to them.

X
INTEREST ON DEMAND DEPOSITS?

Money's lack of a market of its own is more significant than its lack of a price of its own. Bank time deposits and deposits in several types of NFI share with demand deposits and currency the property of being fixed in value in terms of the unit of account. Suppose, now, that demand deposits were also allowed to bear interest. (It is convenient and legitimate here to blur the distinction between demand deposits and currency or to suppose that currency also bears interest.) Would money's interest yield serve as a flexible price equilibrating supply and demand without a painful roundabout process? Would money lose its distinctiveness? (Pesek and Saving do suggest that money loses its monetary quality to the extent that it bears interest.)[32]

Explicit interest on demand deposits would become a new dimension of competition among individual banks, but its rate would not become a price that equilibrated the demand for and supply of money. Even bearing interest, money would remain the means of pricing and paying for everything else. Its supply and demand still would not directly confront each other "at the banks," or on any other particular market. (Supply of and demand for savings and loan deposits, in contrast, do confront each other at the S & L associations; and the interest rate paid on those deposits can function as a kind of deputy for a price.) Money would still lack a single, definite, flexible price whereby its value in goods and services might readily adjust so as to equilibrate its supply and demand. (Possibilities of actually separating the medium of exchange and unit of account form an interesting topic, but one too big for discussion here.)

Since currency is one of the types of bank reserve money, a shortage of it might well count as contributing to a reserve deficiency, which is a supply-side limitation to the creation of deposit money. This point reinforces a denial of any demand-side limitation on the creation of deposit money.

I am indebted to Alan Rabin for raising the questions that this footnote tries to deal with.

32. Pesek and Saving, *The Foundations of Money and Banking*, 105–11.

XI
EXOGENEITY OF THE MONEY SUPPLY

In arguing that the demand for money adjusts to its supply, but by a momentous roundabout process, I have been assuming, or concluding, that its supply is exogenous. That assumption now needs to be qualified and defended. The money supply is "exogenous" if its nominal size is or can be controlled by the monetary authorities and does not automatically change as people make payments or try to build up or run down their money holdings. In financial systems as sophisticated as those of the United States and Great Britain, this is not literally and precisely true. The money supply can vary as recipients cash checks for currency instead of depositing them, for example, or deposit them at banks working with different reserve ratios than the drawee banks. Yet the money supply comes closer to being exogenous than the stock of any other financial asset—closer in a degree that amounts to a difference in kind—and it is a shame to lose this distinction in a morass of quibbles and debating points.

E. V. Morgan presumably was thinking of qualifications like those just mentioned when he specified that for something to count as money, it is not enough that its value should be fixed in terms of the unit of account.[33] "A second necessary condition is that supply should be exogenous, in the sense that the amount issued by any one issuer is not affected by the transactions of any transactor that is not itself an issuer of an asset qualifying as money." (While Morgan's meaning is reasonably clear, his particular wording is open to question. I would have specified an unchanged total amount rather than an unchanged "amount issued by any one issuer.")[34] Morgan's second condition holds if the asset is "perfectly acceptable"—if everyone will accept payment in it rather than insist on or cash it in for some more basic type of money. Merely *partial* acceptability could satisfy Morgan's criterion if accompanied by a further condition: existence of "a mechanism which makes the supply exogenous by off-

33. Morgan, "The Essential Qualities of Money."
34. Ibid., 242.

setting any effect on supply caused by transactors who are not themselves issuers of money."[35] The most plausible such mechanism, it seems to me—and here I part company with Morgan—would be a central-bank practice of offsetting any changes in the total quantity of means of exchange caused by shifts in the public's currency/ deposit ratio, shifts of deposits between banks working with different reserve ratios, or shifts of deposits between banks holding reserves in base money and banks holding reserves in other forms.

The central bank has a more direct control over base money and over demand deposits and currency than over quantities of near moneys. It can influence the latter only indirectly, "through" money. People have to be *induced*—by variations in their accompanying holdings of money and by the influence of the quantity of money on prices and nominal incomes—to demand no more and no less than the stock of near moneys that the central bank might desire to maintain. (Compare Morgan on "what we mean by saying that the supply of bank deposits is determined exogenously, and this is the essential difference between money and money substitutes.")[36]

Not only the quantity of near moneys but also the quantity of money is sometimes said to be demand-determined. That is almost trivially true if the central bank deliberately adjusts the money supply to accommodate demand and avoid the consequences of excess or deficiency. A more meaningful case of a demand-determined quantity of money is one in which the central bank carries out expansionary open-market operations to resist tendencies for market interest rates and the government's borrowing costs to rise. But to say that the quantity of money is demand-determined in such situations is not, as Morgan explains, to deny that the money supply is exogenous. Rather, "the central bank gives overriding priority to the government's desire to maintain a particular level of interest rates even though this is not an equilibrium one. This is not mere hair-splitting; central banks have not always been entirely subservient to governments, and it is important to distinguish the effects of their respective operations."[37]

35. Ibid., 244.
36. Ibid., 247–48.
37. Ibid., 246–47.

XII

FOREIGN INFLUENCES ON THE
MONEY SUPPLY

So far, in treating the quantity of money as exogenous or supply-determined, we have been assuming freely fluctuating exchange rates. Things are different in a country with close ties to world markets and with a pegged exchange rate.[38] Especially in a "small" country, its stock of base money, and through the money-multiplier process its entire money stock, as well as its price level, is dominated by the balance of payments and by linkage to prices abroad. An increase in the demand for domestic cash balances, for example, would tend to satisfy itself through a balance-of-payments surplus and the central bank's creation of additional domestic base money as it bought foreign exchange to keep the exchange rate fixed.

Under such conditions, the country's banking system as a whole is in qualitatively the same position vis-à-vis the outside world as Chicago banks are, considered as a group of their own, vis-à-vis the rest of the United States. The deposits of Chicago banks, like those of a single bank, are *not* exogenously determined. Usefulness of money-multiplier analysis hinges on reasonable stability of the determinants of the multiplier and exogeneity of the monetary base, and the latter is not true of the Chicago area alone.[39] If Chicago banks alone should decide to expand credit, drainage of reserve funds would frustrate them. If Chicago residents should act to build up their money holdings, reserves would flow into their banks through a local balance-of-payments surplus, supporting the desired expansion

38. We should stipulate, further, that the country's currency not be used as an international key currency. Because of the dollar's special international role, the United States monetary system retained, even under fixed rates, the essential domestic characteristics of a system with a floating exchange rate. We should avoid confusion, incidentally, between the meaning of "exogenous" as the term is used in this paper and the nonstandard usage occasionally encountered whereby a money supply is said to be exogenous if it is heavily influenced by impulses coming from outside (exo-) the country.

39. Cf. Masera, "Deposit Creation," 145–46, 155–56. Masera draws parallels among "Chicago banks," domestic NFIs, and the Eurodollar system, and contrasts those institutions with a closed domestic banking system as a whole.

of deposit money. Much the same is true of a country's entire money and banking system under fixed exchange rates.

Even though its quantity is not exogenous in a country with a fixed exchange rate, money does not lose all its distinctive properties. In certain circumstances, as history illustrates, foreign developments working through the country's balance of payments may "impose" on it an imbalance between its demand for and supply of money. This imbalance then has to be adjusted away by the roundabout macroeconomic process mentioned in section 9, since money still lacks a market of its own on which a price of its own adjusts to equilibrate supply and demand. (The foreign-exchange market and rate do not serve this function; and anyway, the exchange rate is fixed.) When the processes of imported inflation "impose" additional money on a country, prices and nominal incomes have to rise until the expanded money supply is demanded after all, and conversely with imported deflation.

Even under fixed exchange rates, money is supplied and demanded in an unusual way and still can be thrust onto or withdrawn from its holders in the aggregate in a way that does not also characterize near moneys. Banks remain unique because of the monetary nature of their demand liabilities. Even under fixed rates, the question "What are banks?" blends into the question of the essential properties that make money macroeconomically so significant.

XIII
THE FUTURE

In conclusion, I return to the institutional developments that seem to be blurring distinctions between banks and other financial institutions and between the medium of exchange and near moneys and even blurring the very concepts of money and its quantity. Perhaps these developments will remain of minor importance; perhaps the trend they suggest is genuine but could be stopped; perhaps resistance would be too costly; those judgments lie outside the scope of this paper. Anyway, if control over the quantity of money *does* become impractical and even conceptually elusive, some substitute must be found. In any monetary system, as Joseph A. Schumpeter explained, some "critical figure," some nominal money magnitude, must be specified from the outside if the purchasing power of the money unit is to be determinate.[40] The method whose possible obsolescence has been worrying us is control of the number of units of medium of exchange in existence. Another is specification of the money price of some commodity or composite of commodities, with that price being kept meaningful by unrestricted two-way convertibility. Belatedly I must admit that the arguments for the gold standard or a composite-commodity standard are more intellectually respectable than I used to think and teach. The relevant arguments go beyond those of this paper.

40. Schumpeter, *Das Wesen des Geldes.*

Individual and Overall Viewpoints in Monetary Theory

THE NEED FOR A
CLEAR DISTINCTION

In or around 1951, while a graduate student at Columbia University, I was privileged to attend an extracurricular seminar on monetary theory conducted by Ludwig von Mises at Washington Square. The concepts that the seminar helped clarify for me included those of the demand for money and factors affecting it, the distinction between actual and demanded quantities of money, the services of or nonpecuniary yield on holdings of money, and diminishing marginal returns on those holdings.[1] Shortly after, I had occasion to ask my monetary theory professor at Columbia a question presupposing the distinction between actual and demanded money holdings. Astonishingly, he was unfamiliar with that distinction and could make no sense of it. Every existing bit of money is held by someone, and held voluntarily, he said, so actual and demanded holdings not merely tend to become equal but are necessarily identical.

Reprinted with permission of Israel M. Kirzner, Department of Economics, New York University, 269 Mercer Street, New York, New York 10003.

1. Other influences on my understanding around this time included Mises's *Human Action* (New Haven: Yale University Press, 1949); and Edwin Cannan, "The Application of the Theoretical Apparatus of Supply and Demand to Units of Currency," *Economic Journal* (1921), reprinted in American Economic Association, *Readings in Monetary Theory* (Philadelphia: Blakiston, 1951), 3–12. W. H. Hutt's "The Yield on Money Held" (an absolutely fundamental contribution, in my opinion) appeared a few years later in the Mises *Festschrift, On Freedom and Free Enterprise*, ed. Mary Sennholz (Princeton: Van Nostrand, 1956).

His error was a specific example of failure to grasp the distinction between individual and overall viewpoints. The importance of that distinction is the theme of this chapter: It seeks to illuminate both the fallacious and the fruitful interplay of viewpoints by bringing together examples of each.

In the demand-for-money example, the error lay in jumping from an aggregative fact to the supposed intentions of individuals. Of course all money belongs to somebody. Of course each holding is voluntary in the sense that the holder has accepted the money voluntarily and has not yet spent or otherwise disposed of it. But this fact does not necessarily mean that the holder is fully content with his cash balance, desiring neither to reduce nor to increase it. People will always accept payment in the routine medium of exchange whether they intend to continue holding it or instead intend to pass it on soon to someone else. Not every inpayment or outpayment represents a deliberate action to increase or reduce one's cash balance. The way that money functions in the economy, including the role of cash balances as buffers absorbing mismatchings of inpayments and outpayments, means that short-run changes in a person's actual cash balance need not reflect any change in his demand for an average cash balance over a span of time. Both for individual holders and for the aggregate of them, therefore, actual holdings of money are no exact measure of desired holdings.

To be sure, a macroeconomic process affecting prices (and usually affecting production and employment also) does tend to bring desired holdings into line with the actual quantity of money.[2] But understanding this process presupposes a firm grasp of the conceptual distinction between actual and desired quantities.

---

2. Both J. M. Keynes and Milton Friedman, separately, called the description of this process the "fundamental" or "most important" proposition of monetary theory. The demanded quantity that tends to be aligned with the actual quantity is expressed in nominal terms; with regard to the real (purchasing-power) quantity of money, the adjustment tends to work the other way around, the desired quantity pulling the actual quantity into line. The "fundamental proposition" referring to nominal quantities presupposes a floating exchange rate; for, with a fixed exchange rate, the demand for money can affect the actual quantity through the balance of payments.

INDIVIDUAL-EXPERIMENTS AND
MARKET-EXPERIMENTS

The sound precept of methodological individualism does not call for rejecting the overall viewpoint in favor of the individual viewpoint. It calls, rather, for building bridges between the two, particularly by relating propositions about all economic phenomena, including the behavior of macroeconomic aggregates, to the perceptions and decisions of individuals.

One example of constructive interplay between the two viewpoints is the relation between individual-experiments and market-experiments, as distinguished by Don Patinkin.[3] In an individual-experiment one considers how some specified change would affect the choices of an individual or a set of individuals or even all members of the economic system considered in some particular capacity (such as actual or potential users of some commodity or as holders of money). It is legitimate in an individual-experiment to postulate alternative values even of some variable that cannot be a datum but rather is an endogenous variable from the standpoint of the economy as a whole. An example is the price of a particular competitively traded commodity. That price cannot simply change apart from underlying causes, apart from changes relatively exogenous to the market process, such as changes in tastes, resources, technology, institutions, and legislation. Still, it is legitimate to conduct the individual-experiment of inquiring, say, how purchases of the commodity desired by individuals or groups would respond to a price change, even though in a different (market-experiment) context that price change cannot simply be postulated by itself. The law of demand and law of supply (asserting downsloping demand curves and upsloping supply curves) are the two most familiar examples of results of individual-experiments. The law of supply and demand, describing how competitive pressures drive price toward the market-clearing level, is an example of the result of a market-experiment. So

3. *Money, Interest, and Prices*, 2d ed. (New York: Harper & Row, 1965), esp. 11–12, 387–95.

is an analysis of how equilibrium price and quantity traded would respond to a specified change in tastes, technology, or available resources affecting the demand for or supply of some commodity.

In monetary theory, an example of an individual-experiment is investigation of how the level of interest rates affects the quantity of money demanded (or, more comprehensively, investigation of the properties of the demand-for-money function). One cannot, however, legitimately try to investigate how the price level and real economic activity, say, would respond to a change in the level of interest rates, postulated by itself. In a market-experiment context, interest rates cannot simply change; their change must result from other changes, including changes exogenous to the market process. A legitimate market-experiment would specify these exogenous changes—perhaps technological developments affecting investment prospects and so the demand for loans—and would investigate their consequences, only one of which would be the interest-rate change. Another example of a market-experiment is investigation of the consequences of an exogenous increase or decrease in the quantity of money. It employs individual-experiment knowledge of the demand-for-money function and traces the consequences of the imbalance initially created between actual and desired holdings of money.

FALLACIES OF COMPOSITION

Probably the best known broad example of confusion of viewpoints is the fallacy of composition, unwarranted generalization from an individual to an overall viewpoint. (Recall the textbook example about standing on tiptoe to see a parade.) Often the fallacy consists of jumping from the result of an individual-experiment to the supposed result of a market-experiment without, of course, even distinguishing between the two types of experiment. The early Keynesian liquidity-preference theory of interest seems to be a case in point: from the inverse relation between the interest rate and desired holdings of money, an inverse relation between the actual money stock and the market-equilibrium interest rate was (invalidly) inferred. Another example is the blurring of distinctions between money and near moneys on the grounds, apparently, that liquid assets in both categories are highly substitutable in the eyes of individual holders.[4] Yet close similarity from the individual point of view does not entail close similarity in the ways that the medium of exchange and near moneys function in the economy as a whole, in the ways that the total quantities of each get determined, or in the ways that the two total quantities affect macroeconomic phenomena.[5] Explaining this point would require a chapter of its own; but, for a simple analogy, consider the close similarity for individual holders between gold coins and redeemable paper money under the historical gold standard, yet the great difference for the performance of the whole economy, especially at a time of balance-of-payments deficit, between having a monetary circulation composed mostly of gold coins and a circulation composed mostly of paper notes backed by only fractional gold reserves.

Some members of the rational-expectations school have recently asserted that increases in the money supply and in federal interest-bearing debt are essentially similar in causing price inflation. "Federal bonds are nothing more than an alternative form of currency—they are promises to deliver currency in the future. Like currency, these bonds are pieces of paper backed by nothing tangible; they are fiat paper." Since the government has no intention of ever retiring its debt, "there is little difference between currency and bonds; both are money." Any increase in the federal budget deficit, whether financed by issue of currency or of bonds, is therefore inflationary. "As is well understood, government can cause inflation by printing more money. It can also cause inflation by printing more bonds. Additions to the stock of money or bonds, by increasing the total amount of nominal wealth, increase private demands for goods and services. The increased demands, in turn, push up the prices of goods."[6] It would seem to follow from this argument that if govern-

4. As in the British Radcliffe Report of 1959; for citations and discussion, see my "Essential Properties of the Medium of Exchange," *Kyklos* 21, no. 1 (1968): 45–69 (reprinted in this volume).

5. I am not forgetting that institutional changes may in fact now be blurring distinctions that formerly were real. That, however, is another story.

6. Preston J. Miller and Alan Struthers, Jr., "The Tax-Cut Illusion," Federal Reserve Bank of Minneapolis, *1979 Annual Report*, 1–9 (preceded by an approving in-

ment deficits are not to be avoided and are inflationary in any case, they might as well be financed in the simplest and cheapest way.[7]

The fallacy in these ideas rests, first of all, on the tacit assumption (reflected in the next-to-last of the sentences quoted) that money affects spending only by being part of its holders' wealth; the real-balance or cash-balance effect consists of nothing but a wealth effect. On this view, whether a good fairy gave a country's inhabitants $1 million worth of blankets (say) or $1 million of new money, spending on other goods and services would respond in the same way. Now, it is presumably true of an individual that his increased spending on goods and services would be unaffected by whether he received a gift of $1 million in cash or a gift of blankets sellable for $1 million after expenses. But it would be illegitimate to generalize from the irrelevance of the form of the gift for the individual to its supposed irrelevance for the behavior of the economy as a whole.

Yet a similar fallacy is committed in practically identifying bonds and money. No matter how wealthy the holders of bonds feel and how many goods and services their perceived wealth prompts them to buy, they can buy only by spending money. (Buying on credit merely delays but does not eliminate payment in money. A comprehensive system of offsetting debts against each other would make a big difference, but the discussion refers to actually existing institutions and practices.) On the warranted assumption that some relation exists between the flow of income and expenditure and desired holdings of the medium of exchange, the quantity of the latter in existence does pose some restraint on the flow of spending. Replacement of a substantial part of the money supply by bonds of equal value could hardly leave total spending unaffected.

When the government finances a deficit by issuing bonds, it finds willing buyers by offering the bonds at a lower price, in nominal

---

troduction by the bank's president, Mark H. Willes); and Preston J. Miller, "Deficit Policies, Deficit Fallacies," Federal Reserve Bank of Minneapolis, *Quarterly Review* 4 (Summer 1980): 2–4. The quotations come from the *Report*, p. 2, and the *Review*, p. 2. In a footnote to the latter, Miller cites other authors who also, he says, perceive the essential similarity of bonds and money. Also see N. J. Simler's letter to the *Wall Street Journal*, 10 August 1981, 19.

7. John Bryant and Neil Wallace, "The Inefficiency of Interest-Bearing National Debt," *Journal of Political Economy* 87 (April 1979): 365–81.

terms, than the sum of their redemption price at maturity and interest payments in the meanwhile. In paying money for the bonds, the buyers forgo other spending or lending. (If it is other lending that the bond buyers forgo, then the other persons to whom they would have made loans must either forgo spending or else compete with still others for the limited supply of loanable funds. If the initial buyers want to cease holding the bonds, they cannot directly spend them on goods and services; rather, they, like the government in the first place, have to provide a price or interest inducement to others to take over the bonds.) Thus bond finance does not increase demands for goods and services and real resources—demands backed up by readiness to pay money—to the extent that the issue of money would have done. New money can be thrust into circulation by being directly spent on goods and services.

This is not to say that bond-financed deficits have no effect on spending. The textbooks explain how the rise in interest rates associated with bond finance will make people choose to hold smaller cash balances than otherwise in relation to income and expenditures; velocity will rise. On the other hand, insofar as people's desired money holdings are positively related to the total sizes of their wealth portfolios—if there is a wealth argument in the demand-for-money function—and insofar as government bonds count as part of the wealth of the private sector, issuing additional government bonds could tend to *increase* desired holdings of money. Conceivably, if not very plausibly, this wealth effect tending to *reduce* the velocity of the (unchanged) money supply could outweigh the above mentioned interest effect on velocity, resulting in *shrinkage* of total spending.[8] No

8. A mathematical formalization of this point, though available, would swell the discussion beyond what is appropriate here. For greater attention to the possibility in question than is usual in textbooks, see Thomas M. Havrilesky and John T. Boorman, *Monetary Macroeconomics* (Arlington Heights, Ill.: AHM Publishing, 1978), chap. 12 and passim.

For an example of a different notion about the relation between money and spending, namely, the erroneous assertion that the total money supply has no significant influence on aggregate spending because individual cash balances, being freely chosen, do not significantly influence spending by their individual holders, see James Tobin, "Asset Holdings and Spending Decisions," *American Economic Review* 42 (May 1952), esp. 115. G. M. Meier quotes this passage with approval in "Some Questions About Growth Economics: Comment," *American Economic Review* 44 (December 1954): 936.

such contractionary effect of a money-financed deficit is even conceivable (without utterly implausible assumptions).[9]

The notorious real-bills doctrine, dating from Adam Smith if not earlier and demolished by Henry Thornton in 1802,[10] keeps getting resurrected and reinvented with new twists. It got its name from the idea that bank lending, even the lending of money created in the process, would be noninflationary if accomplished by discounting short-term real bills, that is, bills of exchange arising from the production or marketing of real goods, as distinguished from mere finance or accommodation bills. The doctrine was also called the "needs-of-trade" theory on the grounds that if the expansion and contraction of money in connection with bank loans were linked to the production and marketing of goods, the quantity of money would be linked to the quantities of goods and thus to the needs of trade. If a bank loan enabled a manufacturer to buy raw materials and process them into goods for the market, the new goods would soon match the new money. Not the mere quantity of money but rather its quality—that is, the manner of its getting into circulation—was the supposed touchstone of sound policy.

Such qualitative regulation would gear the nominal quantity of money to the nominal value of goods rather than to their physical quantity. If prices should somehow happen to rise, then the nominal

9. Another difference between the two types of finance is that bond finance can shift part of the "burden" of government deficit spending to future generations in a way that money finance cannot do. For resurrection of the proposition about burden shifting, which for many years had wrongly been scorned as erroneous, see James M. Buchanan, *Public Principles of Public Debt* (Homewood, Ill.: Irwin, 1958). Buchanan pointed out what this chapter calls a confusion of viewpoints. The conventional wisdom that he attacked was proceeding directly from aggregate and material considerations (such as the fact that real resources cannot be shifted from the future into the present) to judgments about burdens supposedly borne or not borne by individuals in the current and future generations. It went wrong in adopting an insufficiently subjectivist (or even antisubjectivist) conception of burden and in focusing insufficiently on individual persons. The correctness of Buchanan's analysis now seems to be widely, although only tacitly, acknowledged in discussions of the difference between funded and pay-as-you-go programs of social-security financing.

10. *An Enquiry Into the Nature and Effects of the Paper Credit of Great Britain*, ed. F. A. Hayek (1939; reprint, Fairfield, N.J.: Kelley, 1978), chaps. 2, 10. Also see Lloyd W. Mints, *A History of Banking Theory* (Chicago: University of Chicago Press, 1945), 9–11, 25–30, and passim.

volume of lending and money issue supposedly justified by an unchanging physical volume of production would rise in step; monetary expansion in accordance with the doctrine would ratify and reinforce price inflation. A general decline of prices, conversely, would shrink the money supply and reinforce the deflation. Anchoring the money supply to a consequence of itself, namely the price level, means not anchoring it at all.

The real-bills doctrine has further fallacious aspects, but the one most relevant to this paper is its invalid generalization from the individual to the overall point of view. Sure, a loan that expands the money supply may indeed enable the individual manufacturer (or retailer) to market goods that he could not otherwise have produced (or have acquired for his shelves). *His* production or marketing of goods may indeed be geared to his loan. But it does not follow that the total physical production and marketing of goods are geared to the total volume of loans. Real resources are scarce. Except perhaps in a seriously underemployed economy, lending newly created money to business does not so much bring additional productive resources into existence or into use as enable businessmen to bid more eagerly against each other for the resources available in any case.

REVERSE FALLACIES OF COMPOSITION

What might be called the reverse fallacy of composition is the invalid supposition that what is true (or desirable) from an overall viewpoint is therefore true (or desirable) from an individual viewpoint as well. The idea sometimes turns up that the demand for money will tend to adapt itself to the actual quantity in a relatively painless way so that what would otherwise be a deficient money supply (at the going price level) will not constrain transactions, production, and employment after all. Faced with a shortage of coins in particular, people will cooperate to carry out their transactions anyway (the customer will give the retailer the extra dime or two cents needed to hold down the amount of change due). Similarly, George A. Akerlof suggests, people will cooperate to keep their transactions going when total money is in short supply.[11] They may adjust payments schedules or make more use of trade credits; financial institutions may devise new near moneys.

This optimistic argument is mistaken but instructive. A shortage specifically of coins is fairly obvious, and collaboration in coping with it works not only in the general interest but also in one's private interest (to keep one's own transaction going and to earn goodwill). An overall shortage of money is harder for individuals to diagnose. The disequilibrium does not show up on any particular market (whereas coins do have a market of their own in the sense that they exchange against money of other denominations); instead, the monetary disequilibrium shows itself obscurely as a generalized difficulty in selling things and earning incomes. Furthermore—and this is the most relevant point here—the fact that it would be in their common interest for people quite generally to employ money-economizing instruments and practices does not mean that it is in the interest of any individual to do so even before such expedients have already been generally adopted.

A similar point applies to proposals for adopting alternative money systems, such as reckoning in gold units or in units of constant purchasing power as calculated with a price index.[12] The government money might continue to circulate, but the amount changing hands in each particular transaction would be translated from the stable-value amount at the latest exchange rate or price index. Even if such a system would be in the general interest once firmly established, it might not be in the interest of individual transactors to go first in getting the system launched. Consider a bank. Would it be willing to accept deposits repayable in units of gold or of constant

11. "The Questions of Coinage, Trade Credit, Financial Flows and Peanuts: A Flow-of-Funds Approach to the Demand for Money," Federal Reserve Bank of New York, Research Paper no. 7520 (September 1975). A similar argument about money substitutes and a plastic demand for money had already been presented by Jean-Baptiste Say in *A Treatise on Political Economy*, trans. C. R. Prinsep (Philadelphia: Grigg & Elliot, 1836), 133–34.

12. With modifications, the point also applies to Hayek's proposal for encouraging private moneys, whose issuers would compete for holders by achieving records of stability of the purchasing powers of their money units. See a later section of this paper and F. A. Hayek, *Denationalisation of Money*, 2d ed. (London: Institute of Economic Affairs, 1978).

purchasing power before arranging to acquire assets similarly denominated? Would it find borrowers, for example, willing to commit themselves to repaying debt in gold or purchasing-power units before arranging to receive their revenues on such terms? Early users of the parallel money units would be exposing themselves to risk of adverse changes in the exchange rates of those units against the still-dominant government money. Inducements such as appropriately high or low interest rates might be found to make people bear such risks. The point remains, though, that the desirability of some change from the overall point of view does not imply that individuals will have reason to take the initiative in launching the change.

FURTHER CONFUSIONS

The next examples defy easy classification under either the fallacy of composition or its reverse, although the reader may find trying to classify them instructive.

Writers on the Banking school side of nineteenth-century British monetary controversies (including John Fullarton, Thomas Tooke, John Stuart Mill, and James Wilson) expounded a supposed "law of the reflux." An automatic process, they thought, would restrain issue of bank-created money in excess of the "wants of trade" or "needs of trade." Excessive note issues, in particular, would flow back to the issuing banks by way of deposits, repayments of loans, and, less significantly, demands for redemption in coin. (Banking school writers emphasized the first two channels over the third.)[13] Sure, an individual bank trying to get too many notes into circulation (for example, by offering borrowers exceptionally easy terms) would find itself plagued and restrained by what we would nowadays call adverse clearing balances; but the same is not true of the system as a whole. If all banks were moving together in expanding their note and deposit issues, each would be acquiring more and more claims on the

13. Mints, *History of Banking Theory*, 88–94, 134, 207. Mints describes the doctrine and regards it as wrong, but he does not make the confusion-of-viewpoints criticism. He comes close on p. 26, however, where he discusses Adam Smith's errors in connection with the real-bills doctrine and with supposed restraint on overissue of banknotes.

others as well as incurring more and more liabilities to them and so would be avoiding large adverse clearing balances. Furthermore, the effects of the monetary expansion on prices and nominal incomes would be increasing the quantities of money that the public demanded to hold. Apart, therefore, from redeemability requirements and prospects of exhaustion of specie reserves—and these circumstances are not at the core of the supposed law of the reflux—no check on inflationary overissue would operate after all. Determinacy of the money supply and price level presupposes some sort of real anchor or quantitative limitation, such as is provided by redeemability of bank money in base money of limited quantity.

The Yale School's "New View" of money and financial intermediation (in fact hardly new at all) confuses viewpoints in postulating a "natural economic limit" to the size of the money-creating system. Given their wealth and their asset preferences, says James Tobin, people will voluntarily hold additional demand deposits only if yields on alternative assets fall. This also means reduced yields on loans and investments available to the banks, making further lending and investing unprofitable for them beyond some point. In this respect the commercial-banking industry is not different in kind from any other system of financial intermediaries. Even without reserve requirements, the banking system's expansion "would be limited by the availability of assets at yields sufficient to compensate banks for the costs of attracting and holding the corresponding deposits."[14] As Basil Moore expresses the matter, the necessity facing banks, like all other business firms, "of operating at profit, combined with a downward sloping demand curve for bank loans and deposits, serves to restrict output expansion even in the absence of deposit control through reserve manipulation."[15]

14. James Tobin, "Commercial Banks as Creators of 'Money,'" in *Banking and Monetary Studies*, ed. Deane Carson (Homewood, Ill.: Irwin, 1963), 414, 416. Andrew D. Crockett forcefully echoes Tobin's general position in "The Euro-Currency Market: An Attempt to Clarify Some Basic Issues," *International Monetary Fund Staff Papers* 23 (July 1976): 375–86. For further citations and fuller discussion, see my "What Are Banks?" *Atlantic Economic Journal* 6 (December 1978): 1–14 (reprinted in this volume).

15. *An Introduction to the Theory of Finance* (New York: Free Press, 1968), 168–69.

This view slights some familiar contrasts. No obstacle on the demand-for-money side blocks lending and spending new bank demand deposits into existence. (Meeting reserve requirements, if they exist, and in any case maintaining redeemability of deposits in base money, operates on the supply-of-money side. These restraints are too familiar to distinguish any self-styled New View.) No one need be persuaded to invest in the routine medium of exchange before more of it can be created. Bankers do not need to find someone willing to hold it but only someone willing to accept it—if not a borrower, then someone selling a security from his portfolio, or a supplier of furniture or office equipment, or a bank employee. Once a person has accepted new money, he passes it along to others, if he does not want to hold it, instead of somehow making it go out of existence. It is hard to imagine why a bank might find it more profitable to hold reserves in excess of what the law and prudence call for than to buy riskless short-term securities with them. The New Viewers seem to be assuming, tacitly and mistakenly, that the individual bank is wary of bidding down yields on portfolio assets because it is concerned with maximizing not its own profits but those of the banking system as a whole.[16]

Even with regard to the banking system as a whole, something is wrong with the idea that a decline in yields obtainable will check expansion of loans and investments and deposits. That idea overlooks Knut Wicksell's cumulative process. As money expansion raises nominal incomes and prices, the dollar volume of loans demanded rises also, even at given interest rates. The great inflations of history discredit any notion of a natural limit to expansion of money and credit.

A recently popular version of the monetary theory of the balance of payments goes beyond merely recommending attention to the supply of and demand for domestic money holdings in an analysis of balance-of-payments disequilibrium and adjustment; it actually identifies a payments surplus under fixed exchange rates with the process of satisfying an excess demand for domestic money and iden-

16. Paul F. Smith, "Concepts of Money and Commercial Banks," *Journal of Finance* 21 (December 1966): 645–46; Rainer S. Masera, "Deposit Creation, Multiplication and the Euro-Dollar Market," Ente per gli Studi Monetari, Bancari e Finanziari Luigi Einaudi (Rome), *Quaderni di Ricerche* 11 (1973): 151.

tifies a deficit with the process of working off an excess supply of money.[17] Now, an association between money supply-and-demand imbalance and payments disequilibrium is indeed a frequent case and perhaps even the typical case. Their outright identification, however, is fallacious, as could easily be shown by counterexamples (including the historical phenomenon of imported inflation). Actual changes in the money supply are misinterpreted as aggregates of deliberate and desired adjustments in the money holdings of individual holders.

This misinterpretation traces to failure to take due account of the functioning of money as the medium of exchange. It is true that a country's payments surplus or deficit, suitably defined, involves the residents' acquisition or relinquishment, respectively, of domestic money.[18] But these changes may not represent desired adjustments of money holdings. Because money is the routine medium of exchange, people will always accept it even when they do not, individually, desire to go on holding it. But new money does not automatically go out of circulation again just because it is undesired as additional holdings; rather, it touches off an expansionary or inflationary process that tends to make it all desired after all. Conversely, shrinkage of a country's money supply does not necessarily represent the deliberate and desired rundown of individual holdings. Instead, it could be the unintended consequence of money's routine use as the means of payment in a situation in which its domestic holders found purchases of goods and services and securities more attrac-

17. A monetary theory of floating exchange rates, in parallel, identifies a currency's exchange appreciation or depreciation as part of a process of correcting an imbalance between desired and actual holdings of domestic money. For documentation and fuller discussion, see Alan A. Rabin and Leland B. Yeager, "Monetary Approaches to the Balance of Payments and Exchange Rates," *Economic Perspectives* 1 (1979): 173–201. My purpose here is not to explore the error in question fully but merely to cite it as still another example of confusion of viewpoints.

18. A surplus entails creating domestic money as the central bank buys up the country's net receipts of foreign exchange to keep the exchange rate fixed; a deficit entails shrinking domestic money as the central bank sells foreign exchange from its reserves to shore up the home currency's exchange rate. In some cases the central bank might be offsetting this creation or destruction of domestic money in its exchange-rate pegging with money destruction or creation in its domestic operations; but such monetary changes of domestic origin would give superficial support to the (mis)interpretation of the payments surplus or deficit as necessarily due to an excess demand for or supply of domestic money.

tive or more available than sales in transactions with parties other than themselves.

Suppose, for example, that the central bank, committing some colossal blunder, carries out a massive contractionary open-market operation. Private investors buy the securities being offered by the central bank because their low prices and high yields are attractive. These investors pay in money, of course, but probably *without* intending to get along thereafter with a cash balance smaller by that amount. Instead, each probably intends to replenish his cash balance by selling other securities or goods and services to somebody else. These intentions meet frustration, and the excess demand for money resulting from the contractionary open-market operation has disastrous macroeconomic consequences. Now suppose a different blunder with similar consequences: The central bank revalues the home currency upward, cutting in half the pegged home-currency price of foreign exchange. In consequence of all the related price changes, purchases of goods and services and securities abroad become much more attractive and available than sales abroad, the country runs a balance-of-payment deficit, and the home money supply shrinks, with painful deflationary consequences. In brief, by making foreign exchange such a bargain and selling it lavishly out of its reserves, the central bank takes out of circulation the domestic money received in payment. Yet this monetary contraction in no way represents an intentional rundown of private money holdings.

The theory reviewed rests, in short, on a confusion of viewpoints. Specifically, it mistakenly supposes that changes in a country's money supply associated with a balance-of-payment surplus or deficit must correspond (not just may correspond) to aggregates of desired changes in individual holdings.

ILLUMINATING INTERPLAY

Let us turn from castigating errors toward recognizing fruitful interaction between individual and overall viewpoints. A well-known example will serve as a start. How can the economist, observing the whole system of banks operating with fractional reserves, say that the system creates deposit money (when additional reserve funds or cuts in reserve requirements allow it to expand), while the individual banker can nevertheless maintain that he does not create any money at all but rather simply relends money deposited with him, and then not even its entire amount but only the excess over what he must set aside as reserves? What reconciles these contrasting views? Any undergraduate who has passed the money and banking course should know the answer, so I will not presume to repeat it here.[19]

In applying his regression theorem to the so-called circulatory problem, Ludwig von Mises was constructively bridging the two viewpoints. The problem is that money is demanded for its purchasing power: How many nominal units an individual demands to hold depends above all on the price level. Yet the price level is determined by the interplay of money's supply and demand. It is easy to show, as Patinkin has done, that there is no vicious circularity in these propositions.[20] A demand function for money holdings in which the purchasing power of the money units is the principal argument, together with the actual quantity of money, suffices to determine the equilibrium price level in the sense that demanded and actual quantities of money would be unequal at any other price level. This mathematical determinacy or noncircularity does not, however, render Mises's regression theorem otiose. Here, as in the analysis of the difference between near moneys and the medium of exchange, it is necessary to pay attention not only to mathematical functions (such as demand functions for money and other assets) but also to the *functioning* of those assets in the economy and to the processes whereby individuals give effect to their demands for each. Patinkin was con-

19. The correct explanation, in adequate detail, is commonly attributed to C. A. Phillips (*Bank Credit* [New York: Macmillan, 1920]), but he had been anticipated by several others, including Herbert J. Davenport (*The Economics of Enterprise* [New York: Macmillan, 1913]). See Mints, *History of Banking Theory*, 113, 206, 257–58.

20. *Money, Interest, and Prices*, 115–16. Compare Laurence S. Moss, "The Monetary Economics of Ludwig von Mises," in *The Economics of Ludwig von Mises*, ed. Laurence S. Moss (Kansas City: Sheed & Ward, 1976), 13–49.

I am indebted to Roger W. Garrison for correcting my earlier inadequate appreciation of Mises's regression theorem. See his "The Austrian-Neoclassical Relation: A Study in Monetary Dynamics" (Ph.D. diss., University of Virginia, February 1981), 77–81 in particular.

tent with showing that there is no mathematical or logical inconsistency in imagining the individual-experiment that relates the quantity of money demanded to the purchasing power of the unit and then imagining the market-experiment of confronting that demand function with a definite supply of money to determine the equilibrium purchasing power. Mises, however, was mainly concerned with process, with who does what. We may agree that people demand a definite aggregate of holdings of nominal money at each of its conceivable alternative purchasing powers. But which one of the infinitely many alternative levels do people have in mind when they actually decide how much money to hold and try to conduct market transactions consistent with their decisions? Could a new pure fiat money be launched without any clue to its tentative initial value? (Fiat money, in contrast with other things, has no usefulness of its own for people to consider in deciding how much of it to demand.) Suppose the old money were declared invalid and each person were given x units of the new money and told nothing more than to start using it. How would anyone know what prices to ask and offer for things? Would not the launching of the new money be facilitated by some indication of its initial value? If the answer is "yes," Mises was right. He said, we recall, that the demand for money interacting with supply to determine money's value "today" is expressed in the light of money's value "yesterday," which was determined by supply and demand in the light of its value the day before, and so on back in history to the time when some commodity, valuable for its own usefulness, had not quite yet evolved into money. (To say that Mises was right is not to say that Patinkin is wrong, for they were dealing with subtly different questions. Patinkin may be faulted, though, for not pointing out this difference.)

It is important for clear theorizing to distinguish between money's services to society as a whole and its services to an individual holder. On the one hand, in other words, we perceive the advantages of having a monetary rather than a barter economy (advantages that extreme monetary instability undercuts). On the other hand, we perceive the yield—subjective, intangible, and nonpecuniary, but genuine—that an individual holder receives on his cash balance, the yield that is one of the most fundamental concepts of monetary theory.[21]

Advantages of the first type enter into a public-goods aspect of money. Having a stable unit of account in which to conduct one's calculations and possibly to express one's claims and debts is advantageous even to people who do not hold that money and make and receive payments in it. A historical example will help make the point clear. Many business firms in Germany during the extreme inflation of the early 1920s reportedly took to figuring their costs and their selling prices in some relatively stable unit like the United States dollar or the Swiss franc, even though they continued receiving and making payments predominantly in German marks. They translated their stable-money prices into marks at the latest exchange rate at the time of sale. The very existence of the dollar and Swiss franc thus benefited Germans who might never have actually held or received or paid any dollars or francs.

A consideration like this bears on proposals (like that of Hayek, cited in footnote 12) for encouraging the competitive private issue of currencies. Each issuer would have his own unit (ducat, crown, florin, or whatever; the proposal does not envisage rival currencies all denominated in the same unit, such as a quantity of gold); and the different units would be free to fluctuate against each other. Each issuer would have an incentive, supposedly, to restrain his issues to keep the value of his unit stable, thereby attracting wider and wider circles of holders. Virtue would bring its own reward. The larger the real volume of his currency people would willingly hold, the larger the volume of loans the issuer could have outstanding and earning interest. Success in restraining his issue to the volume demanded at a stable value of his unit would itself strengthen that demand, which he could then profitably meet.

Because of the public-good aspect, however—namely, the free availability of his money as a unit of accounting and calculation even to parties who held little or none of it—a well-behaved issuer could not collect compensation for all the advantages he was conferring

21. Compare J. R. Hicks, "The Two Triads," in his *Critical Essays in Monetary Theory* (Oxford: Clarendon Press, 1967), as well as the article by Hutt cited in footnote 1.

on the public in general. The social benefits of his maintaining a stable money would not come fully to his attention. Here we recall the standard argument that the purely private provision of public goods falls short of the optimum, plausibly defined.

This point may not be welcome to those who are looking for monetary reform along private-enterprise lines. It may not be a quantitatively important point. But it is one that reformers should face. And it does illustrate the interplay of viewpoints that is the theme of this paper.

Another sort of relation between viewpoints is that each individual's reasons for using and holding a particular money are strengthened to the extent that others are doing the same. This fact may be relevant to the question whether many or few private currencies or only one would survive in a regime of actual or potential competition. James Tobin has noted an analogy between money and language: "Both are means of communication. The use of a particular language or a particular money by one individual increases its value to other actual or potential users. Increasing returns to scale, in this sense, limits the number of languages or moneys in a society and indeed explains the tendency for one basic language or money to monopolize the field. Theory must give way to history in explaining which language and what money . . . are adopted in any given community." The analogy points to "arbitrariness and circularity" in a money's being accepted: acceptability enhances acceptability.[22] It also affords further insight into the aforementioned difficulties of launching competitive private moneys or a new stable unit to be used optionally in parallel with government money. Early users of a new unit would confer benefits on latecomers, if the reform could succeed, for which the early users could not collect compensation. They thus have inadequate incentives to provide what would be in part a public good.

In a different respect, switching to a new currency creates a public bad if it shrinks demand for holdings of the old one, whose value consequently fluctuates downward more sharply than otherwise.

22. James Tobin, "Discussion," in *Models of Monetary Economies,* ed. John H. Kareken and Neil Wallace (Minneapolis: Federal Reserve Bank of Minneapolis, 1980), 86–87.

This problem of currency substitution might plague a system of competing private currencies even if it could somehow be successfully launched. According to the very logic of the scheme, holders of the different currencies, as well as the financial press, would be alert to signs of unsound management and incipient depreciation of any one of them. Its holders would dump it and fly into others. Sensitive responses of this sort would destabilize the exchange rates between the different currencies, upsetting transactions and calculations. Like bank runs (particularly in the days before deposit insurance), such runs from one currency to another would be harmful from an overall point of view, yet would result from individuals' efforts to protect themselves.

One should be careful, however, about applying such worries to the existing national currencies under floating exchange rates. Yet some writers connected with the rational-expectations school have argued that floating exchange rates are workable only when sensitive international capital transfers are throttled by government controls.[23] The worry seems to be that since fiat currencies lack any intrinsic value and have purchasing power thanks only to the demand for holdings of them in the context of limited supplies, people will make an all-or-nothing choice between one currency or another according to their perceived prospects of escaping inflation. With everyone alert to shift funds, no one can count on his own national currency continuing in general use.

Assessment of this worry requires a careful distinction of viewpoints. If the choice of a general medium of exchange and unit of account were to be made collectively, then there might indeed be an all-or-nothing shift to the prospectively least inflation-plagued currency. But the choice is not made that way. In practice, the shift has

23. John Kareken and Neil Wallace, "International Monetary Reform: The Feasible Alternatives," Federal Reserve Bank of Minneapolis, *Quarterly Review* 2 (Summer 1978): 2–7. To explain away the absence of a flight away from the downward-floating Canadian dollar, Kareken and Wallace refer lamely to expectations that either the Canadian or the United States government would institute controls if such a flight got under way. Gottfried Haberler critically discusses this article in "Flexible-Exchange-Rate Theories and Controversies Once Again," in *Flexible Exchange Rates and the Balance of Payments: Essays in Memory of Egon Sohmen,* ed. John S. Chipman and Charles P. Kindleberger (Amsterdam: North-Holland, 1980), separately reprinted as reprint no. 119 (Washington, D.C.: American Enterprise Institute, January 1981).

to occur piecemeal. As long as one's fellow countrymen are still generally using the national currency, it is awkward and expensive for an individual or firm to try to initiate the shift. With money as with language, inertia tends to perpetuate an entrenched use. Continuing general use tends to maintain the nonpecuniary services that cash balances of the home currency yield. Furthermore, currencies cannot be compared in terms of a single (expected) rate of return on each (gain or loss of purchasing power being appropriately counted in or netted out). The service component of the yield depends at the margin on the size of the individual cash balance. If and as the individual cuts his holding of the home currency, its subjectively appraised yield to him would rise at the margin and rise in relation to the marginal yield on holdings of foreign currency of similar real size. Inflation prospects may reduce the demand for holdings of the home currency, but those prospects would have to be bad indeed to eliminate the demand in an all-or-nothing choice.[24]

Questions about indexing are not unrelated to questions of parallel currencies and of shifts between currencies. Proponents recommend indexing as a way of coping with inflation. A warning is in order, though, against undue projection of advantages from the individual point of view to conclusions about overall feasibility. Clearly it would be convenient for the individual to be able to carry out his accounting and price and cost calculations, receive income, make contracts, accumulate savings, and incur debts all in constant-value units. From the overall point of view, however, parasitism would seem to be a problem. A price index serviceable for defining the constant-value unit and for making conversions between amounts in

24. Haberler, who characterizes Kareken and Wallace's paper as "an extraordinary example of how remorseless logicians can end up in Bedlam, if they get hold of the wrong assumptions," adds some further points: (1) Not everyone has the same expectations. (2) Only the cash, non-interest-bearing portions of different countries' money stocks might be regarded as perfect substitutes for one another. Except in the most extreme inflations, interest-rate differentials would restrain any general rush from assets in one currency to assets in another. Even in the extreme circumstances of Germany in 1920–23, the large-scale substitution of foreign for home money was slow to develop; and in present-day Brazil, where everyone expects the cruzeiro to keep on depreciating, no wholesale substitution of foreign for Brazilian money has occurred (although people would have found a way around the exchange controls if they had felt a strong urge to switch). Haberler, "Flexible-Exchange-Rate Theories," 44–46.

constant units and in current dollars must be compiled from prices determined by the interplay of market forces rather than from prices themselves mechanically calculated according to some formula. Indexing presupposes the prevalence of unindexed prices and wages and is parasitic on them. The more pervasively the index is applied, the more nearly meaningless it becomes in the sense that it is calculated from prices that are themselves calculated according to the index itself (or perhaps its level of a few months earlier).

SOME CENTRAL POINTS OF
MACROECONOMICS

The distinction between viewpoints is vital to some central points of money-macro theory. Disequilibrium between actual and desired holdings of money, together with its macroeconomic consequences—in particular, recession or depression in the case of an excess demand for money—can persist for a long time because there is no specific money market on which a specific price of money adjusts to equilibrate supply and demand. Instead, equilibrating changes in the value of money have to take place through myriad prices of individual goods and services and securities determined on separate though interlocking markets. Imbalance between supply and demand for a particular good or service typically affects not only its price but also its quantity traded and so its quantity produced. An excess demand for money can thus deflate not only prices but also real economic activity; and the less the deflationary impact is absorbed by prices, the more it must be absorbed by production and employment. (The familiar tautology $MV = PQ$ can be helpful in making this point.) Individual and collective rationality can diverge when interlocking wage and price decisions are made, as they realistically must be made, in a piecemeal, decentralized, unsynchronized manner. (The difficulties of maintaining monetary equilibrium through market-determined price-level adjustments form the basis, of course, of the ideal of avoiding monetary disequilibrium in the first place through suitable regulation of the money supply.)

In a depression (and in the absence of sensible monetary policy), it would be collectively rational to cut the general level of costs and wages and prices steeply enough to make the real value of the nominal money stock adequate for a full-employment volume of transactions and production. Nevertheless, the individual agent may not find it rational promptly to cut the particular price or wage for which he is responsible. Instead of initiating cuts in advance of other agents, he may well find it rational to wait for a better reading on the market situation. (The widespread practice of letting what may prove random mismatchings of supply and demand impinge initially on inventories reflects a justified belief that it would be irrational to try to keep supply and demand continuously in balance by prompt and frequent price adjustments.) Instead of going first, the individual agent may rationally wait to see whether cuts by others, intensifying the competition he faces or reducing his production costs or his cost of living, as the case may be, will make it advantageous for him to *follow* with a cut of his own. Here, as in the well-known example of the prisoners' dilemma, the individually rational and the collectively rational may well diverge. Taking the lead in downward price and wage adjustments is in the nature of a public good, and private incentives to supply it are weak.[25]

These observations about depression become relevant to present-day stagflation because of a close analogy holding between the stickiness of a price level and the momentum of an entrenched trend of prices and wages. Restraint on money-supply growth impinges not only on price inflation but also, and earlier, on production and employment. The momentum of wages and prices goes on for a while eroding the real value of the restrained nominal money supply. The momentum derives from the determination of interdependent prices in a piecemeal, unsynchronized manner as people

25. Yet doctrines to the effect that markets are always or should be analyzed as always in equilibrium practically obliterate this distinction of viewpoints. Part of the trouble is their reasoning only in terms of the overall price level or price and wage levels, or distinguishing only between actual and expected average levels (or inflation rates), and not recognizing that these average levels are made up of and can change only by way of millions of separate prices and wages. Such doctrines seem to be gaining popularity in parallel with the doctrine of rational expectations. I have discussed them in "Sticky Prices or Equilibrium Always?" (Paper delivered at the Western Economic Association meetings in San Francisco, 6 July 1981).

attempt to catch up with past increases and to allow for expected future increases in costs and prices and wages other than their own. How can I, an individual businessman, be confident that restraint in my own pricing policy will be matched by restraint in my workers' wage demands and in my suppliers' and competitors' prices? Is it not sensible to continue allowing for past and future increases in all costs and prices that affect me until I get a better reading on how other people may or may not be modifying their price and wage behavior? Of course, if I and all other price setters and wage negotiators were to make our decisions jointly, then it would be in our collective interest to avoid the side effects of monetary restraint by practicing appropriate price and wage restraint. In fact, though, we make our decisions piecemeal, opening the way for divergence between collective and individual rationality.[26] This circumstance is not a defect of the market system but rather an inevitable consequence of the realities that any economic system must cope with, including the fact that inevitably dispersed knowledge can be effectively used only through decentralized decisions whose coordination can hardly be accomplished better than through market processes.

For reasons just implied, the degree of credibility and perceived resoluteness of an anti-inflation policy affects how severe the withdrawal pangs will be. In two alternative situations with objectively the same monetary restraints, the policy will bite more strongly on prices and wages and its recessionary side effects will be milder when the authorities are believed ready to tolerate such effects than when they are suspected of irresolution. It is not the purpose of this paper, however, to pursue such policy issues. Enough has been said to illustrate how the distinction and interplay between individual and collective viewpoints is crucial to understanding the stickiness of price and wage levels and trends, the persistence of monetary disequilibrium, the phenomenon of stagflation, and the problems of stopping inflation.

26. In these circumstances, price or wage restraint is a public good; it confers external benefits for which their creator cannot collect a privately adequate reward. Arthur Okun, among others, recognized these externalities of pricing decisions; see his posthumously published *Prices and Quantities* (Washington, D.C.: Brookings Institution, 1981). Okun also emphasized the role of the "invisible handshake" and of notions of fairness in the stickiness of levels or trends of prices and wages.

OTHER APPLICATIONS OF THE DISTINCTION

Distinguishing between the two viewpoints is more familiar outside than within monetary theory. A mere reminder of a few examples will serve as a conclusion. The distinction is central in analysis of externalities and public goods and their relation to the incomplete specification and application of property rights and pricing. Consider the standard examples of oil capture and overfishing, as well as long waits in line at the King Tut exhibit or for gasoline during shortages. Anyone joining the rush for oil or fish or joining the line for the exhibit or for gasoline is imposing costs on others. Forbearance from joining would be a public good, and "correct" specification and application of property rights and "proper" pricing (as of tickets to the exhibit) would make this forbearance in the private interest of individuals also. (The quotation marks indicate that no premature policy recommendation is intended.) At a cocktail party, speaking in a loud voice is a private good but a public bad, contributing to the state of affairs that makes the shouting privately necessary. During an inflation, keeping one's own selling price or wage rate roughly in line with the general procession is something closely analogous. Divergence between individual and collective rationality is a pervasive fact of life, but this fact does not indict a price system. Rather, it exists because of the impossibility or impracticality of applying property rights and the logic of a price system to so many cases. The consequences of not being able to apply a price system in such cases testify, by the contrast they offer, to the advantages of a price system where it can work.

Concepts akin to those mentioned enter into the application of economics and methodological individualism to the analysis of government. They help explain how programs can get adopted piecemeal whose aggregate has an impact that runs counter to, and could have been expected to run counter to, the public interest in any plausible interpretation of the latter term. They help restrain sentimental exaggerations about how "the people" rule in a democracy and about the value of having affairs taken care of "democratically." They help one understand how democratic government adopts programs with an even less accurate confrontation of costs and benefits than the market process accomplishes even in exaggerated descriptions of market failure; they help explain, in particular, how the governmental decision process is biased toward hyperactivity. Attention to both individual and collective viewpoints reveals the narrowness and the piecemeal nature of so much governmental decision making. It serves for probing into the circumstances, incentives, and actions of the individual participants in this process—the "average voter" (who, as Anthony Downs explained, is "rationally ignorant" about most issues that his vote helps decide on), the special-interest voter, the legislator, the executive, the candidate, the bureaucrat, and the judge.

Ludwig von Mises was an early contributor of ideas in these fields. He appreciated the differences as well as the similarities between voting in political elections and voting with dollars in the marketplace. He contributed insights into the difference between bureaucratic and profit-oriented institutions and into the activities for which each type of institution had a comparative advantage.[27] In monetary theory his contributions were even more fundamental.

27. *Bureaucracy* (London: Hodge, 1945).

Inflation, Output, and Employment: Some Clarifications

(with Dan E. Birch and Alan A. Rabin)

I

INTRODUCTION

The notion has become oddly prevalent that when inflation is said to stimulate output, the stimulus comes from price inflation—*unanticipated* price inflation—and not from the underlying monetary expansion itself. It is hard to believe that such a doctrine has come to be accepted and to require refutation. Yet the literature has reached such a state. Sometimes the obvious—even the equation of exchange—needs to be belabored.

The present paper explicitly distinguishes between unanticipated price inflation and unanticipated money-supply expansion. It denies that price inflation stimulates output and employment, whether expected or not. When nominal spending grows, its impact is split between real activity and prices (falling all on the one or all on the other in the limiting cases). Any real stimulus comes not from price inflation but from its absence (or slightness). The absence of inflationary expectations contributes to a favorable price/output split and enhances the capacity of monetary expansion to provide real stimulus. Of course, monetary expansion cannot go on providing real stimulus indefinitely because resource limitations will make the price/output split increasingly unfavorable; and the development

Reprinted from *Economic Inquiry* 20 (April 1982): 209–21, with permission of the Western Economic Association International, 7400 Center Avenue, Huntington Beach, California 92647.

of inflationary expectations will contribute to the worsening of that split—but this last point is familiar and different from the one we wish to make.

Section II of the paper examines one prominent view of how unanticipated price inflation affects real income and employment. We show that this view has three implications at odds with reality. It also squares poorly with the equation of exchange. We briefly discuss the consequences of deflationary monetary growth; we then analyze the impact of an increase in the rate of growth of money when unemployment is above the natural rate. Finally, this section makes some remarks about rational-expectations models. Section III provides reasons for the stickiness of prices and wages and suggests an alternative explanation of the case of an increase in the money growth rate when unemployment is at the natural rate. Section IV offers concluding observations.

II
UNANTICIPATED PRICE INFLATION
AND UNEMPLOYMENT

While almost everyone now rejects the Phillips curve trade-off between unemployment and inflation, the notion of a trade-off between unemployment and *un*anticipated price inflation seems to have taken its place. In the current fashionable view, unemployment can deviate from its natural level only as a result of unanticipated inflation. We shall call this view the UPI (unanticipated price inflation) theory.[1] The theory hinges on misperceptions of a general inflation. Since businessmen and workers are more aware of increased prices and wages of their own particular products and labor than of increased prices generally, they misinterpret these particular in-

---

1. For a discussion on this point, see Milton Friedman, *Unemployment Versus Inflation: An Evaluation of the Phillips Curve* (London: Institute of Economic Affairs, 1975), 29; Erich Spitäller, "A Model of Inflation and Its Performance in the Seven Main Industrial Countries, 1958–76," *International Monetary Fund Staff Papers* (June 1978): 262; Robert J. Gordon, "Recent Developments in the Theory of Inflation and Unemployment," *Journal of Monetary Economics* 2 (April 1976): 201; and Anthony M. Santomero and John J. Seater, "The Inflation-Unemployment Trade-off: A Critique of the Literature," *Journal of Economic Literature* 16 (June 1978): 519.

creases as real or relative increases, that is, as improvements in their own sales and job opportunities. Outputs and labor supply increase in response. A detached and omniscient observer would say that supply curves have shifted rightward, although businessmen and workers think, mistakenly, that they are simply responding to improved opportunities along their already existing curves.

The following propositions are related to this view that there is a *trade-off* between unanticipated price inflation and unemployment:

1. "Unemployment and output fluctuations thus depend entirely on misinformation."[2] The worker must be "fooled" as to what his real wage is. (Unanticipated price inflation reduces the *actual* real wage but raises the workers' *perceived* real wage.)[3]

2. All unemployment is voluntary because "markets in these models always are in instantaneous equilibrium in the sense that labor suppliers and demanders are always on their supply and demand curves."[4]

3. Causality runs from changes in the money supply to changes in the inflation rate to changes in unemployment. Prices rise and real wages fall before output expands.

Each of the foregoing implications of the UPI theory is open to criticism. First, it is not clear that the worker must be "fooled" in order to have increases in employment. The traditional view that real wages are inversely related to the cyclical utilization of the labor force receives little support from the data examined by Ronald G. Bod-

2. Gordon, "Recent Developments," 196. This appears to be Gordon's interpretation of the UPI theory.

3. Robert E. Lucas, Jr., "Some International Evidence on Output-Inflation Tradeoffs," *American Economic Review* 63 (June 1973): 333. Lucas provides a slightly more general rationale for the expansion of output than that given here. In his model, "the alternative explanation . . . is that the positive association of price changes and output arises because suppliers misinterpret general price movements for relative price changes."

4. Santomero and Seater, "The Inflation-Unemployment Trade-off," 524. Santomero and Seater seem to be referring to the same type of search models as indicated in Gordon's statement.

kin.[5] Second, the UPI theory does not allow for worker dismissals. As Don Patinkin and Robert J. Barro and Herschel I. Grossman recognize, the worker in the short run may indeed be off his supply curve; involuntary unemployment may exist. Third, in general the sequence is the other way around from the one stated above: output rises before prices.[6] In short, the UPI theory is at odds with reality.

It is astonishing that the UPI theory has become so popular even though it contradicts the familiar identity $MV = PQ$. Any increase in nominal spending must be matched by an increase in the value of output, split between increases in prices and in real output. Given a definite price/output split, the greater the inflation rate, the greater the underlying spending expansion so indicated and therefore the greater the output expansion that is complementary with the price increases. Given, however, the degree of spending expansion and with the split a variable, the more the spending expansion goes toward price inflation, the less it can go toward output expansion. Thus, given the degree of spending expansion, the equation of exchange indicates that price inflation is *in rivalry with* output expansion.

We can formulate the UPI hypothesis as follows:

$$\dot{Q} = f(\dot{P} - \dot{P^e}) \quad f' > 0$$

where $\dot{Q}$ is the rate of change of real income and $\dot{P}$ and $\dot{P^e}$ are the actual and expected inflation rates. We maintain, however, in comparable symbols, that

$$\dot{Q} = \dot{M} + \dot{V} - \dot{P}$$

5. Ronald G. Bodkin, "Real Wages and Cyclical Variations in Employment: A Re-examination of the Evidence," *Canadian Journal of Economics* 2 (August 1969): 370. R. A. Kessel and A. A. Alchian ("The Meaning and Validity of the Inflation-Induced Lag of Wages Behind Prices," *American Economic Review* 50 [March 1960]: 43–66) effectively criticize the supposed evidence for the familiar view that wages lag behind prices during and as a consequence of inflation.

6. Don Patinkin, *Money, Interest, and Prices* (New York: Harper & Row, 1965); Robert J. Barro and Herschel I. Grossman, "A General Disequilibrium Model of Income and Employment," *American Economic Review* 61 (March 1971): 82–93. On the last point, see Phillip Cagan, *The Hydra-Headed Monster: The Problem of Inflation in the United States* (Washington, D.C.: American Enterprise Institute, 1969), 39.

where the dots indicate rates of change in the terms in the equation of exchange and where $\dot{V}$ may be taken as zero in the absence of any reason for a change in velocity. This tautology does not prove our view, of course (so further discussion follows); but it does pose an embarrassment for the UPI hypothesis. (UPI theorists might be assuming that price inflation raises velocity, perhaps by raising the cost of holding money, perhaps by hitting different goods and services unevenly and so widening profit margins; but anyone with such a mechanism in mind should spell it out with due emphasis.)

The UPI theory can be carried over to the case of deflation.[7] This theory would say that, following a fall in the money growth rate, prices and wages will fall. Since the worker is fooled into believing his real wage has fallen, he will reduce the supply of labor. Output falls in response to erroneous perceptions.

The UPI theory, which purports to derive from the classical model, implies that rises and falls in employment (given the technology) necessarily involve decreases or increases, respectively, in the real wage rate. Actually, this need not be true. The wage level, the price level, and the level of real income can all be out of line with the nominal quantity of money; and the wage rate need not be out of line with the price level.[8] The main impact of the monetary disturbance falls on real income because wages and prices are slow to adjust. (Section III mentions reasons for the sluggishness of prices.) Hence, in this scenario, (1) it is not a rise in the real wage that causes the unemployment; (2) workers are not necessarily misinformed regarding the level of the real wage; (3) workers are involuntarily unemployed because of insufficient demand in the product market.

Our analysis will now be extended to an increase in the rate of growth of money when unemployment is above the natural rate. After the increase in the nominal money supply, a sub-full-employment level of activity is no longer needed to choke off the demand for money balances. People no longer feel pressed to cut back on

7. The UPI theory on the deflationary side is described in Franco Modigliani, "The Monetarist Controversy or, Should We Forsake Stabilization Policies?" *American Economic Review* 67 (March 1977): 4–5.

8. Compare Patinkin, *Money, Interest, and Prices,* chap. 13, and Barro and Grossman, "A General Disequilibrium Model," 86–87, with Barro and Grossman, *Money, Employment, and Inflation* (Cambridge, England: Cambridge University Press, 1976), 61.

buying to restore or conserve money balances; they now feel freer to spend. Full activity can be restored, and this restoration does not necessarily involve a change in the real wage rate. In this model, the demand for labor increases as producers find that they can sell more output. Barro and Grossman even suggest that the recovery of output and employment may be accompanied by a *rising* real wage: "Thus, disequilibrium analysis of the labor market suggests that real wages may move procyclically. This result differs from the conventional view that employment and real wages must be inversely related."[9]

For real output to increase, it is not necessary to "fool" the worker through unanticipated price inflation. Indeed, monetary changes may restore production to the full-employment level *without price inflation*. The foregoing does not imply, however, that curing a recession by monetary means is free of problems.

Our criticism of UPI theory is related to a similar criticism of rational-expectations models. Several recent papers from that camp have emphasized that government countercyclical monetary policy may be impotent.[10] These models build upon two distinct hypotheses: (1) that expectations are formed rationally (here the word is used as a technical term, in contrast with "adaptively"), and (2) that shifts in aggregate demand will affect output only when the resulting price level differs from the expected one.[11] Contrary to this second hypothesis, we are arguing that what stimulates output is not a divergence between actual and anticipated inflation but rather a monetary change not fully absorbed by price inflation. Thus, sluggishness of price response helps preserve the monetary stimulus. This result obtains regardless of just how expectations are formed.

Moreover, an increase in the money supply could conceivably restore the economy to full employment *regardless of whether or not the*

9. Barro and Grossman, "A General Disequilibrium Model," 87.

10. Bennett T. McCallum, "Price-Level Stickiness and the Feasibility of Monetary Stabilization Policy With Rational Expectations," *Journal of Political Economy* 85 (June 1977): 627–34; and McCallum, "Price Level Adjustments and the Rational Expectations Approach to Macroeconomic Stabilization Policy," *Journal of Money, Credit, and Banking* 10 (November 1978): 418–36.

11. McCallum, "Price Level Adjustments," 418. McCallum even states that the second hypothesis "is a standard neoclassical notion that has been rather widely accepted for several years."

change in the money supply was expected (predictable).[12] The reason is that in a recession there is a full-employment excess demand for money (virtual excess demand for money) which can be satisfied through an actual increase in the money supply. The latter is an alternative to price deflation as a way of increasing the real money supply. Deflation has to work through a sequence of millions of piecemeal price and wage decisions; the alternative of nominal money expansion puts no such demands on the economy's coordinating mechanisms. It is incorrect to assume that predictable changes in money will always go only toward raising prices (although such changes would presumably have whatever effects they do have sooner if expected than if not).

III
RESPONSE TO MONETARY CHANGE

This section contributes to understanding how monetary developments can ever have any real bite at all, and without anyone's necessarily behaving irrationally. In particular, it shows how an increase in aggregate demand can be met at first by increases in output and employment. The mechanism that yields these changes does *not* rely on fooling the worker or employer through unanticipated price inflation. On the contrary, we assume that, and offer several reasons why, wages and prices may respond only sluggishly in the short run to an increase in demand. Our reconciliation of sticky prices with rational behavior relies in part on a crucial distinction between individual and collective rationality. (We regret, by the way, that one camp of economists has practically preempted the word "rational" as a technical term; for we want to use it in its ordinary dictionary sense of "reasonable," "sensible," or "perceived of as advantageous.")

12. This analysis is contrary to the assertions of Barro in "Unanticipated Money Growth and Unemployment in the United States," *American Economic Review* 67 (March 1977): 101–15; and "Unanticipated Money, Output, and the Price Level in the United States," *Journal of Political Economy* 86 (August 1978): 549–80; and Steven M. Sheffrin, "Unanticipated Money Growth and Output Fluctuations," *Economic Inquiry* 17 (January 1979): 1–13.

The theory elaborated in this section is in the tradition of R. W. Clower, Axel Leijonhufvud, and Barro and Grossman.[13] Rejecting such theories because of their alleged presupposition of irrationality blinks the fact that when the purchasing power of money is wrong in relation to the money supply, no single market exists on which adjustment of a single price will restore equilibrium. Why won't prices dependably adjust to keep the real quantity of money equal to the quantity demanded? The absence of the extreme price and wage flexibility that would be necessary is no evidence of villainy on the part of price setters and wage negotiators.[14] On the contrary, it follows from realities: the interdependence of individual prices and wages, yet the decentralized and piecemeal determination of them and their average level.

To say that prices do not readily maintain or restore monetary equilibrium in the face of shocks is no more to complain about "imperfections" of the market system than about villainy. (After all, what is the alternative?) We are simply recognizing the tremendous problems, including the necessity of transmitting dispersed knowledge and mobilizing it for effective coordination, that the market system and money do cope with after a fashion. The remarkable thing about these mechanisms is that they work at all. They can, however, be overtaxed, and with fateful consequences.[15] To expect them to solve the coordination problem automatically is to fail to understand the problem. In reality, corrective adjustments occur only sluggishly after a disturbance.

Neither individual prices and wages nor their average level are determined impersonally by the interplay of supply and demand.

13. R. W. Clower, "The Keynesian Counter-revolution: A Theoretical Appraisal," in *The Theory of Interest Rates*, ed. F. H. Hahn and F. Brechling (London: Macmillan, 1965), 103–25; Axel Leijonhufvud, *On Keynesian Economics and the Economics of Keynes* (New York: Oxford University Press, 1968); and Barro and Grossman, "A General Disequilibrium Model," and *Money, Employment, and Inflation*.

14. Yet villainy does, in essence, seem to be the diagnosis of W. H. Hutt in *Keynesianism—Retrospect and Prospect* (Chicago: Regnery, 1963), and *A Rehabilitation of Say's Law* (Athens: Ohio University Press, 1974).

15. In some contexts, as when, like Don Patinkin (*Money, Interest, and Prices* [New York: Harper & Row, 1965]), we are exploring the bare-bones logic of the quantity theory and the real-balance effect, it is legitimate to abstract from the frictions that obstruct rapid restoration of equilibrium after monetary shocks. For present purposes, though, the frictions of reality are central to the story.

The way that the price of wheat is determined in the wheat pit is the exception and not the rule. Unlike all other goods, money has no price and market of its own. Its value (strictly, the reciprocal of its value) is the average of individual prices and wages determined on myriad distinct though interconnecting markets. Markets are fragmented and price and wage settings are decentralized, as they must be for the effective use of dispersed knowledge.

Under these circumstances, a monetary disequilibrium is not easy for ordinary economic agents to diagnose. It does not show up as any specific frustration of buyers or sellers. Instead, an excess demand for or supply of money expresses itself in quite general restraint or eagerness in buying things. Instead of impinging on one particular market and one particular price, the pressures of monetary disequilibrium are obscurely diffused over myriad individual markets and prices. This very diffusion renders the correction of monetary disequilibrium sluggish.

The holding of inventories (of materials and semifinished and finished products) testifies to the rationality of price stickiness and to the part that incomplete knowledge plays in this stickiness.[16] Buildups and rundowns of inventories absorb random fluctuations and mismatchings of supply and demand. Not every little inventory fluctuation calls for a price change. When, by exception, a fundamental or *non*random supply or demand change does occur, the inventory holder does not immediately recognize its nature, nor is it rational for him that he should, for his being able to do so would have entailed the costs of obtaining and processing detailed knowledge about market conditions and the underlying fundamentals. Even—or especially—when the demand for particular materials or products changes as one aspect of a monetary disequilibrium, the necessity for a price change is likely to go unrecognized for a while.

In a depression associated with a "full-employment excess demand for money," it would be rational to reduce the general level of prices and wages and other costs enough to make the real money stock adequate, provided the decision to do so were made *collectively*

---

16. Some of the points that follow are mentioned in Peter Howitt, "Evaluating the Non-Market-Clearing Approach," *American Economic Review* 69 (May 1979): 60–63, esp. 61.

at one swoop. In view of the piecemeal way in which this general level is actually determined and adjusted, however, the individual agent may not find it rational promptly to cut the particular price or wage for which he is responsible, even though it is above the general-equilibrium level. Instead of acting first, he may rationally wait to see whether cutbacks on the part of others, intensifying the competition he faces or reducing his production costs or his cost of living, as the case may be, will make it advantageous for him to *follow* with a cutback of his own. What is *individually* rational and what is *collectively* rational may well diverge, as the well-known example of the prisoners' dilemma illustrates.[17] This distinction is crucial to our central message. Taking the lead in downward price and wage adjustments is more in the nature of a public than a private good, and private incentives to supply public goods are notoriously weak. These divergences between individual and collective rationality and incentives, together with the interdependence and piecemeal determination of prices and wages and other costs, go a long way toward explaining the stickiness of price and wage levels and the persistence of monetary disequilibrium.

The reader may wonder whether the foregoing argument does not prove too much. How does a disequilibrium price level ever get changed? Well, the argument does not contend that changes never occur. Some sellers will have to cut their prices and even sell at a loss to avoid still greater losses. (An extreme example would be a seller faced with a credit squeeze, growing inventories, and a scarcity of storage space, yet obliged under long-term contracts to accept continuing deliveries of materials.) For sellers in such a position, further delays in price adjustments become less reasonable as time goes on. When they finally do reduce their prices, the attendant changes in costs and competitive conditions make it both easier and more necessary for others to follow.

17. See Thomas C. Schelling, *Micromotives and Macrobehavior* (New York: Norton, 1978); and Mancur Olson, Jr., *The Logic of Collective Action* (Cambridge: Harvard University Press, 1965), for discussions of the important distinction between individual rationality and collective rationality. This distinction gets a lot of play in several strands of microeconomics; we wonder why it has received so little attention in macro.

The above explains why prices and wages may adjust sluggishly.[18] Barro, one of the elaborators of disequilibrium economics, now in a post-Barro-and-Grossman incarnation, joins in the criticism of disequilibrium models. He complains that "the disequilibrium type of model . . . relies on a nontheory of price rigidities."[19] Why does he say "nontheory"? True, the theory is seldom spelled out in detail, but it is available (and has been reviewed in this section).

The roughly opposite cases of depression and expansion beyond natural output (full employment) are similar in exhibiting collective irrationality but individual rationality. We now describe how, starting from general equilibrium, an increase in the money supply can cause a temporary increase in output and employment, and *without* necessarily fooling workers and reducing the real wage rate. The stimulus comes from unanticipated monetary expansion to the extent that it is *not* absorbed by price inflation.

When the money supply and spending increase, businessmen experience an increase in the real demands for their goods. Quite generally, each businessman, or the average businessman, is willing to meet an increase in demand with increased sales, and at a substantially unchanged price, as long as he can get the necessary capital goods, materials, labor, and so forth at unchanged cost.[20] Whether he can get them depends largely on *other* people's willingness to run down their inventories, work their factories more nearly at maxi-

18. Stanley Fischer, in "Long-Term Contracts, Rational Expectations, and the Optimal Money Supply Rule," *Journal of Political Economy* 85, no. 1 (1977): 191–205, explains that wages may be sticky if long-term contracts are made. Edmond S. Phelps and John B. Taylor, in "Stabilizing Powers of Monetary Policy Under Rational Expectations," *Journal of Political Economy* 85, no. 1 (1977): 163–90, rationalize sticky prices by postulating that "firms choose to set their prices and wage rates *1 period in advance* of the period over which they will apply . . . prices and wages are thus 'sticky' in the sense of being predetermined from period to period at successive levels generally different from what would have been established had current business conditions been (correctly) anticipated when the current prices and wage rates were decided." We have provided, however, a better justification for the apparent stickiness of wages of prices.

19. Robert J. Barro, "Second Thoughts on Keynesian Economics," *American Economic Review* 69 (May 1979): 54–59.

20. We recognize that perfect competition does not prevail. Moreover, we by no means deny that price changes may accompany the monetary stimulus to output and employment. Far from being an essential part of the process, however, they are actually in rivalry with the stimulus.

mum capacity, work overtime, take less of a semivacation between jobs, enter the labor force, postpone retirement, etc. To a considerable extent, other people *are* willing to behave that way. Much of the reason for holding inventories in the first place is to be able to accommodate a possibly temporary spurt of demand over supply. Consequently, the increase in demand for goods is met by an expansion of sales and output. (The expansion in sales corresponds partly to the drawing down of inventories of finished goods, goods in process, and materials and partly to workers' postponing the enjoyment of leisure. The businessman is willing to sell from inventory without increases in price because he thinks he can replenish his inventories. The seller of materials is willing to sell from inventories because he thinks he can replenish them.) So now the businessman is willing to hire more workers and buy more materials and plant and equipment. Workers receive more job offers. Even if nominal wages have not gone up, it is an easier search for the worker to find a job as good as he would have considered satisfactory before, since businessmen are bidding more eagerly for labor. (Workers are willing to put in more overtime or to postpone taking some time off between jobs because they think they might as well seize overtime or job opportunities while they are available and postpone their leisure until later on.) At this stage we need not appeal to a rise in nominal wages that appears to the worker to be an increase in real wages. The case is simply that it is easier—it requires less search—to find a job of a given degree of acceptability. That may explain why workers accept more jobs.

In the foregoing story, nothing on the wage side has changed to make expansion more attractive to firms. Rather, the individual businessman sees a chance to do a bigger volume of business. Essentially, the marginal physical product curve of labor has shifted to the right. The marginal product curve for any factor is conventionally drawn against the background of supposedly fixed amounts of other factors. But here the businessman thinks he can add to the amounts of all the factors that he is employing. He is not thinking of a worsened mix of labor in relation to other factors; rather, quantities of other factors contemplated to be in use along with labor have increased. (Capital equipment is not always fully employed; there is some flexibility in the system.) For labor and for, say, cotton alike, the marginal physical product curve shifts to the right because the contemplated quantities of complementary factors employed have also increased. Furthermore, the easier sale of output means that the curves of marginal *revenue* product and of marginal revenue product deflated by price have shifted to the right.

In our model the increase in demand for output will raise the firm's demand for labor. At the same time, workers are able to find jobs more readily; search and transactions costs have decreased. Their response is, in a sense, an increase in the supply of labor. From the above, we cannot predict whether the real wage will increase, decrease, or remain the same. However, if the increased demand is greater than the increased supply, then our model is consistent with a *rise* in the real wage. This may be more in accord with A. W. H. Phillips's original formulation of the Phillips curve, since a *higher* nominal and real wage may now accompany tightness in the labor market.[21]

Since it takes time for price increases to occur, output may expand in the meantime. Thus activity may temporarily be beyond the natural rate level. Perceptions have been at work that eventually result in what superficially looks like a fallacy of composition. Actually, there is none. There would be a fallacy of composition if all businessmen and workers, aggregated together, were making the above-mentioned decisions as a single entity. But they are deciding individually; and each one, from his own point of view, is not committing a fallacy or being fooled. For the individual businessman, his opportunity to do a bigger volume of business at substantially unchanged costs and prices is a genuine opportunity, even though it depends on other businessmen's running down their inventories and on workers' postponing their leisure and even though the opportunity will prove temporary. Why should he pass up the opportunity while it lasts? As for the worker, why should he pass up the opportunity for

21. A. W. H. Phillips, "The Relation Between Unemployment and the Rate of Change of Money Wage Rates in the United Kingdom, 1861–1957," *Economica* 25 (November 1958): 283–99. Note also that we do not deny the possibility that the real wage may rise. The real wage could rise or stay unchanged. Our point is that a rise is not *necessary* to get workers to do more. Note that a rise in the real wage is consistent with the rise in the marginal productivity of labor.

overtime work that he would be glad to do some time or other or pass up the opportunity to find a job easily, even though (or especially though) the opportunity may prove temporary? Why not postpone taking leisure? In other words, in this situation it is rational for businessmen and workers to respond to increased spending by increased sales and output because they have to make their decisions *individually*, even though the behavior would be irrational if the decision to behave that way had been made *collectively*. Thus, no misperception or irrationality is necessarily involved at all. The key to the scenario is that people make the relevant decisions in a decentralized, piecemeal, nonsynchronous manner.

The question may arise: How do we ever get out of this scenario? It looks as if everybody has become happier than before at no cost. However, by its very nature, this situation can persist only temporarily. The inventories available to be run down are not unlimited in size, nor are workers willing without limit to postpone leisure as long as job opportunities are exceptionally abundant. Inflated demands do get transmitted back to primary materials and factors of production, bidding up their prices and creating what superficially looks like a cost-push process throughout the economic system. The inflated flow of spending impinges on basically limited real supplies (and supply schedules), and the economy turns out able to escape only temporarily the impact on prices that standard theory describes. As resource and inventory limitations manifest themselves, as costs and prices and the cost of living rise, and as the initially attractive sales and job opportunities accordingly come to look less attractive after all, the initial quantity impact of the inflated aggregate spending gives way to a price impact. $MV = PQ$ helps us see why Q drops back as P rises, even if MV remains at its new inflated level. In short, real activity drops back to its natural level. For a while, though, there was an expansion of employment and output above their natural rates. The term "above the natural rate" is justified here because the situation was not a sustainable one.[22]

22. It is unnecessary to decide here whether the gain in output and employment should ultimately prove to have been only a borrowing against the future as, later, workers recoup postponed leisure and suppliers rebuild run-down inventories. (We are indebted to an anonymous referee for raising this question, which deserves further consideration.) Even if monetary factors should prove to have af-

In summary, we have seen how physical activity could be gotten above and unemployment below the natural rate temporarily. In this scenario, people are *not* being fooled. They are not mistakenly conceiving the relative price of whatever they are buying or selling to have changed in their favor. They simply have better opportunities to make transactions on terms otherwise as acceptable as before. It is easier for businessmen to find customers willing to meet their terms; it is easier for workers to find jobs meeting their expectations. The key point is *not* that the businessman thinks he is getting a higher relative selling price, nor that the worker thinks he is getting a higher relative wage rate. Rather, each transactor can find trading partners more easily than before.

However, what was possible to each individual worker or businessman from his own point of view for a while turns out not to be lastingly possible for all businessmen and all workers in the aggregate; real limitations on resources and productive capacity ultimately make themselves felt again. Businessmen find that since they are competing with each other to replenish inventories, lay in machinery, and hire workers, it is not as easy as it had been to expand their output at no increase in unit cost. The additional money being spent eventually gets back to bidding up the prices of labor and materials. Costs rise, businessmen find that they must raise their prices, workers find that jobs at the initial wages are not as attractive as they were

---

fected real output only by shifting it in time, the point would remain—and we intended it only as an interesting special case—that monetary factors could indeed have a real bite even on an initial situation of full employment.

Another anonymous referee suggested that the analysis in the text contradicts that of Barro and Grossman ("A General Disequilibrium Model" and *Money, Employment, and Inflation*), who conclude that general excess demand can *shrink* real activity. Actually, there is no contradiction. Our rise in output is avowedly temporary. It hinges on rational decentralized decision making, or workers' postponements of leisure, and on suppliers' rundowns of inventories (using inventories for the buffer purpose for which they are held in the first place). In the model of Barro and Grossman, workers not only do not postpone leisure but withdraw some of their labor because they cannot succeed in spending all of their earnings. Furthermore, Barro and Grossman assume, in *Money, Employment, and Inflation*, that firms do not hold any inventories (and their "General Disequilibrium Model," p. 85, "abstracts from inventory accumulation or decumulation"). We recognize—or certainly could recognize—that an excess demand situation à la Barro and Grossman could develop, with no significant (further) leisure postponements and inventory rundowns taking place and with employment and production reduced below their general-equilibrium levels.

177

when they took them. It turns out to require about as much search as before to find a job of a given degree of real attractiveness. In short, the initial ease of finding customers and suppliers and of finding jobs of given degrees of attractiveness proves to be only temporary as businessmen bid against each other to expand their sales and outputs and as workers-consumers bid against each other to enjoy their money incomes. The monetary expansion does bite on prices and wages, restoring the previous lesser degree of attractiveness of activity for businessmen and workers alike.

IV

CONCLUSION

One of the goals of this paper was to examine the notion of a trade-off between unanticipated price inflation and unemployment. This notion implies, wrongly, that it is the price inflation that causes the reduction in unemployment. Actually, it is the higher rate of money and spending expansion itself that temporarily reduces unemployment; the speedup of price and wage inflation is one of its incidental and counterproductive consequences. David Hume put this central point correctly by saying that in the process of inflation, "it is only in this interval or intermediate situation, between the acquisition of money and rise of prices, that the encreasing quantity of gold and silver is favourable to industry."[23] If, somehow or other, the amount of price inflation were kept down for a given amount of monetary expansion, the reduction in unemployment would be greater.

Yet in the UPI theory it is indeed the unanticipated price inflation that is necessary to reduce unemployment. It does so by reducing the real wage rate and so making employers more willing to hire workers. Therefore, we disagree with the UPI theory's current formulations of the mechanism of adjustment in the short run. Finally, we have shown that even if expectations are formed rationally, monetary changes may affect output in the short run.

23. David Hume, "Of Money" (1752), in *David Hume: Writings on Economics*, ed. Eugene Rothstein (Madison: University of Wisconsin Press, 1970), 38.

Money and Credit Confused: An Appraisal of Economic Doctrine and Federal Reserve Procedure

(with Robert L. Greenfield)

That this doctrine is a very fallacious one, Your Committee cannot entertain a doubt. The fallacy, upon which it is founded, lies in not distinguishing between an advance of capital to Merchants, and an additional supply of currency to the general mass of circulating medium.

—from the passage in the *Bullion Report* of 1810 dealing with the alleged impossibility of overissue

I
INTRODUCTION

It is a serious error to suppose that if the monetary authorities are to alter the actual quantity of money, people must first be persuaded through interest-rate movements to alter the quantity of

Reprinted from the *Southern Economic Journal* 53 (October 1986): 364-73, with permission of the University of North Carolina, Chapel Hill, North Carolina 27599.

While they gratefully acknowledge comments made by David Laidler, James Lothian, John Scadding, Lawrence H. White, and an anonymous referee on an earlier draft of this article, as well as editorial assistance provided by Nancy Greenfield in the revision of that earlier draft and its several successors, the authors bear full responsibility for any remaining faults in analysis or exposition.

money they wish to hold. Nevertheless, the error, in one guise or another, pervades the literature on monetary policy.[1]

"As a result of the Fed's willingness to prevent or moderate a demand-induced movement in the interest rate," write Raymond Lombra and Herbert Kaufman, "shifts in money demand cause shifts in the same direction in reserve supply and therefore money supply."[2] Econometrically determined money-supply functions are thus not what they purport to be. Estimated without account being

1. Chronicling the evolution of Federal Reserve doctrine, Karl Brunner cites Lyle Gramley and Samuel B. Chase as marking the emergence of the supply-and-demand doctrine of money-stock determination, the doctrine we shall criticize. Brunner's observations appear in "Discussion," in *Controlling Monetary Aggregates II: The Implementation,* Federal Reserve Bank of Boston, Conference Series no. 9 (September 1982): 103–14. His discussion is of Gramley and Chase, "Time Deposits in Monetary Analysis," *Federal Reserve Bulletin* (October 1965): 1380–1406. But since the doctrine has much in common with the real-bills fallacy, and since the Federal Reserve has a long history of involvement with that fallacy, the influence of the doctrine undoubtedly antedates 1965. See, for example, Lester Chandler, "The Impacts of Theory on Policy: The Early Years of the Fed," in *Men, Money, and Policy: Essays in Honor of Karl Bopp* (Philadelphia: Federal Reserve Bank of Philadelphia, 1970), 41–53. Brunner's remarking that the doctrine "satisfies an established institution's desire for operational continuity" and "perpetuates the ancient confusion between money and credit" leads us to think that he would concur in our assessment (see Brunner, "Discussion," 4, 111). Other examples of the doctrine's influence within the Federal Reserve system include Stephen H. Axilrod and David E. Lindsey, "Federal Reserve System Implementation of Monetary Policy: Analytical Foundations of the New Approach," *American Economic Review, Papers and Proceedings* 71 (May 1981): 246–52; Steven Leroy and David E. Lindsey, "Determining the Monetary Instrument," *American Economic Review* 68 (December 1978): 929–34; Daniel Laufenberg, "Contemporaneous Versus Lagged Reserve Accounting," *Journal of Money, Credit, and Banking* 8 (May 1976): 239–46; and Henry C. Wallich, "Techniques of Monetary Policy," *Financial Analysts Journal* 37 (July–August 1981): 41–56. Even the *Economic Review* of the Federal Reserve Bank of St. Louis, long a dissenting voice within the system, now seems to acquiesce in the doctrine, as in Daniel L. Thornton, "The Simple Analytics of the Money Supply Process and Monetary Control," Federal Reserve Bank of St. Louis, *Economic Review* (October 1982): 22–39. Examples of the doctrine's influence outside the system include James Tobin, "Commercial Banks as 'Creators of Money,' " in *Banking and Monetary Studies,* ed. Deane Carson (Homewood, Ill.: Irwin, 1963), 408–19; Armen A. Alchian and William R. Allen, *University Economics* (Belmont, Calif.: Wadsworth, 1980), 610–15; William J. Baumol and Alan S. Blinder, *Economics: Principles and Policy* (San Diego: Harcourt Brace Jovanovich, 1985), 241–57; Cambell McConnell, *Economics* (New York: McGraw-Hill, 1984), 303–5; and Warren L. Coats, "Recent Monetary Policy Strategies in the United States." *Kredit und Kapital* 4 (1981): 521–49.

2. Raymond E. Lombra and Herbert Kaufman, "The Money Supply Process: Identification, Stability, and Estimation," *Southern Economic Journal* 50 (April 1984): 1156.

taken of Federal Reserve procedure, they are contaminated by the central bank's response to changes in demand-side factors.

The contention that such an identification problem bedevils earlier empirical estimates of money-supply functions gives us pause. It does so not because we endorse any previous statistical findings (our concern with this matter is not at all a statistical one) but because the idea that the Federal Reserve, taking its cues from incipient interest-rate movements, can cause the quantity of money to accommodate itself reliably to changes in money demand reflects a more deep-seated failure to recognize the true character of monetary disequilibrium. In the Lombra-Kaufman view, the view that mistakenly invokes ordinary supply-and-demand analysis in explaining the money stock's nominal size, any imbalance between actual and demanded quantities of money traces to a disequilibrium interest rate.

II
PERVERSE CHANGES IN THE QUANTITY OF MONEY UNDER INTEREST-RATE TARGETING

We reject the idea that as a result of the Federal Reserve's pursuit of interest-rate targeting, the quantity of money reliably accommodates itself to changes in money demand. We can provide examples to show that interest-rate targeting sometimes renders the central bank a source of *im*balance between money supply and demand.

First, however, we note that an increase in the demand for money cannot be postulated to arise in isolation. Recognition of the two-sidedness of markets warns against such a postulate. A person planning to acquire additional money balances must also be planning to finance that acquisition by less eagerly demanding (or more eagerly supplying) commodities or bonds, or both.

Now, as Don Patinkin explains, interest-rate effects accompany changes in people's preferences for present commodities relative to financial assets (money *and* bonds), even while financial assets, which are vehicles for deferring demand for commodities to the future, remain unchanged in desirability relative to one another. The implied change in people's rates of time preference thus must be recognized.

181

What happens to the equilibrium interest rate depends on whether the demand for money strengthens primarily at the expense of the demand for present commodities, primarily at the expense of the demand for bonds, or equally at the expense of the demand for each. The equilibrium interest rate actually falls, Patinkin concludes, if the demand for money strengthens primarily at the expense of the demand for commodities.[3]

Suppose, then, that the demand for money does strengthen and does so primarily at the expense of the demand for commodities, the interest rate coming under downward pressure. Attempting to maintain its interest-rate peg, the Federal Reserve resists the downward pressure upon the interest rate by selling bonds. The quantity of money actually falls despite the increased demand for money.

Not only can the demand for money increase without there arising upward pressure on the interest rate, but there can also arise upward pressure on the interest rate in the absence of an increase in the demand for money. Suppose, for example, that preferences swing away from bonds and in favor of commodities. People seek to enlarge their present consumption by borrowing, and the interest rate tends to rise. Attempting to maintain its interest-rate peg, the Federal Reserve checks the upward pressure exerted upon the interest rate by buying bonds. The quantity of money grows despite there having arisen no increased demand to hold money.

III
MONEY AND CREDIT CONFUSED

Economists who, like Lombra and Kaufman, regard monetary equilibrium as a matter for ordinary supply-and-demand analysis blind themselves to the disruption attending a policy which links the quantity of money to incipient interest-rate movements. They do not see the disruption that our examples illuminate because they in effect deny the distinction on which those examples center, namely, the

3. Don Patinkin, *Money, Interest, and Prices*, 2d ed. (New York: Harper & Row, 1965), 19, 244–52.

distinction between the demand for money and the demand for credit. Their theory of money-stock determination—the supply-and-demand theory—actually *identifies* the demand for money with the demand for credit.

Consider exactly what the portrayal of the quantity of money as a supply-and-demand-determined magnitude maintains. It maintains, of course, that any actual quantity of money is also a *demanded* quantity. If the actual quantity of money is also a demanded quantity, however, people must be voluntarily borrowing from banks in amounts sufficient to get that actual and, by assumption, demanded quantity of money into existence. This is simply a balance-sheet relation. The supposed supply-and-demand determination of the stock of money and the money-credit identity are two views of the same problem from different sides of the balance sheet.

An arithmetic complication, however, may seem to undermine our ascription of the money-credit identity to economists who embrace the supply-and-demand conception of money-stock determination. After all, changes in the banking system's deposit liabilities may well exceed changes in the quantity of earning assets supplied to the banks by the nonbank private sector; changes in the banks' reserve holdings account for the difference.

Bank reserves' accounting for the complication in question prompts us to wonder what role in money-stock determination reserves (or, more generally, base money) play under the supply-and-demand doctrine. Lombra, James B. Herendeen, and Raymond G. Torto, in their 1980 textbook, spell out the role of bank reserves under the supply-and-demand doctrine quite clearly. In a footnote attached to a chapter that essentially reproduces the widely-cited 1975 Lombra-Torto article on monetary policy,[4] Lombra et al. characterize "the demand for reserves . . . as a 'derived demand'—that is, it is derived from the public's demand for funds. This is analogous to the firm's demand for labor, which is derived from the public's demand for the firm's output. The loans made and the securities purchased

---

4. Raymond E. Lombra and Raymond G. Torto, "The Strategy of Monetary Policy," Federal Reserve Bank of Richmond, *Economic Review* (September–October 1975): 3–14.

are the output of banks and reflect the public's demand for money."[5]

There is no complication after all. Lombra and his collaborators assign to the ranks of supply-and-*demand*-determined variables the quantity of bank reserves itself.[6] They *do* consider an increase in the demand for money to be matched by an equally large increase in the demand for credit, including the demand for central-bank credit in the form of reserves. Banks in their view demand reserves *for the purpose* of supplying bank credit. The supply of and demand for bank credit therefore match one another at each interest rate, leaving the excess demand for credit of the consolidated (banks and nonbanks) private sector just equaling the banks' demand for reserves. The supply-and-demand conception of money-stock determination and the money-credit identity are inextricably intertwined threads of the same doctrine.[7]

5. Raymond E. Lombra, James B. Herendeen, and Raymond G. Torto, *Money and the Financial System: Theory, Institutions, and Policy* (New York: McGraw-Hill, 1980), 457.

6. Earlier in their textbook, Lombra and his coauthors acknowledge the existence of a genuine bond market. Their doing so, however, amounts to no more than a token concession to the distinction we urge; for they then proceed to assert repeatedly that "the interest rate that equates the supply and demand for bonds must also equate the supply and demand for money" (ibid., 282). Similarly, Marvin Goodfriend says that "in [his] model, portfolio equilibrium is characterized by a loan market equilibrium condition. Alternately, portfolio equilibrium could have been characterized by a money market equilibrium condition. See Patinkin, *Money, Interest, and Prices,* chs. IX:4 and XII:4, 5, and 6." (Those familiar with Patinkin's book undoubtedly will question Goodfriend's citing it in this way.) See Goodfriend, "A Model of Money-Stock Determination With Loan Demand and a Banking System Balance Sheet Constraint," Federal Reserve Bank of Richmond, *Economic Review* (January–February 1982): 4.

Now, we recognize that the existence of only a single type of debt means that only a single interest rate need be considered. We also recognize that in general equilibrium, by the very definition of the term, both bond-market and monetary equilibrium prevail. But it hardly follows from these self-evident propositions that to the interest rate falls the task of clearing two markets, a bond market and a "money market," and that a mere interest-rate adjustment can restore partial equilibrium to both. (Actually, Goodfriend's model goes further than his description of it, subscribing not just to this duality of equilibria but to the identity itself.) Supposing that it does involve several errors, by no means the least of which is thinking that the supply of and demand for money confront one another directly in a "money market." Section V picks up the thread of this argument, showing why the quantity of money falls outside the realm of ordinary supply-and-demand analysis.

7. IS-LM-type thinking considers the bond market an acquiescent partner in all market experiments. Diagrammatically, then, the LM locus shifting leftward

IV

THE MONEY-CREDIT IDENTITY IN
FEDERAL RESERVE FORMULATION OF
MONETARY POLICY

Having established that a blurring of money and credit intertwines with the supply-and-demand conception of money-stock determination, we better understand the Federal Reserve's insistence that it controls the quantity of money through its control of interest rates. Federal Reserve staff members Richard Porter, David E. Lindsey, and Daniel E. Laufenberg express the authorities' view of money-stock control within the context of lagged-reserve accounting. "The current stock of demand deposits is determined," they say, "by [the interest] rate interacting with the demand function for demand deposits. . . . [U]nder lagged reserve accounting . . . there is no independent avenue for reserve injections to affect the equilibrium level of deposits in the same week other than by operating through interest rates and deposit demand."[8]

Lombra and Kaufman approvingly quote this statement, though made in 1975, to preview their own use of a "unique data set, derived from internal Federal Reserve (Fed) documents . . . to investigate the relationship between money demand disturbances and money supply responses resulting from the Fed's operating procedures" in the post-1979 period.[9] Neglectful themselves of the distinction between money and credit, Lombra and Kaufman do not see the significance of their correctly suggesting that the Federal Reserve's

---

along a stationary IS locus depicts a disturbance involving an excess demand for money matched *at impact* by an equally large excess supply of bonds. But since this equality limits itself to impact effects, and since disturbances involving commodities and bonds obey the same restriction on impact-effect magnitudes, the IS-LM model is technically free of the money-credit identity. Still, the aggregate-supply–aggregate-demand framework, which takes the IS-LM model as its demand side, leaves much to be desired. Cf. footnote 14.

8. David E. Porter, Richard Lindsey, and Daniel Laufenberg, "Estimation and Stimulation of Simple Equations Relating Reserve Aggregates and Monetary Aggregates" (Unpublished manuscript, Board of Governors of the Federal Reserve System, 1975), 4.

9. Lombra and Kaufman, "The Money Supply Process," 1148.

interest-rate orientation survives the supposed 6 October 1979 transition from a regime of overt interest-rate targeting to a reserves-targeting regime. (Further announcements in 1982 also suggest that 1979 did not bring as significant a change as initially advertised.)

Believing that it can create more money only if people actually demand the additional money in cash balances, the Federal Reserve, choosing to regard prevailing nominal income as a datum, begins its formulation of monetary policy by solving a money-demand equation for the interest rate consistent with the money-stock target. In the authorities' supply-and-demand view "the loans made and the securities purchased are the output of banks and reflect the public's demand for money," to use the wording of Lombra and his coauthors. The Federal Reserve sets about to establish the target-consistent interest rate in the market, then, thinking it capable of inducing nonbank units to supply the appropriate quantity of earning assets to the banking system.

Now, when last period's bank deposits serve as the basis on which the Federal Reserve levies reserve requirements, the quantity of bank reserves held this period becomes a predetermined magnitude. It remains, however, to ask how this predetermined quantity of bank reserves divides into borrowed and nonborrowed components. And in its answer to this question the Federal Reserve sees its influence over the market interest rate and hence the actual (and supposedly demanded) quantity of money.

Equipped with knowledge of reserves required today on the basis of lagged deposits and with an estimate of the sensitivity of bank discount-window borrowing with regard to variations in the federal-funds rate, the Federal Reserve supplies only enough nonborrowed reserves to establish the targeted interest rate in the federal-funds market. When the existing quantity of nonborrowed reserves leaves the banking system unable to fulfill its reserve requirements, the needed additional reserves must be acquired at the Federal Reserve discount window. Administration of the discount window imposes on borrowers nonpecuniary costs that rise with the volume of borrowing; and banks carry their discount-window borrowing to the point at which the nonpecuniary costs of borrowing the last dollar offset fully the explicit advantage of borrowing at the Federal Reserve discount rate rather than at the rate that banks charge one another for reserves lent overnight in the federal-funds market. To lever the funds rate up to its target, then, the Federal Reserve leaves the banks with a reserve deficiency that only the target rate can induce them to remedy voluntarily at the discount window. (Arbitrage keeps the bank-credit and federal-funds rates aligned.)

If the total of borrowed and nonborrowed reserves is insufficient to satisfy reserve requirements against contemporaneously held deposits, then next period, when the Federal Reserve actually uses this period's deposits as the basis on which to compute reserve requirements, upward pressure on the federal-funds rate emerges as banks bid against one another for existing reserves. The higher funds rate results not only in banks' borrowing reserves more heavily at the discount window but also in a smaller quantity of deposits against which reserves must be held, since at the higher interest rate nonbank units borrow from banks in reduced quantities. If either reserve requirements were based on contemporaneously held deposits (the February 1984 reinstatement of "contemporaneous" reserve accounting leaves reserve requirements predetermined on the last two days of any reserve-maintenance period),[10] or a longer-term view taken, the Federal Reserve would combine its knowledge of reserves required against the targeted (rather than lagged) stock of deposits with its estimate of the funds-rate sensitivity of bank discount-window borrowing to compute the quantity of nonborrowed reserves supposedly establishing the market interest rate consistent with the money-stock target. (Even writers sympathetic to the supply-and-demand doctrine may thus express a concern for deposit multipliers.)

Under both the interest-rate-targeting regime and the so-called reserves-targeting regime, the Federal Reserve strives to establish in the market the interest rate which the money-demand equation links to the money-stock target. Viewing the demand for money and the demand for credit as mirror images of one another, the authorities consider that at this interest rate nonbank borrowing from banks

---

10. Under the reserve-accounting system established in February 1984, banks are required to hold reserves in the current reserve-maintenance period against the average of transactions deposit liabilities over the two-week period ending two days before the end of the current maintenance period.

and bank absorption of Federal Reserve credit jointly provide the banking system with assets (including reserves) enough to support the targeted stock of money. The authorities regard their influence over the quantity of money as channeling itself through interest rates.

The money-credit identity thus stands center stage under both policy regimes. Indeed, the two regimes differ only insofar as the Federal Reserve's reaction to a departure from the targeted interest rate is concerned. Under the interest-rate-targeting regime, the Federal Reserve resists a movement, say, above the targeted rate, however caused, by providing more nonborrowed reserves. Under the so-called reserves-targeting regime, the authorities tolerate a movement above the targeted rate, however caused, while accommodating the increased quantity demanded of borrowed reserves.

Monetary policy formulated in this fashion invites the difficulties that our examples of section II illuminate. When, for example, people seek loans to finance investment in plant, equipment, and inventory, creation of new money to satisfy the increase in loan demand temporarily mitigates the upward pressure on the interest rate. But needing reserves to support their new deposits, banks bid more eagerly against one another in the federal-funds market. Under the reserves-targeting regime, the funds rate rises, and they resort to the discount window, further transcending their reluctance to borrow from the Federal Reserve and acquiring the needed reserves. Banks do increase the interest rate they charge on their loan assets, but only to an extent sufficient to cover the increased cost of borrowing reserves.

Eventually, however, incomes and prices rise, in response to the monetary expansion, intensifying the net nominal demand for credit and unleashing the full impact on the interest rate of the strengthened demand for loans. Money creation thus sows the seeds of the reversal of the very restraint it initially imposes on the response of the interest rate to tastes' turning away from bonds and toward commodities. Creation of money ultimately reinforces the enlarged nominal flow of spending and higher prices that develop as people run down their real money holdings in view of the heightened cost of holding them. Federal Reserve procedure, which transmutes an increased demand for credit into an increased quantity of money, makes monetary policy procyclical.

Monetary policy again becomes procyclical when instead of seeking loans to finance their acquisition of commodities, people want to spend away part of their cash balances. Tastes' turning toward commodities and away from financial assets results in a higher equilibrium interest rate, even when the financial asset away from which tastes turn is money.[11] Since Federal Reserve procedure interprets the upward pressure on the interest rate as a signal of a strengthened demand for money, people wind up holding larger quantities of money despite their weakened demands for cash balances.

Notwithstanding his adherence to the supply-and-demand doctrine, Lombra, too, worries about monetary policy's becoming procyclical. Ironically, however, Herendeen, Torto, and he blame that procyclicality on the Federal Reserve's willingness to *accommodate* increases in the demand for money, unambiguous signals of which they find in rising interest rates.

> If the demand for money at a given federal funds rate turns out to be greater . . . than the Fed had estimated, then the actual money supply will also be . . . greater . . . than desired [by the Fed]. With the Fed "pegging" the federal funds rate . . . it is supplying all the reserves banks are demanding at this . . . funds rate. Since bank demand for reserves reflects the public's demand for money, the Fed is also supplying all the money the public wants at this funds rate. . . . Unfortunately, if it supplies more reserves and money, the Fed allows monetary policy to be *procyclical*; that is, the excessive expansion of . . . money and reserves will tend to reinforce and exacerbate the cyclical upswing in economic activity [emphasis in original].[12]

Certainly, a great deal of significance attaches to the quantity of money. But its significance stems from the fact that it sometimes *differs* from the quantity that people wish to hold. An assumed state of uninterrupted monetary equilibrium belies any worries about "excessive expansion of money and reserves."

11. Porter, Lindsey, and Laufenberg, "Estimation and Simulation," 242–52.
12. Lombra, Herendeen, and Torto, *Money and the Financial System*, 459.

V

MONEY'S DISTINCTIVENESS AS THE MEDIUM OF EXCHANGE

The supposition that each existing unit of money is also a demanded unit slights money's distinctiveness as the medium of exchange. Processes susceptible of ordinary supply-and-demand analysis do not govern the nominal quantity of money. The medium of exchange is supplied and demanded in a distinctive way, and imbalances between its actual and desired quantities tend to be eliminated in a roundabout and momentous fashion.[13]

Despite the prevalence of the term, it is highly misleading to speak of the "money market." There is no particular market on which the money stock and the demand for money balances are brought into equality. Nor is there any particular price that adjusts to achieve that equality. The medium of exchange, traded as it is on all markets, is distinct from other goods in not having a market and price specifically its own. Money routinely flows *through* cash balances, people routinely accepting it and routinely paying it out even when not intending, except passively and temporarily, to alter the size of their money balances. Because money balances serve as pools into and from which people receive and make payments and thus serve as buffers against unintended fluctuations in the timing and against short-term fluctuations in the sizes of inward and outward payments, they can rise or fall without these changes' being actively desired.

People are not deliberately acting to increase their money holdings whenever they sell something nor to reduce them whenever they buy something. And this is no less true when people engage in transactions with the central bank. When transactors deal with the central

13. See Yeager, "What Are Banks?" *Atlantic Economic Journal* 6 (December 1978): 1–14 (reprinted in this volume), in which the arguments restated in this section are used to examine critically various expressions of Tobin's "New View" of money and banking. That Tobin's conceiving of a "natural limit" to the size of the money-and-banking system could be billed as a "New View" illustrates the importance of studying the history of economic thought. As our epigraph suggests, the authors of the *Bullion Report*, published in 1810, encountered and refuted this very fallacy in their day.

bank, they do so because they find the price it quotes for bonds attractive to them, not necessarily because they seek to change the size of their money holdings. Furthermore, people uninvolved in central bank transactions find their money balances changed in consequence of them.

When the proceeds of someone's sale of bonds to the central bank are deposited, the bank attracting the deposit finds no shortage of profitable opportunities to rid itself of any unwanted portion of its newly acquired excess reserves. If loan demand should falter, the bank might even use the base money to pay its employees. Which employee refuses a paycheck, thinking it somehow suspicious that the bank is paying by drawing on its excess reserves and worrying that by spending his salary, he contributes to further growth of the stock of money? Once these people accept their checks, the recipients of the resulting expenditures can resist a build-up of their money balances only by refusing to make sales of the ordinary sort. The deposit of these sales receipts leaves a second set of banks in a position to keep the multiple expansion of deposits going. As the money-multiplier/monetary-base formula of the textbooks shows, deposit expansion continues until the resulting reserve requirements coupled with the expansion-related sidetracking of base money for purposes other than supporting the deposit component of the money stock fully absorb the injection of new base money.

No one need be persuaded to invest in the routine medium of exchange before more of it can be created. Once in existence, however, the newly created money engenders its own demand in a roundabout and momentous fashion.

Because money routinely exchanges against everything else, each individual can hold as much or as little money as he effectively demands, despite the authorities' exogenously setting the total of all such holdings. To get more, an individual need only curtail his spending relative to his income, just as someone with excess cash balances can do the opposite. A frustrated excess demand for money, rather than appearing as specific difficulty in buying money, reveals itself as generalized difficulty in selling things and earning incomes. An excess supply of money, to consider the opposite imbalance, touches off a process that raises incomes and prices to the point at which all the existing money winds up demanded in cash balances after all. The supply of and demand for money interact not to determine the nominal quantity of money—that is a supply-determined magnitude—but to determine the nominal flow of spending and eventually the purchasing power of the money unit.[14]

Lombra and Kaufman exhibit great concern for the behavior of the stock of money. Yet that concern squares rather badly with their "money-market" view of monetary equilibrium. Were there actually a money market, a specific market on which an excess demand for money caused direct price/quantity adjustments or away from which frustrated demand turned as people sought to acquire other things instead, the quantity of money would assume the macroeconomic significance of the quantity of refrigerators, a magnitude that really *is* supply-and-demand determined. No effective excessive demand for money and overall deficiency of demand for currently produced output could then ever arise.[15]

VI

CONCLUSION: WHITHER INTEREST RATES?

No demand-side constraint need be satisfied before the authorities can alter the actual quantity of money. To suppose otherwise—to suppose the interest rate to be "the price of money," determined so as to ensure that each existing unit of money is a unit demanded in cash balances as well—is to blur two analytically distinguishable con-

14. The aggregate-supply/aggregate-demand formulation, which combines an IS-LM demand side with a supply side stemming from a labor market equilibrium condition, obscures the specifically monetary nature of business fluctuations. A recession's apparently inadequate spending really reflects difficulties in adjusting the purchasing power of the monetary unit. After all, any nominal spending stream suffices for full employment if combined with an appropriate level of prices. Money's value must change, when it does, however, through adjustments in countless prices determined on myriad distinct but interrelated markets. A price level's or even a price-level trend's becoming entrenched is understandable. Who goes first in altering his pricing?

15. Ibid.; also Yeager, "Essential Properties of the Medium of Exchange," *Kyklos* 21, no. 1 (1968): 45–69; and idem, "What Are Banks?" (both reprinted in this volume).

cepts, money and credit. Nevertheless, many an economist falls prey to the false but apparently considerable temptations of this supply-and-demand doctrine of money-stock determination.

John P. Judd and John L. Scadding, the architects of the Federal Reserve Bank of San Francisco Money Market model, reason along lines that evince the erroneous doctrine's influence. Much as their title "Liability Management, Bank Loans and Deposit 'Market' Equilibrium" suggests, in describing the improvements that their model makes over that used by the Federal Reserve Board, Judd and Scadding seem quite alive to the distinction that we observe falling into such harmful neglect. "Changes in the quantity of bank loans," they write, "have an important by-product: the creation or destruction of deposits. Since changes in credit demand are not necessarily associated with equal changes in deposit demand, the public ends up temporarily holding deposits it does not want.[16]

Yet Judd and Scadding do not disavow the supply-and-demand doctrine. Instead, they attempt to graft onto the doctrine their recognition of the Federal Reserve's tying the quantity of money to credit-market conditions. Their clinging to the supply-and-demand doctrine despite its denial of the very distinction—the money-credit distinction—that they seek to illuminate leads Judd and Scadding to conclude that a *decrease* in the demand for loans causes the interest rate to *rise*. Why? "A decrease in bank loans is illustrated diagrammatically by a leftward shift of the deposit-supply function."[17] (We reproduce as figure 1 the diagram by Judd and Scadding. They describe the supply curve's positive slope as reflecting the additional demand deposits needed to finance a given quantity of loans when an increased interest rate on commercial paper [i_{cp}] makes people less willing to hold banks' managed liabilities.) Despite their title's enclosing the term "Market" in quotation marks, they insist after all upon applying ordinary supply-and-demand analysis to the quantity of deposits.

16. John P. Judd and John L. Scadding, "Liability Management, Bank Loans, and Deposit 'Market' Equilibrium," Federal Reserve Bank of San Francisco, *Economic Review* (Spring 1981): 11, 28.

17. Ibid., 29.

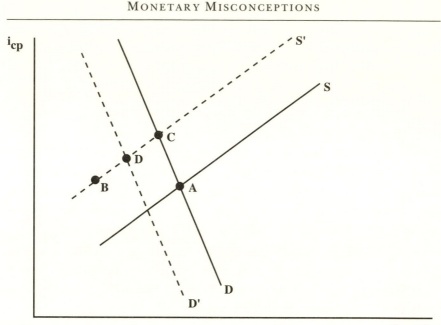

FIGURE 1 The Market for Demand Deposits According to Judd and Scadding (Reproduced from J. P. Judd and L. J. Scadding, "Liability Management, Bank Loans and Deposit 'Market' Equilibrium," Federal Reserve Bank of San Francisco, *Economic Review* [Spring 1981]: 21–44).

Judd and Scadding do seem to recognize that the macroeconomic significance of money hinges upon a divergence between its actual and demanded quantities. Embroidering that idea onto the supply-and-demand doctrine, they consider Federal Reserve procedure's transmuting the weakened loan demand into a reduced quantity of money to "temporarily push the public off its . . . money-demand curve."[18] "This disequilibrium," they say, "reduces interest-rate variability in response to deposit-supply disturbances"; activity in the "money market" moves "from point *A* to point *B* rather than to point *C*," the point to which things would shift if, as assumed in conventional models, the "money market" were to clear instantaneously.[19] Falling prices and incomes, furthermore, because they reduce the nominal demand for money, reduce the extent to which the interest rate rises to clear the "money market."

18. Ibid., 39.
19. Ibid., 29.

But rise it does; or at least it does according to the San Francisco model, whose "money market" settles at its new equilibrium position, point *D*.

The interest rate *rises* when loan demand *weakens?* Money and credit confused.

PART THREE

KEYNESIANISM

AND OTHER

DIVERSIONS

The Keynesian Diversion

Many laymen and even some economists want to label each economist as either Keynesian or anti-Keynesian. Because I am going to make some remarks that may sound anti-Keynesian, I want to disclaim any such predisposition. Before taking any college courses in economics, I was a self-taught Keynesian—poorly taught, perhaps, but enthusiastic. Such works as John Philip Wernette's *Financing Full Employment* gave a monetarist tinge to my early beliefs. In graduate school, as I became better acquainted with Keynesian theory and as I just happened to come across the work of Clark Warburton, I evolved from being rather inconsistently a Keynesian and a monetarist both at the same time to being more definitely a monetarist. For some time I (mis)interpreted Keynes himself as being essentially a monetarist also.

Keynes made many contributions besides what became known as Keynesianism. But his main contribution, as I now see it, was an effective selling job for concern with the problems of employment and effective demand. This concern certainly was not new. Even—or especially—among Chicago school economists in the early years of the Great Depression, this concern led to policy recommendations that seem remarkably Keynesian.[1] But an understanding of the problem was far from general among economists and policy makers, as

Reprinted from the *Western Economic Journal* 11 (June 1973): 150–63, with permission of the Western Economic Association International, 7400 Center Avenue, Huntington Beach, Huntington, California 92647.

This chapter is a slightly shortened version of a contribution to a panel discussion at the convention of the Southern Economic Association in Miami Beach, Florida, 5 November 1971.

1. See J. Ronnie Davis, "Chicago Economists, Deficit Budgets, and the Early 1930s," *American Economic Review* 58 (June 1968): 476–82; and Davis's 1967 University of Virginia dissertation, *The New Economics and the Old Economists* (Ames: Iowa State University Press, 1971).

one can readily verify by browsing through the relevant chapters of Joseph Dorfman's *Economic Mind in American Civilization.*

It is a sad commentary on the American economics profession that the wiles of salesmanship, instead of or in addition to sober analysis, should have been necessary to gain due attention to the problem of effective demand. Keynes, probably to his credit, saw and provided what was needed—enthusiastic polemics, sardonic passages, bits of esoteric and even shocking doctrine. It helps a doctrine make a splash, as Harry Johnson has suggested,[2] if it has just the right degree of difficulty—not so much as to discourage those who thrill at the prospect of being revolutionaries, yet enough to allow those who succeed in understanding it (or think they have) to regard themselves as an elite vanguard within the economics profession.

Keynes's brilliant selling job did not depend on his having a consistent message throughout his *General Theory.* Don Patinkin somewhere condemns the a priori attribution of consistency to an author: it is a fallacy to take for granted that all the different passages in an author's work hang together comfortably and are consistent with a single coherent doctrine. In fact, as Keynes illustrates, an author may be riding several different horses in different parts of even a single book.

In some passages Keynes seems to be a monetarist. Repeating in the *General Theory* what he had said in his *Tract on Monetary Reform* (1923), Keynes calls attention to "the fundamental proposition of monetary theory"—that incomes and prices adjust so as to make desired money balances equal in the aggregate to the actual money stock.[3] Chapter 17 describes the "essential properties" of money that make money the prime candidate for being an asset for which an excess demand matches an excess supply of goods and labor, requiring depression and unemployment to choke off the excess demand for money. "Unemployment develops . . . because people want the moon;—men cannot be employed when the object of desire (*i.e.* money) is something which cannot be produced and the demand

2. "The Keynesian Revolution and the Monetarist Counter-revolution," *American Economic Review* 61 (May 1971): esp. 4–5.

3. John Maynard Keynes, *The General Theory of Employment, Interest, and Money* (New York: Harcourt, Brace, 1936), 84–85.

for which cannot be readily choked off. There is no remedy but to persuade the public that green cheese is practically the same thing and to have a green cheese factory (*i.e.* a central bank) under public control."[4] (Actually, admiration for this chapter properly belongs in large part to Abba Lerner's illuminating exposition of it.)[5]

On rereading the *General Theory* recently, I came away less favorably impressed with chapter 17 than I had been. In describing its "essential properties" that make money a prime candidate for being in excess demand and thereby causing depression, Keynes puts his emphasis on money's yield: its liquidity advantages in excess of carrying costs may well pose a target rate of return that new capital goods could not, in the eyes of potential investors, match. As a result, investment may be inadequate to fill the gap in the spending stream left by saving. Keynes even considers whether assets other than money, such as land or mortgages, might cause the same sort of trouble with an excessively high target rate of return. He does not discuss the special snarl that results when the thing in excess demand is the medium of exchange, so that supply of some goods and services can fail to constitute demand for other goods and services. He does not see the closely related difficulty that money, alone among all assets, has no price of its own and no market of its own.

These omissions on Keynes's part have now been repaired by Robert W. Clower and Axel Leijonhufvud.[6] They have marked out a promising line of advance in macroeconomics and its integration with microeconomics, involving such concepts as the absence of the Walrasian auctioneer, incomplete and costly and imperfect information, false price signals, sluggish price adjustments, quantity adjust-

4. Ibid., 235.

5. "The Essential Properties of Interest and Money," *Quarterly Journal of Economics* 66 (May 1952): 172–93. To Lerner rather than Keynes, incidentally, also belongs credit for the doctrine of functional finance.

6. The most directly relevant citation is Robert W. Clower, "A Reconsideration of the Microfoundations of Monetary Theory," *Western Economic Journal* 6 (December 1967): 1–8, now reprinted in Clower, ed., *Monetary Theory, Selected Readings* (Baltimore: Penguin Books, 1969), 202–11. See also his "The Keynesian Counterrevolution: A Theoretical Appraisal," in *The Theory of Interest Rates*, ed. F. H. Hahn and F. P. R. Brechling (London: Macmillan, 1965), 103–25; and Axel Leijonhufvud, *On Keynesian Economics and the Economics of Keynes* (New York: Oxford University Press, 1968).

ments besides price adjustments, the dual-decision process, and the income-constrained process. This line has already been taken up by such further writers as Donald P. Tucker and Herschel I. Grossman.[7]

The integration of disequilibrium economics with monetary theory in particular seems especially promising to me. Leijonhufvud notes that "the system may be racked by recurrent attacks of Central Bank perversity."[8] As this remark implies, the monetarist evidence about and diagnosis of depressions are perfectly compatible with his and Clower's disequilibrium analysis. Their analysis of cumulative disequilibrium or the income-constrained process helps explain why unsteadiness in the growth of the money supply can throw particularly difficult adjustment burdens onto the price mechanism. Room remains, I believe, for spelling out more fully just why an essential element in cumulative income deterioration is an excess demand for money (or, perhaps more precisely, what *would be* an excess demand for the actual quantity of money at a full-employment level of income).

An adequate quantity of money would offer protection against the cumulativeness of nonmonetary disturbances that could conceivably plague a barter economy. People frustrated in making the exchanges they most desire are prodded, so to speak, into making second-best exchanges. If demands for some goods meet frustration, they spill over into the markets for others. This spillover works better in a monetary economy than under barter, where exchange presupposes a double coincidence of wants. Buying goods with money does not presuppose simultaneous successful selling; exchange of goods can be one-sided for a time. Cash balances that their holders consider excessive burn holes in pockets in a way that idle productive capacity under barter does not do. When, because of disequilibrium prices, demands for some goods are diverted onto other goods in an economy with an adequate total money supply, the main-

---

7. Donald P. Tucker, "Macroeconomic Models and the Demand for Money Under Market Disequilibrium," *Journal of Money, Credit, and Banking* 3 (February 1971): 57–83; Robert J. Barro and Herschel I. Grossman, "A General Disequilibrium Model of Income and Employment," *American Economic Review* 61 (March 1971): 82–93; Grossman, "Money, Interest, and Prices in Market Disequilibrium," *Journal of Political Economy* 79 (September–October 1971): 943–61.

8. *Keynesian Economics*, 399.

tenance or increase of incomes earned in the production of those other goods tends to maintain effective demand for still other goods. Although failure of prices to adjust to an equilibrium pattern distorts resource allocation away from any plausible ideal pattern, it need not unequivocally depress overall economic activity. To see this, suppose that some massive shift in the pattern of demand, perhaps associated with the end of a war, leaves the old pattern of relative prices wrong. The sectors suffering drops in demand for their outputs must curtail their demands for the products of other sectors.[9] Suppose that these cutbacks do initially outweigh the additional incomes and the desired purchases of the sectors favored by the original shifts in demand. The resulting tendency of aggregate income to fall meets resistance. Even with the demand-for-money *function* unchanged, the quantity of money demanded at not yet changed prices would decline with the decline in income. A quantity of money adequate for full employment at the existing level of wages and prices is overabundant for underemployment. People's attempts to reduce their now excessive cash balances would raise the demands for goods either directly or indirectly (by way of the securities markets and interest rates). The spending thus stimulated would go especially toward the goods (or securities) whose prices were, loosely speaking, least too high. It would check the decay spreading from the sectors initially depressed by adverse shifts of demand. Money's intermediary role in the two-stage process of exchanging goods for goods keeps the production of goods to be exchanged from being disrupted as badly as it would be in a barter economy. Demand for goods need not come solely out of currently earned incomes. Goods can be demanded even with money that has not recently (if ever) been received in exchange for goods but that, instead, has been activated out of relative idleness or has been newly created. Frustration in one stage of a desired goods-for-goods exchange need not so immediately spell frustration of the other stage also.

9. In an article reprinted in Clower's *Monetary Theory*, I conceded, citing Hutt, that wrong price ratios could conceivably hamper production and employment even though the average purchasing power of money was correct in relation to the money supply. I now think this conceded too much to the nonmonetary view of depression.

The cash-balance effect just alluded to is more than a Pigou or wealth effect, narrowly conceived.[10] It is more nearly what might be called a Cambridge effect: as their incomes fall, people will not go on indefinitely holding absolutely unchanged and thus relatively increased cash balances.[11] They will economize not only on other goods but also on the services of money. The steps that households and firms take to reduce their money holdings promote the recovery of aggregate income until cash balances no longer seem too large—or serve to check the decline in the first place.

For further insight into how money can block an income-constrained process, let us conceive of a depression in which prices are both stuck too high on the average in relation to the quantity of money and stuck in wrong relations to each other. Now policy expands the quantity of money. If the demands thereby stimulated are frustrated in buying goods whose prices are now relatively too low, they spill over onto other goods. The persons who must content themselves with available substitutes for goods they would have preferred have almost the same impact on the markets as if they had not preferred the goods in short supply and as if their tastes had favored in the first place the goods they wind up buying as substitutes. Monetary expansion could easily be extreme enough to make prices in general no longer too high but instead too low in relation to the money supply. These excessively low prices would not cause or perpetuate "withheld capacity," even though their being stuck in wrong ratios to each other (if they were) would cause "diverted capacity."[12] Wrongness of relative prices need not cause withheld capacity because nonprice rationing of goods in excess demand supplements the rationing function of their excessively low prices. Demands thus blocked shift toward other goods, including ones whose relative prices are too high for general equilibrium.

10. In his December 1967 article, Clower properly criticizes Patinkin and other general-equilibrium writers for treating money as if it influenced market demands only as any other kind of wealth does.

11. Cf. Sir Dennis Robertson, *Lectures on Economic Principles* (London: Collins, Fontana Library, 1963), 443–44.

12. On these terms, see W. H. Hutt, *Keynesianism—Retrospect and Prospect* (Chicago: Regnery, 1963), esp. 21 n, 24, 59–60.

Since monetary expansion in the face of price stickiness could easily be made extreme enough to cause general excess demand for goods and services, a less extreme monetary situation should be possible in which any remaining deficiency of demand for goods and services was at least not a general one. Real disturbances and wrong price ratios need not cause any general deficiency of demand. This possibility of stimulating the effective demand for goods and services by a sufficient supply of money is the reverse side of Clower's point that demands for goods cannot be effective unless backed up not merely by the offer of other goods but by the offer of money in particular.

None of this is to say that monetary expansion can remedy all wastes due to a wrong and rigid pattern of prices. It could not keep prices from conveying misinformation about wants, resources, and technology. In a monetary economy, misallocation waste can persist without idleness waste. (In an extreme barter economy, by contrast, misallocation waste and idleness waste would go together, idleness being an extreme form of misallocation.)

Regarding these wastes, the cases of too little money and too much money in relation to a wrong level and pattern of prices have asymmetrical effects. Both wastes can go with too little money, only misallocation waste with too much. When money is in excess supply, non-price rationing shunts demand onto other goods from goods whose prices are most too low. But when money is in deficient supply, nothing shunts demand around among goods so as to maintain aggregate productive activity. Non-price rationing has no close counterpart in the opposite direction. The possibility that producers frustrated in selling some things may shift into other lines of production offers little benefit when demand was deficient even for the latter products. Again it is crucial that demand, to be effective, must be exercised with money.

The foregoing considerations will perhaps answer the question whether I have not been too preoccupied with depression and too neglectful of inflation. There is no close counterpart in the opposite direction, beyond full employment, of the income-constrained process of deterioration.[13] The economics of disequilibrium has more to tell us about depression than about inflation. The economics of disequilibrium, combined with monetary theory, shows why nonmonetary disturbances alone, even when they leave the existing pattern of relative prices wrong, cannot cause general demand deficiency and unemployment. Maintaining an actual quantity of money equal to the total that would be demanded at full employment and at the existing level of prices and wages would nip a Clower-Leijonhufvud income-constrained process in the bud. It follows that such troubles—though not, of course, all economic troubles—must involve an inappropriate quantity of money.

The prospect of an advance in macroeconomics involving an integration of the theories of money and disequilibrium may be particularly welcome to some of us because it represents a line of advance that does not merely echo or extend the Chicago line, which is so tiresomely often right. The Chicago monetarists have been neglectful so far, and even a bit scornful, of the economics of disequilibrium and of the distinctiveness of money as a medium of exchange. The line of advance marked out by Clower and Leijonhufvud, while reconcilable with the Chicago findings, is refreshingly distinctive.

If this line of advance is not in the Chicago tradition, neither, I submit, is it in the Keynesian tradition. On rereading Clower's and Leijonhufvud's interpretations of Keynes, I was struck by how much of their work is a positive contribution and how little of it is an exposition of what Keynes himself said or can reasonably be interpreted to have meant. They cite remarkably little chapter and verse in support of their interpretations. Instead, they offer intuitions about what Keynes must or should have meant.[14] But if Keynes really wanted to

13. In a fuller discussion, I would include some hedging remarks here about autonomous or inherited price-and-wage inflation. I would also consider an unpublished paper, "Suppressed Inflation and the Supply Multiplier," by Robert J. Barro and Herschel I. Grossman. The authors show why not only prices and wages stuck too high in relation to the quantity of money but also prices and wages stuck too low could cumulatively impair production and employment. Still, major asymmetries remain between the two opposite disequilibrium situations.

14. Clower quotes Keynes's criticisms of classical theory, not passages clearly foreshadowing the Clower-Leijonhufvud theory. Clower envisages a more general

argue that the price system does not maintain or readily restore equilibrium in the face of disturbances because of such elements as costly and incomplete and imperfect information, sluggishness of price adjustments relative to quantity adjustments, the dual-decision phenomenon, the income-constrained process, and all the rest, then why didn't he say so? Without anticipating the specific terminology devised by Clower and Leijonhufvud, he should have been able to get the related ideas across clearly.

Almost as if foreseeing this question of why Keynes didn't say what he supposedly meant, Clower and Leijonhufvud answer with hardly more than excuses for Keynes. In trying to break free from orthodoxy, Keynes was handicapped by the unavailability of the concepts he needed. Furthermore, the orthodox doctrine he was attacking had not been spelled out as explicitly in his day as it now has been in ours.[15] Yet ample excuses for not having done or said something do not, after all, add up to practically the same as having actually done or said it.

On rereading the *General Theory*, I was struck by how much of what Keynes says does resemble the supposedly vulgar Keynesianism of the income-expenditure theory. If Keynes was really a disequilibrium theorist, why did he make so much of the possibility of *equilibrium* at underemployment? Why did he minimize and practically deny the forces that might conceivably be working, however sluggishly, toward full-employment equilibrium? Why did he stress the possibility of chronic unemployment due to a gap between income and consumption that investment might not be able to fill? Recall his comparison of the problems of a poor community and a rich community in filling their saving gaps:

---

theory that Keynes "made *tacit* use of" (279, italics supplied), that Keynes must have had "at the back of his mind" unless "most of the *General Theory* is theoretical nonsense" (290). Clower admittedly "can find no direct evidence in any of his writings to show that he ever thought explicitly in these terms" (290). ("The Keynesian Counter-revolution," page numbers of the reprint in Clower's *Monetary Theory*.) Leijonhufvud, after several pages of trying to read constructive insights into Keynes's criticisms of classical theory, concedes (p. 102 of his book) that Keynes's supposed theory was "obscurely expressed and doubtlessly not all that clear even in his own mind."

15. Cf. Clower, "Counter-revolution," p. 271 of reprint in *Monetary Theory*.

Moreover the richer the community, the wider will tend to be the gap between its actual and its potential production; and therefore the more obvious and outrageous the defects of the economic system. For a poor community will be prone to consume by far the greater part of its output, so that a very modest measure of investment will be sufficient to provide full employment; whereas a wealthy community will have to discover much ampler opportunities for investment if the saving propensities of its wealthy members are to be compatible with the employment of its poorer members. If in a potentially wealthy community the inducement to invest is weak, then, in spite of its potential wealth, the working of the principle of effective demand will compel it to reduce its actual output, until, in spite of its potential wealth, it has become so poor that its surplus over its consumption is sufficiently diminished to correspond to the weakness of the inducement to invest.[16]

Keynes also argues that the more fully investment has already provided for the future, the less scope there is for making still further provision. Recall the following:

The greater . . . the consumption for which we have provided in advance, the more difficult it is to find something further to provide for in advance, and the greater our dependence on present consumption as a source of demand. Yet the larger our incomes, the greater, unfortunately, is the margin between our incomes and our consumption. So, failing some novel expedient, there is, as we shall see, no answer to the riddle, except that there must be sufficient unemployment to keep us so poor that our consumption falls short of our income by no more than the equivalent of the physical provision for future consumption which it pays to produce to-day.[17]

Keynes's hints at the stagnation thesis and at the possible desirability of socializing investment follow along the same line. So do his hints in favor of redistribution of income to raise the overall propensity to consume.[18] In the preliminary summary of his doctrine,[19] and in his emphasis (chapter 8) on his "fundamental psychological law,"

16. Keynes, *General Theory*, 31.
17. Ibid., 105.
18. Ibid., 373.
19. Ibid., 27–31.

Keynes is rather clearly worrying about a deep-seated deficiency of real demand and not about information deficiencies, discoordination, and the like.[20] His emphasis (chapter 10) on a definite quantitative relation between changes in investment and in total income hardly squares with the inherent quantitative vagueness of the cumulative deterioration explained by the income-constrained process of Clower and Leijonhufvud.

It seems significant to me that W. H. Hutt, whose theory of cumulative deterioration in a depression is remarkably similar to the theory of Clower and Leijonhufvud, believes he is expounding a doctrine quite different from what he considers the crudities of Keynes.[21] Hutt describes how changes in taste, technology, or monetary policy can have fateful consequences if prices and wages are not flexible enough to keep plans coordinated in an appropriate new pattern. The drop in sales and production in the sectors first hit spells a drop in real income and real buying power and thus in the real demand for the outputs of other sectors, which suffer in turn, and so on.

The differences between Hutt, on the one hand, and Clower and Leijonhufvud, on the other, are chiefly ones of emphasis. Hutt puts less emphasis than they do on information problems and related reasons why a considerable degree of price and wage stickiness is understandable and rational. He is more inclined to blame the lack of sufficient price flexibility for continuous coordination on villainy on the part of labor unions, business monopolists, and government. He proposed rather drastic action (especially in his earlier book, *Plan for Reconstruction*, 1944) to make the real world more nearly resemble the textbook model of pure and perfect competition. The focus of his positive analysis, though, was failure of the price mechanism to work smoothly and swiftly enough to adjust the plans of all transactors so that they remained consistent with each other in the face of distur-

20. In some afterthoughts published about a year later than the *General Theory* ("The General Theory of Employment," *Quarterly Journal of Economics* [February 1937]: 209–23, reprinted in Clower's *Monetary Theory*), Keynes does put relatively increased emphasis on imperfections of knowledge and foresight; but he still falls far short of articulating anything resembling the dual-decision hypothesis and the rest of the Clower-Leijonhufvud theory.

21. *Keynesianism—Retrospect and Prospect.*

bances, with the result that declines of incomes in some sectors of the economy become contagious throughout the economy.[22]

Like Clower and Leijonhufvud, Hutt does not want actually to rely on general price and wage cuts to cure or forestall depression through some sort of real-balance effect. He stresses the importance of monetary stability or, as he says, maintenance of a money unit of defined value. Still, monetary disturbance is to him just one of a great many disturbances that could make the previously existing price pattern wrong. He therefore blames general disequilibrium and the income-constrained process (the contagion of withheld capacity, as he calls it) not on any particular kind of disturbance but on thwarting of the adjustment mechanism by economic villains of various kinds.

Insofar as monetary expansion can remedy an existing depression, it works, if I understand Hutt correctly, by changing inappropriate prices or wages through some kind of money illusion or trickery. Hutt does not show how an adequate money supply keeps nonmonetary disturbances from causing cumulative deterioration and does not give the reasoning that accordingly puts the blame for such deterioration on money in particular.

Because Hutt's theory is incomplete, and for other reasons, the existence of his book does not detract from the credit that Clower and Leijonhufvud deserve for the major advances they have made. I have mentioned it only as part of my argument that Clower and Leijonhufvud are too modest in attributing their theory to Keynes. Instead of trying to differentiate their product, as all too many scholars do, they are concerned to find continuity with the work of their predecessors. For this concern they deserve only praise. Their generosity to Keynes is rather ironic, though, in view of how Keynes treated his own predecessors. If they were bent on giving away the credit they deserve, they could have found worthier recipients. These include the early twentieth-century theorists of monetary equilib-

22. Mrs. Evelyn Marr Glazier deserves credit for her University of Virginia master's thesis of August 1970, "Theories of Disequilibrium: Clower and Leijonhufvud Compared to Hutt." Mrs. Glazier notes but does not actually tackle the question of who more correctly understands what Keynes really meant. She does, however, show that the three economists named in her title "agree more on some of the fundamental issues of disequilibrium than they do on the history of doctrines" (3).

rium and disequilibrium of whose work Clark Warburton has reminded us.[23]

For brevity, let us consider just one book, by Harry Gunnison Brown. Brown describes a business depression as "a condition of disinclination to purchase."

> each person hesitates to buy—*at existing prices*—lest he cannot sell at a profit; and the reason why each finds it difficult so to sell is that others hesitate to buy. So, also, manufacturers and other employers hesitate to employ their usual number of operatives and other laborers at current rates of wages, lest the output should prove unsalable at a profit.
>
> The difficulty is not . . . that goods absolutely cannot be sold. If they were offered at prices low enough, all goods produced could be sold very easily under almost any conceivable conditions of business.[24]

With prices fallen very low but the nominal money stock maintained, money-holders would find the advantages of spending greatly increased. Only expectations of still further price cuts would motivate postponing expenditure still longer.[25]

Brown clearly recognizes the real-balance effect, broadly conceived:

> at *some* low level of prices, . . . further decline could not be expected. And the amount of potential purchasing power that people will hold indefinitely idle is not indefinitely large. . . . If we assume . . . any definite limit whatever, however remote, to hoarding, we are forced to the conclusion that there must be *some* level of prices low enough to dispose of all goods produced and employ all labor.[26]

23. See, in particular, the papers reprinted in part 1 of his *Depression, Inflation, and Monetary Policy* (Baltimore: Johns Hopkins University Press, 1966).

24. *Economic Science and the Common Welfare*, 5th ed. (Columbia, Mo.: Lucas Brothers, 1931), 84, 85. It is perhaps significant that Brown presents his insights in an elementary text and claims no special originality for them.

25. Ibid., 85–86.

26. Ibid., 86.

Brown sees a restriction of credit and money as the characteristic initiator of cumulative business contractions. He notes why the price system cannot swiftly cope with such a major disturbance. He even alludes to information difficulties of the kind emphasized by Clower, Leijonhufvud, and Armen Alchian. A decrease of credit and spending, he says,

> must, clearly, involve *either* a reduction of prices *or* a decrease of business or both. And we cannot reasonably expect that the entire effect of the decreased expenditure of money and credit will be expressed, immediately, in lower prices. Producers and dealers will not see why they should accept greatly reduced prices for their output or for the goods which they have bought to sell. They will lower their prices only with reluctance. Artisans and laborers will not easily be convinced that there is any adequate reason why they should take lower wages. Persons who have land and buildings to rent or to sell will not readily understand why they should accept lower rents or prices than those which they have come to look upon as reasonable. Speculative holders of vacant land will, in many or most cases, continue to ask the prices they have been asking. But with less money and credit being spent, unless prices-in-general fall in proportion, the volume of business must decline. Continued lack of demand for goods and labor, with unsalableness of the goods and diminished employment for laborers, will force a readjusting reduction in prices and wages. The will to maintain prosperity prices and wages is broken by the compulsion of circumstances. And there is doubtless *some* level of prices, wages, etc., low enough so that, even with greatly diminished spending, business would be active. But the process of readjustment—through lowered prices, lowered discount rates, growing confidence, and increased borrowing—may be one requiring several months or (sometimes) years, during which business is relatively inactive and "depression" is said to continue. [27]

This disinclination to spend current funds and to borrow funds from banks for spending . . . need not bring lessened trade if sellers were universally willing to accept, temporarily, a reduction of prices sufficiently great to carry off of the market all goods, including labor, despite the diminution in the number of dollars expended which characterizes depression. But there are various customary notions of what are reasonable prices for various goods and

27. Ibid., 104.

reasonable wages for labor of various kinds and, furthermore, each person hopes to be able to get the old price or the old wage for what he has to sell and does not want to reduce until sure that his expenses will also be reduced. And so there is a general hesitancy, a holding off for standard prices, wages, and so on, to the inevitable slowing down of business.[28]

Eventually, Brown continues, the inability to sell goods and labor forces reluctant acceptance of lower prices and wages. Hesitancy to buy "comes to express itself . . . not entirely in slack business and not entirely in low prices and wages but partly in each."[29]

Revival would come eventually with progressive decline of prices, wages, interest and rentals, all along the line. With sufficiently low wholesale prices, dealers might slightly extend their purchases. With sufficiently low wages, etc., manufacturers could afford to sell at these low prices. With low retail prices, even low wages would suffice for the purpose of needed consumption goods. A proper proportionate fall all along the line would, then, bring revival. But, in practice, low prices are only a part of the story. If dealers are tempted to buy more largely than they have been buying during the depression, the chances are they will ask for more bank credit in order to do so. This *additional bank credit*, along with the somewhat greater readiness to spend pre-existing credit, enables active buying to occur *without any further fall of prices.*[30]

Modern industry is a vast co-operative undertaking. To a large extent the co-operation is scarcely conscious, the result of voluntary individual action, each individual contributing to the supply of goods or services desired by others, as the best means of securing the money with which to meet his own needs or wants. Yet, to get the best results, it is necessary that our co-operation should be, in part, a deliberate and planned co-operation. . . . We need to extend centralized control . . . *to prevent credit expansion* when such expansion tends merely to raise prices, to encourage speculation and still further expansion, to reduce bank reserves, and to bring later depression. . . . It may be desirable, eventually, to supersede the gold standard as we now know it with a more stable standard of

28. Ibid., 88–89.
29. Ibid., 89.
30. Ibid., 93.

value; but a more intelligent control of credit, by itself, would accomplish very much indeed for business and price stability.[31]

As I trust these passages have shown, Brown views depression basically as a cumulative general disequilibrium touched off by monetary disturbance.[32] As a remedy, he seeks not some impossible and undesirable degree of flexibility in wages and prices, but rather the avoidance of monetary disturbances. On pages 111–15 he contrasts his doctrine with "the theory that business depression is a result of excessive saving." What, he asks, could people ("capitalists or capitalist-employers") do with their incomes? They could (1) spend their incomes on consumption, (2) invest them in durable or production goods, (3) hoard them as unused money or deposits, and (4) throw them into the sea. The choice of possibilities 1 or 2 causes no deficiency of effective demand. If saving and capital accumulation went on indefinitely, asset yields might drop very low, conceivably to zero. But as zero-interest capitalists could only afford to buy fewer goods, other income receivers, such as wage earners or landowners, would have larger incomes and could buy more. In a side comment on possibility 2, Brown notes the question of what happens if a saver buys stocks and bonds instead of actual capital goods and, furthermore, buys the securities not from a corporation newly issuing them but from an earlier holder. The question of what the securities seller does with the money he receives should be handled in much the same way, Brown implies, as the original question of what people can do with their money incomes.

Choice of possibilities 3 or 4 means less money in active circulation, either temporarily or permanently.

> But in *neither* case is there *all-around over-production*. Prices will inevitably become low enough so that what capitalists who have hoarded or thrown away their money, will or can not buy, other classes will buy. . . . If capitalists merely hoard their money, the rest of the community will find prices temporarily reduced in equal degree but prices will in this case tend to rise again if and when the hoarded money gets back into circulation.

31. Ibid., 116–17.
32. He says more on these points than I have quoted.

It is no answer to the argument presented above, to say that decreased money in circulation, together with a general disinclination to accept reduced prices, wages, etc., may lead to depression. *For to say this is to admit that the problem is a monetary and credit problem and is to give away the whole case for all-around over-production.*[33]

Early twentieth-century economists such as Brown had already made good progress toward integrating monetary theory and disequilibrium theory.[34] From their work, Keynesianism, with its worries about savings gaps and inadequate investment, was a backward step. Clower and Leijonhufvud are now putting us back onto a track from which Keynesianism had diverted us. This diversion has held up progress—unless it is true that Keynesianism was necessary to shake economists out of prevalent complacency about effective demand, unless the intellectual conditions of the 1930s and before really made taking one step backward prerequisite to taking two steps forward.

I hope it is clear that these remarks derive from no petty desire to deny glory to Keynes. He has and deserves much anyway. Giving him undue additional credit means depriving others of their share. But this question of glory is relatively trivial. The main thing is to get the story straight for the sake of the cumulative character of the development of economics as a science.

That the promising early twentieth-century theories of monetary disequilibrium should have fallen into neglect, that Clark Warburton's struggles to revive and extend them and their empirical foundation should have been ignored for so many years, that Warburton has even yet not received anywhere near the full credit due him, that the income-and-expenditure Keynesianism, which we now recognize as basically wrong, could for years have seemed to be a new and constructive development, that Keynes should currently be receiving credit for the disequilibrium economics from which he in fact did more than any other economist to divert attention—all these circumstances prompt me to some concluding reflections on the history of

33. Brown, *Economic Science and the Common Welfare*, 115.

34. Another inadequately known economist who merits special mention is Herbert Joseph Davenport. See his *The Economics of Enterprise* (New York: Macmillan, 1913), esp. 291–320.

economic thought. Cultivation of the history of thought is more necessary in economics than in the natural sciences because earlier discoveries in economics are more in danger of being forgotten; maintaining a *cumulative* growth of knowledge is more difficult. In the natural sciences, discoveries get embodied not only in further advances in pure knowledge but also into technology, many of whose users have a profit-and-loss incentive to get things straight. The practitioners of economic technology are largely politicians with rather different motives. (Analogies between the market test and the ballot-box test have been fashionable in recent years, but the differences should not be forgotten.) In economics, consequently, we need scholars who specialize in keeping us aware of earlier contributions and so enable us to recognize earlier successes—and earlier mistakes—when they surface as supposedly new ideas. By exerting a needed discipline, specialists in the history of thought can contribute to the cumulative character of economics.

The Significance of Monetary Disequilibrium

RIVAL THEORIES

Among theories of macroeconomic fluctuations that accord a major role to money, at least three rivals confront each other nowadays. One is orthodox monetarism—"the monetary disequilibrium hypothesis," as Clark Warburton has called it.[1] A second is the so-called Austrian theory of the business cycle. A third builds on notions of rational expectations and equilibrium always. What monetarism offers toward understanding and perhaps improving the world becomes clearer when one compares it with its rivals.

MONETARY DISEQUILIBRIUM THEORY

Fundamentally, behind the veil of money, people specialize in producing particular goods and services to exchange them for the specialized outputs of other people. Any particular output thus constitutes demand, either at once or eventually, for other (noncompeting) outputs. Since supply constitutes demand in that sense, any apparent problem of general deficiency of demand traces to impediments to exchange, which discourage producing goods to be ex-

Reprinted from the *Cato Journal* 6 (Fall 1986): 369–95, with permission of the Cato Institute, 1000 Massachusetts Avenue NW, Washington, D.C. 20001.

For helpful comments on the paper or on pieces of earlier draft, the author thanks David Colander, James Dorn, Daniel Edwards, Roger Garrison, and Alan Rabin; and he apologizes to others whose contributions may have slipped his mind.

1. Clark Warburton, *Depression, Inflation, and Monetary Policy* (Baltimore: Johns Hopkins University Press, 1966), selection 1.

changed. The impediment that most readily comes to mind hinges on the fact that goods exchange for each other not directly but through the intermediary of money or of claims to be settled in money.

As Warburton has argued, a tendency toward market clearing inheres in the logic of market processes.[2] Whenever, therefore, markets are generally and conspicuously failing to clear—when disorder is more pervasive than gluts or shortages of only particular goods or services—some exogenous disturbance must have occurred, one extensive enough to resist quick, automatic correction. It is hard to imagine what that pervasive disruption could be other than a discrepancy between actual and desired holdings of money at the prevailing price level. (It is unnecessary to worry here about just how to define "money." A supply-demand disequilibrium for money broadly defined is very likely to entail disequilibrium in the same direction for money narrowly defined also. Financial innovations may well complicate the task of avoiding imbalance between money's supply and demand, but that complication for policy makers is distinct from the question of diagnosis.)

A discrepancy between supply and demand is likely to develop, Warburton argued, when growth of the money supply falls short of the long-run trend. Actual shrinkage poses the simplest case. People and organizations try to conserve or replenish their shrunken money holdings by restraint in buying and greater efforts to sell goods and services and securities.[3]

Since transactions are voluntary, the shorter of the demand side and the supply side sets the actual volume of transactions on each market. Transactions and production fall off, unless prices and wages promptly absorb the whole impact of the monetary disturbance. Typically they do not. Production cutbacks in response to reduced sales in some sectors of the economy spell reduced real buying power for the outputs of other sectors. Transactions in ultimate factors of production and in final consumer goods and services are far outnumbered by interfirm transactions in intermediate goods—

2. Ibid., selection 1, esp. 26–27.
3. Knut Wicksell, *Interest and Prices*, trans. R. F. Kahn (New York: Kelley, 1965), 40.

materials, parts, equipment, structures, items traded at wholesale, and the like—and this circumstance magnifies the scope for damage from shrinkage of the routine flow of the monetary lubricant. Financial intermediation and trade in financial instruments are similarly vulnerable.[4]

When money is in short supply at the existing nominal price and wage level, why won't people collaborate to economize on money and so keep their transactions, production, and employment going anyway? People do collaborate to economize on coins when they are in short supply. George Akerlof and Alan Blinder and Joseph Stiglitz suggest that the two cases offer similar incentives for collaboration.[5] Yet they are quite different. A shortage specifically of coins is easy to recognize, and collaboration in economizing on coins works not only in the general interest but also in one's evident personal interest (to facilitate specific transactions and to earn goodwill). An overall shortage of money is much harder for individuals to diagnose and to palliate cooperatively in individual transactions.

The rot can snowball, especially if people react to deteriorating business and worsening uncertainty by trying to hold more money relative to other assets and to income and expenditure—if velocity falls, as it typically does in such situations. In depression or recession, what would be an excess demand for money at full employment is being suppressed by people's being too poor to "afford" more than their actual money holdings. Relief of this (suppressed) excess demand for money somehow or other—perhaps by an increase in the nominal money supply, perhaps by growth in real money balances through wage and price cuts—would bring recovery. An excess supply of money, at the other extreme, brings price inflation. The theory extends readily to deal both with stagflation and with the adverse side effects of monetary policy to stop infla-

4. Ben S. Bernanke, "Nonmonetary Effects of the Financial Crisis in the Propagation of the Great Depression," *American Economic Review* 73 (June 1983): 257–76.

5. George A. Akerlof, "The Questions of Coinage, Trade Credit, Financial Flows and Peanuts: A Flow-of-Funds Approach to the Demand for Money," Federal Reserve Bank of New York Research Paper no. 7520 (1975); Alan S. Blinder and Joseph E. Stiglitz, "Money, Credit Constraints, and Economic Activity," *American Economic Review* 73 (May 1983): 299–300.

tion, since an analogy holds between the stickiness of a price and wage level and the momentum of an entrenched uptrend.[6]

This doctrine, or key strands of it, goes back at least to David Hume,[7] and sometimes was the dominant view in macroeconomics. It flourished in the United States in the early decades of the twentieth century, as Warburton has reminded us.[8] W. H. Hutt has long expounded something similar in his own idiosyncratic terminology.[9] Robert Clower and Axel Leijonhufvud rediscovered it,[10] questionably suggesting that it was what Keynes really meant in the *General Theory*.[11] Robert Barro and Herschel Grossman developed some of its theoretical aspects.[12] The doctrine accords well with the statistical evidence of Warburton and Milton Friedman and other monetarists.

It also accords well with narrative history. Many episodes of association between changes in money and in business conditions defy being talked away with the "reverse causation" argument, that is, the contention that the monetary changes were mere passive responses

6. Leland B. Yeager and associates, *Experiences With Stopping Inflation* (Washington, D.C.: American Enterprise Institute, 1981) (partly reprinted in this volume).

7. David Hume, "Of Money" (1752), in *Writings on Economics*, ed. Eugene Rotwein (Madison: University of Wisconsin Press, 1970), 33–46.

8. Clark Warburton, "Monetary Disequilibrium Theory in the First Half of the Twentieth Century," *History of Political Economy* 13 (Summer 1981): 285–99; and Warburton, Manuscript on the history of monetary-disequilibrium theory (George Mason University Library, Fairfax, Va.).

9. W. H. Hutt, *Keynesianism—Retrospect and Prospect* (Chicago: Regnery, 1963); Hutt, *A Rehabilitation of Say's Law* (Athens: Ohio University Press, 1974); and idem, *The Keynesian Episode: A Reassessment* (Indianapolis: Liberty Fund, 1979).

10. Robert W. Clower, "The Keynesian Counterrevolution: A Theoretical Appraisal," in *The Theory of Interest Rates*, ed. F. H. Hahn and F. P. R. Brechling (London: Macmillan, 1965); and Clower, "A Reconsideration of the Microfoundations of Monetary Theory," *Western Economic Journal* 6 (December 1967): 1–8. Axel Leijonhufvud, *On Keynesian Economics and the Economics of Keynes* (New York: Oxford University Press, 1968).

11. Herschel I. Grossman, "Was Keynes a 'Keynesian'?" *Journal of Economic Literature* 10 (March 1972): 26–30; and Leland B. Yeager, "The Keynesian Diversion," *Western Economic Journal* 11 (June 1973): 150–63 (reprinted in this volume).

12. Robert J. Barro and Herschel I. Grossman, "A General Disequilibrium Model of Income and Employment," *American Economic Review* 61 (March 1971): 82–93; and Barro and Grossman, *Money, Employment, and Inflation* (New York: Cambridge University Press, 1976).

to business fluctuations of nonmonetary origin. Warburton and Friedman and Anna Schwartz have assembled episodes from American history.[13]

Episodes appear even in fairly exotic times and places. In several American colonies in the early eighteenth century (that is, even before Hume wrote), issues of new paper money apparently had their intended effect in relieving a "decay of trade."[14] Writing in Sweden in 1761, a time of irredeemable paper money, P. N. Christiernin observed that "reduction in the circulating money supply chokes prosperity," and he went on to amplify that observation. Anticipating Irving Fisher, Christiernin even warned about the interaction between deflation and existing debts.[15] From 1863 through 1865, efforts to deflate the Austrian paper gulden back to its silver parity produced a depression lasting until the Seven Weeks' War of 1866. In the judgment of two modern Austrian economists, the war-related paper-money issues then served as a "deliverance for the entire economy" from the deflation and contributed to the "greatest boom in Austrian history." "The experience gained from the severe economic depression in the wake of [Finance Minister] *Plener's* contractionary measures and from the economic upswing after the expansion of the circulation in the year 1866 confirmed in increasing degree . . . the recognition of a far-reaching connection between the monetary system and the development of business conditions."[16] The association between monetary and business conditions in tsarist Russia is recognized by Haim Barkai, P. A. Khromov, A. F. Jakovlev, and A. Shipov,

13. Clark Warburton, "Monetary Disturbances and Business Fluctuations in Two Centuries of American History," in *In Search of a Monetary Constitution*, ed. Leland B. Yeager (Cambridge: Harvard University Press, 1962); and Milton Friedman and Anna J. Schwartz, *A Monetary History of the United States, 1867–1960* (Princeton: Princeton University Press, 1963).

14. Richard A. Lester, *Monetary Experiments: Early American and Recent Scandinavian* (Princeton: Princeton University Press, 1939), chaps. 3, 5. (Reprint, Newton Abbot, England: David and Charles, 1970.)

15. Pehr Niclas Christiernin, *Summary of Lectures on the High Price of Foreign Exchange in Sweden,* trans. Robert V. Eagly, in Eagly, *The Swedish Bullionist Controversy* (Philadelphia: American Philosophical Society, 1971), 86, 91–94.

16. The quotations are from Alois Gratz and Reinhard Kamitz, in *Hundert Jahre Österreichischer Wirtschaftsentwicklung, 1848–1948,* ed. Hans Mayer (Vienna: Springer, 1949), 254, 147.

and is borne out by available statistics.[17] Relative resistance to depression in the early 1930s by fiat-money Spain and silver-standard China and China's subsequent suffering under the United States silver-purchase program illustrate monetarist theory. So do the consequences of deflation of the stock of cigarette money in a prisoner-of-war camp.[18] These episodes are cited merely as evidence bearing on a theory, not as arguments for populist monetary expansionism.

EARLY RECOGNITION OF PRICE STICKINESS

Since assuming—or recognizing—wage and price stickiness is now widely viewed as a distinctively Keynesian trait in macro theory (a view discussed further below), we should remember that even early monetarists invoked it. David Hume explained that monetary expansion can stimulate production only during a transition period, before prices have risen fully; and, though less clearly, he saw the corresponding point about monetary contraction.[19] "It is easy for prices to adjust upward when the money supply increases," observed Christiernin, "but to get prices to fall has always been more difficult. No one reduces the price of his commodities or his labor until the lack of sales necessitates him to do so. Because of this the workers must suffer want and the industriousness of wage earners must stop before the established market price can be reduced."[20] Henry Thornton was also quite explicit and even noted that wages tend to adjust downward more stickily than prices.[21]

17. Haim Barkai, *Industrialization and Deflation: The Monetary Experience of Tsarist Russia in the Industrialization Era* (Jerusalem: Hebrew University Press, 1969); P. A. Khromov, *.Ekonomicheskoe Razvitie Rossii v XIX–XX Vekakh* (Moscow: Gospolitizdat, 1950), 293–94; A. F. Jakovlev, *.Ekonomicheskie Krizisy v Rossii* (Moscow: Gospolitizdat, 1955), 388–89; A. Shipov, "Kuda i otchego ischezli u nas denjgi?" *Vestnik Promyshlennosti* 9, no. 7 (1860): 33–34, also as quoted in S. G. Strumilin, *Ocherki .Ekonomicheskoj Istorii Rossii* (Moscow: Sots.ekiz, 1960), 479.

18. R. A. Radford, "The Economic Organization of a P.O.W. Camp," *Economica*, n.s. 12 (November 1945): 189–201.

19. Hume, "Of Money," 39–40.

20. Christiernin, in Eagly, *Summary of Lectures*, 90.

21. Henry Thornton, *An Enquiry Into the Nature and Effects of the Paper Credit of Great Britain* (1802, reprint, Fairfield, N.J.: Kelley, 1978), 119–20.

G. Poulett Scrope, under the heading "General Glut of Goods—Supposes a General Want of Money," explained that "epochs of general embarrassment and distress among the productive classes, accompanied . . . by a general glut or apparent excess of all goods in every market . . . are . . . occasioned by the force of some artificial disturbing cause or other," namely money. "A general glut—that is, a general fall in the prices of the mass of commodities below their producing cost—is tantamount to a rise in the general exchangeable value of money; and is a proof, not of an excessive supply of goods, but of a deficient supply of money, against which the goods have to be exchanged."[22]

Like many other diagnosticians of disequilibrium, Scrope did not distinguish as clearly as we might wish between excessive monetary expansion or contraction, on the one hand, and general price increases or decreases, on the other hand—price changes which, along with changes in quantities traded and produced, are symptoms or consequences of the monetary disturbance. These price changes *tend* to correct or forestall the monetary disequilibrium but do not and cannot occur promptly and completely enough to absorb the entire impact of the monetary change and so avoid quantity changes. By clear implication, though, Scrope does recognize the stickiness of at least those prices entering into the "producing cost" of commodities.

It was not a hallmark of classical and neoclassical economics to believe that markets always clear or that automatic market-clearing forces always quickly overpower disturbances to equilibrium. When concerned, as they usually were, with the long-run equilibrium toward which fundamental forces were driving patterns of prices and resource allocation, classical and neoclassical writers (including Ricardo, Mill, and Marshall) did abstract from the shorter-run phenomenon of monetary disequilibrium. But they recognized that such disequilibrium does occur and sometimes paid explicit attention to it.[23]

Turning to early twentieth-century America, we find H. J. Davenport emphasizing the monetary nature of depression:

22. G. Poulett Scrope, *Principles of Political Economy* (London: Longman, Rees, Orme, Brown, Green, & Longman, 1833), 214–15.

23. Warburton, "Monetary Disequilibrium."

It remains difficult to find a market for products, simply because each producer is attempting a feat which must in the average be an impossibility—the selling of goods to others without a corresponding buying from others. . . . [T]he prevailing emphasis is upon money, not as intermediate for present purposes, but as a commodity to be kept. . . . [T]he psychology of the time stresses not the goods to be exchanged through the intermediary commodity, but the commodity itself. The halfway house becomes a house of stopping. . . . Or to put the case in still another way: the situation is one of withdrawal of a large part of the money supply at the existing level of prices; it is a change of the entire demand schedule of money against goods.[24]

Davenport recognizes that the depression would be milder and shorter if prices could fall evenly all along the line. In reality, though, not all prices fall with equal speed. Wages fall only slowly and with painful struggle, and entrepreneurs may be caught in a cost-price squeeze. Existing nominal indebtedness also poses resistance to adjustment.[25]

More generally, uneven changes in individual prices and wages amid a change in their general level, whether downward in depression or upward in inflation or stagflation, degrade the information conveyed by individual prices and in other ways add difficulties for trade and production. Nowadays, theories of "overshooting" of floating exchange rates invoke the stickiness of prices of goods and services.

THE LOGIC OF STICKINESS

In an elementary textbook already in its fifth edition in 1931, Harry Gunnison Brown explains why price reductions would not immediately absorb a contraction of money, credit, and spending. Producers, dealers, and workers do not easily see why they should accept reduced prices and wages; owners of land or buildings will not see why they should accept lower prices or rents. "There are various cus-

24. H. J. Davenport, *The Economics of Enterprise* (New York: Macmillan, 1913), 291–305, 318.
25. Ibid., 319–20.

tomary notions of what are reasonable prices for various goods and reasonable wages for labor of various kinds and, furthermore, each person hopes to be able to get the old price or the old wage for what he has to sell and does not want to reduce until sure that his expenses will also be reduced." People hesitate, holding off for standard prices, wages, and so on. The process of readjustment "may be one requiring several months or (sometimes) years, during which business is relatively inactive and 'depression' is said to continue."[26]

Brown is alluding to the who-goes-first problem. It is illegitimate to suppose that people somehow just know about monetary disequilibrium, know what pressures it is tending to exert for corrective adjustments in prices and wages generally, and promptly use this knowledge in their own pricing decisions. One cannot consistently both suppose that the price system is a communication mechanism—a device for mobilizing and coordinating knowledge dispersed in millions of separate minds—and also suppose that people *already* have the knowledge that the system is working to convey. Businessmen do not have a quick and easy shortcut to the results of the market process. They do not have it even when the market's performance is badly impaired. Money-supply numbers are far from everything they need to know for their business decisions.

Even if an especially perceptive businessman did correctly diagnose a monetary disequilibrium and recognize what adjustments were required, what reason would he have to move first? By promptly cutting the price of his own product or service, he would be cutting its relative price, unless other people cut their prices and wages in at least the same proportion. How could he count on deep enough cuts in the prices of his inputs to spare him losses or increased losses at a reduced price of his own product? The same questions still apply even if monetary conditions and the required adjustments are widely understood. Each decision maker's price or wage actions still depend largely on the actual or expected actions of others. A businessman's difficulties in finding profitable customers or a worker's in finding a job are unlikely to trace wholly, and perhaps not even mainly, to his own pricing policy or wage demands.

26. Harry Gunnison Brown, *Economic Science and the Common Welfare*, 5th ed. (Columbia, Mo.: Lucas Brothers, 1931), 88–89, 104.

Although this point is obvious, many people seem not to grasp its significance; so further emphasis is justified. Suppose that I and a teenage neighbor want to make a deal for him to mow my lawn. Somehow, however, lawnmowers and lawnmower rentals are priced prohibitively high. At no wage rate, then, could my neighbor and I strike an advantageous bargain. The obstacle is not one that either or both of us can remove, and our failing to remove it is no sign of irrationality. Similarly, whether a manufacturer can afford wage rates attractive to workers may well depend on land rents, interest rates, prices of materials and equipment and fuel and transport, prices charged by competitors, and prices entering into workers' cost of living.

The point of these examples is that attaining a market-clearing pattern of prices and wages is not simply a matter of bilateral negotiations between the two parties to each potential transaction. Comprehensive multilateral negotiations are infeasible or prohibitively costly; so groping toward a coordinated pattern of market-clearing prices must take place instead through decentralized, piecemeal, sequential, trial-and-error setting and revision of individual prices and wages.

The economy never reaches a state of full coordination. How close or how far away it is depends on how severe and how recent shocks have been in "wants, resources, and technology"—and monetary conditions. The impossibility of perpetual full coordination is no defect of the market system. It is an inevitable consequence, rather, of the circumstances with which any economic system must cope. One of the market system's virtues is that it does not require or impose collective decisions. The dispersion of knowledge and the fact that certain kinds of knowledge can be used effectively only through decentralized decisions coordinated through markets and prices—rather than coordinated in some magically direct way—is one of the hard facts of reality. It forms part of the reason why monetary disturbances can be so pervasively disruptive: they overtax the knowledge-mobilizing and signaling processes of the market.

Interdependence among individual prices and wages appears in input-output tables. It appears in the attention given to production costs, the cost of living, and notions of fairness in price and wage setting. The holding of inventories (of materials and semifinished and finished products) and buildups and rundowns of inventories testify to the perceived rationality of waiting for further information rather than adjusting one's price in response to every little change in customers' demands.

Even in a depression, when it would be collectively rational to cut the general level of prices and wages and other costs enough to make the real money stock adequate for a full-employment volume of transactions, the individual agent may not find it rational to move first by cutting the particular price or wage for which he is responsible. He may rationally wait to see whether cuts by others, intensifying the competition he faces or reducing his production costs or his cost of living, will make it advantageous for him to *follow* with a cut of his own. The individually rational and the collectively rational may well diverge, as in the well-known example of the prisoners' dilemma. Taking the lead in downward price and wage adjustments is in the nature of a public good, and private incentives to supply public goods are notoriously inadequate. (An analogous argument helps explain people's reluctance to go first in breaking an entrenched uptrend in wages and prices as soon as inflationary monetary growth has been stopped.)

Because wages and prices are sticky, automatic market forces, working alone, correct a severe monetary disequilibrium only slowly and painfully. Extreme flexibility in money's purchasing power not only is infeasible but would even be undesirable in several respects.

Many circumstances make stickiness reasonable from the standpoint of individual decision makers. (A theory does not deserve sneers for being eclectic if its eclecticism corresponds to reality.) The value of long-term customer-supplier and employer-worker relations and notions of implicit contract ("invisible handshake") enter into the explanation.[27] The workers foreclosed from a particular employment by too high a wage rate may well be only a minority of the candidates, victims of a seniority system or of bad breaks. The more senior or the luckier workers who remain employed are not acting against their own interest in refusing to accept wage adjustments

27. Arthur M. Okun, *Prices and Quantities: A Macroeconomic Analysis* (Washington, D.C.: Brookings Institution, 1981).

toward a market-clearing level. For the employer, as well, the costs of obtaining and processing information may recommend judging what wage rates are appropriate by what other people are paying and receiving and by traditional differentials. If changed conditions make old rules of thumb no longer appropriate, it takes time for new rules to evolve. An employer may offer a wage higher than necessary to attract the desired number of workers so that he can screen ones of superior quality from an ample applicant pool. Considerations of morale are relevant to many jobs that involve providing informal training to one's less experienced fellow workers. Performance in this and other respects is hard to monitor, and workers may withhold it if they come to feel that they are being treated unfairly. For some goods and services as well as labor, actual or supposed correlations between price and quality may provide reasons for not relying on market clearing by price alone.[28]

More broadly, money's general purchasing power is sticky because individual prices and wages are interdependent. This interdependence is crucial to the who-goes-first problem.[29] It intertwines with a banal but momentous fact: money, as the medium of exchange, unlike all other goods, lacks a price and a market of its own. No specific "money market" exists on which people acquire and dispose of money, nor does money have any specific price that straightforwardly comes under pressure to clear its (nonexistent) market. Money's value (strictly, the reciprocal of its value) is the average of individual prices and wages determined on myriad distinct though interconnecting markets for individual goods and services. Adjustment of money's value has to occur through supply and demand changes on these individual markets, where these changes can affect not only prices but also quantities traded and produced. In particular, an excess demand for money will tend to deflate not only prices but also quantities—unless prices absorb the entire impact, which is unlikely for the reasons under discussion.

28. Joseph E. Stiglitz, "Equilibrium in Product Markets With Imperfect Information," *American Economic Review* 69 (May 1979): 339–45.

29. Philip Cagan, "Reflections on Rational Expectations," *Journal of Money, Credit, and Banking* 12 (November 1980), part 2, 826–32; and Charles L. Schultz, "Microeconomic Efficiency and Nominal Wage Stickiness," *American Economic Review* 75 (March 1985): 1–15.

For nothing other than the medium of exchange—ranging from Old Masters to the nearest of near moneys—could an excess demand be so pervasively disruptive. A nonmoney does not have a routine flow, lubricating exchanges of other things, to be disrupted in the first place. Efforts to hold more than its actual quantity cannot cause such pervasive trouble. Excess demand for a nonmoney hits its own specific market. The frustrated demand either (1) is curtailed by a rise in the thing's price (or fall in its yield) or (2) is satisfied by a response in its quantity or else (3) is diverted onto other things. No excess demand for a nonmoney can persist, unaccompanied by an excess demand for money, and yet show up as deficiency of demand for other things in general. For the medium of exchange, in contrast, excess demand is neither directly removed nor diverted. Instead, (4) the pressures of monetary disequilibrium are diffused over myriad individual markets and prices, which renders its correction sluggish.

COMPARISON WITH RIVAL THEORIES

We better appreciate monetary disequilibrium theory when we consider how it compares with rival theories and stands up under criticism by their adherents. Criticism from the camp of rational expectations and equilibrium always is relatively explicit. First, though, we shall look at a rival doctrine whose criticism is rather vague, showing up as jabs at "Chicago" economics, at supposedly excessive aggregation, and at supposedly inadequate attention to the nonneutrality of monetary changes.

THE AUSTRIAN THEORY OF THE BUSINESS CYCLE

A particular theory cultivated by Ludwig von Mises and F. A. Hayek in the early 1930s is so widely expounded in speech and print by "Austrian" economists nowadays that I hardly know where to begin or end in giving citations.[30] Some economists may consider that theory too unfamiliar, outmoded, or preposterous to be worth any further attention. Still, I did not want to pass up my present opportunity to reason with its adherents. Their slant on economics has much to offer. I want to support modern Austrianism by helping rid it of an embarrassing excrescence.

Briefly, Austrian cycle theory attributes recession or depression to a preceding excessive expansion of money and credit. It does not flatly deny any possible role of their contraction during the depression; but it insists that misguided expansion has already, before the depression begins, caused the damage fated to follow. The theory, or a hard-core version of it, also suggests that resistance to contraction is then useless or even harmful. Depression must be dealt with early, by forestalling the unhealthy boom in which it originates.

Let us review the supposed process. Perhaps in response to political pressures for lower interest rates, the monetary authorities begin expanding bank reserves through their discount or open-market operations. Business firms find credit cheaper and more abundant. These signals suggest, incorrectly, that people have become more willing to save and so free resources for investment projects that will make greater consumption possible in the future. Accordingly, firms invest more ambitiously than before. In particular, they construct "higher-order" capital goods, goods relatively remote from the final consumer—machine-tool factories, for example, as opposed to retail stores and inventories of consumer goods. Relatively long times must elapse before resources invested in such goods ripen into goods and services for ultimate consumers. This large time element makes demands for higher-order goods relatively sensitive to interest rates. That is why credit expansion particularly stimulates their construction.

Actually—so the Austrian theory continues—the underlying realities have not changed. Resources available for long-term-oriented investment have not become more abundant. Shortages and price

---

30. Richard J. Ebeling, ed., *The Austrian Theory of the Trade Cycle and Other Essays* (New York: Center for Libertarian Studies, 1978). This book was reprinted by the Ludwig von Mises Institute, Washington, D.C., in 1983, and includes essays by von Mises (1936), Gottfried Haberler (1932), Murray N. Rothbard (1969), and F. A. Hayek (1970). It is doubtful that all of these writers in 1986 held to the views they expressed at the dates noted.

increases will reveal intensifying competition for resources among industries producing higher-order capital goods, lower-order (closer to the consumer) capital goods, and consumer goods. This becomes particularly true as workers in the artificially stimulated industries, whose contributions to ultimate consumption are far from maturity, try to spend their increased incomes on current consumption.

Price signals, especially the interest rate, have been falsified. Sooner or later appearances must bow to reality. Shortages or increased prices of resources necessary for their completion will force abandonment of some partially completed capital-construction projects, spelling at least partial waste of the resources already embodied in them. A tightening of credit, with loans no longer so readily available and interest rates no longer so artificially low as they had become, may play a part in this return to reality; for policies of expanding money and credit could not doggedly persist without threatening unlimited inflation.

Cutting back long-term-oriented investment (and even abandoning some partially complete projects) for the reasons just mentioned means laying off workers, canceling orders for machines and materials, and canceling some rentals of land and buildings. The downturn is under way. In the ensuing depression, unwise projects are liquidated or restructured and the wasteful misallocation of resources begins to be undone—but painfully.

THE APPEAL OF THE AUSTRIAN SCENARIO

Some such scenario understandably appeals to Austrian economists. They like to stress that money is not neutral. New money enters the economy through particular channels and only gradually works its effects on all sectors. Meanwhile, it exerts what the Austrians like to call "Cantillon effects."[31] The new money exerts differential effects on individual prices, including the interest rate, and individual types of economic activity. Austrian economists dislike theorizing in terms

31. Richard Cantillon, *Essai sur la Nature du Commerce en Général*, trans. Henry Higgs (London: Macmillan, for the Royal Economic Society, 1931), 158. Cantillon wrote this work in the 1720s, but it was not published until 1755.

of aggregates such as the general price level, total output, and total employment. They disaggregate. They practice "methodological individualism"; they carry their theorizing to the level of the individual business firm, worker, and consumer, investigating how the individual responds to incentives impinging on him, including changes in interest rates and other relative prices.

WHAT EVIDENCE OR ARGUMENT?

A theory's appeal on quasimethodological grounds is not the same thing, however, as evidence supporting it over its rivals. The Austrian scenario of boom and downturn is hardly the only conceivable scenario. Furthermore, it does not explain and hardly even purports to explain the ensuing depression phase. Depression is a pervasive phenomenon, with customers scarce, output reduced, and jobs lost in almost all sectors of the economy. Unlike what might be said of the boom and downturn, the depression phase can hardly be portrayed as an intersectoral struggle for productive resources exacerbated by distorted signals in interest rates and other prices. Austrian economists can explain the continuing depression only lamely, mentioning maladjustments being worked out painfully over time—unless they invoke a "secondary deflation," meaning monetary factors going beyond their own distinctive theory.

My chief objection to the Austrian theory, then, is that it is no more than a conceivable but incomplete scenario. Furthermore, it is an unnecessarily specific scenario: it envisages specific responses to specific price distortions created by the injection of new money, but it demonstrates neither the necessity nor the importance of those specific distortions to the downturn into the depression, let alone to the depression itself. Monetary disequilibrium theory, in contrast, can handle the phenomena of boom and depression with less specific suppositions; unlike the Austrian theory, it does not disregard Occam's razor.

Austrians offer little evidence for their cycle theory beyond its supposed plausibility and its coherence with their methodology. To my knowledge, the chief published exception to this statement is

Charles Wainhouse's article of 1984 (evidently derived from his unpublished New York University dissertation). Using monthly data for the United States for January 1959 through June 1981, all seasonally adjusted except interest rates, Wainhouse investigates whether (1) changes in the supplies of savings and of bank credit are independent, (2) changes in the supply of bank credit lead to changes in interest rates, (3) changes in the rate of change of bank credit lead to changes in the output of producer goods, (4) the ratio of producer-goods prices to consumer-goods prices tends to rise after bank credit starts expanding, (5) prices of producer goods closest to final consumption tend to decline relative to prices of producer goods further away from final consumption after bank credit starts expanding, and (6) consumer-goods prices rise relative to producer-goods prices at the turn from boom to recession, reversing the initial shift in relative prices.

Applying Granger causality tests and other statistical techniques to his data, Wainhouse obtains results he deems consistent with the six hypotheses mentioned. (He also states but does not test three further hypotheses associated with Austrian cycle theory.) Wainhouse does not claim to have actually validated the Austrian theory, of course, but he does suggest that his results warrant further serious study of it.[32]

Stepping back from the details, let us consider just what Wainhouse has found true, or has failed to reject, for the United States from 1959 to 1981. Expansions of money and credit do occur, do affect interest rates, do appear to affect output of producer goods, and do appear to be followed by temporary shifts in relative prices of goods far from and near to final consumption, all of which is compatible with the Austrian theory.

Wainhouse deserves congratulations for going beyond the usual Austrian recitations and looking for actual evidence. (I sometimes get the impression that Austrians recite their favorite cycle theory as a kind of elaborate password for mutual recognition and encouragement.) Wainhouse does not offer any empirical discussion, however,

32. Charles E. Wainhouse, "Empirical Evidence for Hayek's Theory of Economic Fluctuations," in *Money in Crisis*, ed. Barry N. Siegel (San Francisco: Pacific Institute for Public Policy Research, 1984), 37–71.

KEYNESIANISM AND OTHER DIVERSIONS

of the downturn and the ensuing recession or depression. He merely finds several facts consistent with Austrian theory. But innumerable facts are consistent with almost any theory—that Bach lived before Beethoven, that Hebrew is the language of Israel, and that Mars has two moons. My point is that Wainhouse does not find, and as far as I know did not look for, evidence that might discriminate between the Austrian theory and its rivals.

AUSTRIAN THEORY AND DISEQUILIBRIUM THEORY

Wainhouse's statistical results are compatible, in particular, with monetary disequilibrium theory. Most obviously, both Austrian and monetarist theories recognize that expansion and contraction of money affect credit conditions. The specific Austrian scenario is not necessary to understand why demands for capital goods, particularly of higher orders, fluctuate more widely over the cycle than demands for consumer goods and for investment goods close to final consumption. Firms invest in view of prospects for profitable sale of the consumer goods and services that will ultimately result, and investment is more susceptible to postponement or hastening than is consumption. In the short and intermediate term, then, investment can exhibit a magnification of observed or anticipated fluctuations in consumption demands. In a world of uncertainty, furthermore—uncertainty exacerbated by monetary instability—hindsight will reveal some investment projects to have been unwise, some even being abandoned before their completion. The Austrian theory is not needed to account for these facts.

Monetary disequilibrium theorists put less stress than the Austrians on shifts in the interest rate and relative prices. The reason is not that they deny such shifts.[33] The reason, rather, is that such shifts, though crucial to the distinctively Austrian scenario, are mere de-

33. For documented refutation of Austrian charges that mainstream economists deny or unduly neglect relative-price effects, see Thomas M. Humphrey, "On Nonneutral Relative Price Effects in Monetarist Thought: Some Austrian Misconceptions," Federal Reserve Bank of Richmond, *Economic Review* (May–June 1984): 13–19.

tails in the monetary disequilibrium account of the business cycle. Understandably the monetarists emphasize the centerpiece of their story—a disequilibrium relation between the nominal quantity of money and the general level of prices and wages.

Rational Expectations and Equilibrium Always

The Austrians and rational expectations theorists reject traditional monetary disequilibrium theory for different reasons. The Austrians do not mind recognizing the reality of disequilibrium and sometimes even wax scornful of equilibrium theorizing, but they favor a specific scenario of intersectoral distortions tracing to manipulations of money and credit. While belief in rational expectations ("ratex" for short, as in James W. Dean)[34] does not logically entail belief that markets always clear or that one should at least theorize as if they did, there is no denying that the two beliefs often occur together.

Austrians and ratex/equilibrium-always theorists have one thing in common, however—strong methodological influence on their substantive doctrines. This I hope to show.

The challengers of disequilibrium theory ask why stickinesses persist and contracts go unrevised, obstructing exchanges, if people can reap gains from trade by adjusting prices and wages. They find it irrational for people to delay adjustments enabling mutually advantageous transactions to proceed.[35]

Equilibrium-always theorists do not, then, see fluctuations in output and employment as reflecting changing degrees of disequilibrium. Robert Lucas recommends "*equilibrium* models of business cycles . . . in which prices and quantities are taken to be always in equilibrium" and in which "the concepts of excess demands and

34. James W. Dean, "The Dissolution of the Keynesian Consensus," *Public Interest* (1980), special issue on "The Crisis in Economic Theory," 19–34.

35. Grossman, "Was Keynes a 'Keynesian'?"; and Grossman, "The Natural-Rate Hypothesis, the Rational-Expectations Hypothesis, and the Remarkable Survival of Non-Market-Clearing Assumptions," *Carnegie-Rochester Conference Series on Public Policy* 19 (Autumn 1983): 225–46.

supplies play no observational role and are identified with no observed magnitudes."[36] Mark Willes, at the time president of the Federal Reserve Bank of Minneapolis, one of the citadels of the school, waxed enthusiastic about new developments in what he called classical economics, built on "the premises that individuals optimize and that markets clear." The school believes that "the economy is best represented by a model that includes continuous equilibrium. Equilibrium modeling. . . appears able to explain unemployment and the business cycle without discarding what we know about microeconomics. . . . It is not necessary, after the new advances in classical theory, to resort to disequilibrium models in order to account for unemployment, queues, quantity rationing, or other phenomena that accompany the business cycle."[37]

Even Barro, one of the elaborators of disequilibrium economics in the tradition of Clower and Leijonhufvud, subsequently joined in complaining that "the disequilibrium type of model . . . relies on a nontheory of price rigidities."[38]

Why does he say "nontheory"? Though perhaps not often spelled out in detail, the theory is available, as this paper has been trying to show; and if it is eclectic, so be it. Anyway, lack of a theory would not mean absence of the phenomenon. Robert Solow recalls "reading once that it is still not understood how the giraffe manages to pump an adequate blood supply all the way up to its head; but it is hard to imagine that anyone would therefore conclude that giraffes do not have long necks."[39]

Other critics of the ratex school have also interpreted its members as saying just what they do seem to be saying. They take the view, according to Kenneth Arrow, "that all unemployment is essentially voluntary." They "assert that all markets always clear." They work

36. Robert E. Lucas, Jr., "Methods and Problems in Business Cycle Theory," *Journal of Money, Credit, and Banking* 12 (November 1980), part 2, 696–715, esp. 709.

37. Mark H. Willes, " 'Rational Expectations' as a Counterrevolution," *Public Interest* (1980), special issue, 82, 90, 92, 93.

38. Robert J. Barro, "Second Thoughts on Keynesian Economics," *American Economic Review* 69 (May 1979): 58.

39. Robert M. Solow, "On Theories of Unemployment," *American Economic Review* 70 (March 1980): 7.

with "a model in which prices clear markets at every instant."[40] James Dean directs skeptical attention to "the notion that unemployment is best modeled as *voluntary.* . . . [M]ost or all of the unemployed are simply making a free and voluntary choice based on the real wage available to them."[41] An unspoken position of their school "is essentially one of perfect competition, of instantaneously clearing markets."[42] Frank Hahn finds the Lucasians, as he calls them, professing "the notion of involuntary unemployment to be beyond their comprehension and in some way meaningless. I confess that I sometimes hope that they may come to learn by personal experience what the notion is about."[43] Willem Buiter identifies "the *ad hoc* assumption of instantaneous and continuous competitive equilibrium applied so routinely to labour and commodity markets by economists of the 'New Classical School.' "[44] James Tobin reminds his readers of two crucial ingredients in the "new classical macro models": "the assumption of continuous market-clearing equilibrium and the specification of imperfections and asymmetries in the information on which economic agents act and form expectations. The two are connected in the sense that information gaps play in the new macroeconomics very much the same role that failures of prices to clear markets play in the Keynesian tradition, by which I mean the neoclassical synthesis."[45]

Instead of identifying disequilibrium for what it is, ratex theorists suggest that markets still clear as people react to distorted or misperceived prices. Producers or workers misperceive increases in the prices of their own products or labor as genuine increases in real or relative terms even when those increases merely accompany a *general* price inflation. Workers supply more labor (as by reducing their

40. Kenneth J. Arrow, "Real and Nominal Magnitudes in Economics," *Public Interest* (1980), special issue on "The Crisis in Economic Theory," 140, 148, 150.

41. Dean, "The Dissolution of the Keynesian Consensus," 28.

42. Gottfried Haberler, *The Problem of Stagflation* (Washington, D.C.: American Enterprise Institute, 1985), 23.

43. Frank Hahn, *Money and Inflation* (Cambridge: MIT Press, 1985), 105.

44. Willem Buiter, "The Macroeconomics of Dr. Pangloss: A Critical Survey of the New Classical Macroeconomics," *Economic Journal* 90 (March 1980): 41.

45. James Tobin, "Are New Classical Models Plausible Enough to Guide Policy?" *Journal of Money, Credit, and Banking* 12 (November 1980), part 2, 788.

quits or accepting new jobs after shorter searches) because they think they are being offered increased real wage rates. Such misperceptions are likely when inflation comes unexpectedly or at an unexpectedly increased rate. In the opposite case, people cut back work or output because they mistakenly perceive general price deflation as cuts specifically in the prices of their own labor or products. Even a mere slowdown in inflation can cause contraction in this way. Mistakenly thinking that their real wages are being cut, workers may quit their jobs more readily than before and voluntarily engage in lengthier job search. Producers, similarly, may mistakenly perceive a general slowdown of price inflation as declines in the real or relative prices of their own products and may cut production in response. In the sense that workers and producers are still operating "on their supply curves," equilibrium, though distorted, continues to prevail. Even this distortion would be absent if people fully expected and allowed for the underlying change in monetary policy, as self-interest would lead them to do to the extent cost-effectively possible. On this theory, fluctuations in production, employment, and price levels do not represent changes in the degree and direction of any monetary disequilibrium.[46]

The idea of rational expectations is probably useful in many of its applications, but the associated doctrine of equilibrium always is just wrong as macroeconomics. It contradicts the facts of involuntary unemployment and other failures of markets to clear. It unconvincingly challenges a doctrine that has appealed to economists for over two centuries, that fits in well with microeconomic theory, and that is well supported by narrative and statistical history.

No general rule applies in all cases about what simplifying ("unrealistic") assumptions are appropriate. All depends on the particular questions being tackled. In tackling questions about the

---

46. This paragraph alludes to the Phelps-Friedman-Lucas supply function, or Lucas supply function, or "surprise" supply function, so called by Willem Buiter (see footnote 44). See also, for example, Lucas, "Some International Evidence on Output-Inflation Trade-offs," *American Economic Review* 63 (June 1973): 326–34. For further criticism of insistence on seeing quantity changes as occurring only in response to price changes, whether interpreted correctly or incorrectly, see Dan E. Birch, Alan A. Rabin, and Leland B. Yeager, "Inflation, Output, and Employment: Some Clarifications," *Economic Inquiry* 20 (April 1982): 209–21 (reprinted in this volume).

long-run effects on prices and outputs of specified changes in wants, resources, technology, and legislation, one may legitimately neglect intervening disequilibrium to get on with the analysis. But when questions of macroeconomics are at issue—essentially, questions concerning disruptions or imperfections or delays in processes working to coordinate the plans and activities of many different people—then attention properly turns to how quickly and smoothly markets respond when disturbed, to transitional stages, and to the frictions of reality.

Of course markets tend to clear; of course people act to reap gains from trade. But how quickly and effectively? When a monetary disturbance makes price adjustments necessary, how do individual transactors know just what particular adjustments would be appropriate, and what incentives do they have to go first in making them? Such information and incentives do not come to the attention of individual transactors in some magical way, outside the market. The market has work to do. Individuals see the need for price adjustments when they meet frustration in trying to carry out desired transactions at the old prices. Echoing Christiernin, quoted earlier, Charles Schultze notes, "In a world of price and wage setters, firms and workers observe demand shocks principally in the form of changes in their own physical quantities—sales first and then output and employment. . . . [T]he same kind of initial signals—changes in the volume of sales—" is required for "a change in the general level of wages and prices" as for a microreallocation of resources.[47] Even if an exceptional individual did quickly understand the underlying disturbance and the required adjustments, he might see little advantage in adjusting his own price unless others adjusted theirs also.

Anyway, actual or incipient failure of markets to clear is necessary to convey information and incentives. When ratex theorists emphasize that people will adjust prices as necessary to reap gains from trade, they should recognize that they are theorizing about market forces and signals and processes. They have no warrant for assuming that those processes work so fast as to preclude disequilibria in the form of recessions or depressions.

47. Schultz, "Microeconomic Efficiency," 11, 13.

As Haberler has written, quoting Armen Alchian, "even 'in open, unrestricted competitive markets with rational, utility maximizing individual behavior,' substantial or, in case of a sharp decline in monetary demand (depression), 'massive' unemployment is possible. . . . The basic idea is that information about job opportunities is not a free good."[48]

John Boschen and Herschel Grossman employed both preliminary and revised data on monetary aggregates to try to distinguish between responses to anticipated or perceived and to unanticipated or unperceived components of monetary policy. They obtained results "apparently fatal to the equilibrium approach." They find the theory of macroeconomic fluctuations in an "unsatisfactory state." "[E]quilibrium theorizing does not provide an . . . explanation of macroeconomic fluctuations whose implications accord with the apparent facts. The business cycle, consequently, seems mysterious."[49] One must admire the authors' candor, yet wonder at their being mystified.

THE CURSE OF METHODOLOGY

How scholars got their ideas and why they keep urging them are irrelevant to whether those ideas are right or wrong. One should not dismiss ideas because of conjectured motives. But when people persist in an idea—such as a particular interpretation of macroeconomic phenomena—that abundant evidence and argument tell against and for which a well-supported alternative is available, that persistence itself arouses intellectual curiosity. Is persistence among leading scholars some sort of argument for an idea's validity, after all, and a sign of poor judgment on the part of those who reject it? Or is its persistence a genuine puzzle? A puzzle prompts a search for hypotheses that would explain it.

48. Haberler, *The Problem of Stagflation*, 13; and Armen Alchian, "Information Costs, Pricing, and Resource Unemployment," *Western Economic Journal* 7 (June 1969): 117.

49. John F. Boschen and Herschel I. Grossman, "Tests of Equilibrium Macroeconomics Using Contemporaneous Monetary Data," *Journal of Monetary Economics* 10 (November 1982): 329–30.

Setting forth some hunches on these questions may contribute to a dialogue among monetary disequilibrium theorists and equilibrium-always theorists. It may bear on diagnosing the current state of academic economics, including what one might call the curse of methodology. Perhaps sheer fashion has some influence on what ideas are thought acceptable.[50]

Recent writings by Donald McCloskey are helping make it respectable, or so I hope, to question methodological sermons (especially sermons that are insidious because pervasive and tacit), to pay attention to styles of argument, and to regard clarity and even effective rhetoric as virtues. Respectability should not demand one single approved style of modeling or evidence or argument.[51]

To start with a specific example of apparent methodological preconception, I suspect that the Lucas supply function and the idea that sellers are responding to prices according to their supply schedules (rather than sometimes meeting frustration in nonclearing markets) trace to an overemphasis on price signals. People respond to prices, and macroeconomists who do not want to lose contact with price theory should take those responses seriously.

So far so good. That methodological view contributes, however, to the tacit but questionable idea that producers or sellers respond to prices only—rather than also to how readily they are finding customers. That view tends to preclude seeing "positions off the curves," and positions "off" to a greater or lesser extent. Notions of pure competition lurk below the surface: the seller can sell all he wants to at the going price.

Equilibrium-always theorists seem to believe that monetary expansion, for example, and unexpected monetary expansion in particular, can have an impact on real variables only *through* price changes—unexpected and misinterpreted price changes—and not

50. In an apparent allusion to this situation, Edmund Phelps, in "Okun's Micro-Macro System: A Review Article" [on *Prices and Quantities*], *Journal of Economic Literature* 19 (September 1981): 1065, praised Okun for courage—"courage to venture a big theoretical work, in an accessible style, on urgent questions."

51. Donald N. McCloskey, "The Rhetoric of Economics," *Journal of Economic Literature* 21 (June 1983): 481-517; idem, "The Character of Argument in Modern Economics: How Muth Persuades" (Manuscript, University of Iowa, August 1983); and idem, "Economical Writing," *Economic Inquiry* 24 (April 1985): 187–222.

directly, as by giving sellers more customers. The rival monetary disequilibrium theory can readily interpret recovery from depression following expansion of the nominal quantity of money (or, alternatively, following expansion of the real quantity through wage and price cuts) as due to relief of an excess demand for money (strictly, relief of what would have been an excess demand at full employment). But a theorist unwilling to recognize disequilibrium in the first place has to attribute the expansion of output and employment as people's responses to prices along their supply curves.

More generally, the idea seems to be afoot that equilibrium modeling is the thing—the technically advanced thing—to be doing in macroeconomics. Lucas recommends his own brand of equilibrium economics by saying that it employs technical advances in modeling that simply were unavailable a few decades or even a few years earlier. The most important force in recent business-cycle theorizing, he writes, "consists of purely technical developments that enlarge our abilities to construct analogue economies. Here I would include both improvements in mathematical methods and improvements in computational capacity. . . . The historical reason for modeling price dynamics as responses to static excess demands goes no deeper than the observation that the theorists of that time did not know any other way to do it."[52]

Mark Willes notes that the rational expectations school builds on classical premises but has constructed models exhibiting business-cycle features "which the old classical theory couldn't handle. . . . It is not necessary, after the new advances in classical theory, to resort to disequilibrium models in order to account for . . . phenomena that accompany the business cycle."[53]

Also suggesting the influence of sheer commitment to a cherished theoretical tradition, Grossman writes, "The position that strict application of neoclassical maximization postulates is relevant to macroeconomic developments only in the 'long-run' may seem reasonable from an empirical standpoint, but it puts neoclassical economics in a defensive position. It suggests the possibility of a general inability of neoclassical economics to account for short-run economic phe-

52. Lucas, "Methods and Problems," 697, 708.
53. Willes, "Rational Expectations," 90, 92.

nomena." Yet, despite what Grossman seems to imply, disequilibrium is not incompatible with individuals' efforts to maximize.[54]

The idea seems to be in circulation that notions of disequilibrium betray an incomplete model. An economist who talks about disequilibrium is not really talking about failure of market mechanisms but rather, without realizing it, about his own failure as a model builder. A related interpretation views the equilibrium-always doctrine as a methodological exhortation or heuristic rule: do not cop out by speaking of disequilibrium; try to improve your model so that observed magnitudes correspond to solutions to its equations.

In mathematical models, states of affairs or patterns of economic activity are conceived of as solutions to sets of equations, as points on intersecting curves. Disequilibrium states—states represented by points off the curves, so to speak—are messy. It is methodologically unsatisfactory to allow for prices and quantities that are not at their equilibrium values but are only tending toward them at speeds specified only in *ad hoc* ways. In this connection, Lucas scorns models containing "free parameters."[55]

Similar remarks apply to treatment of disequilibrium processes, such as what happens when people try to increase or decrease their cash balances or how the decentralized but intertwining nature of wage and price determination makes for stickiness in the average level or trend of prices. Observation of and reasoning about such processes in the relatively nonmathematical manner in which they are most straightforwardly handled can be stigmatized as casual and loose, so they escape due attention.

Equilibrium-always theorists presumably know as well as anyone else that atomistic competition is and must be the exception rather than the rule in the real world, that sellers are typically not selling as much of their output or labor as they would like to sell at prevailing prices, that most prices and wages are consciously decided upon rather than determined impersonally (even though they are set with an eye on supply and demand), and that these circumstances, among others, make for or reveal price stickiness. But they do not know

54. Grossman, "The Natural-Rate Hypothesis," 240.
55. Lucas, "Methods and Problems."

243

these facts officially—not in what they consider a methodologically reputable way.

They are inclined to invoke a famous slogan, reasonable enough in certain contexts and under certain interpretations, yet much abused: Willes recites that "theories cannot be judged by the realism of their assumptions."[56] Actually, it is necessary to distinguish at least between simplifying assumptions that abstract from facts irrelevant to the question under investigation and assumptions on which the conclusions crucially depend. In critically examining Milton Friedman's position, Alan Musgrave makes enlightening distinctions between negligibility, domain, and heuristic assumptions.[57]

A related bit of methodology tending to discredit notice of unmistakable realities is ritualistic insistence that scientific propositions be testable and conceptually refutable. A supposedly empirical proposition immune to being refuted by any evidence is by that very token beyond the pale of science.

Two kinds of irrefutability, however, must be distinguished. Propositions of the disreputable kind have a *built-in* immunity to adverse evidence. Their ostensible empirical character is a sham. Instead, they convey emotions or the intention to use words in special ways or to follow particular policies. Charles Peirce gives an example: the proposition that the wafers and wine in the Mass turn into the body and blood of Christ while retaining all physical and chemical and other detectable properties of wafers and wine. Another example is the remark attributed to Father Flanagan of Boys' Town that there is no such thing as a bad boy (no matter what horrible crimes he habitually commits, he is fundamentally a good person and worthy of efforts to rehabilitate him). Still another example might be the Marxian proposition about increasing immiserization of the proletariat, with immiserization interpreted flexibly enough to accommodate any evidence.[58]

56. Willes, "Rational Expectations," 91.

57. Alan Musgrave, " 'Unreal Assumptions' in Economic Theory: The F-Twist Untwisted," *Kyklos* 34, no. 3 (1981): 377–87.

58. Charles S. Pierce, "How to Make Our Ideas Clear," in *Philosophical Writings of Pierce*, ed. Justus Buchler (New York: Dover, 1955), 30–31.

A more respectable kind of irrefutability characterizes propositions for which empirical evidence keeps pressing itself upon us every day in such abundance that only with effort can we even imagine a world where those propositions are not true. (But if it turned out that we had been deluded, propositions hinging on our delusions would be refuted after all.) Some examples are that people act purposefully, that resources are scarce in relation to people's practically limitless wants, that more than one factor of production exists and that the law of diminishing returns holds true, that money functions and is supplied and demanded differently than all other goods, that most prices and wages are not determined impersonally and flexibly in atomistic competition, and that markets sometimes do fail to clear. No one will make a scientific reputation by discovering facts like that, of course; but it hardly follows that inescapably familiar facts are by that very token unimportant and deserving of neglect.

THE APPEAL OF EQUILIBRIUM THEORIZING

It is unnecessary to spell out a precise and agreed definition of "equilibrium" to recognize that different and changed meanings of the word are in circulation. Traditionally, and loosely, equilibrium is said to prevail when the plans of different people are meshing in the sense that markets clear. Disequilibrium means discoordination. Market participants may have good reasons from their own points of view for not promptly initiating the price adjustments that would bring markets closer to clearing. Whether or not plans mesh does not hinge only on bilateral negotiations between the potential parties to individual transactions, for what appears acceptable to those parties may well depend on what other parties are agreeing on or failing to agree on for other and perhaps quite different transactions. Some transactions may be falling through because they are not attractive without adjustments to prices not under the control of the parties directly involved. (Some producers may have shut down in a depression, for example, because input prices have not fallen enough for them to cover even their variable costs at a product price low enough to attract customers.) The fact that everyone is behaving rationally from his own point of view does not mean that plans are meshing and markets clearing after all. Each individual may be making the best of the circumstances confronting him—and be in equilibrium in that narrow sense—without the aggregate of such individual positions constituting a general equilibrium for the economy.

Equilibrium-always theorists nevertheless seem to be sliding into the notion that practices making sense for the parties involved constitute an equilibrium. If, for example, advantageous but tacit contracts make prices and wages inflexible in the short run, then the apparent failure of markets to clear need not count as a departure from equilibrium. If, as mentioned above, talk of disequilibrium betrays an incomplete model, then an adequately modeled state of affairs is an equilibrium. Lucas and Thomas J. Sargent even appear to congratulate themselves on the "dramatic development" that the very meaning of the term "equilibrium" has undergone in recent years.[59] Dennis Carlton also seems to use the term "equilibrium" in pretty much the changed sense noted here.[60] Stiglitz speaks of "competitive market equilibrium [without] market clearing," "non-market-clearing equilibria," and "equilibria in which markets do not clear."[61] Sargent expresses satisfaction with "fancier" notions of equilibrium, "much more complicated" notions of market clearing, and "fancy new kinds of equilibrium models."[62] Yet destabilizing the meanings of words, subverting communication, is hardly constructive. (Compare trying to defend the Catholic interpretation of the Mass with "fancier" and "much more complicated" definitions of body and blood, ones that have undergone "dramatic development.")

Perhaps theorists who are uncomfortable with disequilibrium and who change their conceptions of equilibrium do so because they do not recognize that equilibrium is a limiting concept, a theoretical

59. Robert E. Lucas, Jr., and Thomas J. Sargent, "After Keynesian Macroeconomics," in *After the Phillips Curve: Persistence of High Inflation and High Unemployment*, ed. Lucas and Sargent (Boston: Federal Reserve Bank of Boston, 1978), 58.

60. Dennis W. Carlton, "Contracts, Price Rigidity, and Market Equilibrium," *Journal of Political Economy* 87 (October 1979), part 1, 1034–62.

61. Stiglitz, "Equilibrium in Product Markets," 342–43, 345.

62. Arjo Klamer, *Conversations With Economists* (Totowa, N.J.: Rowman & Allanheld, 1983), 67–68.

extreme case. They do not recognize that eqilibrium, like pure competition, although highly useful in theorizing as a benchmark state toward which market forces are tending, is nevertheless not actually and fully reached in the real world. They feel they must define or redefine it so they can say it exists.

Equilibrium in the sense of complete meshing of plans could not prevail outside the abstract world of pure and perfect competition or of a Walrasian (actually, *non*-Walrasian) auctioneer who somehow makes everyone behave like a price taker (and, furthermore, a world without disturbing changes in the data). Nevertheless, it still makes sense to speak of greater or lesser closeness to this limiting state. It makes sense to speak of a state of approximate equilibrium being disrupted by a change in money's supply or demand. This formulation is loose, admittedly, but as Aristotle said, "Our discussion will be adequate if it has as much clearness as the subject-matter admits of, for precision is not to be sought for alike in all discussions, any more than in all the products of the crafts."[63]

Monetary equilibrium or disequilibrium prevails according to whether or not total desired holdings of money equal the actual quantity at the existing purchasing power of the unit. The importance of the distinction does not hinge on anyone's being able to identify monetary equilibrium with precision. Despite real-world difficulties of maintaining or restoring monetary equilibrium, the sheer *concept* of equilibrium is, in one respect, beset with slighter difficulties for money than for an ordinary good or service. A specific national money, the actual medium of exchange, is more nearly homogeneous than an ordinary good or service. The individual transactor is a price taker with regard to it: he must regard its purchasing power as set beyond his control, except to the utterly trivial extent that the price he may be able to set on his own product arithmetically affects money's average purchasing power. This very fact that no one sees himself as having any appreciable influence over the value of the money unit helps explain the sluggishness of the pressures working to correct a disequilibrium value.

63. Aristotle, *Nichomachean Ethics*, in *Introduction to Aristotle*, ed. Richard McKeon (New York: Modern Library, 1947), 309. On inappropriate preoccupation with being precise, compare Karl R. Popper, *The Open Society and Its Enemies*, 2 vols. (London: Routledge & Kegan Paul, 1957), 2: 19–20, 296, 50 n.

Another hunch about the appeal of equilibrium always concerns the apparent notion—reflected in the very title of Barro's "Second Thoughts on Keynesian Economics"—that theories involving price and wage stickiness are Keynesian and therefore, to advanced thinkers, outmoded and wrong.[64] Clower and Leijonhufvud offered their disequilibrium theories as interpretations of Keynes.[65] Arrow casually refers to "disequilibrium theorists . . . stemming from Keynes."[66] Stanley Fischer refers just as casually to "Keynesian disequilibrium analysis."[67] Tobin refers to "the Keynesian message" as dealing with disequilibrium and sluggishness of adjustment.[68] Hahn notes "the present theoretical disillusionment with Keynes" (which, he conjectures, will be reversed).[69] An admirably realistic discussion of nominal wage stickiness is presented by Schultze, generally regarded as a prominent Keynesian.[70]

Actually, as shown earlier, theories of stickiness and monetary disequilibrium far antedate Keynes; and it is ironic to associate those theories with him, especially since he did more than perhaps any other economist to divert attention from them. Economists have been playing musical chairs in recent years, but with doctrines and labels instead of chairs. (Leijonhufvud made some such observation in a witty talk in November 1983.) The abandonment of disequilibrium macroeconomics by players shifting into the ratex/equilibrium-always camp left a partial void into which former Keynesians could move, gracefully discarding their discredited doctrine while keeping their old label. As a result, the label "Keynesian" is now often applied both to non-Keynesian monetary-disequilibrium theorists and to the (former) Keynesians who have recently joined them. Observers should be more careful with doctrinal history and labels.

64. Barro, "Second Thoughts."

65. Clower, "The Keynesian Revolution."

66. Arrow, "Real and Nominal Magnitudes," 149.

67. Stanley Fischer, ed., *Rational Expectations and Economic Policy* (Chicago: University of Chicago Press, for the National Bureau of Economic Research, 1980), 223.

68. Tobin, "Are New Classical Models Plausible?" 789.

69. Frank H. Hahn, "General Equilibrium Theory," *Public Interest* (1980), special issue "The Crisis in Economic Theory," 137.

70. Schultze, "Microeconomic Efficiency."

Mention of theories thought to be "outmoded" prompts a more general remark. Not novelty, not fashion, not even methodological fashion or technical virtuosity or suitability for academic gamesmanship should be the criterion of accepting a theory. Being venerable does not necessarily prove a theory wrong. The contrary is more plausible when human behavior is the subject matter. If observations in widely separated times and places have led many different writers to broadly the same theory, such as monetary disequilibrium theory, that fact counts *something* in its favor. The criterion should be explanatory power and conformity to fact and logic.

A final conjecture about the appeal of equilibrium always is that some theorists are sliding from (warranted) skepticism about activist government policies into (unwarranted) attribution of near perfection to markets.[71] Yet no human institution is perfect. The imperfection of one, the state, does not imply the perfection of another, the market. It does not imply the capacity of the market to cope quickly and painlessly even with severe shocks.

PROSPECTS FOR THEORY AND POLICY

I want to guard against being misunderstood. I am far from condemning the ratex/equilibrium-always school root and branch. It offers improvements in some strands of theory, it makes sound criticisms of Keynesianism as it used to be widely taught and practiced, and it draws sensible policy implications.[72] But those improvements and criticisms and implications can be obtained in a way that better accords with straightforward observation and theory and better maintains continuity with earlier research achievements.

Monetary disequilibrium theory stands up well in comparison with both ratex/equilibrium-always theory and Austrian business-cycle theory. Both those rivals are suffused with methodological preconceptions. (The Austrians deserve credit, however, for facing up

71. For example, Barro, "Second Thoughts," 55.

72. For example, Robert E. Lucas, Jr., "Tobin and Monetarism: A Review Article," *Journal of Economic Literature* 19 (June 1981): 558–67.

to facts of reality that many neoclassicals apparently regard, if they regard them at all, as embarrassing "imperfections.")

Frank Hahn and James Dean may well be right—Hahn in expecting reversal of disillusionment with the disequilibrium approach, Dean in judging that "macroeconomic theory's future probably lies with the Evolutionaries" (which is his term for disequilibrium theorists).[73]

This is not to say that all issues are now settled and that monetary disequilibrium theory should henceforth be held as dogma. Like all theories about empirical reality, it is open to being modified or abandoned in the light of new evidence and argument and newly devised alternatives. I conjecture, though, that it will be fruitful to develop the theory further along lines that recognize how the forces tending spontaneously to restore a disturbed monetary equilibrium are diffused weakly over all sectors of the economy because the medium of exchange lacks a definite market and price of its own on which the pressures of imbalance between supply and demand come to a focus. Quite rationally from their own points of view, individuals behave in ways that add up, macroeconomically, to price and wage stickiness (and, in inflation or stagflation, to persistence of trends). Well-warranted skepticism about activist macroeconomic policies does not justify optimism about the capacity of markets to cope rapidly with monetary disturbances.

The reality and the severe consequences of monetary disequilibrium recommend policies to forestall it. Perhaps the old monetarist rule of steady monetary growth still would be adequate for keeping the supply of money approximately matched to the growing demand. On the other hand, perhaps prolonged disregard of monetarist advice has created complications that the steady-growth rule now could not cope with. Inflation-boosted nominal interest rates interacting with interest ceilings and reserve requirements have induced such a series of financial innovations that we no longer can be confident of how to define money, of whether the Federal Reserve could adequately manipulate its quantity, and of whether the demand-for-money function will remain stable.

73. Hahn, "General Equilibrium Theory," 37; Dean, "The Dissolution of the Keynesian Consensus," 32.

The time has come to consider radically different alternatives. (The contrasts they afford with our existing system can be instructive, even if none of them is ever implemented.) One radical alternative is a version of Irving Fisher's compensated dollar (1920). Two-way convertibility between the dollar and the variable physical amount of gold always equal in actual market value to the bundle of goods and services defining a comprehensive price index would amount to indirect convertibility between money and the bundle. Under that arrangement, the whole price level would no longer have to rise or fall—painfully bucking frictions—to correct monetary disequilibrium; and the actual quantity of money would become automatically responsive to the demand for it. A different reform, the one proposed by Robert L. Greenfield and Yeager, would get the government out of the money business.[74] The unit of account, divorced from the medium of exchange, would be defined as the value of a bundle of many goods. As under Fisher's plan, the price level would be spared pressures tending, sluggishly, to change it. The supply of media of exchange would be left to private banks and investment funds, which would respond to demands for them. These arrangements would preclude monetary disequilibrium as we have known it.

74. Robert L. Greenfield and Leland B. Yeager, "A Laissez-Faire Approach to Monetary Stability," *Journal of Money, Credit, and Banking* 15 (August 1983): 302–15 (reprinted in this volume).

Injection Effects and Monetary Intermediation

Some economists, notably members of the modern "Austrian" school, worry that expansion of the money supply can exert harmful "injection effects" even when it merely satisfies an increased demand for real money holdings accompanying real economic growth and when the general price level would otherwise decline. Their view fails to recognize how the entire monetary system can function as a financial intermediary and how monetary expansion working to stabilize the price level in a growth context, far from emitting false signals about the availability of resources, can facilitate the transfer of resources released by savers into the control of entrepreneurs who will employ them for investment projects. For economists who might still worry about manipulation of the money supply, however, I shall mention how a radically reformed monetary system might achieve a stable price level without such manipulation.

INJECTION EFFECTS AND THE BUSINESS CYCLE

Injection effects, in the broadest sense, can hardly be doubted: monetary expansion cannot leave all real quantities and all relative prices the same as they would otherwise have been. New money enters the economy in particular ways and has differential impacts. The idea traces at least as far back as Richard Cantillon, hence the term "Cantillon effects."[1] The idea is not refuted by a pure-quantity theory,

Printed with permission of the author.

1. Richard Cantillon, *Essai sur la Nature du Commerce en Général*, trans. Henry Higgs (1755; reprint, London: Macmillan, for the Royal Economic Society, 1931), particularly 158ff.

neutral-money result in a model like Don Patinkin's,[2] for the proposition about injection effects refers to processes of transition in the real world and not to a static comparison of long-run equilibria somehow already achieved and differing only in nominal quantities of fiat money.

Worry over injection effects is central to the "Austrian" theory of the business cycle. That theory blames recession or depression on a preceding excessive expansion of money and credit. If the monetary authorities try to reduce interest rates by expanding bank reserves, banks offer cheaper and more abundant loans. These signals suggest (even if incorrectly) that people have become more willing to save and so to free resources for investment projects. Business firms respond by borrowing and investing more ambitiously than before, especially in constructing "higher-order" capital goods. The relatively long times required for such projects to ripen into final consumer goods and services make demands for higher-order goods relatively sensitive to interest rates. That is why the cheap-money policy particularly stimulates their construction.

Actually, the theory continues, resources available for long-term-oriented investment have not become more abundant. Intensified competition for resources to produce high-order capital goods and capital goods closer to the consumer eventually shows up in shortages and price increases. Demands for consumer goods enter this competition as workers in the artificially stimulated industries, whose contributions to ultimate consumption are far from maturity, try to spend their increased incomes.

The initial falsification of market signals is now giving way to reality. Shortages or increased prices of required resources force abandonment of some partially completed capital-construction projects, spelling at least partial waste of the resources already embodied in them. A tightening of credit, with loans no longer artificially abundant and cheap, may play a part in this return to reality; for expansion of money and credit could not persist without threatening unlimited inflation.

2. Don Patinkin, *Money, Interest, and Prices* (New York: Harper & Row, 1965).

Forced cutbacks of investment entail reduced demands for labor, materials, and other productive factors. In the ensuing depression, unwise projects are liquidated or restructured and the wasteful misallocation of resources begins to be undone—but painfully. By now, resistance to this curative process would be worse than useless, at least in a hard-core version of the theory. The artificial boom should have been avoided in the first place.

Neutrality of changes in the quantity of money is unbelievable, of course, not only as long-run comparative statics but especially as short-run dynamics. Harmful injection effects, especially of inflationary monetary expansion, are historically familiar. Monetary expansion has often been unsteady and reversible enough to cause business fluctuations in the manner described by monetary-disequilibrium theory. Inflation has sometimes been "imported" through efforts to keep the domestic currency pegged on the foreign-exchange market at too low a level. Excessive monetary expansion has often been symptomatic of more deep-seated disorders, such as an irresponsible political process.

Theoretical and historical remarks about money's unavoidable nonneutrality constitute no evidence, however, about the nature and importance of the more specific injection effects routinely alleged. Missing from the entire Austrian literature is any systematically presented evidence that those effects are harmful and important and that the business cycle could be avoided by, for example, returning to the gold standard (to mention one familiar recommendation).

It is true that Charles Wainhouse, in an almost unique contribution, has examined statistics that might bear on Austrian cycle theory.[3] His results, deriving from United States data from 1959 to 1981, carry little weight, however, as evidence.[4] In particular, they do not discriminate between the Austrian theory and monetary-disequilibrium theory ("monetarism"). That rival theory not only

---

3. Charles E. Wainhouse, "Empirical Evidence for Hayek's Theory of Economic Fluctuations," in *Money in Crisis*, ed. Barry N. Siegel (San Francisco: Pacific Institute for Public Policy Research, 1984), 37–71.

4. See Leland B. Yeager, "The Significance of Monetary Disequilibrium," *Cato Journal* 6 (Fall 1986): 381–82 (reprinted in this volume).

accords well with the body of economic theory but also finds ample support in the historical and statistical records of diverse times and places.

It is common in the Austrian literature to refer to the United States in the 1920s as illustrating injection effects.[5] The period was one of "inflation," even though the general price level was stable or even gently sagging. In the absence of supposedly excessive monetary expansion, rapid productivity growth would have made the price level fall. The money growth that staved off this price decline caused the distortions that eventually brought on the Great Depression of the 1930s. Murray N. Rothbard decorates this interpretation of the period with many references to persons, ideas, policies, and events. (In places he verges on what I call the Alan Reynolds style of argument: Overwhelm your reader with facts, figures, names, and dates in hopes that he will be so impressed with your profound and wide-ranging scholarship as not to notice the irrelevance of this material to the point at issue.)

Now, innumerable facts are *consistent* with any scientific theory or historical interpretation. Missing from Rothbard's book is systematically mustered evidence, shown to be relevant, that supports his interpretation over rival interpretations. He asserts but does not show or even really argue that monetary expansion, in preventing price deflation, caused the Great Depression. Actually, the United States sank into deep depression *after* a monetary policy targeted on stabilizing the price level had been *abandoned*—if, indeed, such a policy had ever been pursued with any degree of resoluteness in the first place.

INJECTION EFFECTS OF
PRICE-LEVEL STABILIZATION

It is unnecessary to review the usual arguments in favor of a unit of account of stable purchasing power.[6] Here I am more concerned with possible counterarguments. What theory might possibly sup-

5. See, for example, Murray N. Rothbard, *America's Great Depression* (Kansas City: Sheed & Ward, 1975).

6. For a sample of such arguments, see Knut Wicksell, "Penningvárdets stad-

port assertions like Rothbard's? Just what distortions result from injection of new money to keep the price level from sagging? In particular, how does harm result from a monetary policy that resists "real" tendencies toward a decline of the price level by accommodating the growing demand for nominal cash balances associated with growth in population, productivity, and real economic activity?

Critics typically take it for granted that pursuing price-level stability means centralized manipulation of the quantity of government fiat money. Actually, on the contrary, a private-enterprise monetary system that would "spontaneously" accommodate the quantity of means of payment to demands for them at an approximately stable price level is conceivable and even feasible (as briefly explained in a later section). First, though, let us consider centralized management of a fiat money.

Even in the context of productivity improvements or general economic growth, supposedly, monetary expansion to resist a general price decline would itself disturb market equilibrium. Some such effect was apparently the reason why F. A. Hayek, in early publications, was skeptical of stabilization policy. Keeping prices constant despite increased productivity requires banks to expand money and credit by lowering their interest rates. The loan rate that might keep prices from falling is likely to initiate a cumulative and unsustainable investment boom; and the increase in the loan rate that might stop it is likely to reverse it into a downturn, which would require an interest-rate cut before the downturn gains momentum. Hence, an interest-rate policy intended to stabilize the price level would actually entail oscillations, These might spawn a growing assortment of unfinished and abandoned capital processes, and the waste involved might even overshadow the initial rise in productivity.[7]

---

gande, ett medel att förebygga kriser," *Ekonomisk Tidskrift* 10 (1908): 207–14; Lloyd W. Mints, *Monetary Policy for a Competitive Society* (New York: McGraw-Hill, 1950); and W. Lee Hoskins, "Breaking the Inflation-Recession Cycle," Federal Reserve Bank of Cleveland, *Economic Commentary* 15 (October 1989).

7. Friedrich A. Hayek, *Prices and Production* (London: 1931; reprint, New York: Kelley, 1967), lecture 4; Carl G. Uhr, *Economic Doctrines of Knut Wicksell* (Berkeley: University of California Press, 1962), 283.

The most worrisome point about price-stabilizing monetary injections, apparently, is that the expansion of loans and investments whereby new money was put into circulation would artificially lower interest rates, with the consequences described by the Austrian theory of the business cycle.

INJECTION AND INTERMEDIATION

Yet nothing so sinister follows from merely satisfying, and at the existing price level, what would otherwise have been an excess demand for money. Suppose that people in the aggregate are trying to build up their cash balances to accomplish an increased real volume of transactions entailed either by population growth or a rise in productivity. Their very attempts to increase their holdings mean that people want to spend less money than they are currently taking in. They are refraining from buying all the goods and services that their current revenues could buy; they are relinquishing or postponing command over resources. If, now, the money and banking system expands the volume of banknotes and deposits through expanding the volume of its loans to business firms, it is acting as a kind of super financial intermediary. The public, in acquiring new money, is relinquishing command over resources; and the money and banking system, in expanding its loans, is transferring command over these relinquished resources to the borrowers. Money itself is an "indirect security" in the process of financial intermediation. The intermediary institutions acquire "primary securities" issued by the ultimate borrowers or "deficit units" (such as promissory notes signed by business firms borrowing for investment purposes) and issue their own securities, namely banknotes and deposits, to the ultimate lenders or "surplus units," namely, the money accumulators.[8]

8. The concepts and terminology used here come from John G. Gurley and Edward S. Shaw, *Money in a Theory of Finance* (Washington, D.C.: Brookings Institution, 1960). The role of the monetary system as a financial intermediary in the process of economic development is also considered in Ronald I. McKinnon, *Money and Capital in Economic Development* (Washington, D.C.: Brookings Institution, 1973); McKinnon, "Money, Growth, and the Propensity to Save," in *Trade, Stability, and Macroeconomics*, ed. George Horwich and Paul Samuelson (New York: Academic Press,

In the situation described, the monetary system is *not* counterfeiting the availability of resources released by saving; it is *not* falsifying interest-rate signals in the manner envisaged by Austrian business-cycle theory. People building up their cash balances really are relinquishing current command over some of the resources to which their current revenues entitled them, and the money and banking institutions are accomplishing intermediation that transfers that command over resources to borrowers who will employ it for their own purposes, including productive investment.

The standard list of the functions and virtues of financial intermediation is relevant. If the money and banking system did not accommodate the increased demand for money by nominal expansion, then the relinquished command over resources would have to be transferred in some other way—or the relinquishment would fail in the first place. What this other method of transfer might be, and how satisfactory or unsatisfactory, is considered below. What deserves emphasis, meanwhile, is that nominal expansion to accommodate growth in the demand for money need not falsify market signals in some systematically harmful way.

Up to now, we have been considering an increased demand for real cash balances in the context of economic growth. Money accumulators have been spending less than their current revenues and thereby relinquishing current command over resources. What happens, however, if the strengthened demand for money, instead of being expressed in an underspending of revenues, represents a mere intensification of liquidity preference? What if people desire to shift out of holding securities into holding more money without changing their overall saving behavior?[9] Although people are not demanding more financial assets in total—although they are not in that sense expressing an intensified propensity to save—they are in effect de-

---

1974), 487–502, reprinted in *Modern Macroeconomics*, ed. P. G. Korliras and R. S. Thorn (New York: Harper & Row, 1979), 404–13; and Edward S. Shaw, *Financial Deepening in Economic Development* (New York: Oxford University Press, 1973). The literature is reviewed in Maxwell J. Fry, *Money, Interest, and Banking in Economic Development* (Baltimore: Johns Hopkins University Press, 1988).

9. This is the case of an increase in Cambridge *k*, a decline in velocity, precisely the case in which George Selgin, if I understand his argument, would welcome an accommodating increase in the quantity of money. See Selgin, *A Theory of Free Banking* (Totowa, N.J.: Rowman & Littlefield, 1988), chaps. 5 and 6.

manding more intermediation services. In wanting to hold fewer securities and more money, they are implicitly desiring that intermediary institutions take over the securities and provide the money. People's reduced desire to hold securities tends to depress their prices—raise their interest and dividend yields—while their increased demand for money tends to reduce the rate paid on interest-bearing forms of it. By hypothesis, people have become no less willing than before to set free real resources by holding financial assets. Why shouldn't financial intermediaries accommodate what is merely a change in people's preferences between financial assets?

INTERMEDIATION UNDER LAISSEZ-FAIRE

So far I have assumed a money and banking system of our present type, including a central bank that must provide more base-money reserves if ordinary banks are to expand their balance sheets. Intermediation could be accomplished more nearly "automatically" in a system lacking any base money, any government money at all, and any central bank. Robert Greenfield and I call it the "BFH system" to give Fischer Black, Eugene Fama, and Robert Hall credit for ideas borrowed.[10] The unit of account, instead of being a unit of government fiat money or of some single commodity, would be defined by a bundle of goods and services comprehensive enough to have a nearly stable value relative to goods and services in general.

Laissez-faire would allow full scope to innovative financial intermediation. Financial institutions would in effect repackage investment portfolios into convenient media of exchange. Some holdings in these institutions would presumably be dividend-yielding mutual fund equity shares; others would be accounts denominated in the bundle-defined unit of account and bearing interest at competitive rates. In either case, people would stipulate prices and payments and write checks on these holdings in the single, precisely defined, stable unit, *not* in heterogeneous goods and securities.

10. See Greenfield and Yeager, "A Laissez-Faire Approach to Monetary Stability," *Journal of Money, Credit, and Banking* 15 (August 1983): 302–15 (reprinted in this volume).

Checks drawn on and deposits in these institutions, as well as banknotes (and coins) issued by them, would be redeemable, but not directly in bundles of the actual goods and services defining the unit of account, for that would be too awkward for all concerned. Competition would lead institutions to redeem their banknotes and deposits indirectly (and checks, when presenters so desired) in whatever quantities of notes of rival institutions or quantities of agreed redemption media equaled in total market value as many standard commodity bundles as the numbers of units of account denominating the obligations being redeemed. (The redemption media might be agreed securities or possibly gold.)

For convenience, most such redemptions would take place not directly over banks' counters but rather through the operations of clearinghouses, where member institutions would settle net balances due on checks and banknotes presented for settlement. Members would transfer redemption media actually worth as many commodity bundles as the unit-of-account sizes of the balances due. Professionals would make and implement the required calculations every business day, and the ordinary person would no more need to know just what determined the purchasing power of the unit of account than he needs to know what determines the dollar's purchasing power nowadays.

Routine settlements at the clearinghouse would discipline each institution against trying to put more of its monetary liabilities into circulation than the public was willing to hold. Routine settlements would also provide part of the scope for arbitrage that would keep the commodity definition of the unit of account operational.

With the unit no longer defined by government fiat money or any other particular medium of exchange, its value would be established by its commodity definition and by redeemability of instruments denominated in it, not by regulation of any quantity. Quantities of media of exchange would be constrained on the demand side in much the way that operates for mutual fund shares in the United States nowadays, that operated for near moneys until the recent blurring of the distinction between them and demand deposits, and that operates for money itself in a single small country whose monetary unit has a purchasing power dictated by its link to an international gold standard. The sizes of the asset sides and the liability and equity sides of institutions' balance sheets would be influenced and reconciled largely by market-determined interest and yield rates received on the institutions' loans and investments and paid to their depositors and shareholders. The quantity of banknotes and of checkable deposits and mutual fund shares would be determined by the quantity the public desired to hold at the price level corresponding to the definition of the unit of account.

Worry about repeating myself precludes fully explaining the BFH system. I want to warn, however, against a misunderstanding. Ideas applicable to our current system of fiat money, whose unit defines the unit of account, do not straightforwardly carry over to BFH. Under our current system, supply-side expansion of the nominal quantity of money (typically caused or supported by expansion of base money) initiates a process whereby the quantity demanded increases also. Expansion of money beyond the amount the public would otherwise be willing to hold raises the price level, and people wind up holding an increased number of the shrunken money units. Things would be quite different with a unit whose size is defined in goods and services and without reference to any medium of exchange.

The intermediation aspects of the BFH system are instructive. When people are trying to acquire additional holdings of the only kinds of money that exist—bank-issued notes (and coins) and checkable deposits and mutual funds—they are thereby enabling financial institutions to expand their balance sheets, including their loan and investment portfolios. Demands for additional "money" thereby get intermediated into additional supplies of "credit." And this intermediation is appropriate. It does not counterfeit or misrepresent the availability of resources. On the contrary, as people try to build up their holdings of money issued by the financial intermediaries, they thereby forgo current command over resources that they could have exercised; and the intermediaries help route this relinquished command over resources to business (and other) borrowers who do desire to exercise it currently. The intermediaries are repackaging the "primary" securities issued by the ultimate borrowers into the money-like forms desired by the savers.

The BFH system has other advantages as well. It avoids imbalance between the demand for and supply of money and the macroeconomic consequences of that imbalance. It provides the monetary saturation or full liquidity whose absence Milton Friedman regretted. In his 1969 article, "The Optimum Quantity of Money," Friedman worries that the opportunity cost of holding cash balances, the forgone interest, causes waste of resources in tight cash-balance management.[11] Such economizing on cash is wasteful because additional real balances would be nearly costless from the social point of view. The BFH system would nearly abolish the privately perceived opportunity cost of holding them, because competition would prod issuers of checkable deposits and investment accounts to pay interest and dividends at full competitive rates. The system would also avoid certain discouragements to real investment conceived of by Maurice Allais and described in the next section.

Let us return to the case of a shift in the public's preferences from holding securities to holding money. Under the BFH system, the resulting increase in the spread between yields earned on loan and investment portfolios and rates paid on checkable deposits motivates the financial intermediaries to accommodate the desires of the public by themselves holding more securities and providing more money. As in the case of accommodating an increased demand for money associated with economic growth, the intermediary institutions are not misrepresenting the availability of resources or exerting adverse injection effects. On the contrary, they are helping give effect to the desires of the public.

Essentially the same sort of intermediation could be performed by a money and banking system of our current type; it would adjust the actual quantity of money to the quantity of holdings desired at a stable price level. The difference is that such performance by our existing system presupposes centralized management with improbable degrees of cleverness and of freedom from political pressures and bureaucratic motivations.

11. Milton Friedman, "The Optimum Quantity of Money," in Friedman, *The Optimum Quantity of Money and Other Essays* (Chicago: Aldine, 1969).

263

SUPPLYING ADDITIONAL REAL MONEY
THROUGH PRICE-LEVEL DEFLATION

Economic growth raises the demand for real money holdings. Austrian economists, worrying over injection effects, are inclined to rule out meeting that demand by an accommodating nominal expansion. They would prefer to let the price level fall, at least when growth traces to technological progress that cheapens goods in some supposed real sense. An Austrian supporter of the gold standard presumably sees gold not as an ideal regulator of the money supply but as a compromise desirable on partly political grounds. An incipient price-level deflation tends to increase the profitability of producing gold and shifting gold into monetary use, which poses some resistance to the supposedly healthy decline of prices. (F. A. Hayek regretted this resistance in an article of 1928. He had changed his mind by the time of his 1943 article, in which he regretted that the tendency of the gold standard to adjust the money supply *appropriately* for price-level stability was as weak as it was.)[12]

Yet letting additional real money get supplied through price-level deflation may impair the intermediary function of the monetary system and so impair the allocation of resources as savers and investors (and consumers) desire. In 1947 Maurice Allais worried that the availability of money to hold tends to divert people's propensity to save and accumulate wealth away from the construction of capital goods. (James Tobin had similar ideas in 1965.) This worry applies most straightforwardly to money not associated with financial intermediation, such as gold money or government fiat money of fixed nominal quantity whose real quantity can increase only through price-level deflation, or bank money backed 100 percent by gold or fiat money.[13]

12. F. A. Hayek, "Das intertemporal Gleichgewichtssystem der Preise und die Bewegungen des 'Geldwertes,' " *Weltwirtschaftliches Archiv* (1928), no. 2, 33–76; English trans.: "Intertemporal Price Equilibrium and Movements in the Value of Money," in idem, *Money, Capital, and Fluctuations: Early Essays* (London: Routledge & Kegan Paul, 1984), chap. 4; and idem, "A Commodity Reserve Currency," *Economic Journal* 53 (June–September 1943): 176–84.

13. Maurice Allais, *Économie et Intérêt*, 2 vols. (Paris: Imprimerie Nationale, 1947), 1:300–70, and 2:540–90; and James Tobin, "Money and Economic Growth,"

Allais's point becomes clearer through comparison with a more familiar idea: the demand for collectibles as a hedge in times of inflation represents some diversion of people's propensity to save and accumulate wealth away from construction of capital goods or from the purchase of securities issued to finance capital construction. Bidding for collectibles (antiques, coins, and so forth) raises their prices. Their increased value—not merely nominal value but value relative to other goods and services—represents an increase in wealth for individual holders and helps satisfy their propensities to save and hold wealth. Yet the increased values of collectibles do not represent any increase in real wealth from the social point of view. The same point holds for increases in the value of land. (Allais explicitly mentioned land as well as money in his argument about unproductive diversion of the willingness to save; Maxwell J. Fry also recognized the point.)[14] The total market value of wealth, including the value of land and collectibles, appears with positive sign as an argument in the economy's consumption function and with negative sign in its saving function. Other things being equal, the larger this wealth term is, the larger is the volume of consumption out of a given real income and the smaller the volume of resources released by saving for real investment. The more people satisfy their desires to hold savings by holding wealth of a privately genuine but socially spurious kind, such as the bid-up value of collectibles and land, the less they satisfy their desires for savings by holding capital goods (or securities that are a counterpart of capital goods).

Similarly, gains in the purchasing power of gold money or fiat money when strengthened demands for cash balances reduce the price level represent gains in wealth from the private point of view but not so much from the social point of view. Real balances of such money, like other privately held wealth, figure positively in the consumption function and negatively in the saving function; and their growth through price-level deflation makes saving smaller than it would otherwise be. (Compare the theory of how the Pigou or real-balance effect works to hold down saving in a context where worries

---

Econometrica 33 (1965): 671–84, reprinted in *Modern Macroeconomics*, ed. P. G. Korliras and R. S. Thorn (New York: Harper & Row, 1979), 359–69.

14. Fry, *Money, Interest, and Banking*, 17.

center on possible oversaving.) In deterring saving, socially spurious monetary wealth makes real capital formation, and purchases of securities issued to finance it, smaller than they would otherwise be.

It is not clear that this effect is quantitatively important. Relative to the volumes of saving and investment and financial intermediation routinely accomplished anyway, the volumes that might be accommodated by growth of the nominal money supply or be frustrated by its constancy are presumably small. What bears on the issue of price-level stabilization is a qualitative comparison between behavior of the nominal money supply that would and behavior that would not accommodate demands for money holdings at a stable price level in the context of real economic growth. A monetary system accommodating real growth with nominal expansion intermediates growing demands for real money balances into demands for securities and ultimately into real capital formation; but the alternative, deflationary, method of providing real balances impedes that intermediation. Furthermore, deflation actually rewards the holding of money and so strengthens the demand for it.

Mentioning—not endorsing—Allais's policy recommendation will help clinch an understanding of his analysis. He suggested either stamped money or a policy of chronic mild price inflation to discourage money holding and divert propensities to save and accumulate into socially more productive directions. He even suggested splitting the unit of account and medium of exchange. The "franc," the unit of account, would be defined so as to have a stable value. The "circul," or medium of exchange, would continuously depreciate against the stable franc, discouraging holdings of circul-denominated banknotes and deposits. (Use of the circul as unit of account would be "formellement interdit," or flatly forbidden.) Of course, the case for an inflationary policy is far from conclusive.

All sorts of conditions affect the interrelations under discussion here, including the stage of economic and financial development, the rate of technological progress, and the particular characteristics of the production functions and utility functions in which real cash balances might appear as arguments. Still, a general point remains: price-stabilizing monetary growth can be healthy on the basis of plausible value judgments, while letting price deflation occur instead can impede intermediation, capital formation, and growth. These impediments, along with other consequences, count as injection effects of a particular method of increasing the real money stock.

The benefits that Allais hoped for from a depreciating medium of exchange could better be achieved, and with less or no adverse side effects, by the BFH system of free banking sketched out above. (It would meet both the Allais-Tobin worry about too much indulgence in liquidity preference and Friedman's worry about too little indulgence in it.) These benefits of intermediation could also be achieved by a government monetary system cleverly managed to link credit expansion with accommodation of a growing demand for money at a stable price level. Allais himself recognized that creation of new money in ways that tended to favor real investment, as through credit expansion for that purpose, could more or less neutralize the anti-capital-formation effect that he worried about.

It is instructive to consider two opposite extreme cases. (1) Money consists exclusively of a fixed quantity of gold or of a fixed nominal stock of government fiat money. Growth in its real value occurs only through price-level deflation and corresponds to no financial intermediation in any ordinary sense. The propensity to save and accumulate wealth is partially diverted from real capital formation into the accumulation of real money balances. (2) Rapid monetary expansion and price inflation prod people to keep their real balances extremely small. Their services as a factor of production are largely lost; the inefficiencies of getting along on small real cash balances consume resources. Total saving is even discouraged (a) by the unattractiveness of saving through accumulation of money and (b) by disruptions to economic calculation and asset markets by inflation itself, especially unsteady inflation. (If inflation and disrupted asset markets make providing for the future difficult and risky—as illustrated by resort to exotic inflation hedges—why not live for today?) Because the monetary system is so shrunken in real size, little financial intermediation can occur through it. Extreme inflation even yields the government less real revenue than it might reap by inflating at a more moderate rate.

Some situation intermediate between the investment-impairing extremes of case 1 and case 2 would take better advantage of the potentialities of the monetary system as an intermediary. Yet no "optimum" can be specified precisely. One reason is that at least two dimensions are involved: (a) the rates of nominal money growth and of price deflation or inflation, and (b) the degree to which money's "outside" character, on the one hand, or "inside" character, on the other hand, hampers or facilitates monetary intermediation (and here bank reserve ratios are relevant). (The outside/inside distinction is familiar from John Gurley and Edward Shaw.[15] Under the BFH system, money would be inside money to the fullest extent.)

One cannot prove, in particular, that the ideal rate of nominal money growth—or the ideal choice of a BFH unit of account—is the one that just keeps the price level stable. However, stability does have the appeal and the potential credibility of a Schelling point (comparable to the main information booth in Grand Central Station for persons who had agreed to meet in New York City but had neglected to specify exactly where); there is something special about a *zero* rate of price change.

My argument does not presuppose any precise notion of monetary optimum. As for injection effects, even the price-deflation method of real money growth itself unavoidably exerts them. Money simply cannot be neutral, as Austrian economists should be the first to realize. The operational question is what method of real money growth has the least objectionable or most desirable effects on the whole. It is necessary to compare and choose; the issue cannot be settled by reciting the supposed harmful consequences of one particular method only. The method of accommodating a growing demand for money by nominal expansion at a stable price level has the advantage of helping to accomplish financial intermediation and make saving available for capital formation, whereas the deflationary method somewhat impedes this intermediation and this mobilization of saving. (More familiar difficulties with the deflationary method, including the fact that it amounts to "doing things the hard way" in the face of price and wage stickiness—stickiness that, by the way, is eminently reasonable from private points of view—those other difficulties require no discussion here.)

15. *Money in a Theory of Finance.*

FURTHER QUESTIONS ABOUT
STABLE-VALUED MONEY

Instead of exploring all the pros and cons of a stable money unit, I have focused on injection effects as a supposed disadvantage of such a criterion or policy. In realistic circumstances, nominal money expansion to accommodate a growing demand for money does not falsify interest-rate and price signals and does not counterfeit the availability of resources for investment purposes. On the contrary, people's efforts to accumulate additional money holdings represent saving; that is, the freeing of resources from current consumption for more future-oriented purposes. In such circumstances, monetary expansion helps accomplish financial intermediation and give effect to the desires both of savers accumulating money and of investors. Price-level-stabilizing monetary expansion would occur "automatically" under the BFH system, but in principle it could also be accomplished by clever (unrealistically clever) management of government fiat money. The alternative—deflationary—method of accommodating growth in the demand for real money holdings has disadvantages of its own. These include interference with the intermediation necessary for meshing the plans of money accumulators and investors.

Critics of stabilizing money's purchasing power sometimes maintain that while influences on the price level coming from the side of money should be avoided, influences from the side of goods should be allowed their full natural scope. If, for example, increases in productivity expand the aggregate supply of goods, a decline in their prices is the natural response. Yet this distinction bears little weight. Growth over time in income and wealth and in the physical quantities of goods and services to be traded operates as much on the money side, expanding the demand for real cash balances, as it operates on the goods side.

I wonder whether notions about how the "real" cheapening of goods should be reflected in their money prices do not rest on some deep-seated money illusion, some inchoate belief that money has a value of its own distinct from its purchasing power as mirrored in the price level. As for David Davidson and Benjamin Anderson, I have said that these economists indeed tried "to distinguish, though not in a way intelligible to me, between the value of money and its purchasing power, the reciprocal of the price level."[16]

After studying further writings by Davidson, I think I now see what he meant. Davidson challenged Gustav Cassel, who had forthrightly identified changes in the general price level with changes in money's value. A general rise in prices, Davidson objected, can reflect either a rise in the value of commodities or a fall in the value of money—or a rise in the value of both, with commodities gaining value in greater proportion, or a fall in the value of both, with commodities losing value in lesser proportion. Davidson even presented a table purporting to show how much of the rise of prices in Sweden during World War I was due to an increased scarcity value of commodities and how much to a decreased scarcity value of money.[17]

Davidson accepted a real-cost theory of value and was even striving to perfect Ricardo's mainly-labor-input theory. (His article of 1919 addresses the theory of value in general, without special reference to monetary questions. It is a pity, says Brinley Thomas, that Davidson was trying to present a revised version of the classical value theory; for this part of his work brought no fruitful result.)[18] If a general increase in productivity reduces, on the average, the quantities of labor and land and any other primary factors of production necessary to produce a unit of output, then goods have become cheaper, on Davidson's view; and their prices, expressed in money of stable value, would be lower than before.

16. Yeager, "Domestic Stability versus Exchange Rate Stability," *Cato Journal* 8 (Fall 1988): 271–72. See also Benjamin M. Anderson, Jr., *The Value of Money* (New York: Macmillan, 1917); and David Davidson, "Något om begreppet 'penningens värde,'" *Ekonomisk Tidskrift* 8 (1906): 460–68.

17. David Davidson, "Om stabiliseringen af penningens värde," *Ekonomisk Tidskrift* 8 (1906): 460–68; Davidson, "Replik," *Ekonomisk Tidskrift* 11 (1909): 67–68; Davidson, "Några teoretiska frågor," *Ekonomisk Tidskrift* 21 (1919), nos. 10–11, 231; Davidson, "Valutaproblemets teoretiska innebörd, *Ekonomisk Tidskrift* 22 (1920), nos. 3–4, 71–123; Davidson, "Till frågan om penningvärdets reglering under kriget och därefter," *Ekonomisk Tidskrift* 24 (1922), nos. 5–6, 89–114, and *Ekonomisk Tidskrift* 25 (1923): 191–234; and Davidson, "Varuvärde och penningvärde," *Ekonomisk Tidskrift* (1926), no. 1, 1–18. The table is in Davidson, "Till frågan," 197.

18. Brinley Thomas, "The Monetary Doctrines of Professor Davidson," *Economic Journal* 45 (March 1935): 47.

This real-cost doctrine can be more or less reconciled with a marginal-utility theory of value; and Davidson, without going into detail, at least hinted at a reconciliation. If increased productivity makes goods in general more abundant than before, then, precisely in accordance with the principle of diminishing marginal utility, their marginal utility and value decline. If, in the other direction, as illustrated during World War I, developments in world markets worsen Sweden's terms of trade, bringing effects similar to those of a decline in productivity, then goods have higher marginal utility and greater scarcity value than before.

For money, too, lesser or greater scarcity (relative to population, as Davidson occasionally said) entails lesser or greater marginal utility and value. Davidson objected to losing sight of what might be happening, separately, to the values of goods and of money. To be concerned only with their *ratios* of value would be like being concerned only with how the ratio of the average heights of women and men had changed over some period, neglecting what had happened to the average absolute height of the members of each sex.[19] To advocate money not of stable value of its own but of stable purchasing power as indicated by some price index is as "metrologically absurd" as wanting to adjust the definition of the meter according to changes in the average absolute length of objects being measured; it is like wanting a separate meter for children, shorter than the adult meter.[20]

Yet is it not true that all measurement is necessarily relative? There are no utterly absolute standards—are there?—of length or mass or value or anything else. Rising productivity cheapens some goods relative to others (notably, consumer goods relative to human effort), but it can hardly cheapen goods and services in general relative to goods and services in general. It seems reasonable to expect each good's price to express its value relative to others, which is what pricing in a unit of stable general purchasing power does.

Two familiar strands of counterargument, not rehearsed here, involve supposed practical difficulties concerning the specification of

19. Davidson, "Om stabiliseringen af penningens värde," 12.
20. Davidson, "Till frågan om penningvärdets," 113.

the price index to be stabilized and lags bedeviling implementation of monetary policy.

According to another strand, movements of the price level in response to various circumstances would serve fairness among groups of the population better than stability. Davidson offered examples.[21] A stable price level would deprive a creditor of any share of the gains from a general rise in productivity, while someone who had borrowed for productive purposes would unfairly keep the entire gain himself. Or consider two owners of farmland, only one of whom had leveraged his holding by debt. A general rise in the output of land would tend to depress the prices of its products and so not unambiguously press the money value of the land itself either up or down. A policy of stabilizing the product price level, however, would raise the land's money value; and the leveraging landowner would gain differentially, which also seemed unfair to Davidson.

Davidson's notions of objective value bring to mind the idea of a unit of account defined by a representative bundle not of products but of labor and other primary factors of production. More recently, David Glasner has advocated money stabilized in terms of an index of labor wage rates. His chief argument, along with three minor ones, is that a stable wage level would avoid substantial fluctuations in employment. Falling wages in one particular location or industry would signal workers that they might find better opportunities elsewhere. When, in contrast, the general wage level is not stabilized, workers with worsened employment prospects cannot tell whether they face a local-sectoral or a general phenomenon. Employment might suffer from mistaken resistance to general wage cuts made necessary by an adverse supply shock under a product-price-stabilization policy, whereas allowing price increases could accomplish the necessary temporary cuts in real wage wages.[22]

Unfortunately, Glasner says essentially nothing about how a wage-rate index would be specified and calculated, nor whether individual wages would possess the necessary degree of downward flexibility. As

21. Davidson, "Något om begreppet."

22. David Glasner, *Free Banking and Monetary Reform* (New York: Cambridge University Press, 1989), chap. 11.

for monetary responses to severe adverse supply shocks, my comments appear several paragraphs later.

Practical difficulties of stabilizing money against a bundle of primary factors of production led Davidson in 1922 at least to hint at what would in some respects be a rough equivalent—government money managed so as to stabilize average nominal income per member of the population. That policy would make an adequately flexible price level vary inversely with average productivity.

This idea of a nominal-income target for monetary policy has gained support in recent years, although most proposals envisage not a fixed level per capita but a target path of total nominal income or GNP trending steadily upward at a rate thought consistent with average price stability over the long run. (Bennett T. McCallum suggests procedures for implementing such a rule.)[23] Michael Bradley and Dennis Jansen describe nominal-GNP targeting as a straddle between price-level and real-output targeting, the latter being quite inappropriate for familiar reasons (one hopes). Nominal targeting would tend to stabilize "real GNP at its natural rate of output," and "automatically, without monetary policymakers having to know what the natural rate of output actually is."[24]

James Hoehn argues that nominal targeting could help minimize employment distortions that might otherwise occur when labor contracts make nominal wages sticky. If, for example, labor productivity should unexpectedly improve, yet monetary policy kept the price level from falling, firms would expand employment to take advantage of the increased marginal productivity at the unchanged nominal and real wage rate. (Hoehn assumes actual employment to be the amount of labor demanded; he does not consider markets failing to clear because of monetary disequilibrium.) This employment expansion is excessive because firms do not take the increased marginal disutility of labor into account, even though, ideally, real

23. Bennett McCallum, "The Case for Rules in the Conduct of Monetary Policy: A Concrete Example," Federal Reserve Bank of Richmond, *Economic Review* 73 (September–October 1987): 10–18; and idem, *Monetary Economics* (New York: Macmillan, 1989).

24. Michael D. Bradley and Dennis W. Jansen, "Understanding Nominal GNP Targeting," Federal Reserve Bank of St. Louis, *Review* 71 (November–December 1989): 40.

wages should match this marginal disutility. To prevent overemployment in this case of improved productivity, prices should be allowed to fall and the real wage thus to rise. A nominal-income target, as opposed to a price-level target, would promote this result and thus help promote an optimal allocation of employees' time between work and leisure.[25]

It is unnecessary to review Hoehn's other examples of disturbance. His argument involves the welfare effects of volumes of employment associated with real wages above or below what would match the marginal disutility of labor; it seems overly subtle. It illustrates how ingenuity can produce innumerable particular cases in which price-level stability—like any other particular monetary rule or regime—might produce results deemed inferior, on the specific grounds considered, to some alternative rule or regime tailored to the specific circumstances. Yet monetary regimes can hardly be installed and altered from case to case.

George Selgin supposes that technological progress cheapens some particular good whose price figures significantly in the general price level. As a matter of arithmetic, the price level falls slightly (unless monetary institutions or policy resist this spontaneous tendency). This decline of prices on average evidences no excess demand for money being corrected, perhaps sluggishly. By hypothesis, the cheapened good has not been in excess supply, for its producers have cut its price, promptly and painlessly, in line with its reduced cost. The technological advance presumably raises the output of the affected good and perhaps of other goods into whose production factors may be released. Thus the real volume of transactions to be lubricated increases, and so does the associated demand for real cash balances. That increased demand is more or less accommodated automatically, however, through money's rise in purchasing power. (I say "more or less," for only by extreme coincidence would the pattern of interrelated price and quantity adjustments and of people's

25. James G. Hoehn, "Employment Distortions Under Sticky Wages and Monetary Policies to Minimize Them," Federal Reserve Bank of Cleveland, *Economic Review* 25 (1989, Quarter 2): 22–34.

income elasticities of demand for real balances result in an exact accommodation.)[26]

If only one particular good were ever to incur downward price pressure from technical progress, that fact would argue against choosing it as the unit (or medium) of account. (For example, if production of gold alone kept gaining in technical efficiency, a gold standard would be inexpedient.) We would even want to leave that exceptional good out of any bundle of commodities chosen to define the unit of account or leave it out of the definition of any price index to be stabilized. We would see no reason to inflate other prices up to stabilize the average; it would be simpler to let the price of the one exceptional good fall.

More generally, whenever technical progress cheapens one good only, we might like its price to fall while leaving all other prices undisturbed. But what could the unit (or medium) of account be in terms of which prices would behave that way? No such unit is available. All sorts of substitutabilities and complementarities in consumption and production, along with other aspects of general interdependence, make it impossible for any single price to change *alone*. It is pointless to wish for a unit of account with impossible properties (e.g., one whose adoption, besides offering all conceivable economic benefits, would also prevent drug addiction).

It is misleading, furthermore, to consider goods affected by technical progress separately, one by one. Technical progress—along with more pervasive developments that raise productivity, such as capital accumulation and gains in education—is likely to keep on occurring and to affect a wide range of goods. Goods cannot all fall in price relative to each other. The operational question becomes not "Why inflate up other prices when a single price falls?" but rather "Why not neutralize—why not otherwise absorb—a general downward price pressure?" In other words, "Why express money prices in a way that requires most of them to fall when relative prices are tending to change in diverse ways and are under no unequivocal pressure to change in a particular way?" Even if it is reasonable to want to

---

26. George A. Selgin, *Theory of Free Banking*; idem, "The Price Level, Productivity, and Macroeconomic Order" (Discussion Paper no. 101, Department of Economics, University of Hong Kong, October 1988), and personal correspondence.

minimize the number of functionless individual price changes, it seems counterintuitive to suppose that individual price changes would be fewer in the context of a downward-sagging average price level than in the context of a stable average level.

How gains in productivity may affect prices is a far from straightforward matter, as Knut Wicksell pointed out.[27] Inventions or other developments tending to raise productivity may stimulate investment spending and so initially tend to *raise* prices. The question of the time pattern of the effects of changes in productivity thus poses additional complexity for any notion of optimal responsiveness (as opposed to stability) of the general price level.

Perhaps the most embarrassing case for advocates of stable money is a severe *deterioration* of productivity, or the equivalent—an adverse supply shock like or worse than the oil shock of 1973–74, a major calamity, or war. Merely moderate shocks are less worrisome. A long-term uptrend in productivity affords some scope for absorbing them. An adverse shock may merely slow the uptrend of real incomes for a while or reverse the uptrend only slightly and temporarily. Keeping the price level stable may thus require not an absolute decline in nominal incomes but a mere slowdown or temporary interruption of their growth.

If, however, the burden of some severe shock must be allocated over the population somehow or other, an inflationary tax on cash balances and nominal incomes can hardly be ruled out a priori as one way of doing so. (Apparently Wicksell, toward the end of his life, modified his call for a stable price level to allow for such cases.)[28]

Unfortunately, a country's monetary and other institutions cannot be made absolutely invulnerable even to external calamities. Institutions should be chosen to serve and improve the relatively normal conditions in which they have a good chance of flourishing. It seems perverse to try to shape institutions for the worst conceivable cases instead. (The perversity is akin to that of the maximin criterion recommended by John Rawls in *A Theory of Justice* in 1971.)[29]

27. Knut Wicksell, "Penningränta och varupris," *Ekonomisk Tidskrift* 11 (1909): 61–66.

28. Uhr, *Economic Doctrines of Knut Wicksell,* 300–305.

29. John Rawls, *A Theory of Justice* (Cambridge: Harvard University Press, 1971).

One might even argue that stable money provides a better starting point for government borrowing and money issue in rare emergencies than money commanding little confidence in the first place. (Advocates of the gold standard made such an argument during discussions in Russia in the late nineteenth century about reforming the country's floating paper currency.)

In conclusion, though at length, I fear, I want to make one general point. Economic policy fundamentally concerns the choice and modification of *institutions*—the rules and constraints within which individuals and families and firms and government officials carry out their activities.[30] Policy makers have no direct handle on patterns of outcomes—prices, allocation of resources among different lines of production, geographic distribution of productive activities, patterns of employment and unemployment, and distributions of income and wealth. In the realm of monetary regimes, the basic institutional choice is that of the unit of account, the unit in which prices are expressed, accounting conducted, and contracts specified. Is the unit to be some particular commodity or some particular group or composite of commodities, perhaps chosen in view of the expected behavior of its market value relative to goods and services in general? Or is the unit to be some fiat currency whose value depends on its scarcity relative to the demand to hold it, a scarcity somehow regulated by a monetary authority?

Adoption of a fiat currency as unit of account implies choosing some principles for its management but still does not make possible achieving some detailed pattern of the results of economic activity. Of course, one may join David Davidson in thinking up particular constellations of circumstances and propounding ethical judgments according to which fairness between debtors and creditors or fairness among other groups of the population might better be served by a fall (or rise) of the price level than by its stability. If, however, the balance of considerations favors institutions making for a stable monetary unit over alternative monetary institutions, then it is simply irrelevant to think up particular cases in which some other price-level behavior might be deemed preferable. Institutions and rules

30. Rutledge Vining, *On Appraising the Performance of an Economic System* (New York: Cambridge University Press, 1984).

cannot be switched on and off from case to case. It is unreasonable to expect a monetary system to achieve all sorts of good results, including economic justice, in the face of multifarious changes in conditions. Present-day rational-expectations theorists, in particular, must question the idea that the choice of monetary regime can reliably influence real economic outcomes, such as the distribution of real income and wealth among groups.

No single set of institutions can achieve all results deemed good. A monetary system should do what it can reasonably be expected to do, leaving other institutions to undertake tasks more suitable for them. A stable unit of account at least facilitates planning and contracting. As for fairness, savers need not restrict themselves to buying interest-bearing securities of fixed nominal value; they can diversify. They can try to take account of prospective changes in productivity in various industries by investing in equities. They can diversify their asset portfolios, either directly or by investing in mutual funds. Their portfolio choices can express their different degrees of willingness to bear risk in hopes of gain. Likewise, would-be borrowers (business borrowers, anyway) need not borrow only in nominal terms; they can sell stock or obtain loans with equity participations. A sound monetary system can help provide such opportunities by facilitating the development of financial intermediation.

I insist on the question of the unit of account. Anyone condemning the objective of price-level stability is rejecting a unit explicitly or implicitly defined by a bundle of commodities or by the collection of goods and services involved in calculating a broad price index. What unit of account, then, does the critic recommend instead? The case is weak for a unit defined by gold or any other single commodity. Anyone recommending some sort of productivity or money-growth or nominal-income rule—or, at the extreme, recommending the monetary actions deemed best case by case and day by day—must envisage application of the rule or exercise of the discretion by a central monetary authority equipped with the necessary special powers. This means—unless I am committing some gross oversight—that the unit of account is nothing more definite than a unit of government fiat money managed, one hopes, in some way deemed optimal. That choice of unit of account leaves the monetary system vulnerable to the government abuses about which the historical record so eloquently testifies. It precludes a nongovernmental monetary system. Choice of a commodity-defined stable unit of account, on the other hand, makes possible private enterprise and laissez-faire in money along the lines of, for example, the BFH system.

New Keynesians and
Old Monetarists

GAMES WITH NAMES

Developments in macroeconomics remind me of name shifts at the
Library of Congress. In 1980, the original 1897 building became the
Library of Congress Thomas Jefferson Building, and the former Tho-
mas Jefferson Building became the Library of Congress John Adams
Building. (These and the James Madison Memorial Building honor
the presidents involved in establishing the library.)[1]

Like my late father, who never switched from calling Kennedy
Airport by its original name, Idlewild, I am no fan of name changes.
They undercut the purpose of names, impairing communication.
Name-bred confusion over how different doctrines relate to each
other interferes with grasping the realities they refer to. In some
circles nowadays, monetarist economics is handicapped by having
had the label "New Keynesianism" foisted onto it.

Axel Leijonhufvud has brought the Swedish flag into a story of
label shifting.[2] The nine sections formed by a yellow cross on a blue
field correspond to nine doctrinal positions concerning business fluctuations: emphases on three types of impulse —nominal, mixed, and
real or intertemporal—intersect with emphases on three corresponding types of propagation mechanism. The northwest, or nominal-
nominal, section supposedly represents the monetarism of Milton
Friedman, while the southeast, or real-real, section represents Keynes's

Reprinted with permission of the author.

1. Library of Congress, *Information Bulletin* 39 (27 June 1980): 225–26.

2. Axel Leijonhufvud, "Whatever Happened to Keynesian Economics?" (Paper
delivered at a conference on the Legacy of Keynes, Adolphus College, Saint Peter,
Minnesota, 30 September to 1 October 1986).

original position. The New Classical theorists shifted the position of their supposed new generation of monetarists to the northeast, or nominal-real, section of the flag. Even before monetarism conspicuously entered the scene, however, the Keynesians had already moved into the southwest, or real-impulse/nominal-propagation, corner of the flag.

My purpose is not to assess or even further summarize Leijonhufvud's classifications, just to credit him with recognizing a game of musical chairs played with doctrinal positions and labels. Changing the details, I'll offer some embroidery.

KEYNESIANISM

Before examining New Keynesianism, we might recall Keynesianism *sans phrase*. James Tobin has identified four central propositions of the *General Theory*: (1) prices and wages respond only slowly to changed conditions, (2) advanced economies are vulnerable to prolonged involuntary unemployment, (3) capital formation depends on long-run appraisals of profit prospects and risks and on business attitudes, and (4) even if wages and prices were flexible, they would not necessarily provide an automatic stabilizing mechanism.[3]

The distinguished authors of a macroeconomics text describe early or "classical" macroeconomic theories (of Alfred Marshall and A. C. Pigou, for example) as supposing that prices and wages were flexible and would adjust quickly enough to keep labor and machines fully employed.[4] A change in overall demand would affect prices but not output. Keynes "created a new macroeconomic model where shifts in demand *could* influence the level of output. Keynes's idea was to look at what would happen if prices were 'sticky'— meaning that they were not adjusted in response to demand."[5]

Not this particular passage but others like it made Leijonhufvud despair that standards of accuracy respected in mathematics or sta-

3. James Tobin, *Policies for Prosperity: Essays in a Keynesian Mode* (Cambridge: MIT Press, 1987).

4. Robert E. Hall and John B. Taylor, *Macroeconomics* (New York: Norton, 1986).

5. Ibid., 13.

tistics would be applied to the recent history of economic thought. "The fiction, for example, that Keynes himself based his theory of unemployment on 'rigid wages' is now so firmly entrenched in textbooks and journals, and is reprinted with such frequency, that apparently nothing can dislodge it. Today's economics profession, taken as a whole, simply does not care enough about the truth or falsehood of statements of this doctrine-historical kind to enforce reasonable scholarly standards." Leijonhufvud hoped that Keynesianism could "be freed from its unfortunate identification with nominal 'stickiness.'"[6]

NEW KEYNESIANISM

Representative works espousing the "New Keynesian" position include *New Keynesian Economics*, a collection of articles edited by Gregory N. Mankiw and David Romer; Gregory Mankiw's "Quick Refresher Course in Macroeconomics"; Robert Gordon's "What Is New-Keynesian Economics?"; and Alan Blinder's preliminary report on interview studies of pricing.[7] This literature recognizes that fluctuations in total spending, interacting with sticky prices and wages and related market "imperfections," can worsen (or lessen) departures from full coordination of economic activities; and it looks into the sources and microeconomic rationales of these imperfections.

Laurence Ball and David Romer synthesize "two approaches to reviving Keynesian theory"—the one that explains nominal price and wage rigidities by menu costs and so forth and the one that tries to diagnose failures of coordination.[8] Contrary to frequent suppositions, Ball and Romer find those two sets of ideas highly complementary. Some firms' reluctance or willingness to adjust

6. Leijonhufvud, "Whatever Happened to Keynesian Economics?" 24.

7. Gregory N. Mankiw and David Romer, eds., *New Keynesian Economics* (Cambridge: MIT Press, 1991); Mankiw, "A Quick Refresher Course in Macroeconomics," *Journal of Economic Literature* 28 (December 1990): 1645–60; Robert J. Gordon, "What Is New-Keynesian Economics?" *Journal of Economic Literature* 28 (September 1990): 1115–71; Alan S. Blinder, "Why Are Prices Sticky? Preliminary Results From an Interview Study," *American Economic Review* 81 (May 1991): 89–96.

8. Laurence Ball and David Romer, "Sticky Prices as Coordination Failure," *American Economic Review* 81 (June 1991): 539–52.

their prices (and wages) increases other firms' reluctance or willingness to adjust theirs. The advantages of making one's own adjustment are slighter (or negative) when one is adjusting alone than when one is taking part in a general pattern of readjustment. Ball and Romer formalize ideas anticipated by, among others, Charles Schultze in 1985, and Philip Cagan, who has impeccable monetarist credentials, in 1980.[9] More informal anticipations date still earlier, as we shall see.

Joseph Stiglitz interprets New Keynesian economics as emphasizing imperfect information, imperfect markets for capital and risk, imperfect competition, and adjustment costs. In his view,

> the central issue of macroeconomics is not whether there exists an unemployment equilibrium, i.e., a configuration of wages, prices, etc., such that there is no mechanism by which the economy returns eventually to full employment, although elsewhere we have, in fact, shown that to be the case. Rather, the central issue is, are there reasons to believe that adjustment speeds in the response to, say, unemployment are sufficiently slow that the restoration of full employment is a slow and lengthy process? In this sense, the reconciliation of traditional microeconomic general equilibrium analysis and macroeconomic analysis becomes an easier task.[10]

Stiglitz observes that "it takes time to discover certain relationships so that the attainment of a 'rational expectations equilibrium' following a change in certain structural variables may take a long time. Indeed, one might argue that one of the objectives of economics research is to discover relationships which have not been previously discovered."[11]

9. Philip Cagan, "Reflections on Rational Expectations," *Journal of Money, Credit, and Banking* 12 (November 1980): 826–32; and Charles L. Schultze, "Microeconomic Efficiency and Nominal Wage Stickiness," *American Economic Review* 75 (March 1985): 1–15.

10. Joseph E. Stiglitz, "Alternative Approaches to Macroeconomics: Methodological Issues and the New Keynesian Economics," NBER Working Paper no. 3580 (Cambridge, 1991), 35–36.

11. Ibid., 45.

THE OLD MONETARISM

But the ideas and research agenda just described are closer to old-fashioned monetarism than to the macroeconomics of Keynes's *General Theory*. Rarely do self-styled Keynesians still insist that not even in principle do any automatic market mechanisms tend to maintain or restore full-employment equilibrium. (Traditional micro theory, for its part, said nothing about *how fast* in calendar time a new equilibrium emerges after a disturbance. Don Patinkin properly distinguishes underemployment *dis*equilibrium from supposed unemployment equilibrium.)[12] No longer do Keynesians assert their side in the lapsed debate over the relative strengths of fiscal policy and the quantity of money in influencing aggregate demand. Keynesians (or their younger successors) have abandoned their own distinctive position in former controversies for that of their victorious opponents; yet they keep their "Keynesian" label.

As Mankiw and Romer aptly say in introducing their 1991 selection, "much of new Keynesian economics could also be called new monetarist economics."[13] (The adjective "new" applies to monetarism, I think, only because it remains alive, not stopping with mere recitation of old beliefs.)

We should not try to identify and distinguish New Keynesianism and Old Monetarism by their supposed policy recommendations. Notions of how the political system works, not economics alone, color policy preferences. So, perhaps, do personal psychological traits. My concern here is with the economics alone. (Incidentally, the findings of the Public Choice school and its comparisons of government and markets reduce ideological pressures to attribute perfection to markets. The modern Austrian school, to its credit, never has been obsessed with notions of perfect competition and so never has resisted acknowledging market "imperfections," so called by mainstream economists.)

Monetarism—or "monetary-disequilibrium theory," as Clark Warburton liked to call it—did not originate with Milton Friedman,

12. Don Patinkin, *Money, Interest, and Prices* (New York: Harper & Row, 1965), 315, 337–38.
13. Mankiw and Romer, *New Keynesian Economics*, 1:3.

Anna Schwartz, Karl Brunner, and Alan Meltzer, or even with Warburton himself, who anticipated all of them. It can be traced back at
least as far as Richard Cantillon, David Hume, and Pehr Niclas
Christiernin, writing in the eighteenth century. Nineteenth-century
exponents included Henry Thornton, G. Poulett Scrope, and Erick
Bollman. American exponents in the early twentieth century included Joseph French Johnson, Irving Fisher, Herbert J. Davenport,
and Harry Gunnison Brown. More recently, William H. Hutt, an
avowed traditionalist and emphatic opponent of Keynes, combined
an emphasis on price and wage rigidities with recognition of monetary disturbances. Classical and neoclassical writers like Ricardo,
Mill, and Marshall were usually occupied with other topics; but even
they, as Warburton has shown, recognized that monetary disequilibrium does occur, and they sometimes paid explicit attention to it. At
times, Warburton persuasively maintains, monetarism was the dominant view in macroeconomics.[14]

Other economists have recognized that the supposed hallmarks
of the New Keynesianism are well rooted in mainstream economics.
Jacob Viner cites several diagnoses made in Great Britain during or
shortly after the Napoleonic wars of the distress that monetary deflation would cause.[15] Several writers observed that prices do not decline uniformly, which implies the differential stickiness of different
prices; and Thomas Attwood explained that a shrinkage of money,
instead of depressing prices directly, depresses them through first
causing unsalable excess supplies of goods. During the deflation
phase of the bullionist controversies, advocates of an independent
paper standard brought the downward rigidity of factor prices into
their arguments.[16]

14. See James A. Dorn, "The Search for Stable Money: A Historical Perspective," in *The Search for Stable Money*, ed. James A. Dorn and Anna J. Schwartz (Chicago: University of Chicago Press, 1987), chap. 1; Leland B. Yeager, "The Significance of Monetary Disequilibrium," *Cato Journal* 6 (Fall 1986): 369–99 (reprinted in
this volume); and Yeager, "Hutt and Keynes," in *Perspectives on the History of Economic
Thought*, ed. William J. Barber, vol. 6: *Themes in Keynesian Criticism and Supplementary
Modern Topics* (Aldershot, England: Edward Elgar, 1991), 102–16.

15. Jacob Viner, *Studies in the Theory of International Trade* (New York: Harper,
1937), 173 n, 175.

16. Ibid., 186, 195 n, 199, 217.

Arthur Marget shows that, contrary to Keynes's allegation in his *Treatise on Money*, "current economic theory" did *not* assert that all prices changed in equal proportion in response to a change in the quantity of money. On the contrary, *non*proportionality of price changes "has been a commonplace in economic literature since at least the eighteenth century" as well as in "current" textbooks.[17] (Well, nonproportionality of changes *means* that some prices respond relatively sluggishly.) Writers from the mercantilists to Hume recognized money as not only the representative but also the *instrument* of demand and recognized that monetary expansion and contraction affect output.[18]

Keynes in the *General Theory*, notes Marget, charged his predecessors with leaving a serious hiatus between the general theory of value and monetary theory, a defect he claimed to be repairing by presenting a theory of output as a whole.[19] Marget answers Keynes's charges in a three-chapter survey of the earlier literature. The "old" Cambridge school (including Dennis Robertson and A. C. Pigou) *was*, contra Keynes, concerned with "the effects of monetary expansion and contraction upon the level of output as a whole."[20]

Gottfried Haberler, summarizing views of earlier economists and also speaking for himself, repeatedly cited wage and price stickiness as a leading reason why disturbances to money and nominal spending bite on real economic activity instead of just promptly moving wages and prices to new market-clearing levels. By and large, he and the writers he summarized did not think it necessary to explain wage and price stickiness in detail; evidently they felt entitled to invoke a widely observed fact of experience whose approximate rationale, anyway, would become evident on reflection.[21] Echoing F. A. Hayek, Haberler observed that Keynes's warning in 1925 against Britain's re-

17. Arthur W. Marget, *The Theory of Prices*, 2 vols. (New York: Kelley, 1966), 1:500.

18. Ibid., 2:270.

19. Ibid., 2:4.

20. Ibid., 2:83.

21. Gottfried Haberler, *Prosperity and Depression* (London: Allen & Unwin, 1958), 121, 467, 469, 485, 491–92.

turning to the gold standard at the prewar parity "was based on orthodox teaching."[22]

Among conditions eventually favoring recovery from a depression, Haberler noted that, provided the nominal quantity of money has not shrunk too much, price and wage declines make the *real* quantity of money rise until holders feel uncomfortable with its excessive size *relative* to their total wealth and real incomes.[23] (Although he did not, Haberler might well have named these aspects of people's responses the portfolio-balance and Cambridge aspects of the real-balance effect, broadly conceived; the wealth aspect is not the whole story.) In noting how price and wage declines would bring these effects *eventually*, Haberler was again recognizing that these market-clearing adjustments would not occur *instantly*.

Haberler even saw what qualifications had to be set against trusting in the curative powers of the Pigou/Haberler/real-balance effect. Following Irving Fisher and anticipating John Caskey and Steve Fazzari, J. B. De Long and L. H. Summers, and Robert A. Driskill and Steven M. Sheffrin,[24] Haberler recognized reasons, chiefly involving debt burdens and expectations, why a high degree of wage and price flexibility might worsen rather than relieve economic malcoordination in the short or medium run.[25]

FURTHER SAMPLES OF OLD MONETARISM

Ralph Hawtrey, writing in 1913, judged a psychological theory of the business cycle inadequate and presented a monetarist theory.[26] His theory involves a lag of the interest rate behind a turn to rising or

22. Ibid., 469, n. 2.

23. Ibid., 388–90, 403–4.

24. See Irving Fisher, "The Debt-Deflation Theory of Great Depressions," *Econometrica* 1 (October 1933): 337–57; John Caskey and Steve Fazzari, "Aggregate Demand Contractions With Nominal Debt Commitments: Is Wage Flexibility Stabilizing?" *Economic Inquiry* 25 (October 1987): 583–97; J. B. De Long and L. H. Summers, "Is Increased Price Flexibility Stabilizing?" *American Economic Review* 76 (December 1986): 1031–44; and Robert A. Driskill and Steven M. Sheffrin, "Is Price Flexibility Destabilizing?" *American Economic Review* 76 (September 1976): 802–7.

25. *Prosperity and Depression*, 115–16, 243–44, 388–90, 396–401, 404–5, 492, 498.

26. R. G. Hawtrey, *Good and Bad Trade* (New York: Kelley, 1970), vii, 74–77, 183–84, 267–72.

falling prices and a lag of the demand for hand-to-hand currency behind expansion or contraction of credit. The former lag accounts for the inherent instability of credit, while the latter accounts for the considerable length—usually several years—of the resulting oscillations.

Hawtrey recognized that the greater width of cyclical fluctuations in the capital-goods industries than in the consumer-goods industries does not require a real as opposed to monetary explanation of the cycle. Contraction of money restricts spending; sales fall off. Producers can avoid restricting their output only by lowering their prices, which they do only "so far as the existing scale of their expenses will permit. Their expenses depend mainly on the rate of wages, and until the working population will accept lower wages there must be some restriction of output. . . . [Eventually] the pressure of distress due to lack of employment drives the working class to accept lower wages." Meanwhile, though, "customary wages and customary prices resist the change, [and] the adjustment, which is bound to come sooner or later, will only be forced upon the people by the pressure of distress." Moreover, because nominal interest rates do not fully and promptly adjust to expected price-level changes, monetary contraction can further deter investment through the real-interest-rate channel. Transitional obstacles to adjustment through wage and price declines, such as declines in the nominal value of loan collateral and impairment of credit, can also intensify a crisis. (Hawtrey also considered monetary expansion and described its stimulatory effects.)[27]

Evidently something like the Keynesian multiplier was man-in-the-street economics when Hawtrey was writing. But he recognized that the multiplier story is fallacious unless modified to take account of money: "It is frequently argued that the depression of one trade in a country tends to cause depression in the others, inasmuch as the purchasing power of the people engaged in the trade immediately affected is diminished and they are therefore not in a position to buy so much as before of the goods produced by their neighbours." But given no change in the quantity of money (and its velocity, one should add), "this argument is not valid. . . . [T]he aggregate

27. Ibid., 28, 41–43, 49, 93–94, 211–13, 213–15, 265.

demand for commodities remains unaltered and if the demand for some falls off the demand for the remainder is correspondingly stimulated." Hawtrey went on, however, to recognize that the multiplier does indeed operate under the gold standard when, for example, a drop in foreign demand for the country's exports brings gold losses and monetary contraction.[28]

Hawtrey rejected a fiscal-policy remedy for depression on grounds of crowding out, as we would say nowadays.[29]

Another book of 1913 also presents a monetarist position on money, banking, booms, crises, and depression. Though without using the name Say's law, Herbert Davenport recognized both the law's valid central point and also the fallacy of drawing assurance from it that demand for currently produced goods and services could never be deficient. Goods and services exchange for each other through the intermediary of money, for which an excess demand may sometimes develop. "The halfway house becomes a house of stopping." The problem is "withdrawal of a large part of the money supply at the existing level of prices; it is a change in the entire demand schedule of money against goods."[30]

Supplies of bank account money and bank credit typically shrink at the stage of downturn into depression. A scramble for base money both by banks' customers and by banks trying to fortify their imperiled reserves enters into Davenport's story. In passages anticipating Ben Bernanke's celebrated article of 1983 (and making the reader wonder how Bernanke could have thought he was scoring *anti*monetarist points), Davenport explains how flows of credit are disrupted and diverted into poor substitutes for normal channels in the early stages of business contraction. The banks pull back from extending credit, a function in which they normally specialize, forcing this function onto less fit performers. The volume of trade credit expands more or less involuntarily as customers delay payments to their suppliers and even make new purchases contingent on further credit. Credit restriction becomes contagious. Creditors press their debtors

28. Ibid., 134–39.

29. Ibid., 260.

30. Herbert J. Davenport, *The Economics of Enterprise* (New York: Kelley, 1968), 320.

for repayment, who in turn press *their* debtors. Trying to raise funds, debtors dump securities and other assets onto unreceptive markets, depressing the nominal values of collaterals against existing loans and against possible new loans.[31]

Depression could be milder and shorter if prices and wages fell evenly across the board. Inertia, however, is a fact of reality. Wages fall only with painful struggle, perhaps putting entrepreneurs into a cost-price squeeze. Existing nominal indebtedness also poses resistance to adjustment. Like Haberler, Davenport anticipated present-day theories of a catch-22—of how increased price flexibility may in some respects be *de*stabilizing. In particular, expectations of further protracted price declines contribute to deficiency of spending on current output.[32]

Harry Gunnison Brown, whose elementary economics textbook of 1931, *Economic Science and the Common Good*, presents monetarist ideas at length, also published a remarkable but rather hard-to-find article at the depths of the Great Depression. Internal evidence dates it at the beginning of March 1933, just before Franklin D. Roosevelt took office as president.

"We are suffering from bank credit restriction or deflation, and falling prices," Brown wrote. The remedy was not to raise prices by restricting supplies of goods but to expand purchasing power. Yet some theorists were recommending further deflation and "a more complete 'liquidation' as a basis for recovery!" Further deflation of prices and property values would make more and more debtors insolvent. "Deflation to weed out the 'unsound' is as ridiculous logically as it is merciless morally. Deflation *makes* 'unsound' many thousands of debtors whose property, if there were no deflation, would be safely worth far more than their debts."[33]

Brown correctly understood that falling prices, although symptomatic of depression, were not its essence. "A restriction of credit certainly must make for business depression if prices fall, unless and

31. Ibid., 282–83. 285–86, 290–95, 298.

32. Ibid., 299, 313.

33. Harry Gunnison Brown, "Nonsense and Sense in Dealing With the Depression," *Beta Gamma Sigma Exchange* (Spring 1933): 97–107.

until production costs, such as wages and rentals, also fall. But credit restriction must bring business depression no less certainly if prices do not fall. For a decrease of means of purchase, imposed on dealers by bankers' restrictions, must certainly decrease the demand for goods."[34]

"A major cause of the depression," Brown thought, ". . . is an inept policy of those in charge of our Federal Reserve system. . . . [T]he policy followed was definitely and unnecessarily deflationary and tended to produce depression. Those in charge of the system give no evidence of understanding the tremendous control they can exercise over our business prosperity. Apparently they are quite capable of doing, innocently and uncomprehendingly, the very things that conduce to the pitiful disasters of the depression."[35] Brown asked his readers to imagine that, following the prosperity of 1924–29, "some mysterious force spirited away a third of every person's money and bank deposit account. Would not the demand for goods and for labor necessarily decline? Until prices, wages and rentals fell greatly would there not inevitably be dull business, unemployed labor, and idle factories?"[36]

As evidence that the Federal Reserve did not understand what it was doing, Brown quoted from the May 1928 congressional testimony of board member Dr. Adolph C. Miller. When asked whether the sagging of wholesale prices in the mid-1920s had been related to Federal Reserve policy, Miller replied: "I would say emphatically no; emphatically no. I would say that prices were down at that time primarily because they went up so high in the previous period and that the whole movement of prices in this period was one toward the ascertainment of a new level. The prices themselves were, so to speak, finding their new levels."[37]

Brown responded with justifiable sarcasm: "Prices are not *alive* and . . . they cannot 'find' their level as a woodchuck finds its hole. Monetary policies of inflation and deflation, including policies of central banks, do influence prices and do influence general busi-

34. Ibid., 101.
35. Ibid., 99.
36. Ibid.
37. Ibid., 100.

ness conditions." He went on to quote Gustav Cassel, testifying before the same committee just two days after Miller and warning against the potentially deflationary consequences of the policy then being pursued. The Federal Reserve, he judged, was unduly preoccupied with trying to restrain speculation on Wall Street.[38]

Brown warned against insistence that the federal government should balance its budget and avoid borrowing even during the depression:

> On the contrary, the government definitely *should* borrow in order to facilitate the putting of new and additional purchasing power into circulation. When the government pays its civil servants or pays for any sort of public works by funds raised by taxation, the purchasing power of the taxed citizens is reduced by as much as the purchasing power of the government is increased. In periods of prosperity this is as it should be. But at this time of acute depression it is desirable that government spending be increased without compelling a corresponding decrease of expenditure by taxpayers. Fortunately the government can now borrow at a very low interest rate. Why not do so?[39]

Brown argued that government borrowing and spending could rescue the economy from "the vicious circle of falling prices and business and bank failures, and from our depression psychology." The rescue could be achieved, however, only if it "is not balked by an unsympathetic Federal Reserve Board." The new president should compel Federal Reserve cooperation, therefore, through his power of removal. Brown contrasted "the requirements of central banking policy with the requirements of policy for an ordinary bank. In truth the requirements are so far different that experience in the successful management of the ordinary bank may be a definite disqualification for the management of a central bank or the control of Federal Reserve policy!" In contrast with prudent behavior for an ordinary bank when crisis and depression threaten, "the business of a central bank or a central banking system should be to make loans at lower rates and more freely than before, to endeavor to put more money

38. Ibid., 100–101.
39. Ibid., 103.

and checking accounts into circulation rather than to draw money into its own vaults."[40] Brown warned against letting the requirements of that "sacred cow," the gold standard, interfere with the policy he recommended.[41]

Brown waxed prophetic:

> The overturn of the Labor Cabinet in England, the rise of Hitlerism in Germany, and perhaps other events of more or less ominous import, may be the unforeseen consequences of, the result of a discontent really engendered by, a policy of our Federal Reserve Board entered upon with not the slightest premonition of its likely political consequences as well as with no apparent comprehension of its purely economic significance. Whatever else we do, we must institute such control of our money and banking mechanism that it cannot be used to bring us again to such distresses as we are now suffering. We are literally at the mercy—as to our fortunes, our jobs, the care and education of our children—of a Federal Reserve Board which has the power to bring on business depression at almost any time, which has shown that it does not know how to prevent such depression, and which has evinced no support for [remedial] legislation.[42]

In an article of 1948, Brown corrected some careless wording in Gustav Cassel's congressional testimony of May 1928. Cassel should not have implied that "credit restriction by the banks decreases production *because* it reduces prices. Credit restriction must certainly bring reduced production and unemployment if prices are generally rigid or 'sticky' and do *not* fall. And also, of course, reduced production and concomitant unemployment must ensue if prices of commodities do fall while wages do not."[43] (Brown made it clear that his context is money and credit deflation, not increased productive efficiency.)

40. Ibid., 104.

41. Ibid., 105.

42. Ibid., 106.

43. Harry Gunnison Brown, "Two Decades of Decadence in Economic Theorizing," *American Journal of Economics and Sociology* 7 (January 1948): 145–72, reprinted in *Some Disturbing Inhibitions and Fallacies in Current Academic Economics* (New York: Robert Schalkenbach Foundation, 1950), 37–64. The citation is from the reprint at page 44.

Brown saw that a fall of total spending by one-third need not cause depression and unemployment *if* prices, wages, and rentals all fall in the same proportion, and as quickly. (In another passage, he also recognized the proviso to be made about existing nominal debts.) But who would assert that the necessary declines in prices, wages, and rentals would in fact occur quickly enough? No one, Brown implied. He also recognized the possible adverse effects of *expectations* of sagging prices, including adverse effects on borrowing to finance investment projects. "The truth probably is that central banking policy has more to do than anything else with the alternation of prosperity and depression, and that central banking policy affects business activity through affecting the volume of circulating medium."[44] (Brown showed, by the way, but without using the term, that the Keynesian notion of a liquidity trap is preposterous.)[45]

Twelve University of Chicago economists, like Brown, argued in a memorandum of 1932 against relying upon the supposed self-healing characteristics of the economy to get it out of the depression. They stressed the resistance of wages and prices to downward adjustments.[46]

As is evident from some of the examples already presented, monetarist economists do not offer their diagnoses merely by hindsight. Throughout the 1920s, as Ronald W. Batchelder and David Glasner remind us, Ralph Hawtrey and Gustav Cassel, among others, were warning that restoring currencies to their prewar parities without international limitations on the demand for gold might result in deflation and depression. They particularly warned, before 1929, about the working of the gold standard in conjunction with tight-money policies in the United States and France. They continued to condemn the monetary policies that intensified the depression once begun. Yet their analyses are now almost totally forgotten: "The major difference between the Monetarist explanation of the Great Depression and that given by Hawtrey and Cassel is that Monetarists view the monetary shocks (U.S. bank failures) that caused the depression

44. Ibid., 38–39, 41, 54–57.

45. Ibid., 49.

46. J. Ronnie Davis, *The New Economics and the Old Economists* (Ames: Iowa State University Press, 1971), 25–26.

as specific to the United States, whereas Hawtrey and Cassel viewed the Great Depression as a system-wide failure occasioned by shocks occurring in many countries."[47]

A 1991 paper by Thomas Humphrey makes it all the more unnecessary to go on documenting the point that money's nonneutral influence, due largely to price and wage stickiness, was widely recognized long before Keynes. Humphrey cites and quotes writings of David Hume, Henry Thornton, John R. McCulloch, Jeremy Bentham, Thomas Attwood, Thomas R. Malthus, Robert Torrens, and John Stuart Mill.[48] David Ricardo, by exception, attributed little importance to the real effects of money, probably because of his preoccupation with the long view. Yet although he had recommended return of the pound to its pre-1797 par after the Napoleonic wars, Ricardo explained in 1821 that he would never recommend restoration to its old par of a currency that had become depreciated by as much as 30 percent.[49]

NEW CLASSICAL MACROECONOMICS AND REAL-BUSINESS-CYCLE THEORY

New Classical macroeconomics and, more recently, real-business-cycle theories have apparently contributed to counterproductive games with doctrinal names. These doctrines have given Keynesians an improved opportunity to abandon their old position gracefully, shift to the monetarist position on Leijonhufvud's Swedish flag, yet maintain an adversary stance against something called "classical," all while retaining their own label (now qualified as "new"). As Stiglitz notes, Milton "Friedman is, in many ways, closer to the Keynesians

47. Ronald W. Batchelder and David Glasner, "Pre-Keynesian Monetary Theories of the Great Depression: Whatever Happened to Hawtrey and Cassel?" (Paper delivered at the History of Economics Society Meetings, College Park, Maryland, June 1991). Batchelder and Glasner's narrow interpretation of the term "monetarist" seems questionable.

48. Thomas M. Humphrey, "Nonneutrality of Money in Classical Monetary Thought," Federal Reserve Bank of Richmond, *Economic Review* 77 (March–April 1991): 3–15.

49. Haberler, *Prosperity and Depression*, 469, n. 2; Viner, *Studies in the Theory of International Trade*, 204 n, 205 n.

than to the real business cycle theorists. He believes, for instance, that there are short run rigidities (e.g. wage and price rigidities) such that any action by the monetary authority cannot immediately and costlessly be offset by changes in the price level."[50]

This is my main present point about the doctrines that have provided this opportunity, doctrines of extreme satisfaction with how markets operate. I do not have space for substantive summaries that their New Classical authors would consider adequate and fair, nor would my criticisms differ much from those offered by the New Keynesians. I'll merely call attention to some comments.

Already in 1977 James Tobin had identified the main tenets of rational-expectations, equilibrium-always, and New Classical macroeconomics (though without using all those terms). Experience contradicted their tenets: neither involuntary unemployment nor idle productive capacity could be explained as anything like voluntary search. Tobin also expressed skepticism about the argument, invoking expectations of future taxes, that bond-financed government spending could not stimulate total spending. Reality and sound Keynesian theory, he thought, justified stimulation of aggregate demand at times of heavy unemployment.

Even earlier, Gottfried Haberler identified a vogue of stressing "real" factors unduly, to the relative neglect of monetary factors.[51] More generally, and earlier, Harry Gunnison Brown noted that economists, like other people, sometimes cultivate "various trends and fads which have, each, their little day and then give place to others."[52] Some of them may enjoy

the plaudits of other—younger and less noted—economists who may become their admiring disciples, participate in defending their views against dissenting economists, and gain reputations by applying the theories and definitions of their masters to particular cases, or by suggesting minor modifications of these theories.

. . . Yet so soon as it begins to be fairly evident that a particular force or set of forces is the most significant cause of an economic evil and the related theory is sufficiently clarified to make possible

50. Stiglitz, "Alternative Approaches to Macroeconomics," 48 n.
51. Haberler, *Prosperity and Depression*, chap. 13.
52. Brown, "Two Decades of Decadence in Economic Theorizing," 51.

wide public understanding, it appears that not a few professional economists are seized with a desire to direct discussion into the introduction of new terms, into quibbling over trifles, into holding up inconsequential facts as significant causes, and into suggesting as causes facts which may have no causal influence at all.

. . . *Why* must some economists *try so desperately* to trace depressions to causes which are so problematical, so relatively inconsequential and, sometimes, so fantastic, instead of emphasizing particularly a powerful cause, demonstrably capable, in conjunction with price, wage, rental and interest rigidities, of producing severe depression and clearly in operation prior to and even well after the onset of both of these business depressions [1919–21 and 1928–31]? [The situation] is as if, following a violent earthquake, several noted professors concluded that the chief cause of the collapse of a particular building was the backward pressure of the legs of a sparrow who had been observed to take flight from the building's roof only a second before it started to collapse. . . . Perhaps it would be better if more economists would pause, on occasion, from their interest in this or that latest formula or will-o-the-wisp of theory and ask themselves what, after all, economics is chiefly for.[53]

METHODOLOGICAL PRECONCEPTIONS

Hyperclassical doctrines that have given the New Keynesians their opportunities for games with labels show signs of obsession with methodology, often not explicitly articulated. One finds insistence on taking economic theory seriously, insistence on supposed rigor, focus on rational individuals seeking to maximize profit or utility, and the contention that leaving any prices at non-market-clearing levels means irrationally throwing away gains from trade. The slogan about not testing a theory by its assumptions gets recited (even though what assumptions are appropriate depends on the particular questions being tackled).

"It is currently fashionable," Stiglitz observes, "to 'derive' all the functions entering into a macroeconomic analysis from first prin-

---

53. Ibid., 52–53, 63, 64. A footnote on p. 64 cites favorably the work of Henry Simons, George Terbough, and Clark Warburton.

ciples, within the model." Yet economics "is a *cumulative* science. Not every piece of research has to begin at the beginning."[54]

Karl Brunner similarly identifies two fashionable yet counterproductive methodological strands. Both occur among "adherents of rational expectation theory, for example, the Minnesota group. One strand conveys that only a full 'rigorised' formulation can be expected to offer any relevant knowledge. The second strand asserts that only formulations derived from 'first principles' can be assigned (on a priori grounds) any potential cognitive status."[55] Keynes himself happened to hold what Brunner considers a healthier methodological position. That position does not condemn "rigorisation," provided it is not bought by sacrificing content. It recognizes, though, that knowledge can be and has been won without complete rigorization. "It also rejects the Cartesian fallacy of 'first principles.' There are no first principles in this sense." Science begins with empirical problems and regularities, groping for superior hypotheses and acquiring knowledge at each stage.

Insistence on derivation from first principles appears nowadays in anxiety to trace everything to maximization by rational individuals. Often, for example, we are told that we do not understand why money exists and why prices and wages are sticky (if indeed they are): models of these phenomena do not yet measure up to fashionable standards of "rigor."

One response to inexplicable phenomena "is to suggest that because we cannot explain them, they do not exist."[56] Referring to wage and price stickiness in particular, Tobin describes the reaction of rational-expectations theorists: "If we can't explain this phenomenon to our satisfaction within the paradigm, then it doesn't happen."[57] "Even if we do not have a completely convincing explanation for why wages and prices adjust more slowly in the short run than

---

54. Stiglitz, "Alternative Approaches to Macroeconomics," 18, 10.

55. Karl Brunner, "Keynes's Intellectual Legacy," in *Keynes's General Theory: Fifty Years On*, ed. John Burton (London: Institute of Economic Affairs, 1986), 60.

56. Stiglitz, "Alternative Approaches to Macroeconomics," 21.

57. Tobin, *Policies for Prosperity*, 461.

output and employment, the fact is they do, and a central objective of macroeconomics is to explore the consequences of this."[58]

The methodological attitude diagnosed by Brunner and Stiglitz, among others, is an evident example of the "justificationism" that W. W. Bartley finds deeply infecting Western philosophy. Justification-ism insists on accepting no propositions unless they have been justi-fied, demonstrated, proved, or warranted—and other such words that Bartley lists—by appeal to some ultimate authority that com-mands commitment, whether the authority of divine revelation, of reason as conceived by Descartes, or of some other approved method. Justificationism stands in contrast to the "critical rational-ism," "fallibilism," or procedure of conjectures and refutations of Karl Popper and his followers.[59]

As Stiglitz remarks, "Doing rigorous, sophisticated analysis with an obviously incorrect assumption does not make it any more cor-rect." (Stiglitz clearly is not intimidated by perfunctory recitations of the slogan against testing a theory by its assumptions.)[60]

Although the New Classical theorists may believe otherwise, Stiglitz continues, the prestige of theories of general economic equi-librium does not logically impose the assumption that the economy is, or works as if it were, always in equilibrium. What assumptions are appropriate depends on what questions are being asked; and when the subject matter is macroeconomics, which deals with lapses from full coordination, the assumption of equilibrium always lies some-where between question begging and self-contradiction.

Often, in macroeconomics, testing a theory translates into test-ing its conformity with some time-series predictions. "Unfortunately," Stiglitz observes, "there appear to be a plethora of theories which do reasonably well on this criteria [sic]."[61] Our micro-based theories have micro as well as macro predictions; we should see whether they are falsified. If they are, the theory should be rejected or at least patched up. (Parenthetically, Stiglitz adds that "the patching up pro-

58. Stiglitz, "Alternative Approaches to Macroeconomics," 29–30.

59. William Warren Bartley III, *The Retreat to Commitment* (LaSalle, Ill.: Open Court, 1984), app. 2.

60. Stiglitz, "Alternative Approaches to Macroeconomics," 25–26.

61. Ibid., 22.

cess provides a forum for the demonstration of cleverness; and in the end, a judgment must be made whether these have produced a more refined theory, or merely a Ptolemaic exercise.")[62] He continues: "The conformity of a theory to the basic *qualitative* facts of the economy seems to be the first hurdle to which any theory should be subjected. If it fails to meet that test, there is little to be gained from the sophisticated testing of one or two of its implications, for in the end, . . . a theory must be judged by the consistency of all of its implications with the facts."[63]

Still another related methodological notion seems to be that all worthwhile earlier economics is embodied in the latest "frontier" work. Concern for supposedly superseded writings draws contempt in some circles. I hope my present audience needs no lecture on why such contempt is misguided.

CONCLUDING EXHORTATIONS

The title of this concluding section apologizes for what are frankly personal views. Anyway, we economists should not worry as much as we sometimes have about which camp or school each of us belongs to. We should not strain to carry forward the supposedly distinguishing ideas of our own favorite school. Those of us with monetarist sympathies need not be squeamish about observations and arguments that have had a "Keynesian" or "New Keynesian" label foisted onto them. In the present stage of discussion about comparative economic systems, and given the spread of sober analysis about how governments (as well as business firms) operate, an economist need not fear coming across as a socialist or as an eager interventionist merely because he frankly recognizes so-called imperfections of the market. Both in analysis and in assessing remedial policies, we need not shy away from recognizing how these imperfections interact with aggregate-demand shocks in disrupting the coordination of economic activities.

62. Ibid., 23.
63. Ibid., 71–72.

301

We should let our perceptions be determined more by reality and less by methodological fashion. Instead of restricting ourselves to "positive economics," narrowly interpreted, we should practice "Sherlock Holmes inference," being receptive to scraps of evidence of all kinds (Edward Leamer's advice as recalled by Robert J. Shiller in his discussion of Alan Blinder's 1991 paper "Why Are Prices Sticky?").[64] Robin Winks's conception of *The Historian as Detective* can apply to economists also.[65]

Although science does strive to discern uniformities underlying superficial diversities, economists should not strain after mere sham parallelisms. Aggregate demand and supply diagrams provide a case in point. Such constructions evidently appeal to textbook publishers; they appear to teach macroeconomics by building on the student's grasp of micro analysis. But it is better to leave the student ignorant of macro, and aware of his ignorance, than to employ apparatus conveying a serious *mis*understanding. The rationale of aggregate demand and supply curves is much weaker than, and totally different from, the rationale of the familiar micro curves.

Economists should show respect for clear communication, including respect for the integrity of words and labels. If we pay any attention at all to the history of economic thought (as, agreeing with Leijonhufvud, I think we should), we should deign to get that history right.

64. Robert J. Shiller, discussion of Blinder, "Why Are Prices Sticky," in *American Economic Review* 81 (May 1991): 97.

65. Robin W. Winks, ed., *The Historian as Detective: Essays on Evidence* (New York: Harper & Row, 1969).

PART FOUR

AVOIDING

MONETARY

DISEQUILIBRIUM

Monetary Policy: Before and After the Freeze

I

A VIEW BEFORE THE FREEZE

GOVERNMENT FAILURES

My theme is that certain unsatisfactory aspects of the performance of the capitalist economy—inflation, recession, cyclical unemployment, and balance-of-payments crises—are not characteristic of capitalism itself but result, instead, from a defective monetary policy; and monetary policy is a government function.

Some extreme libertarians advocate abolishing all government responsibility for money. A monetary system left entirely to private enterprise is perhaps conceivable, but satisfactory control over the quantity of money would be lacking. In producing ordinary goods and services, private enterprise works for efficiency and abundance. But the serviceability of money depends on its *scarcity*. It is no solution to adopt some commodity like gold as money. First, only by unbelievable good luck would the quantity of the monetary commodity grow at the exact pace needed to avoid both depression and inflation. As Sir John Clapham said, "A currency system which in difficult times depends on the chance occurrence of nuggets in gulches and

Reprinted from the 1971 pamphlet *Monetary Policy and Economic Performance: Views Before and After the Freeze*, with permission of The American Enterprise Institute for Public Policy Research, Washington, D.C. 20036.

gold dust in river sands lacks stability."[1] Second, banking and credit institutions would have incentives to develop substitutes or supplements for gold, leaving the total supply of money under only the loosest restraint.[2] If, therefore, individuals and business firms are to be free to spend or save, invest or hoard, do business for credit or do business for cash, all as they individually see fit, and if a modern market economy, resting on specialization and exchange, is yet to work smoothly, then the total quantity of money must be under control of a monetary authority.

Theories of bureaucracy and politics give ample reason for skepticism about the ability of government to perform *any* function well. But government can perform some functions less badly than unregulated private enterprise. Control of money is one of these. Suitable control over its quantity is technically easy to achieve. The main task is to get the relevant economic theories understood and accepted and the corresponding rules imposed on the money managers. So far, this has not been done, and the consequences are unsatisfactory. This thesis is perhaps not very original, but my task is to report key truths about my assigned topic and not strive for originality at their expense.

In a capitalist economy, or price system, decisions about what goods and services are to be produced, and in what quantities, and about how labor and other resources are to be channeled into the different lines of production—all these decisions are made in response to the spending of money. Businessmen plan production, hire labor, and buy other factors of production with a view to earning profit in money. Prospects of money profit determine whether total production falls short of or keeps rising at the maximum level permitted by real factors (such as the labor force, the stock of capital goods and natural resources, the state of technology, and the degree of efficiency of coordination among economic units). This outcome depends largely on whether the total spending of money is too small, just right, or—in the case of inflation—too great to buy the total po-

1. *The Bank of England* (Cambridge: Cambridge University Press, reprinted 1958), 2: 222–23.

2. A composite-commodity or commodity-reserve standard, often proposed but never (to my knowledge) adopted, would not avoid all of the difficulties of a single-commodity standard.

tential output of goods and services and to hire the available resources at the existing general level of prices and wages. Too little spending logically implies an excess demand for money: people are trying to hold cash balances totaling more than the total quantity of money. Too much spending implies the reverse—an excess supply of money.

Theoretically, an excess demand for or excess supply of money would tend to cure itself through a rise or fall in the buying power of the dollar—but only with delay and after the hardships and injustices of deflation or price inflation. It is "doing things the hard way" to rely passively on such processes to make whatever nominal quantity of money exists have the total real purchasing power just right for a full employment level of total production. To expect adjustments in the general price level to cope with inappropriate behavior of the total nominal quantity of money imposes an unnecessary burden on the capitalist system. As a practical matter, a capitalist economy will perform poorly if the quantity of money grows unsteadily, sometimes spurting, sometimes slowing down, and, in extreme cases, actually shrinking.

MONETARY INSTABILITY

We should not exaggerate the shortcomings of United States monetary policy. It has been much better since World War II than before. Our monetary authorities have learned enough not to repeat the blunders that caused the Great Depression, stretching from 1929 until World War II. During the early and middle 1960s, in particular, monetary policy contributed to prosperity with smooth economic growth. Since 1965, however, the United States has been suffering first inflation and then recession. Recently we have been suffering both at the same time; and now, in the spring of 1971, unemployment and prices both continue rising. Now, as for the inflations and depressions of earlier years, the explanation is unsteadiness in the rate of growth of the money supply.

Several factors seem to account for unsteady monetary growth in the United States. Before 1914 the United States had no central bank; and the money supply was subject to all the accidents of being linked to gold, and through gold to foreign currencies, on a fractional-reserve basis. The Federal Reserve System operated during the first two decades or more of its existence largely under the influence of the "real-bills doctrine." This doctrine focused attention not on the total quantity of money but on the quality of money, or, more precisely, on the supposed quality of the bank loans through which new money was put into circulation. In parallel with this doctrine, the Federal Reserve gave less attention to the quantity of money than to interest rates and related indicators of the so-called ease or tightness of credit conditions. Watching the wrong indicators made it possible to think that monetary policy had been extremely easy, yet had failed, during the Great Depression in the United States. In fact, policy had been extremely tight: the money supply shrank by some one-fourth to one-third (depending on the definition of money used) between 1929 and 1933. The sharp business recession of 1937–38 resulted from a contractionary monetary policy, which the Federal Reserve had imposed because of its wrong theories about the large volume of supposedly excess bank reserves in existence at the time. In truth, the experience of the 1930s demonstrates not the weakness of monetary policy but its potency—and how much damage it can do if it is perverse.

Use of the wrong monetary indicators has persisted into the 1960s and 1970s. The total quantities of currency and bank-deposit money and of "base" money have, it is true, been receiving increased attention. ("Base" or "high-powered" money, as distinguished from bank deposits, is money issued by the government or central bank.) Still, journalists and Federal Reserve officials apparently continue to pay great attention to interest rates and other indicators of credit conditions. Even today, attention to the related concept of "free reserves" has far from lapsed. Free reserves are the amount by which the excess reserves of the commercial banks exceed their borrowings from the Federal Reserve. (If negative, this amount is called "net borrowed reserves.") To an economist who emphasizes the quantity of money instead, the free-reserves view of policy is strange indeed. To the extent that banks are *not* making full use of their reserves to expand their loans and deposits and are holding reserves idle instead, the free-reserve measure indicates an expansionary monetary policy. On the other hand, to the extent that banks are eagerly expanding loans and deposits on the basis of reserves lent to them by the Federal Reserve, the figure for net borrowed reserves indicates a tight monetary policy. This is all quite paradoxical and wrong.

A second apparent reason why unsteady monetary policy persists is the belief that fiscal policy is more important in determining the total level of spending in the economy. A government budget deficit is seen as expansionary, a surplus as deflationary, even apart from what is happening to the quantity of money. This belief, though losing ground as contrary evidence piles up, is not yet dead.

A third reason for unsteady monetary growth is that the money managers have traditionally been overambitious. They are not content to steer a steady course. They see the economy as constantly buffeted by destabilizing developments of a nonmonetary nature: "real" factors sometimes push the economy toward recession and at other times toward inflation. Traditionally the money managers have felt a duty to "lean against the wind"—to tighten or ease monetary policy to compensate for inflationary or deflationary winds originating elsewhere. This view of the economy as inherently unstable is congenial to the authorities: when the economy performs smoothly, they can take credit for successful "fine tuning"; when things go wrong, they can blame nonmonetary developments and suggest that their own judicious intervention has kept the consequences from being even worse.

Actually, since shifts in monetary policy have their main impact on the economy only after long and variable lags, a successful compensatory policy requires "leaning against the wind" as it will be blowing some unknown number of months in the future. Unless the monetary authorities can make and act upon accurate forecasts, their attempts to pursue a compensatory policy result in overreaction. When they see that the economy is in a recession, they tend to pursue an expansionary policy so vigorously and so long that an inflationary boom develops. Then, in an effort to check the inflation, they step on the monetary brakes so hard and so long as to cause another recession. Each time the authorities tend to go too far in trying to compensate for the consequences of their earlier errors in the opposite direction. Naturally, this is not the way that the Federal

Reserve officials themselves interpret the several episodes of this kind that the United States has experienced since World War II.

Finally, under the heading of overambitiousness, comes an itch constantly to be doing something. The money managers, like most people, want to think of their jobs as important, complicated, and demanding. They are actively alert to signs of the supposed need for delicate adjustments in policy. They are eager to meet their important responsibilities. As I shall mention later, central bankers behave similarly on the international scene.

SINCE 1965

Let us look more closely at the unsteadiness of monetary policy since about 1965, following several comparatively satisfactory years. The Vietnam escalation brought swollen deficits to the United States government budget. Conceivably the government could finance its deficit by selling its bonds at whatever interest rates were necessary to find buyers for them. Instead of expanding the money supply at a rate incompatible with price-level stability, the government would be bidding loan funds away from other potential borrowers, "crowding out" their spending projects. Such deficit financing would be inflationary, if at all, only to a minor extent. In reality, however, governments and central bankers are unwilling to see interest rates rise as high as this approach might entail. Particularly at the time of a new issue of government securities, the Federal Reserve is inclined to facilitate their sale and keep them from jolting the credit and bond markets. For this purpose it is likely to buy existing securities itself, thereby expanding bank reserves and in turn the money supply. Until recently, anyway, it tended to overlook how, in the longer run, inflation would actually raise interest rates.

Ideally, the monetary expansion caused by this practice of "even keeling" is intended to be temporary only. In practice, though, with new issues of government securities repeatedly requiring such support, the expansion continues instead of being reversed. For this reason, large and chronic government budget deficits tend to promote rapid expansion of the money supply. For the sake of sound theory and sound interpretation of the historical record, however, it is important to distinguish between government deficits themselves and the creation of money that may finance them.

By the spring of 1966, price inflation had become so noticeable that the Federal Reserve, overreacting as usual, almost entirely halted the growth of the money supply until around the end of the year. Whatever indicators and targets of policy besides the money supply the Federal Reserve may have had in mind, it behaved so as to stop its growth. A pause in economic activity ensued in late 1966 and early 1967, threatening for a time to turn into a recession. The Federal Reserve reversed itself, however, and brought about an exceptionally rapid expansion of the money supply in 1967 and 1968.

Table 1 shows the annual rates of change of the money supply, prices, and production during certain periods since 1959. By itself, this table does not prove that monetary changes have been having the effects that I have asserted. Evidence on that score appears in studies of the sort mentioned later. The table merely provides some

TABLE 1 ANNUAL PERCENTAGE RATES OF CHANGE IN U.S. MONEY SUPPLY, INDUSTRIAL PRODUCTION INDEX, AND CONSUMER PRICE INDEX OVER SELECTED PERIODS, 1959–1971

MONEY SUPPLY		INDUSTRIAL PRODUCTION INDEX		CONSUMER PRICE INDEX	
Jul. '59–Jun. '60:	−2.8	Jun. '59–Dec. '60:	−3.9	Jul. '59–May '61:	+1.1
Jun. '60–Apr. '62:	+2.4	Dec. '60–May '62:	+9.8	May '61–Sep. '62:	+1.6
Apr. '62–Sep. '62:	−0.7	May '62–Dec. '62:	+1.7	Sep. '62–Feb. '63:	0.0
Sep. '62–May '65:	+3.9	Dec. '62–May '65:	+7.4	Feb. '63–May '65:	+1.4
May '65–Apr. '66:	+6.3	May '65–Oct. '66:	+8.6	May '65–Oct. '66:	+3.2
Apr. '66–Jan. '67:	−0.5	Oct. '66–Jun. '67:	−3.5	Oct. '66–Jul. '67:	+2.3
Jan. '67–Jan. '69:	+7.6	Jun. '67–Jul. '69:	+5.7	Jul. '67–Mar. '69:	+4.6
Jan. '69–Feb. '70:	+3.0	Jul. '69–Nov. '70:	−5.7	Mar. '69–Jun. '70:	+6.1
Feb. '70–Jan. '71:	+5.5				
		Nov. '70–May '71:	+7.3	Jun. '70–May '71:	+4.2
Jan '71–May '71:	+13.6				

SOURCE: Federal Reserve Bank of St. Louis. Underlying figures for money supply (demand deposits and currency) and industrial production, but not for consumer prices, are seasonally adjusted.

orientation and, in particular, gives an idea of how big certain changes have been. It gives an impression, for example, of the severity of recent United States price inflation: though severe by United States standards, its rate would count as mild indeed in many countries.

Among other reasons why rapid monetary expansion continued in the second half of 1968 was the belief of some monetary officials that the income-tax surcharge enacted in June would cause "fiscal overkill." Monetary ease was thought advisable to compensate for deflationary fiscal policy. As a consequence of this episode (about which more will be said later), inflation gained momentum.

INFLATIONARY RECESSION

Around the end of 1968 and early in 1969 the Federal Reserve took actions that sharply slowed the rate of monetary expansion. (Defined to include time deposits as well as currency and demand deposits, the money supply actually began shrinking.) This new reversal brought on a mild recession that began late in 1969 and worsened in 1970, with a slow recovery apparently beginning late in the year. President Nixon received blame not only for the inherited problem of the Vietnam War but also for the equally inherited economic difficulties. At first the Nixon administration talked of ending the inflation gradually while avoiding a recession. As signs of recession became unmistakable, the line shifted to arguing that any recession would be mild and brief and that victory over inflation was in sight. By the time a recession had become unmistakable, a slowdown in inflation had not; only careful scrutiny of the price indexes would reveal encouraging signs. The opposition had the opportunity to hold the administration responsible not only for recession and inflation at the same time but also, in view of its earlier optimistic talk, of not having a clue to what was going on.

A more realistic line, it seems to me, would have been safer for the administration. President Nixon should have stressed from the outset that the inflation he inherited had been going on for several years and would be hard to stop. It was to be expected from earlier experience that price inflation would persist for some time even if efforts to check it brought on a recession. Prices were continuing to rise in response to *earlier* excessive monetary expansion. This phenomenon illustrated and further supported the monetary doctrines of the "Chicago school," led by a man who had been an important economic advisor to the Republicans, behind the scenes, in the 1964 presidential campaign and during the early part of the Nixon administration.

As buyers become accustomed to repeatedly paying increased prices and as they find it increasingly difficult to compare the prices asked by rival sellers, their sensitivity to price competition weakens. Sellers become accustomed to passing actual and even expected cost increases on to their customers without meeting too much buyer resistance. Inflationary expectations prompt big wage demands by labor and acquiescence by employers. Even if a businessman should experience some drop or lag in his sales that he might attribute to his prices being too high, he could think that the continuing general inflation of costs and prices would soon make his current prices competitive and acceptable after all. Why reverse a slightly premature price increase when customers will soon be willing to accept it?

Another reason why inflation persists is that not all prices rise uniformly. Some, such as land and building rents and contractual wage rates, are set for months or years at a time, and the opportunity to revise them does not occur until existing contracts expire. A similar lag affects governmentally regulated prices, exise taxes, and the like. Furthermore, a business firm typically raises its selling prices in response to a rise in its costs; at least, a firm is likely to delay a price increase until it can point out to its customers, as an excuse, an increase (or clearly impending increase) in its costs.

The standard response of a firm to a rise in demand for its products is to try to expand quantities available for sale. A retailer will order more goods at wholesale. A manufacturer will order more materials, seek more labor, and perhaps try to expand his plant and equipment. Each individual businessman might think that, given time for adjustment, he could accommodate the increased demand for his product without raising prices. Yet as businessmen transmit the increased demands for final products back to the factors of production, competing against each other for materials, labor, and plant and equipment, they bid up these cost elements.

To the individual businessman, then, the chief factor justifying and requiring a rise in his selling prices is the rise in his costs. From his standpoint, the inflation may look like a cost-push process, even though costs are in fact rising as inflationary demands for final products are transmitted back to factors of production. In at least some stages of the inflation process, then, costs tend to rise first and prices to follow with a lag. A related reason for the sequential aspect of the inflation process is that prices charged by some business firms are costs of others.

For these and other reasons, a change in monetary policy and in the flow of money demand for final goods and services does not have its full impact at once. It spreads out over many months, even years. If monetary policy were to be tightened and an inflationary expansion of demand checked, much of the adjustment of prices to the earlier demand inflation would remain to be completed. Prices would continue rising for—in summary—at least three reasons. First, buyers and sellers would be acting on expectations formed during the period of active monetary inflation. Second, contractual prices would be renegotiated as contracts expired. Third, costs and prices would interact in sequences complicated by the fact that some firms' prices are other firms' costs.

When a switch to monetary restraint finally halts expansion of the total flow of money expenditure, or cuts it back to a rate consistent with growth in the economy's physical capacity to produce goods and services, the restrained flow of spending measured in nominal dollars becomes a shrunken flow of real purchasing power. The continuing process of delayed price adjustment shrinks each dollar in purchasing power and shrinks the total real quality of goods and services that the nominal flow of spending can buy. A recession develops. In terms of the equation of exchange, MV comes under restraint while P goes on rising with a momentum of its own; so T, the real volume of economic activity, has to fall.

It is in a situation like this that the case for a so-called incomes policy—formal or informal controls over wages and prices—is relatively best. To the extent that such a policy can check the momentum of wage and price increases, the restrained total flow of nominal money spending can go toward buying a full-employment output of

314

goods and services rather than toward buying a stagnant or shrinking total output at rising prices. Yet even in this situation, the case for an incomes policy is not very good.

Unfortunately, there is no easy and quick way to shake people out of expectations bred by several years of rapid inflation. Something rather convincing has to happen. Price consciousness has to be restored. Businessmen must realize that they cannot go on blithely consenting to wage increases and other cost increases in the expectation of successfully passing these increases on to docile customers. Gluts of goods, production capacity, and labor have to appear. In other words, a recession is indispensable, or almost so. Experience shows that changes in monetary policy work with lags and that its effects stretch out longer for price movements than for production. A tightening of money-supply growth shows up for the most part first in dampening physical activity and only later in slowing and eventually stopping price increases.

The Nixon administration should have emphasized from the start that the economic damage it inherited had been done months and years before. All the country could now hope to salvage was a lesson—a lesson about the consequences of unstable monetary policies and about the lagged relations among movements in money and in production and prices. If taken to heart, this lesson would keep the monetary authorities from repeating similar mistakes in the future. In trying to hide this lesson by blaming the Nixon administration for inflationary recession, the administration's critics were doing the country a disservice. But since the administration itself muffed the opportunity to teach this lesson, it is not surprising that it is being blamed for an inherited problem.

RENEWED INFLATION?

Partly because the lesson has not been learned, the United States now finds itself, in mid-1971, facing another example of monetary overreaction to short-run developments. Preoccupied with the recent recession, policy makers have been concentrating their efforts on hastening recovery almost without regard, apparently, for longer-run consequences. During the first five months of 1971 the Federal Reserve system allowed the money supply to expand at a rate of 11 percent a year, a rate which, if maintained much longer, could hardly fail to rekindle the fires of inflation. This policy is almost tragic. The country has gone through a period of exceptionally high interest rates associated, first, with expectations of continued price increases and then, also, with an anti-inflationary tightening of monetary growth. That policy switch has brought recession and unemployment. We have paid the bulk of the price for checking inflation and were just beginning to see signs of at last getting what we had paid for. Now, after so much effort, pain, and patience, it would be particularly ironic to throw away our victory over inflation. If we do, the recession of 1970 will appear in retrospect as an episode of pointless masochism in a period of inflation stretching unbroken from the mid-1960s to the mid-1970s and perhaps beyond.

What explains this turn of events? One possibility is that President Nixon is determined to hasten recovery from the recession and get unemployment down to an acceptable figure. Since prices respond more slowly than production and employment, there is some hope that price inflation will not speed up unmistakably before late 1972. Even if this were the administration's view, it is hard to see why the Federal Reserve should go along, since its officials are not under the direct control of the administration. Perhaps the Federal Reserve is overreacting again and is independently giving priority to rapid recovery from the recession. Perhaps it is still paying too little attention to the quantity of money and too much attention to other supposed targets and indicators of policy. Some newspaper and magazine articles have suggested that the rapid growth of the money supply in the first half of 1971 is a surprise even to the Federal Reserve itself.[3] Pending further evidence, I'll lamely have to leave its recent inflationary behavior as a genuine mystery.

3. According to *Business Week* (19 June 1971, 34), "For weeks, the Federal Reserve has been fighting gamely to slow the rate of growth of the nation's money supply without letting the cost of money go through the roof." This remark is interesting because it suggests that concern with interest rates has again overridden concern with the quantity of money. The writers of the First National Bank's *Monthly Economic Letter* (June 1971): 1–2, also mention this possibility as they wonder about reasons for the recent misbehavior of the Federal Reserve.

INTERNATIONAL MONETARY POLICY

Domestic and international monetary policies intersect in ways that are sometimes awkward. Worries about the United States's balance of payments and cries of "dollar imperialism" are familiar. The Bretton Woods system of fixed-but-adjustable exchange rates imparts an inflationary bias to the world economy; at least, the case for this proposition, centering on the concept of imported inflation, seems persuasive. Balance-of-payments disequilibriums interfere with domestic stabilization policies, while, on the other hand, divergences among countries in business-cycle movements and in the underlying domestic monetary policies cause balance-of-payments disequilibriums. International short-term capital movements have been particularly troublesome in recent years. With currency transactions substantially free of controls and with fixed exchange rates trusted, flows of funds become highly sensitive to differences in interest rates. With currency transactions substantially free of controls and with fixed exchange rates trusted, flows of funds become highly sensitive to differences in interest rates. When fixed exchange rates come under suspicion and are thought likely to be altered, speculation motivates massive transfers of funds. Troublesome capital flows occur, then, under either of two extreme conditions—trust and distrust of the levels at which exchange rates are fixed.

Let us recall the chief international monetary crises of the last four years—not to go back any further. The fall of 1967 saw a crisis leading to devaluation of the British pound in mid-November. In March 1968 a flight from the dollar into gold led to abandonment of the inter-central-bank gold pool and adoption of a two-price system for gold. Later that spring a flight from the franc developed, and the Paris foreign exchange market was closed from May 20 to June 7. The franc was not devalued at that time, but various exchange controls were imposed or tightened. On Wednesday, November 20, 1968, the principal European foreign-exchange markets were closed for the remainder of the week while the finance ministers and central-bank governors of the Group of Ten met in emergency session in Bonn. Exchange-rate adjustments were generally expected, including at least a devaluation of the franc and possibly a revaluation of the mark. But Sunday, No-

317

vember 24, DeGaulle surprised the world with his decision not to devalue. Germany adopted various palliative measures in lieu of revaluation. In the spring of 1969, renewed speculation on revaluation of the mark brought massive inflows of funds into Germany. Between the end of April and May 9, German reserves rose by some $4.1 billion, including $2.5 billion on May 8 and 9 alone.[4] On May 9 a German government spokesman announced that there would be no revaluation and that the existing parity of the mark was valid for "eternity." Further substitute measures were adopted. "Eternity" lasted until Wednesday, September 24 of the same year. After the close of that day's foreign-exchange trading, the authorities announced that the market would remain closed through the German election the following Sunday. This move forestalled an inflow of funds that might otherwise have approached the massive proportions of November 1968 and May 1969. The mark was allowed to float during most of October and was revalued 9.3 percent above the old parity on Friday, October 24. Meanwhile, on August 8, the French franc had been devalued by 11.1 percent. The foreign-exchange markets appeared to accept this measure with relief, since speculation against the franc had been rocking the markets repeatedly since the events of 1968. Relative calm returned in 1970, though the floating of the Canadian dollar at the end of May is noteworthy. During the same year the United States ran a deficit on the official-settlements basis of a record $9.8 billion. Announcement of this figure in February 1971 gave fresh impetus to a heavy outflow of funds already under way from the United States. The most obvious cause of the flow had been the differential emerging between American and European interest rates. Declining interest rates in the United States (together with restored ability to sell certificates of deposit at home) had encouraged United States banks to repay mammoth loans obtained earlier in the Eurodollar market. These repayments depressed Eurodollar interest rates and gave investors in short-term liquid assets an incentive to move their funds out of dollar claims and put them into Germany and other European countries where interest rates were higher. Furthermore, continental businessmen, notably Germans, had an incentive to borrow on the Eurodollar market and then sell the borrowed funds for local currency.

4. *Federal Reserve Bulletin* (March 1970): 229.

It is ironic that a decline in American interest rates should have promoted a flight from the dollar, for the decline was due chiefly to the recession the United States had suffered in efforts to stop inflation. These efforts should have tended, fundamentally, to strengthen the dollar. When the recession became unmistakable, Federal Reserve policy reinforced the decline of interest rates to promote business recovery. As interest-motivated transfers gathered momentum and as the reserves of the German Bundesbank grew massively, the flow of funds became increasingly speculative. Talk of a possible upward revaluation or upward float of the mark—talk to which German officials contributed—helped swell the dumping of dollars onto the Bundesbank to an estimated total of $2.2 billion on Tuesday, May 4, 1971, and the first forty minutes of trading on Wednesday morning. Then the Bundesbank stopped supporting the dollar. The market was closed for the rest of the week. When it reopened on Monday, May 10, two currencies had been revalued upward, two were floating, and one was on a two-tier system. The uncertainties that remained about future policies are still with us.

By the time of these revaluations and floats, international monetary experts had finally come to realize the paradoxical role of central bankers in the Eurodollar market. (The involvement of the Eurodollar market in the crisis should be of interest to East Europeans because of their own role, back to the late 1950s, in initiating the growth of the market.) It turned out that central bankers had themselves been contributing to interest-rate differentials and to the multiplication of the dollars whose inflow into their own reserves had been troubling them so much. The typical European central bank had been depositing on the Eurodollar market, either directly or through the intermediary of the Bank for International Settlements, some of the dollars that it had been reluctantly acquiring. This action tended to depress interest rates on the Eurodollar market and so increase the incentive for European businessmen to borrow dollars cheaply there and then sell them for their own local currencies. Furthermore, dollars deposited by a central bank in a Eurodollar bank were available for relending, including relending to borrowers who would convert them into their local currencies. Thus, dollars would come back into the possession of central banks, be again deposited in the Eurodollar market, and so on and on. As a result, central banks were reluctantly buying up dollars in amounts several billion dollars larger than the amount of increase in United States liabilities to foreign central banks. In effect, the Europeans themselves to a large extent had been manufacturing the dollars whose influx they had been so bitterly blaming on the United States. This weird situation was a feature not of capitalism as such or of the Eurodollar market, but of government intervention—in particular, of exchange-rate pegging and of practices of acquiring and holding dollar reserves.

Professor Machlup has written an article about "The Magicians and their Rabbits." When an ordinary magician pulls a rabbit out of a hat during a stage performance, he knows that he has put it there in advance. But the dollar-multiplying central bankers are a particularly naive breed of magician: when they pull a rabbit out of a hat, they are as astonished as the audience.[5] Yet these naive magicians have been bitterly criticizing private speculators for troubles that they themselves had intensified. These magicians number among the officials to whom we are now expected to look for controls over the Eurodollar market and for solutions to international monetary problems in general.

IMPLICATIONS OF RECENT EXPERIENCE

The crisis of May 1971 has generated much talk about policies likely to be adopted to forestall further troubles. These include (1) greater flexibility, though not free flexibility, of exchange rates; (2) a greater degree of coordination of financial policies, partly to limit interest-rate differentials, with increased emphasis on fiscal rather than monetary policy for domestic stabilization purposes; a world central bank could conceivably promote this coordination; (3) tighter controls over international capital movements.

5. Fritz Machlup, in *Morgan Guaranty Survey* (May 1971): 3–13. In its forty-first *Annual Report*, published 14 June 1971, the Bank for International Settlements mentions in several places—though of course does not emphasize—the role of central banks, and its own role, in the multiplication of dollars. The report even acknowledges (e.g., 164, 166) that central banks made large deposits in the Eurodollar market to obtain attractive interest yields on their foreign-exchange reserves.

Yet this would be an inappropriate combination of policies. If exchange rates were to be held rigid, a relatively plausible case could be made for trying to coordinate monetary and interest-rate policies and to control capital movements. But with exchange rates flexible, coordination of domestic policies is not only unnecessary but questionable (and so, in particular, is the idea of achieving domestic objectives with fiscal rather than monetary policy). Control over capital movements would be not only unnecessary but also likely to hamper various kinds of arbitrage and speculation needed for the smoothest possible working of free foreign-exchange markets. Admittedly, though, it may be academic to worry just now about interferences with the smooth working of freely floating exchange rates, since what policy makers have been toying with is not free flexibility but manipulated flexibility (which, one might plausibly argue, is likely to combine the worst features of floating and pegged rates).

Many years probably must elapse before the lessons taught by experience with domestic and international monetary policies finally get learned and heeded—or before a new generation of central bankers succeeds the present one. So far, central bankers seem to have the same itch to meddle actively on the international scene as on the domestic scene—and for the same bureaucratic motives.[6]

6. As Milton Friedman implies, the problems caused by pegging exchange rates are *fun* for central bankers and government officials:

> Floating exchange rates would put an end to the grave problems requiring repeated meetings of secretaries of the Treasury and governors of central banks to try to draw up sweeping reforms. It would put an end to the occasional crisis producing frantic scurrying of high governmental officials from capital to capital, midnight phone calls among the great central banks lining up emergency loans to support one or another currency.
>
> Indeed this is, I believe, one of the major sources of the opposition to floating exchange rates. The people engaged in these activities are important people and they are all persuaded that they are engaged in important activities. It cannot be, they say to themselves, that these important activities arise simply from pegging exchange rates.

Milton Friedman and Robert V. Roosa, *The Balance of Payments: Free Versus Fixed Exchange Rates* (Washington, D.C.: American Enterprise Institute for Public Policy Research, 1967), 15–16.
Richard H. Timberlake, Jr., citing Robert Roosa and others, also conjectures that monetary officials have a taste for the system of fixed exchange rates because of their own "essential" roles in it; see his "The Fixation With Fixed Exchange Rates,"

The chief lesson is this: If only the authorities would stop trying to be so clever in their interventions on domestic and international money markets and would play a less grandiose role; if only, for example, they worried less about maintaining so-called orderly conditions on the credit and securities markets and aimed, instead, at a smooth moderate growth of the domestic money supply; and if only they would keep their hands off the foreign-exchange markets; then several supposed defects of the capitalist system would substantially vanish. We would see the end of serious inflations and recessions and of international currency crises.

It is unlikely, of course, that most capitalist countries will heed this lesson any time soon. This is just one more reason for not linking them all together through some sort of international coordination of policies. Let those countries that are in the vanguard of heeding the lessons of monetary theory and experience put them into effect alone, without being dragged into continuing disorders by countries that are slow in learning. Time will then afford a growing number of examples of how well a capitalist economy can perform if only its monetary authorities behave themselves.

II
A VIEW AFTER THE FREEZE

DOMESTIC LESSONS

If I were rewriting my "before the freeze" section I would increase its emphasis on the danger of throwing away the only thing—a lesson—to be salvaged from the botched monetary policy of recent years. That botch caused an inflationary recession for which there simply was no quick and easy cure. We might avoid similar mistakes in the future by taking to heart what went wrong. Yet the New Economic Policy (NEP) adopted on August 15 threatens to obscure even that lesson.

Southern Economic Journal 36 (October 1969), esp. 139. For specific examples of the enjoyment of "frantic scurrying" and "midnight phone calls," see John Brooks, "In Defense of Sterling," *New Yorker* 44, 23 March 1968, 44ff.; and 30 March 1968, 43ff.

One way it does so is by appearing to recognize, act on, and dignify an unduly sharp distinction between demand-pull and cost-push inflation. As part 1 explains, individual businessmen may well see even an outright demand-pull inflation as a cost-push process. This appearance grows even stronger as wage-and-price inflation continues with a momentum of its own for months, even years, after actual excess demand has been turned off, and even after recession has developed. (For several reasons noted below, price trends respond to monetary changes with longer lags than physical activity does.) The excessive monetary expansion that initiated the problem some time earlier tends to be forgotten. Publicity in favor of the NEP reinforces this forgetfulness.[7] The long-persisting disorders caused by an unsteady monetary policy develop, ironically, into ones for which the monetary authorities superficially appear to have no responsibility.

The NEP also undermines the lesson of experience by seeming officially to recognize a supposed failure of "monetarist" doctrine and policy. Shortly after assuming office, wrote Leonard Silk in the *New York Times* of August 23, 1971, President Nixon "began a crucial test of an economic theory which maintained that a moderately growing money supply, coupled with a moderately restrictive budgetary policy, could gradually stop the inflation Mr. Nixon had inherited from the Johnson Administration" and set the stage, before the 1972 election, for strong expansion with full employment and stable prices. This experiment ended with the freeze of wages, prices, and rents. The monetarist doctrine had not only proved politically unrealistic but had "also failed economically, in its own terms. Inflation did not fade away." Monetarism had proved wrong. Silk said, in supposing that "inflation could be caused only by too much money, not by too much private power in the marketplace."

In the same newspaper just one week later (August 30, 1971), Pierre Rinfret, one of the country's most prominent economic consultants to business, echoed this theme. Hailing Nixon's "daring, dy-

---

7. For example, a newsletter of 3 November 1971, issued by Citizens for a New Prosperity, carries a stop-sign emblem labeled "Stop Inflation" and reports with satisfaction on various grass-roots efforts to do just that, including a nationwide voluntary wage-price freeze that an Arlington, Virginia, housewife was "ordering." Such efforts almost surely do more to undermine than to promote public understanding of what causes and what would cure inflation.

namic and delightful economic program" with "joy and elation," Rinfret expressed pride in "a President who had the courage, stamina and strength to move forward vigorously. . . . Political economics," he continued, "has prevailed over economics per se. The day when Government policy is based solely on some obscure economic theory espoused by some obscure economist out of some obscure Midwestern university has come to an end. The academicians are through. The President has opted for the pragmatists, for the practitioners, for the doers, for the realists."[8]

Besides being anti-intellectual and revealing an infatuation with what the Mexicans call "machismo," such comments have the further defect of obscuring how well recent experience actually supports monetarist doctrine. Changes in monetary growth do work with lags, as Professor Friedman long has stressed; and resulting changes in physical economic activity, particularly in the downward direction, tend to precede changes in price trends. No one ever promised that a switch to steady monetary growth would quickly repair the damage done by several years of zigzagging. On the contrary, the monetarists at the Federal Reserve Bank of St. Louis have been openly pessimistic about an early end to both inflation and unemployment, whatever stable rate of growth were belatedly adopted.[9] Monetary steadiness is a necessary condition for satisfactory economic performance but not a sufficient condition, and especially not a quickly sufficient condition. To reject monetarist doctrine and policy merely because it does not promise or deliver quick and happy results is like rejecting medical science because it does not promise or deliver a sure cure for cancer—and like resorting, instead, to magical incantations and salves made of ground-up bats' wings.

To recommend monetary steadiness, by the way, is not necessarily to insist on a specific rate of money-supply growth rigidly locked in by law. It is all too easy and familiar for champions of unfettered discretion to score some empty debating points by caricaturing the

8. One might well ask: if the quantity theory of money, Milton Friedman, and the University of Chicago all are obscure, then what theory, economist, and university *are* well known?

9. Leonall C. Andersen and Keith M. Carlson, "A Monetarist Model for Economic Stabilization," Federal Reserve Bank of St. Louis, *Review* (April 1970): 7–25, and articles in later issues.

monetarist position. Without detouring into this rules-versus-authorities debate, we can recognize a world of difference between a steady policy, even with the target rate of monetary growth subject to smooth and gradual revision in the light of sustained experience, and the zigzag policy of frequent shifts in strength and direction in efforts to offset economic fluctuations—fluctuations largely caused by earlier efforts of the same kind.

Far from failing, monetarist policy has not yet had a full-fledged trial. In January 1970, it is true, directives of the Federal Open Market Committee did begin giving increased attention to desired growth rates of certain monetary aggregates. Even so, the monetary growth rate did not become the immediate target; instead, it was supposedly to be controlled *through* the money-market conditions that have traditionally preoccupied the Federal Reserve.[10] "Despite the stated policy to place emphasis on the monetary growth rate in 1971," the Council of Economic Advisers observed,

> actual operations were designed to influence interest rates and conditions in short-term money markets, with the intention of thereby achieving the desired monetary growth rate. In practice the Federal Reserve operated most directly on the interest rate on loans among banks, called the Federal funds rate, relying on its appraisal of how monetary growth rates would respond to various levels of the interest rate. If the money stock responded to the Federal funds rate in a way that differed from the expected response, the monetary growth rate would differ from that desired.[11]

Despite, therefore, any supposed change or partial change of policy in accordance with monetarist doctrine, monetary zigzags have

10. Jerry L. Jordan and Neil A. Stevens, "The Year 1970—A 'Modest' Beginning for Monetary Aggregates," Federal Reserve Bank of St. Louis, *Review* (May 1971): 14–32. Toward the end of 1970, as this article notes, the committee appears to have shifted its emphasis back from monetary aggregates onto money-market conditions.

11. *Annual Report of the Council of Economic Advisers* (Washington, D.C.: Government Printing Office, January 1972), 57–58. Actually, the words "respond" and "response" go too far toward adopting the rather misleading language often used in Federal Reserve descriptions of money-supply behavior. The money supply responds not so much to interest rates as to Federal Reserve actions, whose immediate aim may be some desired behavior of interest rates.

continued during the Nixon administration. Monetary growth slowed severely early in 1969, speeded up again around February 1970, and slowed again briefly in the last quarter of the year. In the first half of 1971, growth became alarmingly rapid. More recent information tends to bear out the conjecture made in part 1 that the supposed inability of the Federal Reserve to control this growth stemmed from its overriding preoccupation with trying to resist the rise of interest rates. August brought a sharp switch to several months of substantially zero money-supply growth; a downturn in interest-rate trends seemingly contributed to this change in Federal Reserve actions."[12]

The excessive money-supply growth in the first half of 1971 apparently reinforced the inflationary expectations that had been helping sidetrack the growth of nominal spending largely into paying increased wages and prices rather than into supporting recovery of employment and production. Businessmen may well have become so alert to inflation that they no longer reaffirmed or revised their expectations about its pace only after looking at price indexes; they may have seen the money growth rate itself as a significant and earlier indicator. Several bank newsletters paid explicit attention to this rate in 1971 and noted what it implied for future price trends. Interest rates were reflecting price expectations, and "[i]nterest rates have risen on signals that the rate of growth of the money supply was increasing." Robert Mundell has also alluded to this direct monetary influence on expectations, adding that monetary expansion cannot promote real economic expansion unless it has rigidities to bite on— price and wage rigidities and money illusions. Experience with rapid inflation itself tends to dissolve normal rigidities, leaving monetary acceleration to have its main impact on price trends rather than on real economic activity."[13]

12. These statements, as well as remarks and the table in part 1, refer to seasonally adjusted money-supply figures. Use of adjusted figures seems to be standard practice in monetarist and nonmonetarist writings alike, including those of the Federal Reserve. It must be admitted, however, that intrayear growth patterns of adjusted and unadjusted money diverge widely. Furthermore, the very meaning of seasonal adjustment of figures on anything so subject to policy control as the money supply is open to serious question. The fact remains, though, that the money supply, measured in any plausible way, has grown very unsteadily.

13. The quoted sentence comes from A. James Meigs and William Wolman, "Central Banks and the Money Supply," Federal Reserve Bank of St. Louis, *Review*

This last point about monetary policy's losing its bite does not, of course, refute monetarist policy advice. Far from recommending active switching back and forth in an attempt to control real activity, that doctrine counsels against such disruptions.

Still another danger of misreading the lessons of experience hinges on imposition of the NEP in precisely the situation in which controls have relatively the best chance of seeming to work as intended.[14] What part 1 said deserves amplification now. Well-warranted expectations of continuing price inflation had raised the rate of either unemployment or inflation necessary to keep the other rate down to any specific figure. (In short, expectations had worsened the Phillips curve.) An incomes policy, especially if accompanying a moderate monetary policy, could counteract this worsening and contribute to stopping inflation with less unemployment during the transition than would otherwise occur. Controls could conceivably substitute for business recession as the "something rather convincing" (mentioned in part 1) that was necessary to dampen inflationary expectations, restore price consciousness, and make businessmen realize that they could not continue to count on shifting cost increases to docile customers. So far as controls could check the upward momentum of wages and prices, a restrained flow of spending could go toward buying a full-employment output of goods and services rather than toward simply paying increased prices and wages. Ideally, by reducing the

---

(August 1971): 26. Mundell's ideas appear in *The Dollar and the Policy Maker: 1971*, Princeton Essays no. 85 (Princeton: Princeton University Press, 1971). A. A. Walters makes similar reference to a direct effect of money on expectations in "Consistent Expectations, Distributed Lags and the Quantity Theory," *Economic Journal* 81 (June 1971): 273–81.

14. Professor Abba Lerner unintentionally illustrated this danger in a panel discussion on 5 November 1971, during the Southern Economic Association meetings in Miami Beach. How we had gotten into the present mess did not matter, he said; the important thing was to understand how wage and price regulation could help us get out. (He distinguished between "regulation," aimed at improving the operation of markets by preventing wages and prices from rising in the absence of excess demand, and "controls," which impede the operation of markets by trying to suppress the consequences of current demand inflation. This distinction in terminology is not, however, generally recognized.) Lerner to the contrary, attention to how we got into the mess *is* important; for what is at stake is the chance to learn from past errors.

unemployment and loss of output associated with checking price inflation and by reducing the expected-inflation component of interest rates, the controls could even help make the necessary monetary restraint politically feasible.

To be sure, controls—and especially an outright freeze—leave individual prices and wages in wrong relations with each other by arresting the process of their mutual adjustment. But this, in the rationale of the policy, might be only a minor difficulty: with goods and labor still generally in excess supply, the wrongness of their relative prices could safely be left for correction later, after the general upward momentum had been broken.

An incomes policy, as just conceived, is quite different from trying to suppress wage and price increases in the face of a continuing monetary inflation. Rather, it aims to counter a temporary worsening of the unemployment-or-inflation trade-off dramatized in the form of inflationary recession.

Controls: For and Against

Experience with temporary controls in these special circumstances may be misread, unfortunately, as evidence in favor of controls maintained permanently and in other circumstances. For several reasons they may appear to succeed. First and most obviously, price indexes will not rise as fast under controls, and especially during a freeze, as they had risen before. When a surveyor from the Bureau of Labor Statistics visits a store to gather current prices, he will hardly be told that they have risen to an illegal degree. If prices spurt after a freeze is thawed or controls lifted, the controls will look deceptively good in comparison. In future years, some econometricians' equations will no doubt include a dummy variable representing controls "on" or "off" and will suggest to naive readers that controls significantly improved economic performance. Actually, controls should be appraised by their total consequences, not just their most superficially measurable consequences or the consequences observed only during the periods of control.

Second, some improvement on the price front might have appeared, anyway, for reasons other than the controls. Unemployment and productive slack during 1970 and 1971 were already working against the momentum of wage and price inflation. For a time, in fact, close scrutiny of price indexes could even yield some encouragement. The renewed acceleration of money-supply growth in the first half of 1971, on the other hand, tended to support this momentum.

Third, output and employment were already recovering from the recession. Besides the controls, fiscal stimulus, including the import surcharge, was part of Nixon's new package. It is a usual feature of recovery from recession, furthermore, for businessmen to make fuller use of their productive plant in combination with their labor forces and so to spread their overhead costs over increased volumes of output. Showing up as improvements in productivity, these developments (the reverse of those suffered on the way down into recession) help check cost-and-price increases.

To some extent, the controls may even have genuine, and not just apparent, good results. The announcement of August 15 bred some sheer unreasoning and temporary optimism, presumably tending to spur purchases and production of consumer and investment goods. Further, the freeze presumably tempered inflationary expectations. The ensuing decline in interest rates also makes it easier for the Federal Reserve—given the indicators and targets it employs and the political pressures it feels—to hold the line on the money supply.

Because the NEP imposed controls as a temporary expedient in the exceptional circumstances of inflationary recession, it is an experiment that appeals to the intellectual curiosity of economists. It furnishes material for future doctoral dissertations. On the other hand, economists have reasons to regret the NEP. It may well sap the meaning of econometrically fitted functions by changing the underlying behavioral relations. It impairs the meaning of economic statistics themselves, particularly prices and price indexes.

And there are other, more substantive, grounds for regretting the policy. (Mentioning them is not necessarily to condemn it totally, or even on balance; after all, I have been trying to figure out what a respectable rationale for the policy might be.) It hampers adjustments of relative prices, threatening shortages of items whose prices are held most too low. It causes inequities of familiar kinds; and it accustoms people to look to the government to upset, in their favor, contracts voluntarily made. Remembering it, wage and price setters will have an incentive, in future episodes of inflation, to rush increases into effect before a new freeze is imposed, as well as to avoid price cuts they might otherwise have made. (In this respect, a current improvement in the unemployment-or-inflation trade-off comes at the expense of a worsened trade-off in the future.)

Controls reward invention of increasingly ingenious evasions as time goes on; and in this respect, the most conscientious and public-spirited people suffer to the advantage of evaders. Particularly after relaxation into being "voluntary," controls tend to waste the scarce and precious spirit of voluntary decency. Far from giving the American people healthy exercise for their moral muscles, such controls tend to undermine morality by breeding confusion about the supposed wickedness of seeking profit or of adjusting particular wages or prices upward. Actually, such actions are essential in a market economy.

"Voluntary" controls help blur the distinction between what is voluntary and what is compulsory, sabotaging the English language. Legal and social philosophers have cause for alarm when extralegal sanctions are held in reserve and are sometimes employed and when the executive branch of government can obtain the effects of legislation or constitutional amendments by bypassing legislative or constitutional processes. It is ominous when supposedly patriotic appeals can blackmail potential critics of a policy into silence and when businessmen find it advisable to give an incumbent administration free political publicity, as by posting signs reading "We fight inflation. We support the U.S. economic program." The considerations relevant to appraising economic policies go far beyond narrowly economic ones.

Over the long run, especially, the case is weak for controls to improve the unemployment-or-inflation trade-off. Steadiness in monetary growth offers a healthier contribution. To the ways suggested in part 1, I would now add that steadiness would avoid the unneces-

sary obsolescence of knowledge of market conditions and the resulting inefficiency caused by spurts and slumps of aggregate demand.[15]

Another thing to add is that steadiness would reduce the appearance of power that labor unions enjoy when an inflationary environment makes winning wage increases easy. Insofar as apparent power
helps unions to enlist the support of workers and to intimidate employers, monetary steadiness would do something to impair even
their actual power.

Recommending monetary steadiness does not imply rejecting all
measures that might be recommended under the name of incomes
policy.[16] Various structural reforms, unlike wage and price controls,
could join in reinforcing rather than undermining the character of
our price and market system.

INTERNATIONAL LESSONS

On the international scene, the flare-up of the chronic crisis in August 1971 again illustrated the defects of the Bretton Woods system.
Once again the major foreign-exchange markets closed, this time for
the entire week of August 16–20. After reopening, the markets were
plagued by the uncertainties of unsystematic government interventions (the floating exchange rates were "dirty floats"), import sur-
charges, fears of retaliation and trade war, governmental blustering
and tense negotiations, and prospects of officially imposed ex-
change-parity changes (such as were in fact made by the Smithsonian Agreement of December 1971).

15. For comments on how monetary disorders wastefully disrupt communication of market information, see Karl Brunner. "The Monetarist View of Keynesian
Ideas," *Lloyds Bank Review* (October 1971), esp. 40.

16. Under the name of a "second type" of incomes policy, Gottfried Haberler
has extended some earlier suggestions of Federal Reserve Chairman Arthur Burns.
Haberler recommends changes in minimum-wage laws, stopping public subsidiza-
tion of strikes through welfare and unemployment benefits, discontinuing various
anticompetitive activities of government, positive actions to strengthen competition, and other measures "to strengthen the market and to work with and through
the price mechanism." See his *Incomes Policies and Inflation* (Washington, D.C.:
American Enterprise Institute for Public Policy Research, 1971). Haberler's case for
such measures is persuasive, but it invites confusion to call them an "incomes policy,"
since that term is usually understood to cover wage and price controls.

The overhang of dollars accumulated by foreign central banks as they engaged in massive pegging and intervention during past exchange crises now impairs the functioning of the new provisional system of adjusted and somewhat more flexible exchange rates. It contributes to the danger of renewed crisis. If a system of free exchange rates should eventually be introduced, the problem of the overhang of officially held dollars—itself the product of the opposite system practiced earlier—would presumably persist and would plague the free-rate system and impair the proper interpretation of its performance.

Disorders such as experienced in 1971 cast further discredit on the ritualistic slogan that pegged exchange rates are essential because free-market rates hamper trade and investment through uncertainty, breed destabilizing speculation, and so forth. Businessmen could cope more easily with moderate fluctuations in free markets than with risks of major parity changes imposed overnight and than with the risks that intervention-plagued markets will be actually closed down.

Why are the practicing "experts" so slow to see this? Perhaps the London *Economist* had a point when it editorialized that

> the staff of the IMF derive their jobs and their degree of power from policing fixed exchange rates, and through laying down conditions (of varied quality) when granting IMF credit to countries that foolishly borrow to protect overvalued rates; they therefore naturally want the main industrial countries in the Group of Ten to agree formally to a new pattern of fixed rates . . . , no doubt with some wider permitted bands of fluctuation as a sop.[17]

The United States now has an opportunity to be free of its (real or imaginary) worries about gold—or had that opportunity until it muffed it by entering into the Smithsonian Agreement. Still, we Americans can be alert for a similar opportunity to arise again. With the link cut between the dollar and gold, we no longer need (if we ever did) to impose restrictions on trade and payments for the sake of our balance of payments. (The particular way we shed our obligations concerning gold in August 1971 may be regrettable, but that is

17. *Economist*, 28 August 1971, 9–10.

now water over the dam.) Efforts to browbeat foreign countries, including the indiscriminate and heavy-handed but fortunately only temporary import surcharge, catering to misguided protectionist sentiment at home, are particularly regrettable. How could we go on running a payments deficit unless foreigners kept on accumulating dollars? Suppose they did. What would be so bad about that for us? If we try to form a definite conception of precisely what balance-of-payments catastrophes we fear, we will realize how vague our fears have been.

We need only express sympathy for, and give a little advice to, countries absorbing more dollars than they want, thereby suffering imported inflation and other troubles. We should advise their central banks and governments to stop paying such high local-currency prices for dollars that they accumulate too many of them. Let them revalue their currencies upward against the dollar or allow them to float freely. (We Americans do not have the option of unilaterally floating the dollar because it is overwhelmingly the foreigners, not we, who have been pegging or manipulating the exchange rates between it and other currencies.) Genuinely "clean" floats, with no controls blocking arbitrage and speculation from their equilibrating functions, would solve the bulk of international monetary problems.

If foreign countries stopped buying up unwanted dollars, currencies hitherto undervalued against the dollar would then appreciate against it. The United States government would not need to press the foreigners for such a result; their unwanted accumulations of dollars exert pressure enough, especially in combination with the awkward uncertainty about the future exchange-rate system that remains until they do act. (Because foreign trade plays such a relatively smaller role in our economy than abroad, we could live with this uncertainty more easily than the foreigners could while they are making up their minds.)

It is conceivable that foreign countries might go beyond merely floating or moderately revaluing their currencies; at the extreme, they might sell off their accumulated dollars at prices low enough to get them entirely absorbed on the private markets. What would this unlikely event mean for us? Most of the dollars unloaded onto private markets would be spent on American goods, services, and securities; our balance of payments would move heavily into surplus during the period when the unloaded dollars were coming home. Although most people seem to regard a surplus as a good thing, one developing under such circumstances, especially if developing suddenly, could admittedly be awkward. We would simply have to put up with this transition toward steadier conditions of international trade, taking it philosophically as a delayed consequence of the unfortunate earlier system of exchange-rate pegging. We could not with good grace limit the spending of dollars that foreign countries had accepted in good faith, even though in pursuit of mistaken policies.

Just as we do not need the import surcharge to browbeat foreign countries into helping us with our balance of payments, neither do we need to raise the price of gold as an inducement. The Smithsonian Agreement shows, unfortunately, that this point is still not generally understood. Raising the price of gold may give a new lease on life to misconceptions about the role of gold in monetary systems. It further entrenches the farce that a fixed official price of gold is somehow important, even though people are not free to buy the stuff at that or any other price. It goes along with restoring the old crisis-prone system of fixed parities—or nearly fixed parities; widening the bands of fluctuation a bit is not a fundamental change. It is a step away from the ultimate solution to international monetary problems—"clean" floats. And a rise in the price of gold is objectionable on still other grounds. As for the contention that a token increase in the dollar price of gold is necessary for international political reasons, the childishness of the people who put stock in such gestures only underlines the futility of looking to such people for solutions to international monetary problems. Rather than consent to either a substantial or a token increase in the official gold price, the United States would do better to abandon any official price, as well as all restrictions on private ownership of gold.

We should take the position, in short, that we are not pegging the dollar to gold or to foreign currencies. With us doing no pegging, our balance of payments will be self-equilibrating—unless foreigners continue to engage in pegging. And if, contrary to our advice, they peg their currencies at values too low in relation to the dollar, then their resulting accumulations of dollars are their worry, not ours.

Although we would not be pegging the dollar to anything, our intelligent action to maintain its purchasing power would work both in our own interest and as a major contribution to a smoothly working international monetary system. This result requires that our monetary authorities follow sensible rules.

Stable Money and
Free-Market Currencies

The assigned title of this paper suggests that my task is to survey proposals that the title brings to mind rather than devote the paper to a single one of them. Even if none of the proposed reforms ever is adopted, examining how they might work may promote progress in monetary theory. Some properties of actual monetary systems are illuminated by contrasting them with imaginary systems.

OUR PREPOSTEROUS DOLLAR

On reflection, our existing monetary system must seem preposterous. It is not difficult to understand how individually plausible steps over years and centuries have brought us to where we now are, but the cumulative result remains preposterous nevertheless. Our unit of account—our pervasively used measure of value, analogous to units of weight and length—is whatever value supply and demand fleetingly accord to the dollar of fiat money.

If balance between demand for and supply of this fiat medium of exchange is not maintained by clever manipulation of its nominal quantity at a stable equilibrium value of the money unit, then any correction of this supply-and-demand imbalance must occur through growth or shrinkage of the unit itself. Money's purchasing power—the general price level—must change. This change does not occur swiftly and smoothly. Money's value must change, when it does, through a long-drawn-out, roundabout process involving millions of separately determined, though interdependent, prices and wage

Reprinted from the *Cato Journal* 3 (Spring 1983): 305–26, with permission of the Cato Institute, 1000 Massachusetts Avenue NW, Washington, D.C. 20001.

rates. Meanwhile, until the monetary disequilibrium has been finally corrected in this circuitous way, we suffer the pains of an excess demand for or excess supply of money.

Fundamentally, behind the veil of money, people specialize in producing particular goods (and services) to exchange them for the specialized outputs of other people. Since supply of goods constitutes demand for goods in that sense, any problem of apparent deficiency of aggregate demand traces to impediments to exchange, which discourage producing goods to be exchanged. Probably the most serious impediment—to judge from all the evidence supporting the "monetarist" theory of business fluctuations—hinges on the fact that goods exchange for each other not directly but through the intermediary of money (or of claims to be settled in money). Trouble occurs when a discrepancy develops between actual and desired holdings of money at the prevailing price level. Such a discrepancy can develop when the actual growth of the money supply falls short of the long-run trend or, more simply, when money actually shrinks. People and organizations try to conserve or replenish their deficient money holdings by exhibiting reduced eagerness to buy and increased eagerness to sell goods and services and securities. Since transactions are voluntary, the shorter of the demand side and the supply side sets the actual volume of transactions on each particular market. Production cutbacks in response to reduced sales in some sectors of the economy spell reduced real buying power for the outputs of other sectors. Elements of price and wage stickiness, though utterly rational from the individual points of view of the decision makers involved, do keep downward price and wage adjustments from absorbing the full impact of the reduced willingness to spend associated with efforts to build or maintain cash balances. The rot snowballs, especially if people react to deteriorating business and growing uncertainty by trying to increase their money holdings relative to income and expenditure. In depression or recession, what would be an excess demand for money at full employment is being suppressed by people's being too poor to "afford" more than their actual money holdings. Relief of this (suppressed) excess demand for money somehow or other—perhaps by an increase in the nominal supply, perhaps through price and wage reductions that create the additional real money balances demanded at full employment—would bring recovery. An excess supply of money, at the other extreme, brings price inflation.

This theory of monetary disequilibrium can be extended to deal with stagflation and with the adverse side effects of anti-inflationary monetary policies by working out a close analogy between the stickiness of a price and wage *level* and the momentum of an entrenched upward *trend*. General interdependence or input-output-type interdependence helps account for this momentum. Not all cost pass-throughs can occur instantly. (But this does not mean that inflation is a cost-push phenomenon.) The momentum of price and cost increases makes it possible for excessive growth of the money supply in the past to produce a situation in which, once nominal money growth has been stopped or slowed (or even only its acceleration reduced), the money supply in purchasing-power terms is currently insufficient for a full-employment volume of economic activity.

The point relevant to what concerns us here is that imbalance between the actual quantity of money and the total of desired cash balances cannot readily be forestalled or corrected through adjustment of the price of money on the market for money, because money, in contrast with all other things, does not have a single price and single market of its own. Monetary imbalance has to be corrected through the roundabout and sluggish process of adjusting the prices of a great many individual goods and services (and securities). Because prices do not immediately absorb the full impact of the supply and demand imbalances for individual goods and services that are the counterpart of an overall monetary imbalance, quantities traded and produced are affected also. Thus, the deflationary process associated with an excess demand for money, in particular, can be painful.

Yet even if, and perhaps especially if—contrary to reality—the purchasing power of the money unit were sufficiently flexible to forestall imbalance between money's supply and demand, and if potential imbalances kept calling this flexibility into play, the resulting instability of the unit of account would impair coordination. Capricious redistributions between debtors and creditors and the further-reaching effects of changed real debt burdens are not the whole story by far. More than the meeting of minds between prospective debtors and creditors is impaired; for the unit of account is used pervasively in expressing bids and offers and the terms of transactions, in assessing costs and benefits, and in business and personal planning. Not merely coordination but, more broadly, economic calculation is at stake.

Consider how difficult constructing a house would be (ordering and fitting together the components, appliances, and all the rest) if the unit of length, the meter or the foot, kept changing and accordingly were perceived by different persons to have different sizes. Consider how preposterous it would be for the length of the meter to fluctuate according to supply and demand in the market for meter-sticks. Yet our dollar suffers from a comparable absurdity—or a worse one, in view of the associated macroeconomic disorders.

The remedy is to be sought in somehow arranging for the quantity of money always to match the demand for it at a stable value of the unit. Alternatively, the value of the unit must be stabilized and the quantity of the medium of exchange made appropriately responsive to the demand for it through decoupling the unit of account and the medium of exchange from each other.

Reformed Government Money

I shall say only a little here about remedies within the realm of government money and I shall say nothing about a governmental gold standard, partly because such a standard is very likely to be a mere pseudo gold standard rather than a real one (to make Milton Friedman's important distinction).[1] Anyone serious about the gold standard should favor leaving it to private enterprise, protected against governmental ruination. (I'll say a little about this later on.)

I used to favor the familiar monetarist quantity rule, but lately doubts have been plaguing me. Recent and ongoing financial innovations (money-market funds, sweep accounts, overnight RPs, over-

---

1. Milton Friedman, "Real and Pseudo Gold Standards," *Journal of Law and Economics* 4 (October 1961), reprinted in his *Dollars and Deficits* (Englewood Cliffs, N.J.: Prentice-Hall, 1968), 247–65.

night Eurodollars, highly marketable credit instruments, cash management devices, and all the rest) are rendering the very concept of money hopelessly fuzzy and the velocity of whatever constitutes money hopelessly unstable and unpredictable. So, anyway, goes a view that I cannot confidently dismiss.

If this view should be or should become correct, the monetarist rule would have become inapplicable precisely because of failure to adopt it unequivocally, credibly, and in due time. The troublesome financial innovations represent attempts to wriggle around interest ceilings and reserve requirements made particularly costly by inflation-boosted nominal interest rates, the inflation tracing in turn to disregard of monetarist advice. Rejection of a prescribed treatment may allow a disease to develop to a stage at which the original prescription would no longer work and at which some quite different treatment becomes necessary. This does not mean that the doctors who made the original prescription—here, the monetarists—have anything to apologize for.

Anyway, the old proposal for targeting monetary policy on a broad price index deserves a fresh look. Underlying this proposal is the idea that incipient monetary disequilibrium would tend to show itself in prices. Movements away from a previously stable price level are symptoms of excess demand for or excess supply of money, either of which, but especially the former, impinges on real activity as well as on prices. Monetary policy aimed at price-level stability would coincide with resisting unemployment due to general deficiency of spending while not creating too much new money in a doomed attempt to cure unemployment of some other kind. This idea is not crucially dependent on any particular definition or measure of money, since imbalances between its supply and demand, and not those quantities separately, are what are to be detected and corrected.

The standard objection stresses time lags between the need for and the taking of corrective policy actions and then lags between the actions and their results. A price index, like individual prices, responds sluggishly. Because of these lags, results might run in the wrong direction by the time they appeared. This difficulty would bedevil a sharply shifting policy, however, more than a steady and consistent one. Ways might be found, furthermore, to mitigate the problem of lags, perhaps through attention to particularly sensitive commodity prices and to future prices.

INDEXING AND BASKET CURRENCIES

Even so, proposals for nongovernmental remedies intrigue me more. First I shall consider some proposed remedies that, while not free of government involvement, do or could have private aspects.

Proposals for a stable unit of account come to the fore in times of severe inflation.[2] Under widespread indexing, the dollar of base-

---

2. And not only then; some were published during the nineteenth century when price levels were trending downward. After mentioning earlier proposals by Joseph Lowe and G. Poulett Scrope, W. Stanley Jevons recommended "a tabular or average standard of value," to be based on an index number. *Money and the Mechanism of Exchange* (New York: Appleton, 1875), chap. 25. Alfred Marshall recommended expressing debts and the interest on them, pensions, taxes, salaries, and wages in units of the purchasing power possessed by one pound sterling at, say, the beginning of 1887; eventually "the currency would . . . be restricted to the functions for which it is well fitted, of measuring and settling transactions that are completed shortly after they are begun." "Remedies for Fluctuations of General Prices," *Contemporary Review* (1887), reprinted in *Memorials of Alfred Marshall* (1925), 197–99, and extracted in Milton Friedman, *Monetary Correction* (London: Institute of Economic Affairs, 1974), 36–38. Friedman's booklet, pp. 39–45, also contains Brian Griffiths, "English Classical Political Economy and the Debate on Indexation." Walter Bagehot criticized Jevons's proposal in "A New Standard of Value," *Economist*, 20 November 1875, reprinted in *Economic Journal* 2 (September 1892): 472–77. Aneurin Williams, anticipating Irving Fisher's proposal of three decades later for a "compensated dollar" (*Stabilizing the Dollar* [New York: Macmillan, 1920]), proposed adjusting the gold content of the pound sterling in line with changes in the purchasing power of gold so as to keep the purchasing power of sterling constant. "A 'Fixed Value of Bullion' Standard—A Proposal for Preventing General Fluctuations of Trade," *Economic Journal* 2 (June 1892): 280–89. Robert Giffen criticized Williams's proposal in "Fancy Monetary Standards," *Economic Journal* 2 (September 1892): 463–71.

In recent years, though perhaps not still today, the most prominent advocate of indexing has been Milton Friedman. (See his *Monetary Correction*, as well as his "Using Escalators to Help Fight Inflation," *Fortune* 90 [July 1974]: 94–97, 174, 176.) Friedman's chief argument appears to be that indexing would help break the sheer momentum of wage increases and would thereby lessen the unemployment associated with a program of slowing down monetary expansion and eventually returning to price-level stability. Trying to appraise that particular argument would be rather aside from the main topics of this paper.

year purchasing power—we might call it the "constant"[3]—would be the unit of account, while the ordinary dollar in which demand deposits and currency are denominated remained the medium of exchange.[4]

Separate proposals by Jacques Riboud and by nine prominent European economists may be understood as variants of the proposal for a unit of base-year purchasing power.[5] The "Eurostable" or "Europa," as the new unit would be called under the respective proposals, would initially be defined as a composite of specified amounts of each of several national currencies. For convenience in arithmetic, we might think of the initial definition of *one hundred* Eurostables as g German marks plus f French francs plus i Italian lire plus u United States dollars, and so on. We may think of one hundred Eurostables as the total value of several little piles on a table, each of a specific national currency. Now, as national price levels rise (or fall) over

3. The name comes from Ralph Borsodi's proposal for a unit of steady purchasing power whose nominal dollar value would rise in step with the Consumer Price Index. Actually, Borsodi envisaged not just a mere unit of account but also a medium of exchange denominated in constants. The question arises, however, of whether such a system of indexing does not presuppose the continued existence of ordinary dollar prices and dollars in circulation. Such questions are considered later in this paper.

Anyway, a small-scale trial of Borsodi's proposal was begun in June 1972 in Exeter, New Hampshire, where two banks made available checking accounts and even currency denominated in constants. The experiment was discontinued in January 1974, supposedly because of the elderly Mr. Borsodi's physical weakness, because of doubts about legality, and because earnings on the assets (mainly Treasury securities) matching the constant liabilities did not fully cover expenses plus the indexed growth in the dollar value of the liabilities. See "Paying with constants instead of dollars," *Business Week*, 4 May 1974, 29.

4. If only bonds and other long-term contracts were denominated in "constants," then the base-year dollar would be serving only as the standard of deferred payments but not as the general unit of account. The old textbook distinction between those two functions is perhaps not empty after all. (Alfred Marshall evidently had it in mind; see footnote 2.) Perhaps we should retain the distinction, especially if the idea of universal use of an index-defined stable unit of account turns out to be self-contradictory.

5. Jacques Riboud, *Une Monnaie pour l'Europe: L'Eurostable* (Paris: Editions de la R.P.P., 1975); and idem, *Eurostable*, Bulletin du Centre Jouffroy pour la Réflexion Monétaire (March–April 1977); Giorgio Basevi, Michele Fratianni, Herbert Giersch, Pieter Korteweg, David O'Mahony, Michael Parkin, Theo Peeters, Pascal Salin, and Niels Thygesen, "The All Saints' Day Manifesto for European Monetary Union," *Economist* 1 (November 1975), reprinted in *One Money for Europe*, ed. Michele Fratianni and Theo Peeters (London: Macmillan, 1978), 37–43. My present purposes do not require sharply distinguishing the features of these different proposals.

time, the amount of currency in each pile is increased (or reduced) in proportion to its country's price index. The nominal amount of currency in each pile varies to keep its purchasing power unchanged; so the combined purchasing power of all the piles on the table remains constant also. Adjustments of this kind would be carried out at least as frequently as every month. Riboud envisages daily adjustments calculated with projections of the national price indexes and with whatever minor corrections proved necessary being made as the latest figure for each index became available. Constancy of the purchasing power of the Eurostable is defined with reference not to a single national price index only but to several specified indexes. In effect, the constant purchasing power of the Eurostable is the aggregate of the purchasing powers possessed by specified amounts of marks, francs, lire, dollars, and so forth *in the base month*.[6]

With details depending on the particular scheme in question, central banks or commercial banks would accept deposits and grant loans denominated in Eurostables or Europas. To be safe in incurring deposit obligations denominated in purchasing-power units and thus perhaps having to be honored in greatly increased nominal

---

6. It seems to me that the following formulas would apply to the Eurostable system. The value of 1 Eurostable (or perhaps of 100 Eurostables, as suggested in the text) is

$$\sum_{i=1}^{n} u_i P_i$$

where u_i is the number of units of the ith country's currency in the base-period basket and P_i is the ith country's price index on the basis of its base-period figure being 1. The number of countries, currencies, and indexes involved is n. To consider exchange rates, let r_{jE} = number of units of currency j worth 1 Eurostable. (Currency j is a particular one of the currencies indicated by subscript i.) Let r_{ji} = number of units of currency j worth 1 unit of currency i; u_i and P_i have the meanings already indicated. Then:

$$r_{jE} = \sum_{i=1}^{n} u_i P_i r_{ji}$$

The Eurostable or Europa is quite different from the Special Drawing Right of the International Monetary Fund and the Eureo and other composite units described in Joseph Aschheim and Y. S. Park, *Artificial Currency Units: The Formation of Functional Currency Areas*, Princeton Essays in International Finance no. 114 (Princeton: Princeton University Press, 1976). These artificial units are defined as baskets containing *fixed* nominal amounts of national currencies; instead of having fixed purchasing power, they lose it along with the national currencies composing their baskets.

amounts of national currency, banks would have to hold assets similarly denominated. The question arises whether borrowers would be willing to incur debts perhaps repayable in unpredictably swollen nominal amounts of national currency. What would induce borrowers to incur such debts unless they could already count on receiving their incomes in such units? Especially low interest rates might constitute the inducement, but the low rates would be a disadvantage from the bankers' point of view.

We shall set aside the point that the two proposals mentioned, but the Europa scheme more so than the Eurostable scheme, envision that the new stable unit would serve not only as a standard of deferred payments and unit of account but also, increasingly, as a medium of exchange. Our concern here is just with how a separation of functions would work.

SEPARATION OF FUNCTIONS AND ITS THEORETICAL APPEAL

History can give us little direct help toward answering this question. Separation is, to be sure, far from unprecedented. In Germany during the hyperinflation after World War I, some bonds were denominated and some prices calculated in centners of rye, Swiss francs, or grams of gold. In ancient times and in the Middle Ages, the money circulating in commercial centers was a hodgepodge of variously denominated coins from both local and far-away mints;[7] so the unit of account and medium of exchange could not have been unified. Even in the United States, until beyond the middle of the nineteenth century, foreign as well as American coins were in use; and the notes of the shakier or less well known state-chartered banks circulated at various discounts. But though examples of separation of functions, these were not cases of a single unit of account, distinct from the circulating medium, being in *general* use. Clearly they provide no example of a unit of account defined so as to have a stable purchasing

7. Heinrich Rittershausen, *Bankpolitik* (Frankfurt: Knapp, 1956), esp., 58–60; Carlo M. Cipolla, *Money, Prices, and Civilization in the Mediterranean World, Fifth to Seventeenth Century* (Princeton: Princeton University Press, 1956).

power. The medieval "ghost moneys" described by Cipolla were not such units, either;[8] instead, they appear to have been multiples or fractions of some currently or formerly circulating coin used for convenience in arithmetic and accounting before the days of calculators.

What concerns us here is a different state of affairs; namely, how things would work with something like the Eurostable or Europa in general use as the unit of account and distinct from the medium of exchange. We may as well analyze the simplest case, in which the "basket" defining the unit contains just one national currency, whose nominal quantity would be periodically adjusted upward in proportion to a single index of prices quoted in terms of the circulating currency. The dollar of base-year purchasing power, Borsodi's "constant," would then be the unit of account. (The Eurostable/Europa scheme is essentially the same except in defining a stable unit with reference to several price indexes instead of only one.)

The idea of separating the unit of account and medium of exchange has appeal as conceivably a way not only of achieving a stable measuring rod for economic coordination and economic calculation but also of avoiding the macroeconomic disorders mentioned earlier by giving the medium of exchange a flexible, market-clearing price of its own.

The separation of functions might also, for good or ill, help wear down money illusion and inflation illusion. Money illusion, in the old sense of the term, is the tacit assumption that a dollar is a dollar, that money is a stable measure of value, and that changes in the general price level reflect disorders from the side of goods rather than from the side of money. What might be called inflation illusion is the related perception of inflation as a sort of plague affecting wages and prices rather than as the specifically monetary disorder that it really is. These illusions are supported by money's lack of any specific market (other than the foreign-exchange market, anyway) on which it is straightforwardly quoted and can be seen to be deteriorating. Money is quoted on millions of different markets in millions of different ways; but this very multiplicity of markets and of prices, many of which

8. Cipolla, *Money, Prices, and Civilization*, chap. 4.

would be changing anyway even apart from any monetary disorder, obstructs any simple view of what is happening to money itself.

Things might be different if a Eurostable or some other index-defined constant existed against which national currencies were quoted every day. Such quotations would be the result of calculations, however, rather than of a direct market process; ordinary money still would not have an actual market specifically its own.

DIFFICULTIES WITH A CONSTANT UNIT AND INDEXING

We still are left wondering whether general cost accounting, pricing, and contracting in terms of Eurostables or constants, while ordinary money continued to serve as the medium of exchange, could help overcome the macroeconomic difficulties associated with money as we have known it.

Before facing more fundamental questions, let us, for completeness, recognize a couple of minor difficulties. A scheme involving use of a price index might create temptations to rig the index. Also, how would the use of stable units of account get launched? What would induce borrowers to incur debts in such units? If people are going to undertake commitments to make future payments or repayments denominated in a stable unit, they will want to count on receiving income denominated in the same unit. They want to be obligated to pay the sort of money they expect to receive—except insofar as they are persuaded to gamble on doing otherwise, perhaps by an interest rate lower than on ordinary loans.

Here is a chicken-and-egg or Alphonse-and-Gaston problem. The more payments people are already scheduled to receive in a particular money, the more readily will they take on commitments to make payments in the same money. The spread of a practice facilitates its further spread,[9] but its not yet having gotten a good start hampers

9. With money as with language, acceptability enhances acceptability. "The use of a particular language or a particular money by one individual increases its value to other actual or potential users. Increasing returns to scale, in this sense, limits the number of languages or moneys in a society and indeed explains the tendency for one basic language or money to monopolize the field." James Tobin, "Discus-

its ever getting started. Early users of a new unit would confer benefits on latecomers, if the reform could succeed, for which the early users could not collect compensation. They thus have inadequate incentives to provide what would be in part a public good.

A more fundamental difficulty is illuminated by supposing, or trying to suppose, that the practice has become quite general of not only expressing debts and other contracts but also pricing goods and services in constants. Prices in ordinary dollars, supposedly continuing to serve as the medium of exchange, are translated from the prices set in constants according to the current level of the price index whose "basket" of goods and services defines the constant. That is to say, if the current month's index of prices in ordinary dollars happens to stand seven (say) times as high as the index in the base period—if the standard basket costs seven times as many dollars as it did in the base period when, by definition, the dollar and the constant were equal in purchasing power—then the current exchange rate is seven dollars per constant, and multiplication by seven translates prices set in constants into current dollar prices.

But isn't there a contradiction here? If dollar prices are determined by applying the price index to translate prices set in constants, what is the meaning of the dollar price index? It expresses the average level of dollar prices calculated by means of the index itself (or by means of its latest published value, which may express the level of prices a few weeks earlier). In short, the dollar price level is the arithmetical consequence of itself or of its own recent value. A rise in the index arithmetically raises its component prices and thus itself, and so on. The level of dollar prices is adrift, giving itself further momentum as it moves. It would be, anyway, unless a restricted quantity of medium-of-exchange dollars somehow provided it with an anchor after all. We shall return to this question, or the closely related question, of the real quantity of the medium of exchange.

Meanwhile, there does seem to be an internal contradiction in the very notion of all-around indexing; that is, of all-around price-setting in a constant unit related to the ordinary medium of exchange by calculations with a price index. If indexing comes to be

sion," in *Models of Monetary Economies*, ed. John H. Kareken and Neil Wallace (Minneapolis: Federal Reserve Bank of Minneapolis, 1980), 86–87.

employed not only in long-term contracts but also in general pricing, then it kills off the market-determined prices necessary for the construction of meaningful indexes. Employed beyond a certain degree, it destroys itself. This degree is analogous, in a way, to the critical mass of fissionable uranium or plutonium. To avoid the contradiction, indexing must not be employed quite generally, but only to provide a stable standard of deferred payments. Indexing is parasitical on its *not* being applied in setting most (or many) prices. It presupposes that most of the prices entering into the calculation of the index are determined by market forces—by people's bids and offers—directly in terms of the medium of exchange.

Yet the very meaning of generally setting prices in index-defined constants—which is what we have been trying to imagine—precludes people's continuing to express their bid and ask prices only in medium-of-exchange dollars without reference to their exchange rate against constants. Does this imply, then, that people would be negotiating prices in constants? That, too, is bedeviled with contradictions. Pricing and costing and bargaining in terms of constants would seem to be trying or threatening to change a historical datum, the constant itself; that is, the purchasing power that the dollar had in the base year.

All-around indexing, or pricing in constants, runs counter to free-market pricing in another way. It would replace current supply-and-demand determination of individual prices with *calculations*, calculations presumably applied to a pattern of prices established some time in the past. Unless somehow modified, it would freeze relative prices and remove them from the influence of up-to-date market conditions.

A further difficulty arises when people are trying to build up or run down their holdings of the medium of exchange. If the level of prices translated into medium-of-exchange dollars is adrift as a consequence of all-around indexing, as noted above, and if the quantity of medium of exchange is exogenously determined, then no process would seem to be at work tending to equate the actual and desired quantities of it. The exchange rate between dollars and constants, being a calculated number, is hardly something directly determined on the market by an equilibrating process.

Suppose that at its current purchasing power (however determined), people want to hold more of the medium of exchange than actually exists. How do they go about building up their holdings? They might start by bidding and asking lower prices for goods and services than translation from constants (calculations with the price index) would indicate. That would be a departure from the hypothesized all-around indexing. They might bid and ask lower prices in constants, thereby tending to alter the purchasing power of the constant. But since the constant is defined as a dollar of base-year purchasing power, changing its purchasing power means changing a historical datum—a contradiction in terms. Neither approach is compatible with what we are trying to conceive of—general pricing in terms of constants.

A conceivable alternative is that people, in trying to build up their cash balances, would not alter the prices they bid and asked but would simply hold back from buying things. (Their increased eagerness to sell things, not expressed in reduced selling prices, would have little operational meaning.) The outcome would be a recession in real economic activity of such degree that people no longer, after all, felt able to "afford" holding more than the actual quantity of medium of exchange. In that case, the joint existence of the constant and the medium-of-exchange dollar and the index-calculated exchange rate between them, far from providing a mechanism for painlessly ensuring monetary equilibrium, would pose an obstacle by making prices more nearly rigid or, perhaps more exactly, by making prices more nearly the arbitrary result of arithmetical calculations.

None of the ideas reviewed so far, then, would give the medium of exchange a price of its own determined on a market of its own in such a way as to keep its supply and demand painlessly in equilibrium. Widespread indexing as a stage of transition to something else might be conceivable, but the idea of universal indexing permanently associated with an ordinary medium of exchange verges on nonsense.

A more ambitious reform scheme might go beyond introducing a unit of account distinct from the medium of exchange. It might introduce demand deposits and even currency denominated in constants. Their issuers would presumably stand ready to redeem them in equivalent amounts of the ordinary medium of exchange, equivalences being calculated with a price index. There is no obvious reason why the market exchange rate between the two media of exchange should diverge significantly from the calculated rate; arbitrage should prevent that. If deposits and currency denominated in constants should totally displace the ordinary medium of exchange, the question would arise of what would be left for them to be redeemable in. Issuers might conceivably promise to add to everyone's holdings of these new media of exchange in proportion to the rise in the price index. But then the nominal money supply and the price level would be indeterminate (as in a monetary system managed fully in accordance with the fallacious real-bills doctrine); increases in each would call for increases in the other, indefinitely.[10]

SEPARATE BUT ACTUAL UNITS

Now that we have abandoned the idea of a generally employed abstract stable unit with a price-index-calculated exchange rate against ordinary money, let us suppose that the separate and stable—but now only relatively stable—unit of account actually exits as a commodity, say gold, or as a foreign currency.[11] Suppose that Americans came to use German marks or grams of gold as units of account while still making and receiving payments in ordinary dollars. (Offhand, no fundamental difference is apparent between using the mark and using gold as the other unit alongside the dollar, but this question may require further thought.) One difference from all-around indexing and similar schemes is that a currently market-determined exchange rate, and not just a calculated translation rate, does exist between the parallel unit and the domestically circulating dollar. Does this exchange rate and the market on which it is determined serve as a price and market "of its own" for the domestic medium of exchange in such a way as to solve or mitigate the macroeconomic problems previously reviewed?

10. Cf. William Baumol, "The Escalated Economy and the Stimulating Effects of Inflation," *Rivista Internazionale di Scienze Economiche e Commerciali* 12 (February 1965): 103–14.

11. As Heinrich Rittershausen says, a separation between the functions of money does occur on the international scene. *Bankpolitik*, 61–62, 67–69.

Suppose, for definiteness, that Americans undergo a change in tastes and desire increased *real* holdings of dollar cash balances. Under ordinary circumstances and with the nominal supply of dollars unchanged, a deflationary process sets in that cuts production and employment as well as prices. Under the separation of functions, however, the dollar appreciates against the mark or gold, meaning that the total quantity of the medium of exchange grows in terms of the unit of account. (Alternatively, though perhaps less plausibly, the level of United States prices expressed in the marks or gold falls directly. In either case, the dollar money supply gains in purchasing power over goods and services.) The separation of the unit of account and medium of exchange, with translation between them at a flexible, market-determined price, does appear to be a way of avoiding or relatively painlessly correcting a monetary disequilibrium. But this conclusion requires further pondering.

We must ask, also, whether such a split system would be durable. Would it come into use in the first place if the general purchasing power of the mark or gold were only slightly less unstable than that of the dollar? And if the dollar were much more unstable, would it nevertheless persist in use as the medium of exchange? Since unification of money's functions is a convenience for its users, the mark or gold might then well displace the dollar as the medium of exchange also.

Durable or not, the system just mentioned is worth considering, for F. A. Hayek recognizes something similar as a preliminary step to the ultimate reform that he recommends (which is discussed below). Hayek would permit people in each country to use foreign currencies as units of account and media of exchange; these would be free to compete with the national currency.

PRIVATE MONEY

Realistically, private money must mean money that is *predominantly* so. The government would still be involved—in repressing force and fraud and in enforcing contracts. (I cannot go all the way with libertarians of the anarchist wing.)

As a libertarian, I favor allowing free banking—the competitive private issue of notes and deposits redeemable, presumably, in gold. Notes and deposits would be backed by merely fractional reserves, for efforts to enforce 100 percent banking in the face of contrary incentives and private ingenuity would require unacceptably extreme government interference.

For people serious about a gold standard, the monetary unit should be a physical quantity of gold, such as the gram or milligram, and not some abstract unit whose definition in terms of gold is subject to change. Yet I have doubts about whether such a system could catch on. How would the voluntary use of gold units catch on? If bankers are to issue note and deposit liabilities denominated in gold, they will want to hold assets—loans and investments—also denominated in gold. The problem of motivating people to go first in using new units, already noted in connection with index-defined units, arises here too.

Furthermore, a gold monetary unit is preposterous in the same way as a fiat unit, although in lesser degree. The unit of value still lacks objectivity and dependability. Its size (purchasing power) depends on interaction between supply of and demand for an industrially rather unimportant substance being supplied and demanded predominantly for monetary purposes (that is, in association with the demand for money more broadly defined). The real size of a gold unit, as of a fiat unit, is changeable and undependable. Imbalance between the demand for and supply of monetary gold, like such imbalance for government-issued fiat base money, touches off a roundabout and sluggish process of adjustment in the unit's real value, a process with painful macroeconomic side effects. Furthermore, lapses of confidence in banks operating with fractional reserves could touch off a self-aggravating scramble for the gold on which the system is based.

Better alternatives are available. The government cannot avoid giving some encouragement to one or another system of private money. It is bound to do so by the manner in which it disengages itself from the present government-dominated monetary system. Therefore, the advantages and disadvantages of the different private systems are bound to be a topic of policy discussion. To say "Let the market decide" is no adequate answer.

F. A. Hayek would authorize the issue of competing private fiat moneys. He has set forth the advantages of his proposal in some detail and has also tried to foresee and deal with difficulties.[12] My concern with his scheme is to ask the sorts of questions raised about indexing and other schemes already reviewed. What would determine the value of each money unit? How would price levels and the exchange rates among the different private currencies be determined? Would money acquire a price and market of its own in such a sense that the supply of and demand for each money would be equilibrated relatively painlessly?

Under Hayek's scheme, each issuer would have his own unit (ducat, crown, florin, or whatever; the proposal does *not* envisage rival currencies all denominated in the same unit, such as a quantity of gold, although gold-dominated currencies could figure among the competing units). The different units would be free to fluctuate against each other. The value of each unit would not be a matter of sheer definition (as would be true of an index-defined abstract unit) but would depend on supply and demand. Each money would exist in some definite quantity. Each issuer would supposedly have an incentive to restrain his issues so as to keep the purchasing power of his unit stable, thereby attracting more and more holders. (Rather than go further and try to engineer an actual deflation of prices in terms of his money, he would presumably pay explicit interest on holdings.) The larger the real volume of his currency people would willingly hold, the larger the volume of loans the issuer could have outstanding and earning interest. Success in restraining his issue to the volume demanded at a stable value of his unit would itself strengthen that demand, which he could then profitably meet. Virtue would bring its own reward. Conceivably a single money might

12. Hayek describes his proposal in *Choice in Currency*, Occasional Paper 48 (London: Institute of Economic Affairs, 1976), and *Denationalisation of Money*, Hobart Special Paper 70, 2d ed. (London: Institute of Economic Affairs, 1978). Cf. Thomas Saving, "Competitive Money Production and Price Level Determinancy" [*sic*], *Southern Economic Journal* 43 (October 1976): 987–94; Benjamin Klein, "The Competitive Supply of Money," *Journal of Money, Credit, and Banking* 4 (November 1975); Gordon Tullock, "Competing Moneys," *Journal of Money, Credit, and Banking* 7 (November 1976); Benjamin Klein, "Competing Moneys: Comment," *Journal of Money, Credit, and Banking* 7 (November 1976).

become the dominant or the only one used in a given territory. Its issuer would remain disciplined, though, by potential competition.

Under Hayek's scheme, separation of functions in one sense is lost—separation between the unit of account and medium of exchange—but separation is gained among the different monetary units, each of which would perform both functions.

If people wanted to acquire additional holdings of particular Hayek currencies, these would begin rising in value on the intercurrency exchange market and probably in purchasing power over goods and services also, leading their issuers to expand their amounts. If people wanted to reduce their holdings of particular currencies, they would fall in exchange value and probably in purchasing power, prodding their issuers, anxious to preserve their reputations, to try to reduce their outstanding issues, in the first instance by repurchasing them with reserves of other currencies. Through exchange-rate, purchasing-power, and quantity changes, then, and notably through quantity responses, equilibrium between desired and actual amounts of particular currencies would be maintained or restored.

But what happens if people desire to build up their real holdings of all currencies, or desire to build up the total real purchasing power that they hold in currencies in general? This desire might strike some currencies earlier or in greater degree, so that the same changes and incentives as mentioned above would occur. But suppose, instead, that the real demand for currency holdings increased uniformly. Well, currencies would tend to gain in purchasing power (approximately uniformly, with exchange rates approximately unchanged). This would motivate their issuers to expand their circulations. However, the purchasing power signals would appear more slowly and more sluggishly than the exchange-rate signals would appear in the alternative case of only some currencies being directly affected.

But this may be a point in favor of the scheme: In practice, changes in the real demands for holdings of various currencies will not occur uniformly, and exchange rates will change, motivating changes in the issues most affected. In other words, just as nowadays, there will be no single market on which and single price at which currencies in general exchange against other things. However, people will no longer be dealing with money in general. Each currency will have a market and price of its own—the exchange market and its exchange rate.

In considering stable units of account or gold units serving in parallel with ordinary money as the medium of exchange, we noted the difficulty of getting such a system launched. People would have weak incentives to supply the public good of being its early users. The same would be true of trying to launch Hayek's system.

Another public-good aspect of a prudently managed currency is that, once well launched, it provides even people who do not hold it and do not make and receive payments in it with a stable unit of account in which they might conduct their calculations and express their claims and debts. Because of the free availability of his money as a unit of accounting and calculation even to parties who held little or none of it, a well-behaved issuer could not collect compensation for all the advantages he was conferring on the public in general. The social benefits of his maintaining a stable money would not come fully to his attention. The standard argument seems relevant that the purely private provision of public goods falls short of the optimum, plausibly defined.[13]

These points about public goods and externalities suggest that private-enterprise money would be at a disadvantage relative to government money. While the government incurs the costs of running a monetary system, it also more or less covers them from the seigniorage yielded by its quasi-monopoly position. These considerations may not be quantitatively important. (All sorts of private activities generate positive externalities without themselves being made unprofitable—for example, the benefits that relatively lazy shoppers get from the careful shopping of others, or free rides obtained on

13. Referring more to money in general than to specific currencies, Herbert Grubel notes that money saves resources otherwise consumed in accomplishing barter transactions, and it promotes productivity by encouraging specialization. Most of these benefits accrue to society as externalities. Herbert G. Grubel, *International Economics* (Homewood, Ill.: Irwin, 1977), 449.

For further distinction between the public and the private benefits of money, see J. R. Hicks, "The Two Triads," in his *Critical Essays in Monetary Theory* (Oxford: Clarendon Press, 1967), 1–60.

the information generated or publicized by organized markets.) Still, monetary reformers should face these points.

In a different respect, switching to a new currency creates a public *bad* if it shrinks demand for holdings of the old one, whose value consequently zigzags downward more sharply than otherwise. This problem of currency substitution might plague a system of competing private currencies even if it could somehow be successfully launched. According to the scheme's very logic, holders of the different currencies, as well as the financial press, would be alert to signs of unsound management and incipient depreciation of any one of them. Its holders would dump it and fly into others. Responses of this sort would destabilize the exchange rates between the different currencies, upsetting transactions and calculations. Like bank runs in the days before deposit insurance, such runs from one currency to another would be harmful from an overall point of view, though resulting from individuals' efforts to protect themselves.[14] (To recognize these disruptively sensitive responses is not to deny, however, that current and expected future purchasing-power parities would no doubt be the main systematic determinants of exchange rates.)

A possible variant of Hayek's schemes comes to mind. According to the original proposal, private issuers would strive to keep their moneys stable in value by suitable regulation of their quantities but would not keep them redeemable in anything in particular. (To get their moneys launched in the first place, issuers might promise to redeem them in definite amounts of government money; but as inflation continued to eat away the value of government money, redeemability in it would become more and more a dead letter.) Now,

---

14. For a description of this possible problem, though not for its relation to Hayek's proposal specifically, see Marc A. Miles, "Currency Substitution, Flexible Exchange Rates, and Monetary Independence," *American Economic Review* 68 (June 1978): 428–36.

The problem of instability from currency substitution seems more likely to characterize rival currencies competing even within countries than ordinary national currencies floating against each other on the foreign-exchange market. As long as one's fellow countrymen are still quite generally using the national currency, it is awkward and expensive for an individual or firm to try to initiate the shift to some other country's currency as its routine unit of account and medium of exchange even in domestic transactions. With money as with language, inertia tends to perpetuate an entrenched use.

issuers might find it to their competitive advantage (or might conceivably be required) to promise redemption of their currencies on demand in gold (or in some other one or more commodities or even securities). The quantity of gold (or other redemption medium) per currency unit would not be physically fixed, however, but would be whatever quantity had a fixed purchasing power over the goods and services composing a specified bundle. That amount of gold would be recalculated each month (or day) from the open-market price of gold and from the prices of the various goods in the bundle. Issuers might also undertake to issue their currencies in exchange for the calculated amounts of gold, perhaps instituting a slight spread between their selling and buying prices of gold to cover expenses. Convertibility of this sort would give additional operationality to the expectation that issuers would strive to keep their money units stable in purchasing power; they would now be required to *do something* at the initiative of the money holders.[15] Furthermore, if the different issuers kept recalculating the constant-purchasing-power amounts of gold in which their currencies were redeemable with reference to a common basket of goods and services, then an inconvenience of Hayek's system—that of a multiplicity of units of account, analogous to multiple systems of weights and measures—would be avoided. The operating properties of this variant system, however, remain to be explored.

A Single Stable Unit Distinct From the Medium of Exchange

By saving until now the reform that I currently prefer, I have avoided letting it monopolize the paper. Robert Greenfield and I have described it in detail elsewhere, provisionally calling it the "BFH system."[16] Like the reform proposed by Hayek, it would almost com-

15. This idea draws some inspiration from Aneurin Williams's and Irving Fisher's proposals, cited in footnote 2, for what Fisher called a "compensated dollar," and from Willford I. King, *The Keys to Prosperity* (New York: Distributed by the Committee for Constitutional Government, 1948), 209–10.

16. Robert L. Greenfield and Leland B. Yeager, "A Laissez-Faire Approach to Monetary Stability," *Journal of Money, Credit, and Banking* 15 (August 1983): 302–15

pletely depoliticize money and banking. By the manner of its withdrawal from its current domination of our current system, the government would give a noncoercive nudge in favor of the new system. It would help launch a stable unit of account free of the absurdity of being the supply-and-demand-determined value of the unit of the medium of exchange. The government would define the new unit, just as it defines units of weights and measures. The definition would run in terms of a bundle of commodities so comprehensive that the unit's value would remain nearly stable against goods and services in general. The government would conduct its own accounting and transactions in the new unit. Thanks to this governmental nudge, the public-good or who-goes-first problem of getting a new unit adopted would largely be sidestepped. The government would be barred from issuing money. Private enterprise, probably in the form of institutions combining the features of today's banks, money-market mutual funds, and stock mutual funds, would offer convenient media of exchange. Separation of a unit of account of defined purchasing power from the medium—or rather media—of exchange, whose quantity would be appropriately determined largely on the demand side, would go far toward avoiding macroeconomic disorders and facilitating stable prosperity. Lacking any base money, whether gold or government-issued money, on which ordinary money would be pyramided on a fractional-reserve basis, the BFH system would not share the precariousness and vulnerability of ordinary monetary systems.

Although I do not have the space for a full description of the BFH system and do not want to repeat myself by providing one here, I would like to forestall a few misconceptions that, as experience shows, are likely to arise. The BFH system is not a variant of the often proposed composite-commodity or commodity-reserve system of government money. It is not a variant of the tabular standard (widespread indexing). Questions about whether the BFH system involves convertible or inconvertible money—questions presupposing some familiar answer—are inapplicable to it. The definition of its unit of account does not require "implementation" through convertibility of

_____

(reprinted in this volume), in which writings of Fischer *B*lack, Eugene *F*ama, and Robert *H*all are given credit for some component ideas.

any familiar sort, any more than does maintenance of the defined length of the meter. (Of course, ordinary business practice would force people to make and receive payments for current purchases and sales of goods and services and in settlement of debts in property actually worth the specified number of units of account. Whether this counts as "convertibility" is a mere question of terminology.)

The BFH system would lack money as we now know it. People would probably make payments by writing checks—checks denominated in the defined unit of account—on their holdings of shares of stock in institutions combining the features of mutual funds and banks. (These shares would have market-determined flexible prices.) These practices would not entail the textbook inconveniences of barter. The advantages of having a single definite unit of account and convenient methods of payment would be retained and enhanced. The absurdities of linking the unit of account and medium of exchange in the manner now familiar to us would be avoided. (By contrast with the situation in which both paper dollars and gold, say, were temporarily serving as both unit of account and medium of exchange, the conditions promoting convergence onto a single money serving both functions would be absent.)

Unlike the monetarism we are familiar with, which requires an accurate adjustment of the quantity of money to the demand for it and must therefore be suspicious of innovations that alter the supply-demand relation and even blur the concept of money, the BFH system can positively welcome deregulation and financial innovation. The government can take just as much a laissez-faire stance toward the financial system, once it has offered and promoted a particular definition of the unit of account, as it can take toward ordinary businesses that happen to employ a defined unit of length in their operations.

CONCLUDING REMARKS

It is easy to say that the best reform of all would institute a single worldwide money of assuredly constant purchasing power serving all four of money's traditionally listed functions. But recommending such a money would be empty unless we could specify how to achieve and maintain it. A monetary system is a set of institutions, sustained by laws, not a laundry list of desirable features. An abstract wish for ideal results does not itself chart a way out of present-day disorders.

It is easy, also, to point to complications and costs and nuisances associated with Hayek's and other reform schemes. In part, these would be open manifestations of complexities already existing but hidden in governmental monetary systems uniting the several functions of money (for example, distortions of information through inflation). These complications are different in detail under each scheme from what they are under unified government moneys. There is much to be said for having the complexities and costs evident, rather than keeping them as hard to perceive and cope with as they are nowadays.

With government no longer obscuring the relevant costs and benefits and no longer impeding financial innovation in efforts to shore up its own preposterous monetary system, we could expect private ingenuity to develop a monetary system—or a system transcending money—with features perhaps even more attractive than any we can now imagine.

A Laissez-Faire Approach
to Monetary Stability

(with Robert L. Greenfield)

This paper develops some diverse hints for a new monetary system offered separately by Fischer Black, Eugene Fama, and Robert E. Hall. (For reasons that will become evident, though, we should perhaps say "payments system" instead of monetary system.) None of the economists mentioned has actually proposed the particular system set forth here nor examined all its properties, and we call it the "BFH system" not to implicate them but only to give credit for some component ideas and to have a convenient label.[1] Regardless of who

Reprinted from the *Journal of Money, Credit, and Banking* 15 (August 1983): 302–15, with permission of the Ohio State University Press, © 1983. All rights reserved.

The authors thank the Institute for Humane Studies for the opportunity to work together on this and related topics and James M. Buchanan, James P. Cover, and Kaj Areskoug for written comments on earlier drafts, Robert E. Hall, Joseph T. Salerno, and William Breit for discussion, and Lawrence H. White for large and valuable amounts of both. Buchanan suggested the story of the fungus that we shall use and contributed to explaining how what he called "indirect convertibility" might be said to characterize the BFH system.

1. We do not claim to be offering an accurate summary or synthesis of particular persons' proposals. Instead, we are picking and choosing among ideas and modifying and extending them. (Incidentally, we would welcome suggestions for a name more descriptive than "BFH system.") While Fischer Black and Eugene F. Fama do consider using commodities as numéraire (and Fama even considers using spaceship permits), they mainly discuss how an unregulated financial system would operate. While Robert E. Hall also champions deregulation, he stresses his idea of a unit of account defined by a bundle of commodities. He would define the unit in terms of a small number of commodities whose amounts would be adjusted from time to time to stabilize a general price index. (He thus extends Irving Fisher's idea of a "compensated dollar" of adjustable gold content.) We, however, consider a unit defined once and for all in terms of so many commodities that its stability in terms of the unchanging bundle would come close to stability of its general purchasing power. See Fischer Black, "Banking and Interest Rates in a World Without Money," *Journal of Bank Research* (Autumn 1970): 8–20; Eugene F. Fama, "Banking in the Theory of Finance," *Journal of Monetary Economics* 6 (1980): 39–57; and Robert E. Hall, "The Government and the Monetary Unit" (Unpublished manuscript, 1981).

if anyone may actually advocate the system, contemplating it is instructive. It illuminates, by contrast, some characteristics of our existing and recent systems.

Briefly, the idea is to define the unit of account physically, in terms of many commodities, and not in terms of any medium of exchange whose value depends on regulation of its quantity or on its redeemability. (We use the terms "unit of account," "value unit," and "pricing unit" as synonyms, preferring one or another according to the particular emphasis intended.) Apart from defining the unit and enforcing contracts, the government would practice laissez-faire toward the medium of exchange and the banking and financial system.

Remarks by readers of our drafts have alerted us to the danger of being misinterpreted, no matter how clearly we say what we mean. This danger is understandable. People absorb ideas, and even sense impressions, by classifying them in relation to their earlier experiences.[2] People then sometimes react more to the pigeonholes they use than to the ideas themselves. We must insist, therefore, that the system we describe does not fit into familiar pigeonholes. We must warn our readers against preconceptions and urge them to await what we actually say.

The BFH system is not a variant of the often-proposed composite-commodity or commodity-reserve money. It is not a variant of the tabular standard (widespread indexing). Questions about whether the BFH system involves convertible or inconvertible money—questions presupposing some familiar answer—are inapplicable to it. The definition of the BFH unit of account does not require "implementation" through convertibility of any familiar sort, any more than does maintenance of the defined length of the meter.

Although the BFH system would indeed lack money as we now know it, it would not entail the textbook inconveniences of barter. The advantages of having a definite unit of account and convenient methods of payment would be retained and enhanced.

---

2. Friedrich A. Hayek, *The Sensory Order* (London: Routledge & Kegan Paul, 1952).

Also false is the notion that the BFH system is impractical because it somehow runs counter to the natural evolution of monetary and financial institutions. Our existing system is far from the pure product of any such evolution. Dismantling it would require legislation, whose specific provisions would be bound to nudge subsequent developments one way or another. That is why it is not self-contradictory to assess alternative payments systems even from a laissez-faire position.

I

SYSTEMS COMPARED AND QUESTIONS ILLUMINATED

We gain better understanding of a given payments system by comparing it with alternatives. Walter Eucken and Heinrich Rittershausen have emphasized crucial differences between systems that unite and those that separate the unit of account and the medium of exchange.[3] Separation, though familiar in the Middle Ages, is unfamiliar nowadays, a fact that makes the separated system we shall describe particularly instructive. In one type of monetary system, properly so called, the unit of account is the unit of the medium of exchange, whose value depends on the demand for it as such and on restriction of its quantity. This is our present system of fiat money. Under a second type of system, money is denominated in a unit kept equal in value to a definite quantity of some commodity by interconvertibility at a fixed ratio. The monetary commodity has a "natural" scarcity value; unlike fiat money, it cannot be simply printed or written into existence. This is the logic of the gold standard. The same logic applies, and more powerfully, to the often proposed composite-commodity or commodity-reserve standard, which would make the money unit interconvertible not with a single commodity but with a physically specified bundle of commodities.

A third type of payments system is the one examined here. It resembles the composite-commodity standard in its definition of the

3. Walter Eucken, *The Foundations of Economics*, trans. T. W. Hutchison (London: Hodge, 1950); Heinrich Rittershausen, *Bankpolitik* (Frankfurt: Knapp, 1966).

unit of account but differs from that standard in lacking any government-issued or government-specified medium of exchange and in lacking any claims obligatorily redeemable in bundles of the specific commodities defining the unit. One fundamental difference between this third (BFH) system and either ordinary system relates to the supply and demand that determine the value of the unit of account. Under both fiat money and an ordinary commodity standard, the unit's value is determined by supply of and demand for money or a monetary commodity, with the demand being wholly (for fiat money) or largely (for commodity money) of a monetary character. Under the BFH system, in contrast, the demand for the many commodities defining the unit is almost entirely nonmonetary. Under fiat money or an ordinary commodity standard, an imbalance between actual and desired money holdings can develop and (barring adroit remedial money-supply management) can call for adjustment of the real value of the unit of account. Pressures for this adjustment may work only sluggishly and therefore painfully because of stickiness in many individual prices and wages. Under the BFH system, in contrast, because of the almost wholly nonmonetary character of the demands for and supplies of the commodities defining the unit and because of the unit's separation from the medium of exchange, no monetary pressures can come to exert themselves, either sluggishly and painfully or otherwise, on the value of the unit. The BFH system offers much less scope than an ordinary monetary system for destructive monetary disequilibrium.

Comparison of the BFH system with others should help forestall misapplication of propositions true under one system to another system under which they do not apply. It should aid in pondering several interrelated questions. What are the possibilities and consequences of separating the unit of account and medium of exchange? What are the similarities and the differences between a unit of value and other units of weights and measures? What is necessary for an operationally meaningful definition of the pricing unit and for a determinate price level? By what processes does the value of the money unit change? Under what circumstances, if any, is the real-bills or needs-of-trade doctrine valid, and is James Tobin's notion valid of a natural economic limit to the nominal size of the money and banking system? Under what circumstances and in what senses is it true that the supply of money tends to create its own demand and that the demand for money tends to create its own supply? What is the role of base money when the bulk of the circulating medium consists of demand obligations backed by fractional reserves of it? What market processes tend to forestall or correct an imbalance between money's supply and demand, and what circumstances impair these processes, permitting painful macroeconomic consequences? Most broadly, what are the merits and defects of different systems?

II
THE BLACK-FAMA-HALL SYSTEM

The BFH system would get rid of any distinct money existing in a definite quantity. The government would be forbidden to issue obligations fixed in value in the unit of account and especially suitable as media of exchange. It would not give legal-tender status to any particular means of payment but would simply enforce contracts in which the parties themselves had specified what would constitute fulfillment. No longer would there be any such thing as money whose purchasing power depended on limitation of its quantity. No longer, then, could there be too much of it, causing price inflation, or too little, causing depression, or a sequence of imbalances, causing stagflation. A wrong quantity of money could no longer cause problems because money would not exist.

But without money, how would prices be quoted, contracts expressed, and financial records kept? The answer is that there would be a defined unit of value, just as there are defined units of length, weight, volume, time, temperature, and energy. Business practice, left to itself, might eventually converge on a specific definition of the unit. The government could hasten and probably improve the choice, however, by noncoercively offering a definition, just as it does with weights and measures. The unit would be defined by a suitable bundle of commodities. Just as the meter is defined physically as 1,650,763.73 wavelengths of the orange-red radiation of krypton 86, so the value unit would be defined physically as the total market value of, say, 50 kg of ammonium nitrate + 40 kg of copper + 35 kg of aluminum + 80 square meters of plywood of a specified grade (the four commodities mentioned by Robert Hall) + definite amounts of still other commodities. The prices of the individual commodities would not be fixed and would remain free to vary in relation to one another. Only the bundle as a whole would, by definition, have the fixed price of one unit. (For a unit of convenient size, however, the bundle might be designated as worth *one thousand* units.) The bundle would be composed of precisely gradable, competitively traded, and industrially important commodities, and in amounts corresponding to their relative importance. Many would be materials used in the production of a wide range of goods so that adopting the bundle as the value unit would come close to stabilizing the general level of prices expressed in that unit.

The commodities defining the unit would have the characteristics envisaged in the composite-commodity or commodity-reserve proposal, with one exception. They would not have to be storable, that is, capable of being held as monetary reserves, since the BFH scheme does not require any direct convertibility of obligations into the particular commodities defining the value unit. This difference—this lack of dependence on any particular base money— deserves emphasis. The more familiar proposal calls for an ordinary commodity standard in the sense that standard commodity bundles would be exchangeable for newly issued money and money would be redeemable in bundles at a fixed ratio. That proposed system differs from the gold standard chiefly in that a bundle of commodities takes the place of a single one. It, like the gold standard, is vulnerable to abandonment or to devaluation of the money unit. When the gold standard is abandoned or the gold content of the money unit is cut, the old unit keeps its functions, and people regard gold as a commodity whose price has risen. Part of the beauty of the BFH system, in contrast, is that the value unit remains stable in terms of the designated commodity bundle because its value never did depend on direct convertibility into that bundle or any specific commodity. Instead, its value is fixed by definition. It is free of any link to issues of money that might become inflated.

The BFH system bears a superficial resemblance to the proposed tabular standard of value, that is, widespread indexing, in that both involve specifying a standard bundle of goods and services. The latter system, however, presupposes the continued existence of an ordinary medium of exchange whose unit also serves as the ordinary unit of account. The total price of the standard bundle quoted in that ordinary unit—or, rather, changes in that price level—is what the price index measures. Use of the index to calculate current ordinary-money equivalents of certain debts and payments erects a unit of constant purchasing power, corresponding to the price index employed and its commodity bundle, into a unit of account rivaling the ordinary money unit. This rival unit presumably serves mainly in contracts spanning substantial periods of time (it is a "standard of deferred payments," as the older textbooks used to say). The BFH system, in sharp contrast, abolishes any ordinary money in terms of which a price index might be calculated and so avoids any rivalry between distinct units of account.[4]

Robert Hall suggested an analogy between the yard and the proposed value unit (in his taped panel discussion; what follows here embroiders on what he actually said). Both are units of measurement—one of length, the other of value. Both are defined in physical terms. Neither unit has any quantitative existence. It is nonsense to ask how many yards or how many value units there are in existence. Another element of the analogy is that no one seeks to maintain the size of the yard or of the value unit by maintaining any direct convertibility, as between cloth and yardsticks or between money and specific commodities. (Issuers of demand obligations, like other debtors, would be concerned about maintaining the value of their own obligations, but that is not the same as their bearing responsibility for the real value of the unit of account itself.)

Of course, an analogy is just that and not an identity. There are differences between units of length and value, just as between units of length and weight. The key similarity is that both are *defined* units whose definitions do not change or stop being applicable because of

4. Further discussion of the tabular standard and of why it is parasitical on the continued existence of ordinary money and unindexed prices appears in Leland B. Yeager, "Stable Money and Free-Market Currencies," *Cato Journal* 6 (Spring 1983): 305–26 (reprinted in this volume).

changes in some quantity or because of other physical or economic events.

With no money quantitatively existing, people make payments by transferring other property. To buy a bicycle priced at one hundred value units or pay a debt of one hundred units, one transfers property having that total value. Although the BFH system is barter in that sense, it is not *crude* barter. People need not haggle over the particular goods to be accepted in each transaction. The profit motive will surely lead competing private firms to offer convenient methods of payment.

Under laissez-faire, financial intermediaries blending the characteristics of present-day banks and mutual funds would presumably develop. People would make payments by writing checks (or doing the equivalent electronically) to transfer the appropriate amounts —value-unit-*worths*—of shares of ownership in these funds. (Convenience would dictate writing checks in numbers of value units, not in numbers of shares of heterogeneous funds.) The funds would invest in primary securities (business and personal loans and stocks and bonds) and perhaps in real estate and commodities. They would seek to attract customers (owners of their shares) by compiling records of high earnings, safety, and efficiency in administering the payments (checking) system. The funds would presumably charge for their checking services, so that investors would not be subsidizing customers using them mainly as checking accounts. Payment and investment institutions like these would arise unless entrepreneurs devised even more convenient ones that we have not been able to imagine. Different funds would specialize in different fields and services.

A customer's holding in his fund would not have to be fixed in size in value units. Apart from his adding to it or drawing it down, his holding would rise or fall in value as his fund received earnings and made capital gains or as it suffered losses on its asset portfolio. (In effect, holdings would bear interest or dividends at fluctuating rates, possibly sometimes negative.) Despite these fluctuations in value, the customer could watch his holding closely enough to avoid writing too big a volume of checks. He would probably be using the fund partly as an investment vehicle, anyway, and would not want to keep his holding down to the minimum required for transactions.

Furthermore, funds might well arrange to honor overdraft checks by making automatic loans to their drawers.

Funds would have to make settlements with one another, as banks do nowadays, for the differences between the value amounts of checks written on each one and of checks on others deposited with it. How would the funds do this? Remember, there is no base money—neither government-issued fiat money nor monetary stocks of particular commodities. Again, competition would favor efficient practices. Funds would presumably agree, under the auspices of their clearinghouses, on what portfolio assets—perhaps specified securities—would be acceptable in settlements.

The question of settlements leads into the question of what would happen if many owners of a particular fund wanted to get out of it. The departing owners would presumably write checks against their old fund and deposit them in their new funds. The shrinking fund would have to transfer assets to the growing ones. Loss of owners and of the value of assets and shareholdings would punish poor management. The discipline of competition would favor good performance.

What would serve as hand-to-hand currency? Fund shares of fluctuating value— some of them—could take the physical form of coins and circulating paper. It would probably prove convenient, however, for currency to be denominated in the unit of account. (The distinction between *evaluation* and *denomination* deserves attention. All property can have its current value, changeable or not, measured in units of account. An asset so denominated, however—like a ten-dollar bill of today—has its value *specified* as so many units.)

Nowadays, by way of a minor administrative detail or public-relations device, most money-market mutual funds fix the value of their shares at one dollar each and take account of earnings (or losses) by adjusting the number of shares in each owner's holding. If, similarly, BFH funds kept their shares worth one unit of account each, then some bearer shares could circulate as coins and notes. Only a small fraction of all shares would presumably take that form, however, unless some convenient way were devised for adjusting not merely the number of book-entry shares but also the number of shares circulating as currency to reflect the earnings or losses of individual funds. Alternatively, instead of being ownership shares, the circulating currency (and also some deposits) could be debt instruments issued by funds and other organizations and denominated in units of account.

III
ADVANTAGES

Considering its possible advantages will serve further to contrast the BFH system with our existing system and to provide a focus for certain questions. First, the system would provide a stable unit for pricing, invoicing, accounting, economic calculation, borrowing and lending, and writing contracts reaching into the future. The government, second, would come under financial discipline. It would have to borrow on the same basis as any other borrower and could no longer acquire resources by issuing money and otherwise imposing inflationary "taxation without representation." Competition under laissez-faire, third, would spur innovation in finance and the payments system and would exert discipline on banks and investment funds. Institutions would evolve, yes, but would no longer exhibit the socially unproductive instability hitherto associated with continual attempts to wriggle around changing government regulations.

A fourth set of advantages follows from the fact that the medium of exchange (i.e., readily transferable property) would not be redeemable in any particular base money, whether commodity money or government fiat money. No multiple expansions and contractions of ordinary money could occur in response to changes in the amount of any base money held as fractional reserves. No runs on financial institutions could occur of the self-aggravating type that used to be familiar (especially before government insurance of bank deposits, which, by the way, would be inappropriate under the BFH system). No scramble for base money of limited total quantity could make suspicion of particular institutions spread to others. Suspicion would be more nearly concentrated on poorly managed funds, holdings in which would depreciate in value, particularly as settlement of checks drawn by customers shifting to other funds stripped the shrinking funds of their most readily acceptable assets. Runs would be less catastrophic under the BFH system than under an ordinary banking system for reasons resembling the reasons for the differences between runs on national currencies under a system of pegged exchange rates and the more nearly self-restraining runs under floating exchange rates.

A related advantage is avoidance of multiple expansions and contractions of money supplies through the balance of payments. No longer could a payments deficit drain away base money and impose multiple deflation of a country's ordinary money supply. A country under the BFH system would have no fixed exchange rate (unless, quite exceptionally, and sacrificing key features of the system, it chose to define its unit of account as an amount of some foreign currency). Foreign currencies would be free to fluctuate in value against both the country's physically defined unit of account and its various media of exchange. A deficit on current account would necessarily mean either that foreigners were acquiring financial claims on the country or that its residents were disposing of financial claims on foreigners. No balance-of-payments surplus, to mention the opposite disorder, could impose imported inflation.

IV

AVOIDING MACROECONOMIC DIFFICULTIES

Our existing monetary system is subject not only to inflation but also to stagflation, deflation, and depression because the unit of account and the medium of exchange are tied together and because the actual quantity of money can fail to correspond to the total of money holdings desired at the existing price level (or entrenched price trend). Market-clearing forces do not work very well to maintain or restore equilibrium between money's supply and demand because money does not have a single price of its own that can adjust on a market of its own. Instead, the medium of exchange has a fixed price in the unit of account (each dollar of the money supply has a price of exactly one dollar). With no specific price and market to impinge upon, imbalance between money's supply and demand must oper-

373

ate upon the dollar's purchasing power, that is, on the whole general price level. This process requires adjustments on the markets and in the prices of millions of individual goods and services, leaving scope for quantities traded and produced to be affected. Prices and wages respond far from promptly enough to absorb the full impact of imbalances; they are sticky—some more so than others—for reasons that make excellent sense from the standpoints of individual price setters and wage negotiators. Under these realistic circumstances, failure to keep the quantity of money correctly and steadily managed can have momentous consequences.[5]

Inadequate effective demand for goods and services is sometimes blamed on oversaving. That as such, we insist (without repeating in detail what we have written elsewhere), is not what threatens general deflation of economic activity. The trouble comes, rather, from attempts to save by acquiring money, a good for which excess demand can develop and persist because it has no price of its own that could adjust on a market of its own to equilibrate supply and demand. Since money routinely facilitates exchanges of goods for one another, impairment of its circulation obstructs those exchanges and in turn obstructs the production of goods to be exchanged. In these respects money has no close counterpart in the BFH system.

In avoiding these monetary difficulties, the BFH system offers yet a fifth set of advantages. The unit of account no longer has its value dependent on the quantity of the medium of exchange. The unit's general purchasing power, being practically fixed by definition, is never called upon to undergo adjustment through a process exposed to the hitches characteristic of our existing system. The very concepts of quantity of money and of possibly divergent actual and demanded quantities become inapplicable. What serves as the medium of exchange is indefinite, plastic, and subject to the desires of market participants. As in a barter world, no clear line separates media

5. To avoid repetition, we refer to three papers by Yeager: "Essential Properties of the Medium of Exchange," *Kyklos* 21 (1968): 45–69, reprinted in *Monetary Theory: Selected Readings*, ed. Robert W. Clower (Baltimore: Penguin, 1969), 37–60, and in this volume; "What Are Banks?" *Atlantic Economic Journal* 6 (December 1978): 1-14 (reprinted in this volume); and "Sticky Prices or Equilibrium Always?" (Paper delivered at the meetings of the Western Economic Association, San Francisco, 7 July 1981.)

of exchange from other assets. Most owners of funds would be holding shares both as checking accounts and as investments. They could reclassify portions of their holdings as serving one purpose or the other as suited their changing circumstances and desires (if they ever bothered to make such a classification in the first place). Media of exchange would no longer have a fixed price in the unit of account (anyway, not all of them would). No longer could the pressures of imbalance between money's supply and demand be tending to change the purchasing power of the unit—but only sluggishly, with adverse side effects on quantities of goods and services traded and produced.

These macroeconomic advantages are worth a closer look. Actual quantities of media of exchange (liquid assets, readily transferable property) would adjust to the demand for them. In our existing world, by contrast, the nominal quantity of a country's medium of exchange is primarily determined on the supply side in the way described by the money-multiplier analysis of the money-and-banking textbooks (the analysis involving the quantity of base money and reserve and currency/deposit ratios). The real (purchasing-power) quantity of the medium of exchange does tend to be determined on the demand side, but through the roundabout and possibly sluggish and painful process of adjustment of the whole general price level. (For familiar reasons, this proposition about supply-side determination of the nominal quantity of money and demand-side determination of the real quantity applies strictly only to a closed economy, a country with a floating exchange rate, or a key-currency country in the special position that the United States enjoyed even under the Bretton Woods system. Under a fixed exchange rate regime, demands for money holdings can affect even the actual nominal quantity in a non-key-currency country through the balance of payments.)

In the BFH world, the (near-) fixity of the purchasing power of the unit of account obliterates any distinction between determination of real and determination of nominal quantities of assets usable as means of payment. No base money exists to constrain or support their quantities from the supply side. The fuzziness of the dividing line between these and other assets, furthermore, obviates the distinction that does hold in our actual world between the predominantly supply-side determination of nominal amounts of money and the supply-*and-demand* determination of nominal as well as real amounts of near moneys and nonmoneys.

V
RESPONSES OF QUANTITIES OF MEDIA OF EXCHANGE

With money of our present kind, the nominal quantity is determined on the supply side, with the nominal demand for it falling passively into line (subject to the standard exception for an open economy under fixed exchange rates). The unit's real size tends to adjust appropriately, but through a roundabout and possibly painful process.

With BFH fund shares serving as the media of exchange, their actual quantity, measured in units of account, is determined by interaction of demand with supply. Interest rates, broadly interpreted, play a role in the equilibration. By divorcing the unit of account and medium of exchange, the BFH system avoids supply-side determination of the latter's quantity. Just as even the nominal money supply is demand-determined in an open economy with a fixed exchange rate whose price level is dictated to it by the world market, so the volume of media of exchange is demand-determined in a BFH economy whose unit of account has a purchasing power dictated by its multi-commodity definition.

Space permits only few examples of the process at work. Suppose people's tastes shift away from holding fund shares and in favor of holding "bonds." (Here we stretch the term to cover all primary securities—stocks, bonds, promissory notes, mortgage obligations, and the like issued by the users of the resources so obtained—and even to cover any real estate and other physical assets in which funds might invest.) Accordingly, the rate of return paid on fund shares rises, while the the bond rate falls, the latter being an average rate of return on "bonds" in our stretched sense of the word. That is to say, the spread of the bond rate over the share rate—the price of intermediation services—falls, as is to be expected in consequence of the postulated decline in demand for those services. The unit-of-account volume of fund shares supplied goes down, matching the decline in demand for them.

For an example of an automatically accommodated increase in demand for media of exchange, suppose that some development expands the real size of the economy at full employment. Under an ordinary monetary system, an accommodating expansion of the nominal money supply is limited by the monetary base (as determined by policy or by the workings of a commodity standard) and by the determinants of the money multiplier. Under the BFH system, no such limitation or contingency impedes the expansion of fund shares. On the liability or equity side of their balance sheets, funds find their owners willing to hold more shares. On their asset side, funds find business firms willing to borrow more and issue more securities to finance taking advantage of the increased labor supply (if that, e.g., had been the element making for real growth) and of expanded markets for output.

Finally, let us suppose, or try to suppose, something analogous to expansion of an ordinary money supply at the initiative of issuers. Under our existing system, the central bank expands the stock of base money, the banking system responds, no one refuses payment in the newly created money, and spending and respending of the expanded money supply raises prices until it all is demanded as cash balances after all.

Under the BFH system, by way of an analogy that will prove incomplete, the funds step into the financial markets to grant loans and buy securities, paying with their own newly created shares. The more imprudently expanding funds face adverse clearing balances and the necessity of surrendering assets acceptable in interfund settlements. This happens not only because of their relatively great expansion of shares against which checks are now being written but also because doubts about their soundness lead owners to shift their holdings into more prudent funds. Both the asset portfolios of and shareholdings in the relatively imprudent funds decline not only in amount but also in price in terms of the unit of account, especially as those funds must part with their least dubious assets in interfund settlements. The settlement assets gained by the relatively prudent funds are not a close counterpart of base money under our existing system and cannot support a multiple expansion of assets and shares by those funds.

The crucial part of the story, however, is still to be told. As funds in general seek increased earnings by expanding at their own initiative, the firms and individuals borrowing from them or selling securities to them move to spend the shares thereby acquired. Shares accordingly depreciate against commodities, the unit of account, and funds' portfolio earnings. Just as would be the case were tastes simply to shift away from shareholdings and in favor of current consumption, share rates of return and then bond interest rates rise, discouraging the funds' supply of shares to the public and issuers' supply of primary securities to the funds. The funds' efforts to expand meet restraint after all.

Under both our existing system and the BFH system, the real volume of media of exchange is determined by demand (interacting with supply); and under the BFH system, fixity of the unit of account means that the volume measured in it, the nominal volume, is demand-determined also. This condition shields the BFH system from the macroeconomic disorder that does accompany an excess demand for or supply of money in our existing system. The BFH system has no clearly distinct medium of exchange that routinely flows to lubricate transactions in goods and services in such a way that expansion or restriction of its flow would do great damage. The medium of exchange—or a major part of it, shareholdings in funds—has a flexible price in terms of the stable-by-definition unit of account. (Recall the distinction between an asset's being denominated in a unit and its having a value expressible in that unit.) The total quantity of the medium of exchange—if that total is meaningful at all, in view of the vague and shiftable distinction between the exchange medium and investment assets—tends to adjust, as we have seen, to accommodate the demand for it. (Thus, the "natural economic limit" attributed by James Tobin,[6] erroneously, to the nominal size of a money and banking system of our current type *would* operate under the BFH system.)

6. James Tobin, "Commercial Banks as Creators of 'Money,' " in *Banking and Monetary Studies*, ed. Deane Carson (Homewood, Ill.: Irwin, 1963), 408–19.

VI
OPERATIONALITY AND DETERMINACY

Some readers may still be wondering whether the physical definition of the unit of account has operational meaning and whether the level of prices expressed in that unit is determinate. Determinacy, as Joseph A. Schumpeter said of a monetary system,[7] presupposes the specification from outside the market process of some "critical figure," some nominal magnitude (as by control of the number of money units in existence or, alternatively, by operational specification of the money price of some commodity or composite of commodities).

In the BFH system, that "critical figure" can only be the commodity-bundle definition of the unit of account. That definition leaves the individual prices of the items in the bundle free to respond to supply and demand changes. Could market conditions, then, establish prices that, when multiplied by the specified quantities, add up to more (or less) than one unit of account, contradicting the unit's definition?

Our reassuring answer does not rest on a circular argument. We do suppose—but on empirical grounds, namely, the tremendous convenience of a generally employed unit of account—that people take the government-suggested unit seriously in expressing prices, debts, and accounts. That unit has no plausible rivals. In an ordinary monetary system, the unit in which the medium of exchange is denominated remains available as an alternative to any proposed commodity-bundle unit. The BFH system, however, happily lacks any homogeneous medium of exchange denominated in units of itself.

Suppose that the BFH bundle were defined as 1 apple + 1 banana + 1 cherry. Prices are to be paid and debts settled in bundles-worths of convenient payment property. Now, apples are struck by a fungus. What market forces arise to accomplish the appropriate changes in relative prices while still enforcing the unit's definition?

7. Joseph A. Schumpeter, *Das Wesen des Geldes*, ed. Fritz Karl Mann (Göttingen: Vandenhoeck & Ruprecht, 1970).

We know that apples should rise in price relative to miscellaneous goods and services and to bananas and cherries also. By hypothesis, bundles are now more difficult to obtain. And if it is more difficult to come by a BFH bundle, then it is more difficult to come by anything worth a BFH bundle. People therefore offer bundles—or bundles-worths of payment property—less eagerly than before in trying to buy miscellaneous commodities, whose prices therefore fall relative to the bundle itself.

Now, the banana and the cherry, besides being components of the bundle, are themselves desired commodities. They therefore number among the goods for which people bid less eagerly in view of the hypothesized increased difficulty of obtaining bundles and so bundles-worths of payment property. The resulting fall in the prices of bananas and cherries counterbalances the increased unit-of-account price of apples.

This view of the market process that maintains the commodity-bundle definition of the unit of account emphasizes the advantages of defining the BFH bundle in a more comprehensive way. In our simple example of a three-fruit bundle, the general price level comes under substantial downward pressure when apples are attacked by the fungus. Such pressure, confronting sluggishly adjusting disequi-librium prices, can impede exchange and so impede production and employment. This impediment, however, is a consequence of utiliz-ing such a narrowly defined bundle.

If the bundle were more widely defined, the undisturbed supply conditions of the other items composing it would mitigate the defla-tionary impact of the worsened apple-supply conditions. Bundles and bundles-worths of property would become only marginally more difficult to come by, and as a result, the general price level would come under only slight deflationary pressure. Thus, the wider the definition of the bundle, the greater the degree to which appropri-ate changes in relative prices are effected by change in the unit-of-account price of any particular bundle component struck by altered supply or demand conditions. A widely defined bundle thus concen-trates the impact of such changes, avoiding widespread and possibly painful repercussions.

The absence of convertibility of a familiar type lacks the ominous consequences that it might have in a monetary system with a homogeneous medium of exchange. Under the often-proposed composite-commodity standard, for example, in which the paper dollar is set equal in value to a certain bundle of commodities, tension arises between regarding the paper dollar and regarding the commodity bundle as the unit of account. In such a system, two-way convertibility must be maintained to prevent a divergence of the two units. The BFH system, however, lacking as it does any paper dollar that might rival the commodity bundle as the unit of account, never permits such tension to arise. Absence of a rival unit makes the BFH system's lack of convertibility of the usual sort irrelevant to the system's operationality and determinacy. Worries about lack of convertibility reflect an understandable but inappropriate carryover of concepts suited to existing monetary systems instead.

The BFH system of sophisticated barter does seem to avoid the disadvantages both of crude barter and of money as we have known it. We postpone considering a transition to the BFH system. It is a type of reform whose success does not hinge on its early adoption. (In contrast, one might plausibly argue that delay in adopting the program of today's monetarists threatens to entrench a situation in which rapid institutional change and the blurring of the very concept of money will have made that program no longer workable.) Regardless of whether the BFH system ever is adopted, the proposal offers a fresh slant on some crucial aspects of actual monetary systems.

Deregulation and
Monetary Reform

In the past we could distinguish sharply between currency and checkable deposits, on the one hand, and savings accounts and other near and nonmoneys, on the other hand. Unambiguously defining money and measuring its quantity has now been growing more difficult. Inflation-boosted nominal interest rates have promoted wriggling around requirements for non-interest-bearing reserves and around interest rate ceilings. Responses include money market funds, money market deposit accounts, NOW and Super-NOW accounts, overnight repurchase agreements, aspects of the Eurocurrency market, and cash-management accounts offered by brokerage houses. Deregulation has been blurring the distinction between banks and nonbanks and between things that do and things that do not function as media of exchange.

The late Robert Weintraub, among others, used to argue that despite institutional changes, the functional relation between nominal *GNP* and the quantity of money will remain stable—money being properly defined.[1] Adjusted definitions and adjusted demand or velocity functions can continue yielding good fits. Weintraub expected continuing success with money defined as fully checkable accounts in depository institutions plus currency in circulation and nonbank travelers' checks.

But does such a possibility warrant confidence in being able to conduct a quantity-oriented monetary policy from month to month

Reprinted from the *American Economic Review* (May 1985): 103–6, with permission from The American Economic Association, 2014 Broadway, Nashville, Tennessee 37203.

1. Robert Weintraub, "The New Role for Gold in U.S. Monetary Policy," in *Money in Crisis,* ed. Barry N. Siegel (San Francisco: Pacific Institute for Public Policy Research, 1984).

and day to day? What accounts should be deemed *fully* checkable? Which institutions count as *depository* institutions? Figuring out, *ex post*, how money should have been defined and regulated is not the same as knowing how to do so currently. (Thomas Simpson, John Wenninger, and Gillian Garcia offer recent discussions by Federal Reserve economists.)[2]

Robert Hall has expressed skepticism about the old idea of quantity control:

> Monetary regulations imposed by the American and British governments of the past century create a more-or-less stable relation between a certain class of assets called money and nominal spending . . . , but different regulations would alter that relation. . . .
>
> Regulation of financial institutions . . . had . . . implications for the stability of the demand for money. . . . [M]ost important, a wide variety of methods of carrying out transactions and holding wealth were regulated out of existence. . . .
>
> . . . [T]he money stock itself is a creature of inefficient regulation.[3]

I do not say that the monetarists were wrong in advocating their steady-growth rule. But their remedy was not taken in due time, the disease has grown more complicated, and their old prescription may no longer be the best.

Rolling deregulation back might conceivably restore stable links between money and other variables. However, deregulation is no mere product of ideology. Regulations have been succumbing to powerful market incentives not easily overcome. Conceivably, also, new monetary linkages might stabilize after the current process of transition has run its course. Who can foretell the future?

2. See Gillian Garcia, "The Right Rabbit: Which Intermediate Target Should the Fed Pursue?" Federal Reserve Bank of Chicago, *Economic Perspectives* (May–June 1984): 15–31; and Thomas D. Simpson, "Changes in the Financial System: Implications for Monetary Policy," *Brookings Papers on Economic Activity* 1 (1984): 249–65 (followed by comments by James Duesenberry, Robert Hall, Benjamin Friedman, Ralph Bryant, and Edmund Phelps).

3. Robert E. Hall, *"Monetary Trends in the United States and the United Kingdom:* A Review From the Perspective of New Developments in Monetary Economics," *Journal of Economic Literature* 20 (December 1982): 1552–55.

I

THE BFH SYSTEM

Prudence recommends being ready: we should contemplate radical alternatives to our existing and changing monetary regime. Even reforms never adopted may provide contrasts affording insights into our present unsatisfactory method of giving determinacy to our unit of account.

The unit in which we quote prices, express debts and terms of other contracts, and keep accounts is the value of the dollar of fiat money, the scruffy dollar bill. This unit is analogous to units of weight and length and is at least as often used in everyday activities. Yet its size is determined in a haphazard, precarious, and downright preposterous manner.

I wish time permitted detailing the absurdities of making our unit of account be the supply-and-demand-determined value of the unit of the fiat medium of exchange. Supply and demand fail to balance smoothly and continuously because they do not meet on a specific market and determine a specific price. "The money market" is just a figure of speech, not a reality; so monetary disequilibrium gets corrected only in a roundabout and often painful way.

One radical contrast with our existing system appears in what Robert Greenfield and I call the BFH system (crediting Fischer Black, Eugene Fama, and Robert Hall for ideas borrowed). The unit of account would no longer coincide with the unit of the medium of exchange. No homogeneous medium of exchange would exist as a possible rival unit. The government would define the new unit, just as it defines units of weights and measures. The definition would run in terms of a bundle of commodities so comprehensive as to have a nearly stable value against goods and services in general. The items in the bundle would be precisely specifiable ones with continuously quoted prices.[4]

4. Robert L. Greenfield and Leland B. Yeager, "A Laissez-Faire Approach to Monetary Stability," *Journal of Money, Credit, and Banking* 15 (August 1983): 302–15 (reprinted in this volume).

The government would exert a nudge against the inertia of old practices by conducting its own transactions and accounting in the new unit. The government is bound to influence a new system by the particular way it disengages from its domination of the current one, so policy makers can hardly avoid considering what sort of reform is desirable. Apart from promoting the new BFH unit, the government would practice *laissez-faire* toward the financial system. It would be forbidden to issue money. (The reform is quite different from the often-proposed composite-commodity money.)

Deregulation would give full scope to innovative financial intermediation. Private enterprises would, in effect, repackage investment portfolios into convenient media of exchange. No one can confidently predict future details. It seems likely, though, that institutions would emerge combining the features of today's banks, money market funds, and stock mutual funds. Some holdings in these institutions would presumably be dividend-yielding equity shares; others would be accounts denominated in the BFH unit and bearing interest at competitive rates. In either case, people would not only stipulate prices and payments but also write checks on these holdings in the single, precisely defined, stable unit, *not* in heterogeneous goods and securities.

Would checks drawn on and deposits in financial institutions be redeemable? (The same question applies to currency, for some institutions would presumably issue notes and even coins denominated in the BFH unit.) It is unlikely—because so awkward—that institutions would offer and customers demand redemption in bundles of the actual commodities defining the unit. "Indirect redeemability," as James Buchanan has suggested calling it, is more likely. Competition might lead institutions to cash checks and redeem their currencies and deposits in whatever quantities of gold or of specified securities equaled in total value as many standard commodity bundles as the numbers of units of account denominating the obligations to be redeemed.

It is important that institutions would similarly settle net balances due on account of checks (and banknotes) presented at their clearinghouse. They would transfer gold or securities actually worth as many commodity bundles as the numbers of units of account to be settled. Professionals would make and implement the required calculations every business day, and the ordinary person would no more need to know just what determines the purchasing power of the BFH unit than he needs to know what determines that of the dollar nowadays.

Furthermore, routine settlements at the clearinghouse would provide part of the scope for arbitrage that would maintain the operationality of the unit's commodity definition. Suppose, with Arthur Okun, that the standard bundle consists of 1 ball + 1 orange (the principle illustrated is the same with a multi-item bundle). Suppose, further, that market forces make 1 ball worth 3 oranges. Then the BFH unit is worth $1\frac{1}{3}$ balls and, equivalently, 4 oranges. Prices are U.75 for a ball and U.25 for an orange, totaling U1, as they should. Any discrepancy would provide an opportunity for profitable and corrective arbitrage. Numerical examples could readily be given if space permitted.[5]

Although practices under the BFH system would displace money as we now know it, they would not entail the textbook inconveniences of barter. The advantages of a single definite unit of account and convenient methods of payment would be retained and enhanced. Apart from crucial differences in the unit and in the media for redeeming their obligations, financial institutions would be practicing something similar to free banking under a gold standard.[6]

With the unit of account and media of exchange divorced, the unit's value (like the meter's length) would be established by definition, not by regulation of any quantity. Quantities of media of exchange would be limited by the real (unit of account) quantities people were willing to hold. Quantities would be constrained in much the way operating for mutual fund shares nowadays, for near moneys until the recent blurring of the distinction between them and circulating media, and for money itself in an individual small country to which the purchasing power of its unit is dictated under an international gold standard. The sizes of the asset sides and the

5. Arthur Okun, *Prices and Quantities* (Washington, D.C.: Brookings Institution, 1981), 290.

6. On the success of free banking in Scotland up to 1845 and for analysis, see Lawrence H. White, *Free Banking in Britain: Theory, Experience, and Debate, 1800–1845* (New York: Cambridge University Press, 1984).

liability and equity sides of institutions' balance sheets would be influenced and reconciled largely by market-determined interest and yield rates received on the institutions' loans and investments and paid to their depositors and shareholders.

Trouble in understanding this demand-side (as well as supply-side) limit to quantities stems, I conjecture, from carrying ideas over from our present system of fiat money, whose unit is also the unit of account. Under this system, expansion of the nominal supply causes the nominal amount demanded to increase also through shrinkage of the unit's real size. Things would be quite different with a unit defined without reference to any medium of exchange.

With quantities of media of exchange determined by demand and supply and with checkable deposits and equity holdings in financial institutions having market-clearing flexible yields or prices of their own expressed in the BFH unit, monetary disequilibrium as we have known it could no longer occur. With the value of the unit of account spared from sometimes coming under strong but sluggishly working upward or downward pressure, painful macroeconomic disorders would be practically forestalled.

Besides macroeconomic advantages, the BFH system would provide the monetary saturation whose absence concerned Milton Friedman in his 1969 article, "The Optimum Quantity of Money." Since media of exchange would bear interest or dividends at competitive rates, high opportunity costs would no longer press holders to spend real resources economizing on cash balances.[7]

A further advantage is absence of any base money distinct from more abundant ordinary money. No longer could scrambles to get out of ordinary money into base money cause panics and deflation. Any distrust would be concentrated on specific financial institutions. Investments in them would decline in price and quantity. Competition would favor the more prudently managed institutions. Deregulation would appropriately extend to abolishing government deposit insurance.

Mention of base money reminds us of perhaps the greatest difficulty with the BFH system, that of making the transition. The appear-

7. Milton Friedman, "The Optimum Quantity of Money," in Friedman, *The Optimum Quantity of Money and Other Essays* (Chicago: Aldine, 1969).

ance of attractive alternatives would collapse the demand to hold money of the present type. Holdings of and liabilities on bank-account dollars would pretty well match. The problem is the collapse of demand for Federal Reserve notes and deposits and Treasury coins. Either this base money would lose its value, expropriating its holders, or else the government would have to replace it by ordinary, interest-bearing, burdensome government debt.

I see no satisfactory answer to this problem of transition. Still, the BFH system is worth understanding for the light it sheds on our existing system. Futhermore, if the existing dollar should be destroyed anyway—perhaps by persisting government fiscal irresponsibility—it would be a shame to reconstruct the same old failed system.

II
FISHER'S PROPOSAL, MODIFIED

The awkwardness of shifting away from government money recommends considering a second-best reform. Abandoning any quantity rule, it would combine a price-index rule with gold redeemability in a manner reminiscent of Irving Fisher's "compensated dollar."[8]

The monetary authority would be required not only to target a comprehensive price index but also to redeem its money on demand in the (changeable) weight of gold actually worth, at current prices, the bundle of goods and services used in specifying the index. The authority would also be required to issue new money in exchange for the calculated amount of gold, with perhaps a slight spread between its selling and buying prices of gold to cover expenses.

The standard objection to irredeemable fiat money managed so as to stabilize a price index centers on lags and the attendant danger of overshooting and of oscillations around the target. Lags supposedly intervene between an incipient money-supply-and-demand imbalance and its reflection in the price index and between movements of the index and policy responses and their corrective effects. Under

8. See Irving Fisher, *Stabilizing the Dollar* (New York: Macmillan, 1920); cf. Willford I. King, *The Keys to Prosperity* (New York: Committee for Constitutional Government, 1948), 209–10. The present proposal differs from Fischer's only in details and in the rationale offered.

the system suggested here, though, two-way convertibility plus arbitrage would keep the dollar always equal in value to the (variable) quantity of gold that was in turn equal in value to a specified bundle of goods and services. The problem of lags would thus be circumvented (or so it seems to me).

Convertibility of the sort described would tie the dollar to the specified bundle. The system would not be a gold standard. Some other commodity, or some one or more securities, might well be the redemption medium instead; gold serves here only as an example. No such self-aggravating and devastating scramble for gold could occur as can occur under an ordinary gold standard with fractional reserves. Any scramble would reflect itself in an increased price of gold both in money and relative to other goods and services, thereby automatically reducing the physical quantity of gold in which the dollar was redeemable.

Incidentally, the monetary authority would not necessarily be restricted to issuing and retiring money only against quantities of redemption medium offered by or demanded by the public. It could aim open market operations in securities at stabilizing the price index directly and so hold down the volume of actual conversions. Still, two-way convertibility would be available to keep the dollar stable against commodities.

Convertibility of this sort would be more than merely decorative. It would impose an additional discipline on the monetary authority by requiring it actually to *do something* at the initiative of money holders. If excessive money creation had raised the price index from the target level of 100 to 120, people would be redeeming money of $100 face value in gold (or some other redemption medium) quoted at $120, selling the gold for $120 and redeeming that money in gold worth $144, and so on. Threatened with running out of gold, the government would have to buy more. In bidding up the dollar price of gold, it would be tending in that particular way to hold down the physical quantity of gold in which the dollar was redeemable. To avoid further debasing the purchasing power of money and further endangering its gold reserves, however, the government would have to pay for its gold purchases otherwise than by issuing or reissuing money. It would have to raise the necessary funds by cutting expenditures or by taxes or noninflationary borrowing. Such discipline would constrain overissue in the first place.

Monetary management would no longer depend on accurate conceptualization, measurement, and regulation of the quantity of money. The logic of this system of a modified compensated dollar, like the logic of the BFH system, would recommend complete deregulation, including free banking. By the way, the BFH system might be interpreted as a nongovernmental, decentralized, and competitive version of the system just described.

A Real-GNP Dollar

(with Robert L. Greenfield)

Monetarists long have advocated committing the Federal Reserve to a quantity-of-money rule. Milton Friedman, Karl Brunner, and Allan Meltzer, to name but the most prominent among the monetarists, for years advocated a rule requiring the Federal Reserve to increase the quantity of base money at a fixed annual rate, the rate consistent with price-level stability. Brunner and Meltzer still hold to this position. Friedman, however, has broken ranks: he would have the Federal Reserve freeze the monetary base.[1]

Freezing the monetary base, Friedman argues, would bring us closer than we have ever been to having a money supply "determined by the market interactions of many financial institutions and millions of holders of monetary assets."[2] We, too, see considerable merit in having market forces determine the quantity of money. For that very reason, however, we consider Friedman's proposal, radical though it may sound, not imaginative enough. In the present state of knowledge, as Friedman likes to say, economists can hope to do better.

This paper, building on an old idea of Irving Fisher's, describes the kind of changes needed to make the money supply capable of taking care of itself. Our variation on Fisher's proposal offers macroeconomic advantages that bring to mind the advantages that Friedman and other monetarists see in a floating exchange rate.

Reprinted with permission of the authors.

1. Milton Friedman, "The Case for Overhauling the Fed," *Challenge* (July–August 1985): 4–12.

2. Ibid., 11.

MACROECONOMIC DISEQUILIBRIUM

Sometimes, even economists forget why money matters. When we sweep aside "the veil of money," we see that each person specializes in the production of a single good or service. The producer intends to exchange most, often all, of what he produces for the products of other specialists. Goods and services do not exchange directly for goods and services, however; they exchange indirectly through the intermediary of money.

Each person (and firm) holds a store of the monetary lubricant, the quantity directly depending upon the magnitude of receipts and expenditures. Money balances held add up to "the money supply"; and provided that the money supply measures up to desired money balances, transactions can proceed without monetary impediment.

Sometimes, however, the money supply falls short of the demanded quantity. A person seeking to replenish or enlarge his holdings of money will curtail his expenditures and push his sales. On the markets for goods and services, then, excess supplies prevail; markets fail to clear. Lacking customers, producers lay off employees. Lacking income, both producers and employees cease being customers. The problem snowballs. At some reduced level of real income, people feel unable to afford holding money balances any larger than those they have; poverty chokes off what, at full employment, anyway, would be an excess demand for money. A surpressed monetary disequilibrium prevails.

Any nominal quantity of money, of course, however small, would suffice for full employment, provided that the general level of prices and wages fell far enough to make that small nominal quantity of money adequate in real terms. The general level of prices and wages changes, when it does, however, through changes in the individual prices and wages that compose it. Individual price setters and wage negotiators have good reason not to want to take the lead in what cannot be other than a piecemeal and decentralized downward adjustment of prices and wages. The wait for the wage-and-price-level adjustment needed to restore full employment, therefore, can be long and painful.

Monetary Misalignment

The general deficiency of effective demand for currently produced goods and services traces to the money supply's having become too small in relation to the prevailing wage-and-price level. How can such a misalignment occur? Well, the money supply might just shrink, as it did during the early 1930s. The fear of bank closings led depositors to the teller's window, wanting to hold a particular kind of money, namely, cash (as opposed to deposit money). To accommodate a depositor's request for cash, a bank has to give the depositor not only the reserves being held against his deposit dollar but also the reserves being held against several other deposit dollars. The other deposit dollars, stripped of the reserves needed to back them, get canceled, as banks attempt to repair reserve deficiencies by selling off assets. Between 1930 and 1933, one of every three dollars was canceled.

Freezing the monetary base, as Friedman now recommends, would contribute nothing to easing problems associated with wide-scale bank runs. When depositors make cash withdrawals, the monetary base—total bank reserves plus currency outside banks—does not change. As a result of the redistribution of base money away from banks, the existing monetary base can no longer support as large a total quantity of money, currency outside banks and deposits, as before. No one has argued more vigorously than Friedman himself that faced with the bank runs of the early 1930s, the Federal Reserve should have conducted massive open-market purchases; the Federal Reserve, that is to say, should have greatly *expanded* the monetary base and thereby permitted the banking system to accommodate the demands for cash while at the same time maintaining the stock of deposits.

The Bank Run as a Pricing Problem

An economist would be quick to diagnose the bank-run problem, were the problem cast in nonmonetary terms. If, when the demand for something supplied in a fixed quantity strengthened, the total quantity supplied proved inadequate, then the price adjustment needed to equilibrate supply and demand must somehow have been jammed, perhaps through a price ceiling. Recast in these ordinary supply-and-demand terms, the bank run should pose no greater a diagnostic challenge than that presented by the gasoline lines of the 1970s.

Suppose, for example, that the government saddled hotel owners with an Old Master requirement. To operate a hotel, a person must afford his guests adequate opportunity to cultivate an appreciation of art. Of every twenty hotel rooms, therefore, at least one room would have to have a genuine Old Master gracing its walls. Old Masters are supplied in a fixed quantity, and that quantity would constrain the availability of hotel space.

Suppose, now, that the government's art-appreciation program were so successful that hotel owners had opportunities to sell their Old Masters at irresistible prices. The sale of the Old Masters would obviously cut into the availability of hotel space. How could the art lovers' demand for Old Masters be met without necessitating a reduction in hotel space?

The answer lies in expressing the Old Master requirement in value rather than in physical terms. Rather than requiring hotel owners to hang an Old Master in at least 5 percent of their rooms, require hotel owners to hang Old Masters *worth* at least 5 percent of a year's full-capacity rent. Require quality, not quantity. As the market price of Old Masters rose, a reduced number of Old Masters would permit hotel owners to keep the same number of hotel rooms available.

Return now to a monetary context. Assume that only one bank existed. Call it the Federal Reserve, and suppose that the Federal Reserve fulfilled reserve requirements expressed in gold. Under an ordinary gold standard, such a reserve requirement would constrain the quantity of money. When a depositor turned in his banknote or deposit dollar for redemption, the total number of dollars would fall by a multiple of the withdrawal. How could the bank accommodate the redemption request yet avoid the loss of reserves and the subsequent multiple-note-and-deposit contraction?

Again, think in value terms. Suppose the Federal Reserve obligated itself to convert each thousand dollars into enough gold to buy the basket of goods and services defining the fixed-weighted price index for Gross National Product (the implicit GNP price deflator, though more familiar, comes closer to being a Paasche index than to being a Laspeyres index). If the price of the items included in the basket added up to one thousand dollars, and if the price of gold were one thousand dollars per ounce, the Federal Reserve would redeem each of its dollar liabilities in one ounce of gold.

A bank run and the associated scramble for gold would tend to push up the price of gold. Suppose that the price of gold rose to two thousand dollars per ounce, while the market basket defining the fixed-weighted price index for GNP continued to have a cumulative one-thousand-dollar price. The Federal Reserve would have to convert each dollar liability into one-half ounce of gold, because one-half an ounce of gold would have market value equal to that of the standard market basket. The price of the redemption medium itself, here gold, would vary in terms of the medium of exchange, the Federal Reserve's currency or deposit dollar. A reduced holding of gold thus would enable the Federal Reserve to keep in existence an unchanged total number of dollars (just as a reduced number of Old Masters permitted hotel owners to rent the same number of rooms).

Under an ordinary gold standard, under which each Federal Reserve dollar would be convertible into a prespecified physical quantity of gold, discoveries of new gold fields or improved methods of gold extraction would put downward pressure on the market price of gold. Miners would then be able to sell gold to the Federal Reserve for a higher price than they otherwise could have obtained on the market. The stock of monetary gold would increase, enlarging the quantity of money and producing inflationary pressures.

Under standard-bundles-worths convertibility, by contrast, a straightforward price adjustment would keep gold discoveries from unduly enlarging the money supply. A discovery of gold would reduce the market price of gold, and, as a result, each dollar would be redeemable in a larger physical quantity of gold. The Federal Reserve, watching the gold market, would merely reduce the price at which it bought and sold gold.

Suppose, for example, that as a result of these gold discoveries, the market price of gold headed toward five hundred dollars per ounce. The Federal Reserve, remember, promised to keep one thousand dollars convertible into enough gold to buy the standard market bundle. How many ounces of gold now would have market value equal to that of the standard bundle? Since the price of gold fell to five hundred dollars while the price of the standard bundle remained at one thousand dollars, two ounces of gold would have market value equal to that of the standard bundle. The Federal Reserve would reduce the price at which it bought and sold gold to five hundred dollars per ounce, the market price. No incentives would develop to move gold from industrial and ornamental to monetary use. The gold discoveries thus would not produce inflationary pressures.

Redemption in real-GNP bundles-worths of gold would tie the dollar to the bundle of goods and services that define the fixed-weighted price index for GNP. If at prevailing market prices, the Federal Reserve always redeemed one thousand dollars in enough gold to purchase the bundle defined by the fixed-weighted price index for GNP, then one thousand dollars would always purchase that bundle. If $A = B$ and $B = C$, then $A = C$.

The system that we describe is not an ordinary gold standard. Gold here serves as the redemption medium, but anything else would be equally serviceable. The Federal Reserve might have chosen interest-bearing securities, for example, as its redemption medium. The objective would be to tie the dollar (or some number of dollars) to a standard market basket of goods and services. The redemption medium would provide the adherence by changing hands in *value* amounts rather than in prespecified physical amounts. The particular item chosen to serve as the redemption medium, however, would be irrelevant.

PARALLELS

In some respects, the argument in favor of the real-GNP dollar parallels the argument that Friedman and other monetarists have offered in favor of a floating exchange rate. Under a fixed exchange rate, restoration of equilibrium after, say, a movement of world demand away from a country's exports and the cancellation of money caused by exchange-rate pegging requires downward adjustment of that country's entire wage-and-price level. The customary (and understandable) stickiness of wages and prices will translate these deflationary pressures into reduced output and employment. A floating exchange rate takes pressure off the general level of wages and prices and focuses it upon a single, rather easily changed price, namely, the foreign-exchange rate.

In much the same way, the real-GNP-dollar system would take pressure off the general *level* of wages and prices and focus it upon one particular price, the price of the redemption medium. To calculate the price of the redemption medium, the Federal Reserve would simply keep an eye on the various goods-and-services markets and on the gold market. Calculating the price of the redemption medium would entail no more than a piece of simple arithmetic.

Irving Fisher recommended much the same thing when he proposed his compensated-dollar scheme, whereby periodically (every two months) the government would alter the gold "content" of the dollar.[3] He naturally thought in terms of gold as a redemption medium, because he lived in a gold-standard world. Fisher, however, seems to have been less interested in macroeconomic stabilization than in an "honest dollar," that is, a dollar that over time would have unchanged meaning or purchasing power. To enhance the macroeconomic stabilization capacity of the scheme, we recommend but two minor modifications to Fisher's proposal: first, that the price of the redemption medium be calculated on more or less a continuous basis (nowadays, the technology needed for continuous calculation presents no obstacle), and, second, that in calculating the price of the redemption medium, the Federal Reserve take into account not only changes in the standard bundle's cumulative price but also changes in the market price of gold.

Although the real-GNP-dollar system, even if gold were adopted as the redemption medium, would not actually be a gold standard, the scheme would accommodate the money supply to changes in the demand for money, just as an ordinary gold standard would. Sup-

3. Irving Fisher, *Stabilizing the Dollar* (New York: Macmillan, 1920).

pose, for example, that the general public wanted to enlarge its money holdings. As usual, spending flows would shrink and prices would come under downward pressure. Suppose, although things would never get this far, that both the price of gold and the cumulative price of the standard bundle fell to five hundred dollars. The arbitrage opportunities would be obvious. The Federal Reserve, remember, promised to give you one thousand dollars in exchange for as many ounces of gold as are actually worth, at market prices, one standard bundle. You therefore could buy an ounce of gold for five hundred dollars and then bring it to the Federal Reserve, where you would sell it for one thousand dollars. The money supply would grow and thus accommodate itself to the increased demand for money.

WHAT TO FREEZE?

If private, commercial banks sprang up and issued deposit dollars convertible into the Federal Reserve dollar, then rigidity of the redemption medium's price would again became a problem. Bank deposit dollars would exchange for Federal Reserve dollars at a fixed price, one bank dollar for one Federal Reserve dollar, just as they do today. Wide-scale efforts to turn privately issued deposit dollars into Federal Reserve dollars would cause a multiple contraction of those deposit dollars. Because it would keep its dollar convertible into whatever quantity of gold had $\frac{1}{1,000}$ the value of the bundle of goods and services that define the fixed-weighted price index for GNP, however, the Federal Reserve could meet a scramble for its notes without worrying, as apparently it worried in the 1930s, that it was jeopardizing the convertibility of its own monetary liabilities. Nevertheless, the system would lose some of its self-regulating advantage.

To achieve macroeconomic stability, monetary reform, if it freezes anything, should freeze not the quantity of *base money* but the quantity of the *redemption medium*. The market value of the redemption medium, however, must be free to fluctuate. Friedman's proposed freeze of the monetary base would invite disequilibrium by constraining the redemption system in two dimensions, price and quantity. Only by having a fluctuating price can the redemption medium, if fixed in quantity, fasten the monetary unit to the standard market bundle.

To illustrate how a more fully developed financial system could exhibit the desired elasticity, suppose, for example, that the Federal Reserve decided to close its doors. Suppose, however, that before going out of business, the Federal Reserve temporarily recalled its notes, erased the inscription "one dollar," and replaced it with the inscription "one greenback." Suppose as well that the Federal Reserve converted its deposit liabilities to banks in the same way, replacing the banks' deposits with notes bearing the inscription, "one greenback." These greenbacks still would have value, not as money, however, but as antiques, collectibles, reminders of a bygone era. They would have become Old Masters.

Only by sheer coincidence, of course, would these greenbacks have value in proportion to the denominations they formerly carried. What had been a ten-dollar bill, for example, probably would not wind up being ten times as valuable as what had been a one-dollar bill. Suppose that to sidestep this problem, the Federal Reserve, when it sends greenbacks to former holders of currency, sends only one type. A person who had been holding a ten-dollar bill would therefore receive ten greenbacks, suitably rumpled for authenticity.

Suppose that encouraged by the governmental exhortations, people, rather than switching to a "greenback standard," clung to the dollar as their pricing unit. The government itself, trying to set an example, would continue to use the dollar in its own accounting and contracting and tax collecting. Suppose that to give the dollar determinate purchasing power, the government, noting that yesterday the cumulative price of the items going into the fixed-weighted price index for GNP was one thousand dollars, defined the dollar as $\frac{1}{1,000}$ the market value of that bundle.

Banks would continue to operate, meeting the demand for notes and checkable deposits. Banks would repackage primary assets, such as stocks, bonds, and, yes, perhaps even antiques, into moneylike liabilities. The firms' inducement to perform in this intermediary capacity would be the extent to which the yields they earned on their assets exceeded the rates competition would force them to pay on deposits and equity holdings. (Notes could conceivably earn interest, perhaps through some kind of lottery feature.)[4]

The elimination of the Federal Reserve's paper dollar would not saddle anyone with the textbook disadvantages of barter. You would buy things just as you always have, namely, by handing the merchant the appropriate number of dollars. Those dollars could take the form of notes or, instead, dollar-denominated checks.

To have their notes and checkable deposits and equity holdings taken seriously, however, banks would have to keep them convertible into something. (Nowadays, to have their particular brand-name deposit dollars taken seriously, banks must keep them convertible into the dominant Federal Reserve dollar.) Assume that each bank kept its dollar liability redeemable in as many greenbacks, the collector's item, as had $\frac{1}{1,000}$ the market value of the standard basket. A person who wanted to redeem a ten-dollar note would be given as many greenbacks as had $\frac{1}{100}$ (i.e., $\frac{10}{1,000}$) the market value of the standard bundle.

The great bulk of such redemptions doubtless would take place at the clearinghouse, where professionals would undertake the necessary calculations. A bank facing a one-hundred-dollar adverse clearinghouse balance, for example, would pay over as many greenbacks as had $\frac{1}{10}$ (i.e., $\frac{100}{1,000}$) the actual market value of the standard bundle. The purchasing power of the pricing-unit dollar would not have to change to accommodate an increased demand for money; the "dollar" would mean $\frac{1}{1,000}$ the value of the standard GNP bundle. Notes and checks denominated "one dollar," by definition made operational by value convertibility, would continuously have purchasing power equal to $\frac{1}{1,000}$ the value of the standard bundle. The quantity of money would respond directly to changes in demand through the interest-rate-spread channel, supplemented by the arbitrage called into action if the standard bundle began to lose contact with its one-thousand-dollar price tag.

Any change in supply or demand conditions, as they pertain to greenbacks, would alter the price at which banks redeemed their dol-

4. J. Huston McCulloch, "Beyond the Historical Gold Standard," in *Alternative Monetary Regimes,* ed. Colin D. Campbell and William R. Dougan (Baltimore: Johns Hopkins University Press, 1986), 73–81.

lar liabilities. A nostalgia craze, which produced a run on antiques, including the greenback, for example, would raise the dollar price of the greenback and thus would reduce the number of greenbacks a bank had to pay out in redeeming its note or deposit denominated "one dollar." The dollar price of the standard bundle, however, would not change, because the greenback would not be a base money and thus would not constrain the total quantity of exchange media. The quantity of exchange media could not get out of line with the general level of wages and prices, which, as a result, no longer would be called upon to undergo across-the-board change.

Suppose, however, that antiques in general and greenbacks in particular fell from favor relative to goods and services in general. Each dollar-denominated note or deposit would have to be redeemed in a larger number of greenbacks. Would this downside risk discourage a bank's undertaking dollar-denominated liabilities, when "dollar" means $\frac{1}{1,000}$ the value of the standard bundle? Would the redemption medium's fall in price bring an operating real-GNP-dollar system down?

Downside risk inheres in the very nature of business, not just banking. The miller who purchases wheat in effect wagers that the price of flour will not fall. Should the miller be particularly averse to risk, he could hedge his position by selling wheat short.

Bankers assume a bullish position on anything they hold as an asset. Part of the art of banking is putting together a portfolio that will pan out. If under the real-GNP-dollar system the banker were unduly worried about the fate of the redemption medium, then he could sell quantities of the redemption medium short and thereby hedge his position.

Today, the deposits of even a technically insolvent bank can continue as money, provided the bank can meet its clearinghouse balance and whatever demands for cash present themselves. Standard-bundles-worths convertibility would tend to make the system behave as if it were one bank with depositors so loyal that they stuck with the bank despite its technical insolvency.

This advantage, of course, would pertain to the system, not to the individual bank. If, say, the clearinghouse members were to discover that one particular bank's greenbacks were not authentic, then that single bank would face a problem. Holders of its notes, deposits, and checkable equity holdings doubtless would want to switch to another bank. But if greenbacks *in general* became nearly worthless, the banks together, under the auspices of their clearinghouse, would simply switch to another redemption asset. As a redemption medium, the greenback offers nothing unique. Interest-bearing securities, for example, which the banks would also hold, would do just as well. Since the greenbacks themselves would not have been money in the first place, no scramble for them would develop. It would do a person no good to get greenbacks. The only available alternative to the one bank's notes, deposits, and checkable equity holdings would be another bank's. No base money would exist that people could scramble for. Any suspicions about the banks *in general* would show up not as a scramble for greenbacks but as pure disintermediation, a shift of tastes away from media of exchange and in favor of the primary assets that the banks had been repackaging into those media, and a resulting shrinkage of the quantity of exchange media. Any pressure upon the price level, and, where frustrated, upon quantities produced, would be nipped in the bud.

THE TRANSITION

Once operational, the real-GNP-dollar system would provide monetary and macroeconomic stability. We imagined that to install a variably priced redemption medium, the Federal Reserve converted its dollar deposit and currency liabilities into greenbacks. Greenbacks would have value not as money but as Old Masters. The problem, of course, is the possibility that they would be worth less as collectibles than they were as money and that, as a result, certain persons would be harmed in the transition to the real-GNP-dollar system. Reserves held by banks would pose a similar problem. If the price of a greenback turned out to be less than one dollar, then a bank's net worth would tend to turn negative. To negate these problems, the government would have to make good these losses with interest-bearing debt. The Federal Reserve's holdings of government bonds might be redistributed as compensation for these losses. (A person would suffer no loss on account of holding dollar-denominated bank deposits, however, because the dollar would be defined as having its prevailing purchasing power.) Perhaps another and even easier way of overcoming this transitional problem awaits discovery. If we economists can find it, we can hasten the day when monetary and macroeconomic disequilibrium becomes a thing of the past.

Can Monetary Disequilibrium Be Eliminated?

(with Robert L. Greenfield)

MACRO DISEQUILIBRIUM

"Real" factors, such as the oil shocks of 1973–74 and 1979, can play some role in macroeconomic fluctuations.[1] Yet even such shocks have a monetary aspect. Our task, however, is to focus on monetary disturbances to business activity and on their possible elimination through private-enterprise-oriented reform.

The monetarist diagnosis of price inflation is too compelling to require further mention here, but the diagnosis of business slumps may be worth reviewing.[2] People produce their own particular goods and services to exchange them for the outputs of other specialists, currently or later. These exchanges occur not by barter but through the intermediary of money or of claims ultimately to be settled in money. Money routinely circulates to accomplish these transactions, and people (and firms) hold it in amounts related to their receipts and payments. Desired money balances depend, in large part, on the physical volume of transactions contemplated and on the prices at which

Reprinted from the *Cato Journal* 9 (Fall 1989): 405–19, with permission of the Cato Institute, 1000 Massachusetts Avenue NW, Washington, D.C. 20001.

1. See James D. Hamilton, "A Neoclassical Model of Unemployment and the Business Cycle," *Journal of Political Economy* 96 (June 1988): 593–617; Steven Strongin, "Real Boats Rock: Monetary Policy and Real Business Cycles," Federal Reserve Bank of Chicago, *Economic Perspectives* 12 (November–December 1988): 21–28, and work cited therein.

2. On booms, see Dan E. Birch, Alan A. Rabin, and Leland B. Yeager, "Inflation, Output, and Employment: Some Clarifications," *Economic Inquiry* 20 (April 1982): 209–21 (reprinted in this volume).

goods and services change hands. Actual money balances add up to the money supply, and if it equals the total of desired money balances, the flow of transactions continues without monetary impediment.

If the actual money supply somehow falls short of desired money balances, people act to build up their money holdings by displaying reduced eagerness to buy and increased eagerness to sell on the markets for goods and services and securities.[3] On these markets, by and large, quantities demanded fall short of quantities supplied at the old pattern of prices. Since transactions are voluntary, the short side of each market prevails: Actual transactions fall off. Frustration of exchanges discourages production of goods destined for exchange and discourages purchases of labor and other inputs: The business decline feeds on itself. At some reduced volume of employment and production and transactions, people would no longer effectively desire money balances totaling more than the actual money supply: A monetary quasi-equilibrium—an unpleasantly suppressed disequilibrium—would be reached.

In principle, any actual quantity of money, however small, would suffice for full equilibrium, if prices of goods and services would fall far enough to make an otherwise insufficient nominal quantity suffice to satisfy the demand for real money balances at full employment. It takes time, however, for prices fully to achieve this position. Many prices (and wages) are sticky, with the consequence that markets for many goods and services fail to clear quickly.

By "stickiness," we do not mean rigidity; we do not mean that prices are unresponsive to market imbalances.[4] Different prices (and wages), however, are responsive in different degrees. Because prices are interdependent, yet necessarily are set in a decentralized and piecemeal manner, it takes time for them to achieve a new equilibrium pattern after a pervasive disturbance.

Stickiness in this sense is a fact of reality. It presupposes no irrationality. Reasons for it are readily understandable, including those set

3. Knut Wicksell, *Interest and Prices*, trans. R. F. Kahn (New York: Kelley, 1965), 39–41.

4. Axel Leijonhufvud, *Information and Coordination* (New York: Oxford University Press, 1981), 59–60, 110–12, passim.

forth by Arthur Okun[5] and George Akerlof and Janet Yellen.[6] Stickiness *would* suggest irrational behavior on the part of one benevolent and omniscient auctioneer capable of simultaneously adjusting all prices and wages to their new general-equilibrium values, but it suggests no irrationality on the part of the many decentralized price setters and wage negotiators of the real world. It is a misconception to blame these people for irrationally throwing away gains from trade by leaving prices at non-market-clearing levels (see "The Significance of Monetary Disequilibrium," in this volume). We do not think it is helpful, by the way, to maintain the thesis of cleared markets and continuous equilibrium by redefining the terms involved.

In recent years, "advanced" thinkers have disparaged recognition of price stickiness. Supposedly, the alleged phenomenon is unexplained by any theory.[7] The disparagement seems to rest on two notions: first, that belief in stickiness is distinctively Keynesian —which is a gross misreading of the history of thought[8]—and, second, that Keynesianism is discredited and out of fashion.

Abolition of price stickiness, even if it were possible, contrary to fact, would hardly dispel the problem of monetary disturbances in a system of decentralized decision making. Great volatility of the price level would undercut the rationale of money itself and could even aggravate miscoordination, as through expectations and debt burdens.[9]

---

5. Arthur Okun, *Prices and Quantities* (Washington, D.C.: Brookings Institution, 1981).

6. George Akerlof and Janet L. Yellen, "A Near-Rational Model of the Business Cycle With Wage and Price Inertia," *Quarterly Journal of Economics* 100 (1985 supplement): 823–38.

7. Robert J. Barro, "Second Thoughts on Keynesian Economics," *American Economic Review* 69 (May 1979): 54–59.

8. Ludwig von Mises, *The Theory of Money and Credit*, trans. H. E. Batson (Indianapolis: Liberty Fund, 1981), 133–36.

9. Abba P. Lerner, "The Essential Properties of Interest and Money," *Quarterly Journal of Economics* 66 (May 1952): 172–93; Robert A. Driskill and Steven Sheffrin, "Is Price Flexibility Destabilizing?" *American Economic Review* 76 (September 1986): 802–7; J. Bradford De Long and Lawrence H. Summers, "Is Increased Price Flexibility Stabilizing?" *American Economic Review* 76 (December 1986): 1031–44; and John Caskey and Steve Fazzari, "Aggregate Demand Contractions With Nominal Debt Commitments: Is Wage Flexibility Stabilizing?" *Economic Inquiry* 25 (October 1987): 583–97.

An economy beset by monetary disturbances faces a catch-22: It is damned whether or not it exhibits great flexibility of wages and prices.

Ample evidence justifies emphasis on the question of balance or imbalance between actual and demanded quantities of money. The pervasiveness of brisk or depressed business conditions throughout most sectors of an economy, together with the persistence of such conditions for many months or even years, testifies to some pervasive and not quickly remedied condition. For over two hundred years, monetarist writers have pointed to associations between money-supply and business fluctuations and to apparent leads of the one over the other. Many episodes of money supplies' being changed by causes independent of income and price levels discredit the "reverse causation" argument concerning the alleged low evidential value of the observed associations.

Recent experience is widely said to discredit monetarism. The evident lack of any tight, dependable relation between money supplies and prices and nominal and real incomes—notably, the puzzling decline of money's velocity since about 1981—helps vindicate, once again, the insistence of "Austrian" economists that economic life exhibits no quantitative relations comparable to the constants of the natural sciences. In particular, the old monetarist proposal for steady monetary growth looks like a dubious idea.

But we must distinguish between policy prescriptions, on the one hand, and theory and evidence, on the other. Doubts about the money-growth rule in no way discredit the theory and historical experience that justify insisting on the monetary aspects of business fluctuations.

How might the actual quantity of money come to fall short of demanded holdings? (For brevity, we hasten over the more readily understandable case of an excess supply of money.) Most obviously, an actual shrinkage could leave money in excess demand. A policy blunder might be the cause; or, under an international gold standard, a drop in foreign demand for the home country's exports, bringing loss of base money through a balance-of-payments deficit, could cause the shrinkage. An excess demand for money can result from a mere slowdown in nominal growth as money demanded at the prevailing price level continues growing because of normal growth in population and productivity and in the full-employment volume of transactions. (Clark Warburton places emphasis on this case.)[10] Erratic monetary growth can cause periods of stagflation, when nominal demands for money associated with the catching-up of wages and prices to earlier rapid monetary growth now impinge on reduced nominal growth.

Our existing monetary system is absurd in having a unit of account the size (purchasing power) of which is the supply-and-demand determined value of a fiat medium of exchange. (William Warren Woolsey describes what he calls unit-of-account and medium-of-exchange problems. They involve, respectively, a unit of account that is away from its equilibrium value—a disequilibrium price level—and an excess demand for or supply of the medium of exchange. Under a system of our existing type, of course, the two problems go hand in hand.)[11]

Most of us employ or think in terms of the dollar at least as often each day as we employ units of length and weight. Yet the size of this essential unit is whatever value the scruffy dollar bill happens to possess; its size is defined poorly if at all and is maintained precariously. Its undependability impairs the meeting of minds between borrowers and lenders and other transactors; it impairs economic calculation and coordination.

A related absurdity of our existing system concerns the *manner* in which the supply of and demand for money interact in determining and altering the dollar's value. They do not meet on a single, specific market and determine a single, specific price (like, say, the market for and price of copper). Since monetary disequilibrium cannot be corrected by straightforward adjustment of a single price on a single market, its correction requires adjusting myriad separate but interdependent prices on myriad separate markets, a process that can be drawn out and painful.

Disequilibrium between the supply of and demand for money can persist as long as it sometimes does because, for one thing, nomi-

10. Clark Warburton, *Depression, Inflation, and Monetary Policy* (Baltimore: Johns Hopkins University Press, 1966).

11. Warren William Woolsey, "The Black-Fama-Hall Payments System: An Analysis and Evaluation" (Ph.D. diss., George Mason University, 1987).

nal supply does not adjust "automatically" to meet the nominal demand. (*Real* supply does tend to meet real demand, but only through the roundabout, protracted, and possibly painful price-level process.) The nominal quantity of money in the United States nowadays is determined predominantly on the supply side in the manner the textbooks describe in terms of the quantity of base money and the money-multiplier formula. (Using this formula does not, of course, imply belief that the parameters in it are fixed in some nonsubjective manner.)

MONETARY REFORM

An ideal reform would presumably accommodate nominal supply to nominal demand—not, however, in the determinacy-robbing sense of the real-bills doctrine but rather in the sense of accommodating the nominal quantity of money to the quantity demanded at full employment *and* at the existing, independently determinate, price level. Conceivably, of course, the central bank could practice a policy of always deliberately adjusting the supply of fiat money to the full-employment demand for it at the existing price level, and much scope does remain for instructive discussion of the old proposal for a price-level-stabilization rule. So far, however, we have not had such a policy; and we have reason to consider ways of getting its result in a manner that would be durably independent of governmental blunders.

We ourselves have a proposal, which we call (admittedly somewhat unsatisfactorily) the BFH system to acknowledge some ideas borrowed, modified, and recombined from the writings of Fischer *B*lack, Eugene *F*ama, and Robert *H*all.[12] (Incidentally, we cringe at being associated with some other ideas these writers may have been advocating.)

Government would be banished from any role in the monetary system other than that of defining a unit of account or numéraire. We envisage a unit defined by a bundle of goods and services com-

---

12. Compare Robert L. Greenfield and Leland B. Yeager, "A Laissez-Faire Approach to Monetary Stability," *Journal of Money, Credit, and Banking* 15 (August 1983): 302–15 (reprinted in this volume).

prehensive enough for the general level of prices quoted in it to be practically steady. Merely by conducting its own accounting and transactions in this Unit—we tentatively so name it, with a capital *U*—the government would give private parties a strong incentive to adopt the same Unit.

Freed from any special regulation, financial institutions would meet demands for media of exchange by supplying banknotes and checking deposits denominated in the bundle-defined Unit. They would quite probably also offer equity shares in mutual funds lacking fixed nominal values, funds on which shareholders could draw checks, much as shareholders can draw checks on money market mutual funds nowadays. By holding assets including loans, bonds, stocks, and possibly even real estate and other investments and by issuing note and deposit liabilities and checkable equity claims, these institutions would in effect be repackaging their loans and investments into media of exchange.

No longer would the size of the numéraire, our Unit, be determined by the supply of and demand for any medium of exchange. The Unit would be defined by goods and services having supplies and demands of an almost entirely *non*monetary character.

For customers to take its banknotes and deposits seriously, each issuing institution would have to keep them redeemable. Because redemption in the actual bundles of goods and services defining the Unit would be inconvenient for customers and banks alike, redemption would very probably be promised and accepted in some convenient redemption medium, say gold, in amounts actually worth, at prevailing market prices, as many standard bundles as the Unit denominations of the banknotes and deposits being redeemed. A one-hundred-Unit note, for example, would be redeemed in property actually worth one hundred standard bundles.

The great bulk of such redemptions would probably take place in settlement of net balances due at clearinghouses, where each bank would routinely present notes issued by and checks drawn on other banks acquired from its own depositors. As a medium of settlement among themselves, banks might conceivably use gold (transferring it in amounts valued in Units rather than in prespecified physical amounts); but they would probably find it more advantageous to use interest- and dividend-bearing securities or shares in mutual funds operated by the clearinghouses for just such use in settlements. Clearinghouse members would transfer these settlement media among themselves in amounts worth, at actual market prices, as many standard bundles as the Unit-denominated sizes of the net balances being settled. If Bank A owed Bank B one hundred Units, for example, Bank A would transfer to Bank B interest-bearing securities actually worth one hundred standard bundles.

Under such a system, no bank could keep more of its note and deposit liabilities in circulation and of its checkable equity accounts outstanding than the public was willing to hold. A temporarily over-expanded bank would experience adverse clearing balances and the resulting transfer of both assets and liabilities to banks with which the public was more willing to do business.

The country's financial system as a whole, furthermore, would also experience market pressures tending to keep its monetary liabilities (including checkable equity accounts) no larger and no smaller in Unit volume than the public desired to hold at the price level corresponding to the commodity-bundle definition of the Unit. The demand for media of exchange would govern their actual quantity.

The situation would partially resemble that of a small country under an international gold standard. World-market conditions and its fixed exchange rate would dictate its price level to the gold-standard country; and its gold-based money supply would respond to the demand for money balances. An excess demand for or supply of money tends to be adjusted away by a balance-of-payments surplus or deficit and the associated inflow or outflow of gold.

The situations would not be entirely the same, however, for a gold-standard country could experience money-supply growth or shrinkage caused not only by an increase or decrease in the domestic demand for money but also by some other disturbance to its balance of payments (or some other influence on its monetary gold stock, such as new gold discoveries). The money supply of a country on the BFH system would be determined more nearly completely on the demand side. No base money—nothing comparable to gold or to government fiat money—would exist to serve as the foundation for a total money supply that would contract or expand in the manner described with the aid of a money-multiplier formula. No such supply-side constraint or impetus would control the country's money supply.

In the BFH country, the stock of banknotes, deposits, and checkable equity funds would be the product of business firms engaged in financial intermediation. (Of course, "country" need not be taken literally. We mean a territory or a set of transactors within which the BFH system prevails.) These media of exchange would represent, as we said, the "repackaging" of the earning assets acquired by the intermediary firms. The firms would supply their intermediation services in response to the public's demand for them, neither constrained nor driven by considerations associated with any stock of base money. The firms' inducement, the price paid for their services, would be the excess of the yields they obtained on their earning assets over the interest and dividend rates that competition would require them to pay to the holders of their moneylike liabilities.

Suppose that the public became more liquidity-minded, less willing to hold bonds and stocks and other "primary securities" (to use the terminology of Gurley and Shaw),[13] and more anxious to hold media of exchange. In consequence, yields would tend to rise on primary securities, whereas interest and dividend rates on checkable deposits and equity funds necessary to retain or attract holders would tend to fall. The spread in favor of financial intermediaries, the price of their repackaging services, thus would rise. How small an actual rise would materialize would depend on how price-elastically the intermediaries supplied their services. Anyway, the intermediaries would wind up holding more primary securities than before and having issued a greater volume of media of exchange, all of which would be appropriate to the postulated change in the public's tastes.

Or suppose, similarly, that growth in population and productivity raised full-employment real income and the associated demand for media of exchange. By that very token, the volume of business available to intermediary firms would expand. Again, they would wind up holding more primary securities and having issued more banknotes and checkable deposits and fund shares.

13. [The reference is to John G. Gurley and Edward S. Shaw, *Money in a Theory of Finance* (Washington, D.C.: Brookings Institution, 1960), 72–73—Ed.]

For a different example, suppose that some development reduced the demand for money. Higher interest rates on deposits would become necessary to retain holders; and thus faced with a shrunken net reward for their services, intermediaries would shrink the volume of their media of exchange supplied, which would befit the shrunken demand for them.

These examples illustrate one channel, that involving the banks' spread of earnings on assets over interest paid on monetary liabilities, which is to say the price of intermediation services, whereby the supply of money would adjust to the demand for money balances. Another channel involves the arbitrage that would occur if the general price level, and particularly the total price of the BFH commodity bundle, should begin to deviate from the one corresponding to the definition of the Unit. We should reemphasize that the real size of the Unit, quite unlike that of the dollar under our existing system, would not derive from the demand for and restricted supply of any base money (the nonexistence of a base money underlies the main advantages of the BFH system). Instead, the Unit's size would derive from its commodity-bundle definition, made operational by the banks' competition-imposed commitment to what might be called indirect convertibility, as explained above.

Suppose, now, contrary to all likelihood, that a drop in the demand for money and eagerness to spend it on commodities should raise the price of the standard bundle above its definitional level of U1.00 to as much as U1.20. Under these conditions, holders of Unit-denominated notes and deposits could do much better than simply spend them on goods and services. Exercising their redemption privileges at the issuing institutions, holders would redeem each one-Unit note and deposit in as much gold or whatever else the redemption medium might be as actually equaled in value, at current market prices, the total of the components of the bundle. In the supposed abnormal situation, holders would take away a quantity of the redemption medium quoted at U1.20. They could sell this medium for notes and deposits denominated at U1.20, redeem these in redemption medium salable for U1.44, and so on.

To engage in such arbitrage, people would try to obtain notes and deposits for redemption by exhibiting reduced eagerness to buy goods and services and increased eagerness to sell them, all of which would put appropriate downward pressure on the general price level and on the total price of the standard bundle. The hypothesized deviation from what corresponded to the definition of the Unit would vanish. At the same time, the volumes of money and intermediation services would shrink, as befitted the shrunken demands for them.

No scramble for the redemption medium would pose a problem; the redemption medium would not be analogous to a base money. It is unlikely, anyway, that one single thing, like gold or like one specific security issue, would have been chosen as the sole redemption medium in the first place. More likely, several widely used suitable commodities or, still more likely, several actively traded investment-grade securities would be chosen as alternative redemption media. These media, furthermore, would probably not be demanded solely or even mainly for this purpose; instead, they would be widely used as industrial materials or, more probably, widely held as investments. Most important, these media would have prices of their own that are free to move in equilibrating their own supplies and demands. In the redemption of Unit-denominated notes and deposits, remember, these media would change hands by *value* and not in prespecified physical amounts. They would serve as mere go-betweens in the process of indirect redemption whereby each one-Unit note or deposit would operationally be kept equal in value to the bundle, and kept equal much more conveniently than by redemption directly in its component goods and services.

Suppose, now, an opposite but equally improbable discrepancy: A strengthened demand for media of exchange has deflated the price of the bundle to U0.80, with corresponding deflationary pressures on the general price level. Nobody would want to exercise the redemption privilege. On the contrary, banks would hasten to expand their loans and investments and perhaps to buy real estate and other assets at their currently depressed prices, paying with newly issued notes and deposits and knowing that each one Unit of these is redeemable in redemption media currently purchasable for as little as U0.80. Such behavior would reverse the hypothesized downward deviation of the price level and also satisfy the strengthened demand for money.

These examples merely illustrate the possibilities of corrective arbitrage, which would no doubt be multifarious. Much of the arbitrage would no doubt involve the operations of the banks at their clearinghouses. Stabilizing expectations would play a role. The examples should not call to mind inflationary and deflationary episodes that only subsequently get reversed. They suggest, rather, kinds of market forces that would operate continuously in the first place to nip price-level deviations in the bud and to adjust actual quantities of media of exchange to the demand for them.

Besides pointing out the interest-rate-spread and price-arbitrage channels of "automatic" adjustment of money supply to money demand, we should make one more point. Because deposits and checkable equity accounts would bear interest and dividends at competitive rates (and possibly even banknotes as well, through a lottery feature),[14] these things would serve not only as media of exchange but also as investment assets. Holders could adjust their holdings of what they consider money not merely by adjusting their total holdings of such assets but also by shifting, in their own minds, the dividing line between what they consider money and what they consider investments. The very concept of a quantity of money would become radically fuzzy in a BFH world. This fuzziness would not spell price-level indeterminacy because, to repeat, the purchasing power of the Unit, instead of being determined by interaction between supply of and demand for money, whether defined broadly or defined narrowly as base money, would be determined by the Unit's commodity definition.

Misconceptions

Next we must deal with several misconceptions that have appeared about the BFH system. They are not all compatible with one another. First comes the notion that since the system would abolish money *as we have known it*, especially base money, and since it would

14. J. Huston McCulloch, "Beyond the Historical Gold Standard," in *Alternative Monetary Regimes*, ed. Colin D. Campbell and William R. Dougan (Baltimore: Johns Hopkins University Press, 1986), 73–81.

"separate" the medium of exchange and unit of account—which in a certain sense it would do—it must entail the textbook inconveniences of barter.[15]

Yet "separation" in no way means that people would be making and receiving payments, awkwardly, in miscellaneous commodities and securities with fluctuating values that would have to be translated into numbers of Units on each occasion. Instead, people would be using coins, banknotes, and checking accounts furnished by banks and denominated in Units.

People would also probably be drawing checks on equity accounts offered by some banks as an investment and transactions medium combined, accounts not denominated in Units. (Shares in these accounts, incidentally, would have flexible market-determined prices; and to the extent that these shares constituted part of the total stock of media of exchange, their price flexibility would contribute to "automatic" equilibration of money's supply and demand.) Checks drawn on these equity accounts, however, instead of being denominated in the miscellaneous shares themselves, would be denominated, like other checks, in Units. (Compare checkable money-market mutual funds nowadays.) When such a check cleared, its writer's account would be reduced by however many shares then had the same market value as the denomination of the check.

Banks would be freed from any special regulation. With competition spurring innovation, the payments system would become more efficient than the one we now know.

People would have a stable Unit, moreover, in which to carry out their pricing, contracting, accounting, and cost/benefit calculations. They would no more need to understand the operations that keep the Unit's purchasing power in correspondence with its commodity-bundle definition, including routine redemption of net balances due among banks on account of notes and deposits presented at the clearinghouses, than they need to understand Federal Reserve operations and other influences on the value of the dollar nowadays.

15. Lawrence H. White, "Competitive Payments Systems and the Unit of Account," *American Economic Review* 74 (September 1984): 619–712; Gerald P. O'Driscoll, Jr., "Deregulation and Monetary Reform," Federal Reserve Bank of Dallas, *Economic Review* (July 1986): 19–23; and O'Driscoll, "Money, Deregulation, and the Business Cycle," *Cato Journal* 6 (Fall 1986): 587–605.

"Separation" simply means that the Unit would be defined independently of any particular medium of exchange. Various media would hitch onto the Unit. In the United States nowadays, in contrast, the dollar as unit of account is defined in fiat base money issued by the government (Federal Reserve); most concretely, it is defined by the dollar bill, the real size of which depends, rather haphazardly, on supply and demand.

Before 1933 the dollar was defined by 23.22 grains (1.5046 grams) of pure gold. The linkage established by direct convertibility ordinarily forestalled the question whether the unit of account was the government dollar or the gold it "contained." When a government cut the gold content of its money or went off its metallic standard entirely, then people stuck with the government unit and not with the metal as their unit of account. Many historical examples testify to this amply understandable response.

Under the BFH system, the Unit would not be defined by any dominant medium of exchange or base money because none would exist. No particular one of the several or many competing private banknote issues would define it—not the one-Unit notes of this or that or any other particular bank. The Unit would be defined independently of any money issues by the standard commodity bundle. Each bank, to have its coins and notes and the checks drawn on itself taken seriously, would have to denominate its issues in Units and honor validly drawn Unit checks. It would have to maintain its issues at their full values by restricting their quantity to the quantity the public was willing to hold at the values denominating them and by undertaking indirect redeemability. The great bulk of redemptions would probably take place routinely at the clearinghouses in settlement of net balances due among financial institutions.

If any particular bank should blunder into overissue so badly as to default on fully settling its balances at the clearinghouse, that bank's notes and checks on its deposits would come to be accepted at a discount only, if at all. The overissuing bank could not count on anyone continuing to accept its notes and deposits at their full Unit values, regarding its one-Unit notes as *defining* the unit of account (while the issues of competing banks and the commodity bundle itself came to be quoted at a premium). Not at all. Competition demands pru-

CAN MONETARY DISEQUILIBRIUM BE ELIMINATED?

dence and would make the situation of each issuer of media of exchange sharply different from that of government, a monopoly issuer of base or dominant money.

Note that we refer to monopoly issue of *base* or *dominant money*. Of course we do not deny David Meiselman's contention that already, today, the bulk of the United States money supply, namely, checking-account money, is issued competitively by thousands of private banks.[16] We merely do not find that fact as reassuring as Meiselman seems to find it. Competition determines the quantities of these various bank-issued dollars *relative* to one another. Their subordination to the dominant Federal Reserve dollar, however, means that their *total* quantity gets determined predominantly on the supply side and in the manner described by the money-multiplier analysis of the textbooks.

Nonanalytical sloganeering against "a governmental money monopoly" and in favor of "free banking,"[17] besides conveying the erroneous impression that merely dropping reserve requirements and allowing private banks to issue banknotes would eliminate monetary disequilibrium, invites reactions like Meiselman's. Such a reaction skirts the question of how the *total* money stock gets determined. Our existing system determines the quantity of money on the supply side rather than in response to the demand for money balances. This condition would remain even if private banks were allowed to determine their own reserve ratios and to issue notes, provided a dominant or base money continued to exist on which bank money was pyramided and in which it was redeemable.

Another misconception is that the BFH system amounts to hardly anything different from a privatized composite-commodity standard.[18] That proposed standard is an instructive but nevertheless old idea that reformers have been independently inventing for many decades. It is a particular proposal for the regulation of government

16. David Meiselman, "Is Gold the Answer?" in *The Search for Stable Money,* ed. James A. Dorn and Anna J. Schwartz (Chicago: University of Chicago Press, 1987), 257–60.

17. Don Lavoie, "Introductory Notes," *Market Process* 7 (Spring 1988): 1.

18. Bennett T. McCallum, "Bank Deregulation, Accounting Systems of Exchange, and the Unit of Account: A Critical Review," *Carnegie-Rochester Conference Series on Public Policy* 23 (1985): 13–45.

currency, which would continue to be the base money, in which banks and other financial intermediaries denominated their notes (if any) and their deposits and onto which they pyramided these monetary liabilities.

The BFH system, in radical contrast, would abolish base money, governmental or otherwise. Its commodity bundle, far from constituting a base money or serving in its regulation, would merely define the unit of account, and define it independently of any particular medium of exchange. Absence of any base money and thus of any particular reserve medium would radically change the problem of bank runs and the supposed necessity of a central bank as lender of last resort. Absence of any particular base money and reserve medium that banks and their depositors might scramble for in times of distrust would get rid of this kind of contagion of runs. (No scrambles for assets used as redemption media and clearinghouse settlement media would cause problems, either; for, as explained above, they would change hands in value amounts rather than in physically specified amounts; and their own flexible prices, furthermore, would work to equilibrate their supplies and demand.)

Still another misconception is that prices and the price level would be indeterminate under the BFH system (and even that its advocates consider this supposed indeterminacy an advantage).[19] Such a notion may partly derive from quantity-theory thinking and from recognition that the quantity of BFH money would not be pinned down either by a link to gold (which exists only in definite amounts and is costly to produce) or by deliberate regulation. As Joseph Schumpeter explained around 1930, anticipating the equivalent of Don Patinkin's analysis, some "critical figure," some nominal magnitude determined otherwise than by ordinary market processes, is necessary for the determinacy of a monetary system.[20] The most familiar examples of setting such a critical figure are specification of some price (such as the dollar price of gold, made operational by two-way convertibility) or control of some nominal quantity (such as

19. Ibid., 34–35.

20. Joseph Schumpeter, *Das Wesen des Geldes*, ed. Fritz Karl Mann (Göttingen: Vandenhoeck & Ruprecht, 1970); Don Patinkin, "Financial Intermediaries and the Logical Structure of Monetary Policy," *American Economic Review* 51 (March 1961): 95–116.

the quantity of government fiat money; control of nominal GNP, if feasible, would also do the trick). The BFH system would provide determinacy by defining the unit of account with a commodity bundle, by setting the bundle's total price at one Unit. This definition would be made operational by indirect convertibility of notes, deposits, and checks.

Even so, at least one critic, Kevin D. Hoover, has questioned whether merely *indirect* convertibility would suffice for determinacy.[21] Supposedly, holders of notes and deposits would have to have the right to require their direct redemption in the actual goods and services composing the bundle. In reply, we might insist on the inconvenience for all concerned and on the extreme unlikelihood that anyone would want all those commodities, and want them in the exact proportions in which they entered the bundle. We might point out that the rare money presenter who did so want them could obtain them, if not by simply spending his money on them in the first place, then by selling the redemption medium he initially received and buying the commodities with the proceeds, leaving open the question of whether he or the money issuer should cover his transactions costs. Or we might modify our description of the BFH system by postulating that competition would compel money issuers to offer the option of actual direct redemption in commodities, even though hardly anyone would exercise that option. We do not want, however, to take this cop-out. We want to face the analytical issue: Would merely *indirect* redeemability of notes and deposits denominated in the BFH Unit suffice to give them definite purchasing powers? Notes and deposits thus kept equal in value to an amount of redemption property in turn worth one thousand (say) bundles would themselves be worth that many bundles; if A and C are each equal to B, then A and C are equal to each other—is that not true?

We may develop our argument by considering Irving Fisher's compensated dollar.[22] That dollar would always be redeemable in a definite amount of gold. The amount, however, would be subject to adjustment every two months or so in view of a price index. Adjust-

21. Kevin D. Hoover, "Money, Prices, and Finance in the New Monetary Economics," *Oxford Economic Papers* 40 (March 1988): 150–67.

22. Irving Fisher, *Stabilizing the Dollar* (New York: Macmillan, 1920).

ability surely would not keep the dollar from having a determinate value corresponding to its gold content at each time. Now consider a privatized and decentralized and otherwise modified version of the compensated dollar: The amount of gold in which the dollar is redeemable would be adjustable not just every two months but, say, every hour of each business day; and the adjustment would take account not only of the market prices of the goods and services entering into the calculation of the price index but also of the price of gold itself. Although the dollar would have a changeable gold content, the content would be definite at each instant; and the dollar's purchasing power should be correspondingly determinate.

So far as determinacy is concerned, there seems to be no essential difference between the compensated dollar as described by Fisher himself and the modification described here, which is the BFH system. Neither in Fisher's system nor in the BFH system would it matter whether the redemption medium is gold itself or some other convenient asset.

Fisher's idea applied to government base money is still worth considering as a live option because of transitional difficulties involved in moving to a completely privatized and decentralized system. (In particular, getting rid of government base money would either require its repudiation, perhaps through inflation, expropriating its holders, or else require its replacement by interest-bearing, burdensome government debt.) Two modifications to Fisher's own proposal for compensated government base money seem worth recommending: Adjustments in the dollar's gold content should be made in view not only of incipient changes in the target price index but also of changes in the price of gold itself; and adjustments should be made not just every month or two but almost continuously, perhaps several or many times each day. High-tech communications and data-processing capabilities not available in Fisher's day would make continuous compensation technically feasible. The International Market Index of fifty foreign stocks traded in the United States, for example, is recalculated every *fifteen seconds* during the United States trading day.[23] The same point about technology also would apply, of course, to the BFH system.

23. *Wall Street Journal*, 16 December 1988, C11.

The continuously compensated dollar, resting on a commodity- or index-defined unit of account and two-way interconvertibility between unit-of-account worths of a convenient redemption medium, would bypass the difficulties commonly cited as objections to a price-level-stabilization rule for monetary management. Or so it seems to us. Admittedly, however, this solution seems suspiciously simple, and we await instruction on just what may be wrong with it

CONCLUSION

The full-fledged BFH system, complete with privatization and decentralization, would offer advantages beyond those we have space to explain here. It would bypass, for example, two actual or supposed disadvantages of a monetary system of the ordinary type—the anti-capital-formation effect of money, which concerns Maurice Allais and James Tobin, and the waste of real resources in tight cash-balance management, which concerns Milton Friedman. Apart from the puzzle of how to get rid of government base money gracefully, we can answer "yes" to the question that our title poses: Through institution of a privatized system under which the supply of money responds to the demand for it, and at a stable price level, monetary disequilibrium can indeed be eliminated.

INDEX

Abs, Hermann, 69n

Accounting systems, assumption of stable money and, 35

Akerlof, G. A., 128–29, 145–46, 219, 409

Alchian, Armen A., 35n, 166n, 180n, 212, 240

Allais, Maurice, 263, 264–67

Allen, William R., 180n

Andersen, Leonall C., 23, 324n

Anderson, Benjamin M., Jr., 269–70

Areskoug, Kaj, 363n

Argentina, 51, 72, 74, 78–79, 82

Aristotle, 247

Arrow, Kenneth, 236–37, 248

Art objects, investment in, 38

Aschheim, Joseph, 114n, 115n, 344n

Asset preferences, asymmetrical, 94–97

Attwood, Thomas, 286, 296

Austria, 36, 75, 81, 221

Austrian theory of the business cycle, 229–35, 249–50, 253–56, 264, 285, 410

Autonomous expenditures, 22–23

Axilrod, Stephen H., 180n

Bach, George L., 17n

Bagehot, Walter, 342n

Balance of payments: currency depreciation due to, 47; disequilibriums, 317; monetary theory of, 149–51

Ball, Laurence, 283–84

Bank of the United States. *See* Second Bank of the United States

Bank reserves. *See* Reserves

Bank runs as pricing problem, 395–98

Barber, William J., 286n

Barkai, Haim, 25n, 221, 222n

Barro, Robert J., 166, 167n, 168, 169n, 170, 173, 177n, 206n, 220, 236, 248, 249n, 409n

Bartley, William W., 300

Basevi, Giorgio, 343n

Basket currencies, 343–46

Batchelder, Ronald W., 295–96

Baumol, William J., 180n, 351n

Bentham, Jeremy, 296

Bernanke, Ben, 290

BFH system, 251, 267, 279, 358–60, 363–81, 385–91, 412–25; advantages of, 372–73, 388; analogy of yard and proposed value unit and, 369–70; avoidance of macroeconomics difficulties by, 373–76; barter aspects of, 370; compared with other systems, 365–67; concept of, 364, 385–86, 412–13; defined unit of account in, 367–68; difficulty with, 388–89; financial intermediaries and, 370–71, 386, 413–14; hand-to-hand currency in, 371–72; interest-rate-spread channel of "automatic" adjustment of money supply to money demand in, 415–16;

427

BFH system (*continued*)
  intermediation aspects of,
  260–63, 415; lack of dependence
  on any particular base money of,
  368, 414–15; misconceptions
  about, 359–60, 364–65, 418–25;
  operationality and determinacy
  in, 379–81; price-arbitrage
  channel of "automatic"
  adjustment of money supply to
  money demand in, 416–17;
  quantity of money in, 367,
  387–88; responses of quantities
  of media of exchange, 376–78;
  settlements in, 371, 386–87,
  413–14; vs. widespread indexing,
  369
Birch, Dan E., 238*n*, 407*n*
Black, Fischer, 260, 363, 385, 412
"Black box" criticism of
  monetarism, 25
Blinder, Alan S., 180*n*, 219, 283,
  302
Bodkin, Ronald G., 165–66
Bolivia, 72, 75–76, 81, 82
Bollman, Erick, 286
Bond-financed deficits, fallacies of
  composition and, 141–44
Boorman, John T., 143*n*
Borsodi, Ralph, 343*n*, 346
Boschen, John, 240
Bradley, Michael D., 273
Brainard, William C., 96*n*
Brazil, 59, 77, 82
Brechling, F., 170*n*, 201*n*, 220*n*
Breit, William, 363*n*
Bresciani-Turroni, Costantino, 37*n*,
  47*n*
Bretton Woods system, 317, 331,
  375
Brown, Harry Gunnison, 53,
  211–15, 224–25, 286, 291–95,
  297–98
Brunner, Karl, 30*n*, 49*n*, 69*n*, 98*n*,
  113*n*, 118*n*, 180*n*, 286, 299, 300,
  331*n*, 393

Bryant, John, 142*n*
Bryant, Ralph, 384*n*
Buchanan, James M., 144*n*, 363*n*,
  386
Buiter, Willem, 237, 238*n*
Bullion Report of 1810, 179
Burma, 72
Burns, Arthur F., 40, 331
Burstein, M. L., 95–96*n*
Business-cycle theory, 4. *See also*
  Austrian theory of the business
  cycle; Depression
Business habits, assumption of
  stable money and, 35

Cacy, J. A., 113*n*
Cagan, Phillip, 28, 50*n*, 65*n*, 166*n*,
  228*n*, 284
Campbell, Colin D., 402*n*, 418*n*
Cannan, Edwin, 6*n*, 137*n*
Cantillon, Richard, 231*n*, 253, 286
Cantillon effects, 231, 253. *See also*
  Injection effects
Carlson, Keith M., 324*n*
Carlton, Dennis W., 246
Carson, Deane, 90*n*, 113*n*, 148*n*, 180*n*
Carter, Jimmy, 71
Cash balance holders, reaction to
  inflation by, 34–35
Cash-balance interpretation of
  depression, 3–17; advantages of,
  3–4; empirical evidence of (*see*
  Monetarism); equilibrium in
  stock vs. flow sense and, 6;
  Keynesian theory and, 7–9; near
  money and, 12–15; Pigou effect
  and, 9–12; policy and, 15–17;
  price-and-wage inflation and
  deflation and, 10–11; Say's law
  and money, 4–6; stickiness of
  value of money and, 7, 9–11, 17
Caskey, John, 288, 409*n*
Cassel, Gustav, 270, 293, 294, 295
Catt, A. J. L., 101, 102*n*
Central bankers, Eurodollar market
  and, 319–20

Chandler, Lester, 180n
Chase, Samuel B., Jr., 30n, 91–92n, 118n, 180n
Chicago economists, 206, 295, 313. *See also* Monetarism
Chile, 51, 73, 82
China, 222
Chipman, John S., 156n
Christiernin, Pehr N., 221, 239, 286
Cipolla, Carlo M., 345n, 346
Circularity problem, interaction between individual and overall viewpoints and, 151
Claassen, Emil, 41n, 44n
Clapham, Sir John, 305–6
Clower, R. W., 95n, 170, 201–7, 209, 210, 212, 215, 220, 248, 374n
Coats, Warren L., 180n
Coghlan, Richard T., 118n, 386
Colander, David C., 54n, 60n, 74n, 79n, 80n, 217n
Collectibles, investment in, 38
Colombia, 82
Commercial banks: cost-and-revenue analysis, difficulties for, 119–22; deregulation and, 383; exogeneity of money supply and, 131–32; foreign influences on the money supply and, 133–34; interest on demand deposits example, 130; issue of, 111–12; macroeconomic properties of demand deposits and currency, 126–29; how money supply creates its own demand, 116, 121–23; "natural economic limit" postulation of New View and, 91, 117–18, 148, 366–67, 378; New View of, 90–94, 112–14, 149; reserve requirements argument, 123–26; uniqueness of, 111–35; unsatisfactory criticisms of New View, 114–15
Compensated dollar system, 251, 389, 423–24; modified, 389–91.

See also BFH system; Real-GNP dollar
Composite-commodity standard, 135, 367
Composition, fallacies of, 140–45; reverse, 145–47
"Constant" unit of account, 146–47, 341–51, 369
Consumption, money supply and, 21–23
Contractionary monetary policy, 308
Cooper, Richard, 45
Cost-and-revenue analysis of size of money and banking system, 119–22
Costanzo, G. A., 39, 43
Cost-of-living increases, 51, 51–52, 61, 63
Cost-price interactions, inflation and, 60–65
Cost-push inflation, 43, 44
Council of Economic Advisors, 325
Cover, James P., 363n
Credit: Austrian theory of the business cycle and, 229–34; bank creation of, money issue and (*see* Commercial banks, uniqueness of); confusion with money (*see* Supply-and-demand doctrine of money-stock determination, criticism of); monetarism and (*see* Monetarism); reaction to inflation by holders of, 35
Creeping inflation, 49
Crockett, Andrew D., 111n, 112–13, 118, 124
Culbertson, John M., 29n, 92n, 93n
Cumulative deterioration in a depression, theory of, 209
Cumulative process, 94, 120
Currency: in BFH system, 371–72; depreciation of, unfavorable balance of payments and, 47; macroeconomic properties of, 126–29; private money, 154–55;

Currency (*continued*)
  substitution, 156–57, 357. *See also*
  Medium of exchange; Money;
  Unit of account

Davenport, Herbert J., 152*n*, 215*n*,
  223–24, 286, 290–91
Davidson, David, 269–73, 277
Davis, J. Ronnie, 199*n*, 295*n*
Dean, James W., 235, 250
Debt monetization, 33
Decontrol, inflation and, 72–73
Deflation: monetary, 10; price-and-
  wage, 10–11; unanticipated price
  inflation (UPI) theory and, 167,
  169
DeGaulle, Charles, 318
De Long, J. B., 288, 409*n*
Demand: for current output,
  deficient, 102, 103; effective,
  Keynes and, 199–200; for goods
  and services, deficient, 108; for
  money (*see* Money demand)
Demand deposits, bank, 111–13; vs.
  deposits in nonbank institutions,
  115–17; interest on, 130;
  macroeconomic properties of,
  126–29; New View of money and
  banking and, 91, 112–13,
  117–18, 148; supply-and-demand
  doctrine of money-stock
  determination and, 185, 186
Depression: Austrian theory of the
  business cycle and, 229–35,
  254–56; Brown (Harry
  Gunnison) on, 211–15;
  cumulative deterioration in,
  theory of, 209–10; Davenport (H.
  J.) on, 223–24; as excess demand
  for money (*see* Cash-balance
  interpretation of depression);
  integration of monetary theory
  with disequilibrium economics
  and, 202–7; interplay between
  individual and collective
  viewpoints and, 158–60

Deregulation, 383–91
Diversification demand for actual
  money, 94–95
Doctrinal names, games with,
  281–302; Keynesianism, 281–83,
  285, 287–88; methodological
  preconceptions, 298–301; New
  Classical macroeconomics,
  296–97; New Keynesianism,
  283–86, 296, 298; Old
  Monetarism, 285–96; real-
  business-cycle theories, 296–97
Dollar. *See* Unit of account
Dorfman, Joseph, 200
Dorn, James A., 217*n*, 286*n*, 421*n*
Dorrance, Graeme S., 81
Dougan, William R., 402*n*, 418
Downs, Anthony, 162
Driskill, Robert A., 288, 409*n*

Earley, James S., 113*n*
Ebeling, Richard J., 230*n*
*Economic Mind in American
  Civilization* (Dorfman), 200
*Economic Science and the Common
  Good* (Brown), 291
Eder, George Jackson, 81
Edge, Stephanie K., 22*n*
Edwards, Daniel, 87*n*, 217*n*
Effective demand, Keynes and,
  199–200
Equilibrium-always theory, 235–50,
  297. *See also* New Classical school
Equilibrium in stock vs. flow sense, 6
Eucken, Walter, 365
Eurodollar market, 319–20
"Europas," 343–45
"Eurostables," 343–45
Excess demand: for actual money,
  88, 102–8, 126–29, 338–39;
  depression or recession and (*see*
  Cash-balance interpretation of
  depression); Keynesian theory
  and, 200–201; for nonmoney,
  128, 229; Say's law and, 4–5

Exogeneity of money supply, 131–32. *See also* Supply-and-demand doctrine of money-stock determination

Expectations, inflation and, 56, 64–68, 70, 71. *See also* Rational-expectations theory

Expenditures, autonomous, 22–23

Fama, Eugene, 260, 363, 385, 412

Fazzari, Steve, 288, 409n

Federal Bank of Minneapolis, 77–78

Federal Open Market Committee, 325

Federal Reserve, 26, 28–30, 45, 69, 292, 293, 308–12, 315–16, 319, 326, 329. *See also* Monetary policy; Supply-and-demand doctrine of money-stock determination, criticism of

Federal Reserve Bank of St. Louis, 324

Fellner, William, 54n, 67, 74n

Fetter, Frank Whitson, 41n

Fiat money, 277, 337–40, 365, 366, 385, 411

Financing Full Employment (Wernette), 199

Finland, 81

Fiscal policy, 20, 309, 312

Fischer, Stanley, 173n, 248

Fisher, Irving, 251, 286, 288, 358n, 359n, 389, 393, 399, 423–24

Foreign-exchange holdings, 38

Foreign-exchange losses, inflation from, 43–44

Foreign exchange rates: Bretton Woods system of, 317, 331, 375; flexible, 320, 321; floating of, 72, 156, 321, 331, 333, 398–99; monetary crises of 1967–71 and, 317–18, 331–32; removal of controls on, 72–73; stabilization of, 75–76

Foreign influences on the money supply, 133–34

France, 69, 71, 83, 295

Fratianni, Michele, 343n

Free reserves, 308–9

Frictional unemployment, 15

Friedman, Benjamin, 384n

Friedman, Irving S., 81–82

Friedman, Milton, xiv, 19–21, 25, 29n, 37n, 79n, 96n, 121, 127, 138n, 164n, 220, 221, 244, 263, 281, 285, 296–97, 321n, 324, 340, 342n, 388, 393, 395, 398, 400

Frisch, Helmut, 45n

Fry, Maxwell J., 259, 265

Fukuoka, Masao, 16n

Fullarton, John, 147

Functional distinction between money and nonmoney, 97–102

Fundamental proposition of monetary theory, 121–22, 127, 138n, 200

Gaines, Tilford C., 113n

Garcia, Gillian, 384

García, Valeriano, 42n

Garrison, Roger W., 152n, 217n

General Theory of Employment, Interest and Money, The (Keynes), 8–9, 102, 103n, 121n, 200–201, 207–9, 220, 282–83, 287

Germany: imported inflation in, 71–72; inflation of the 1920s in, 37, 38, 46, 47, 69, 83, 154, 345; monetary crisis of 1969 in, 318; post–World War II repressed inflation in, 69

Giersch, Herbert, 61n, 343n

Giffen, Robert, 342

Glasner, David, 272, 295–96

Glazier, Mrs. Evelyn Marr, 210n

Gold, price of, 334

Gold monetary unit, 351–53, 356

Gold standard, 135, 264, 265, 277, 288, 294, 295, 340, 353, 365, 368, 397

Goldthorpe, John H., 36n, 45n

Goodfriend, Marvin, 184n

Goods, deficient demand for, 108
Gordon, Robert J., 164*n*, 165*n*, 283
Government, analysis of, 161–62
Government deficit spending, 33, 41–43, 45–46, 310–12
Government failures in monetary policy, 305–7
Government money remedies, 340–42
Gradualism vs. quick fix approach to stabilization, 76–84
Gramley, Lyle E., 29–30*n*, 91–92*n*, 118*n*, 180*n*
Gratz, Alois, 25*n*, 221*n*
Great Britain, 47, 286–88
Great Depression, 307, 308
Greenfield, Nancy, 179*n*
Greenfield, Robert L., 179–95, 251, 260, 358, 363–81, 393–405, 407–25
Griffiths, Brian, 342
Grossman, Herschel I., 166, 167*n*, 168, 170, 177*n*, 202, 206*n*, 220, 235*n*, 240, 242, 243
Gross national product, 24
Grubel, Herbert G., 356*n*
Gurley, John G., xvi, 90, 93*n*, 94, 258*n*, 268, 415
Guttentag, Jack M., 114*n*

Haberler, Gottfried, 4*n*, 49–51, 69, 156*n*, 157*n*, 237*n*, 240, 287–88, 296*n*, 297, 331*n*
Hahn, F. H., 25*n*, 170*n*, 201*n*, 220*n*, 237, 248, 250
Hall, Robert E., 260, 359*n*, 363, 369, 384, 385, 412
Hamberg, D., 4*n*, 12*n*
Hamilton, James D., 407*n*
Harcourt, G. C., 37*n*
Harrod, Roy, 95–96*n*
Hart, Albert Gaylord, 7*n*
Havenstein, Rudolf, 47
Havrilesky, Thomas M., 143*n*
Hawtrey, Ralph, 288–90, 295–96

Hayek, F. A., xvii, 144*n*, 146*n*, 154, 229–30, 257, 264, 287, 354–55, 361, 364*n*
Helfferich, Karl, 47
Herendeen, James B., 183, 184*n*, 189
Hicks, John R., 13, 35*n*, 36, 154*n*, 356*n*
Higgs, Henry, 253*n*
Hirsch, Fred, 36*n*, 45*n*
Historian as Detective, The: Essays on Evidence (Wink), 302
Hoehn, James G., 273–74
Hoover, Kevin D., 423
Horwich, George, 113*n*, 258*n*
Hoskins, W. Lee, 257*n*
Howitt, Peter, 171*n*
Hume, David, xiv, 178*n*, 220, 286, 287, 296
Humphreys, Thomas M., 234, 296
Hutt, W. H., 87*n*, 109*n*, 137*n*, 170*n*, 203, 204*n*, 209, 220, 286

Imported inflation, 40, 42–45, 71–72, 134, 255
Income, oversaving and cyclical fall in, 7–9
Income-constrained process, 202–7, 209
Incomes policy, 314–15, 327–28
Income taxes, 41
Income velocity of money, 42
Indexing, 157–58, 342–51, 369, 389–91
Individual-experiments and market-experiments, 139–40
Inflation, 33–84; analogy between levels and trends of prices, 52–58, 66; Bretton Woods system and, 317; classifications of, 48–52; conditions favorable and unfavorable for stopping, 69–72; costs of, 34–40; as excess supply of money (*see* Cash-balance interpretation of depression; Monetarism); from foreign-

exchange losses, 43–44; foreign exchange rate stabilization and, 75–76; government deficit spending and, 33, 41–43, 45–46, 310–12; gradualism vs. quick fix and, 76–84; imported, 42–43, 45, 71–72, 134, 255; inflationary momentum and the side effects of trying to stop, 58–69; interplay between individual and collective viewpoints and, 158–60; monetary, 10–11; New Economic Policy (NEP) of 1971 and, 327–28; Nixon administration and, 312–16, 326; price-and-wage, 10–11; price and wage controls and, 73–75, 80–81, 327–31; price and wage decontrol and, 72–73; rational expectations/equilibrium always theory, 238; sources of, 40–48; unanticipated, unemployment and, 164–69; unconstrained cumulative process and, 120
Inflation illusion, 346
Injection effects, 253–80; business cycle and, 253–56; further questions about stable-valued money, 269–79; intermediation and, 258–60; intermediation under laissez-faire and, 260–63; of price-level stabilization, 256–58; supplying additional real money through price-level deflation, 264–68. *See also* Cantillon effects
Interest rates: Austrian theory of the business cycle and, 229, 230, 233, 254; cash-balance interpretation of depression and, 13–14; deposit, ceilings on, 125–26; Federal Reserve targeting of (*see* Supply-and-demand doctrine of money-stock determination, criticism of); functional distinctions between

money and nonmoney and, 101–2; inflation and, 36; international monetary policy and, 318–19
Intermediation: injection effects and, 258–60; under laissez-faire, 260–63
International monetary policy, 317–22, 331–35
Investment: cash-balance interpretation of depression and, 8–9; injection effects and, 230, 231, 254, 255
Italy, 71

Jakovlev, A. F., 25n, 221, 222n
Jansen, Dennis W., 273
Japan, 24
Jevons, W. Stanley, 342n
Johnson, Harry, 25n, 40–41, 122n, 200
Johnson, Joseph French, 286
Jordan, Jerry L., 23, 325n
Judd, John P., 193–95

Kafka, Alexandre, 59, 70n, 77, 80
Kahn, R. F., 408n
Kalecki, Michael, 36n
Kamitz, Reinhard, 25n, 221n
Kareken, John H., 30n, 155n, 156n, 348n
Katz, Samuel I., 111n
Kaufman, Herbert, 180, 181, 185–86, 192
Keller, Robert R., 74n
Kennedy, John F., 50
Keran, Michael, 28n
Kessel, R. A., 166n
Kessel, Reuben, 35n
Keynes, John Maynard, xiii$n$, 8–9, 21, 102–3, 121, 127, 138n, 199–200, 248, 299, 409
Keynesian theory, xiii–xiv, 199–216; cash-balance interpretation of depression and, 7–9; Clower's and Leijonhufvud's

Keynesian theory (*continued*)
interpretation of, 201–7, 209,
210, 215, 248; cumulative
deterioration in depression
theory and, 209–10; doctrinal
position shifting and, 281–83,
285, 287–88; evidence
supporting monetarism and, 22,
200–201; fundamental
proposition of monetary theory
and, 121–22, 127, 138n, 200;
*General Theory of Employment,
Interest and Money, The* (Keynes),
8–9, 102, 103n, 121n, 200–201,
207–9, 220, 282–83, 287. *See also*
New Keynesianism
Khromov, P. A., 25n, 221, 222n
Kindleberger, Charles P., 156n
King, Willford I., 358n
Kirzner, Israel M., 137n
Klamer, Arjo, 246n
Klein, Benjamin, 354n
Korean War, 50
Korliras, P. G., 259n
Korteweg, Pieter, 343n
Küng, Emil, 9n

Lagged-reserve accounting, 185
Laidler, David, 179n
Laissez-faire approach to monetary
stability (*see* BFH system)
Lange, Oscar, 5
Latin America, 41, 43
Laufenberg, Daniel, 180n, 185,
189n
Lavoie, Don, 421n
Leading business indicators, index
of, 24
Leamer, Edward, 302
Leijonhufvud, Axel, 37n, 65n, 170,
201–2, 206, 207, 209, 210, 212,
215, 220, 248, 281–82, 302, 408n
Lerner, Abba P., 10, 17n, 74n, 79n,
80n, 103n, 104n, 201, 327n, 409n
Leroy, Steven, 180n
Lester, Richard A., 221n

Leutwiler, F., 44
Lindsay, Robert, 114n
Lindsey, David E., 180n, 185, 189n
Liquidity, 87–90
Liquidity-preference theory, 13, 140
Loeb, Harold, 103n
Lombra, Raymond E., 180, 181,
183–86, 189, 192
London *Economist*, 332
Lothian, James, 179n
Lowe, Joseph, 342n
Lucas, Robert E., Jr., 165n, 235–36,
238n, 242n, 243n, 246, 249n

Machlup, Fritz, 44, 320
Macroeconomic disequilibrium,
394, 407–12
Maier, Charles S., 36n
Malthus, Thomas R., 296
Mankiw, Gregory N., 283, 285
Mann, Fritz Karl, 124n, 422n
Marget, Arthur, 287
Market-experiments and individual-
experiments, 139–40
Marshall, Alfred, 282, 286, 342n,
343n
Masera, Rainer S., 119n, 122n,
133n, 149n
Mayer, Hans, 25n
McCallum, Bennett T., 168n, 273,
421n
McClosky, Donald, 241
McConnell, Cambell, 180n
McCulloch, J. Huston, 402n, 418n
McCulloch, John R., 296
McKeon, Richard, 247n
Medium of exchange, separation
from unit of account: in BFH
system (*see* BFH system);
indexing, 342–51, 389–91;
separate but actual units, 351–52.
See also Currency; Money; Unit of
account
Meier, G. M., 122n, 143n
Meigs, A. James, 326n
Meiselman, David, 21n, 22, 25, 421

Meltzer, Alan H., 28n, 49n, 69n, 98n, 286, 393
Methodological individualism, 87
Miles, Marc A., 357n
Mill, John Stuart, 147, 286, 296
Miller, Adolph C., 292
Miller, Preston J., 141n
Mints, Lloyd W., 144n, 147n, 152, 257n
Mises, Ludwig von, 137, 152, 153, 162, 229–30, 409n
Modified compensated dollar system, 389–91. *See also* Real-GNP dollar
Modigliani, Franco, 167n
Momentum, inflationary, 58–69
Monetarism, 19–31; Austrian theory of the business cycle compared with, 229–35, 249–50; concept of, 19; diagnosis of business slumps, 407–10; evidence supporting, 19–24; fundamental theory, 217–22; looseness of links between Federal Reserve actions and money-supply behavior, 30–31; New Economic Policy (NEP) of 1971 and, 323–31; Old, 285–96; opposition to, 25–29; origins of, 285–86; rational expectations/equilibrium always theory compared with, 235–50
Monetary deflation, 10
Monetary disequilibrium, 217–22, 394, 407–12; early recognition of, 222–24, 285–86; Keynesian economics and, 103–5, 215, 248; persistence of, 158, 171–72; Say's law and, 5–7. *See also* BFH system; Equilibrium-always theory; Price stickiness; Stable unit of account
Monetary indicators, 308–9
Monetary policy: analogy between levels and trends of prices and, 57; cash-balance interpretation of depression and, 15–17;

conditions favorable and unfavorable for stopping inflation, 69–72; deregulation, 383–91; foreign exchange rate stabilization, 75–76; government failures in, 305–7; inflationary momentum and, 58–69; injection effects and (*see* Injection effects) international, 317–22, 331–35; monetarism and, 26–31; monetary instability, 307–10; money vs. near money and, 110; New Economic Policy (NEP) of 1971, 322–31; noninflationary, political and sociological impediments to, 45–46; price and wage controls (*see* Price controls; Wage controls); price and wage decontrol, 72–73; price indexing (*see* Price indexing); radically different alternatives, 251; real-bills doctrine, 47–48, 144–45, 308; real-GNP dollar and (*see* Real-GNP dollar); supply-and-demand doctrine of money-stock determination (*see* Supply-and-demand doctrine of money-stock determination, criticism of); unsteadiness from 1965 to 1971, 310–16; view after the freeze, 322–35; view before the freeze, 305–22. *See also* Stable unit of account
Monetary reform: modified compensated dollar system, 389–91, 389–91. *See also* BFH system; Real-GNP dollar; Stable unit of account
Monetary systems: BFH (*see* BFH system); fiat money, 277, 337–40, 365, 366, 385, 411; gold standard, 135, 264, 265, 277, 288, 294, 295, 340, 353, 365, 368, 397. *See also* Unit of account
Monetary systems, alternative, 146–47

Monetary theory: of balance of
payments, 149–51; fundamental
proposition of, 121–22, 127,
138n, 200; integration of
disequilibrium economics with,
202–15; viewpoints in (*see*
Viewpoints in monetary theory)
Money: distinctiveness of, supply-
and-demand doctrine of money-
stock determination and,
190–92; services to society as
whole vs. services to individual
holder, 153–55. *See also* Currency;
Medium of exchange; Money
demand; Money/near money
distinctions; Money supply; Unit
of account
Money demand: "automatic"
adjustment of money supply to,
in BFH system, 415–17; confused
with credit demand (*see* Supply-
and-demand doctrine of money-
stock determination, criticism
of); created by money supply,
116, 121–23; excess, depression
as (*see* Cash-balance
interpretation of depression);
excess, for actual money, 88,
102–8, 126–29, 410; Say's law
and, 5
Money illusion, 79, 346
Money managers,
overambitiousness of, 309–10
Money-market view of monetary
equilibrium, 190–95
Money-multiplier formulas, 113–14,
289–90
Money/near money distinctions,
87–110; adjustments of
imbalances between supply and
demand, 122–23; asymmetrical
asset preferences, 94–97;
example of claims on nonbank
intermediaries, 90–94; excess
demand for actual money, 88,
102–8; fallacies of composition

and, 140–41; functional
contrasts, 97–102; liquidity and
money, 87–90; macroeconomic
properties of demand deposits
and currency, 126–29;
transactions costs, 109–10
Money supply: Austrian theory of
the business cycle and, 229–35,
254–55; "automatic" adjustment
to money demand in BFH
system, 415–17; creation of own
demand by, 116, 121–23;
deficient, collaboration in coping
with, 145–46, 219; excess,
inflation as (*see* Cash-balance
interpretation of depression;
Monetarism); exogeneity of,
131–32; foreign influences on,
133–34; increase in rate of
growth when unemployment is
above the natural rate, 167–68;
increase in rate of growth when
unemployment is at the natural
rate, 173–78; injection effects
and (*see* Injection effects);
monetarism and (*see*
Monetarism); real-GNP dollar
and (*see* Real-GNP dollar);
unanticipated price inflation
(UPI) theory and, 163–69;
unsteady growth of, 307–10
Moore, Basil J., 118, 120n, 123n,
148
Morgan, E. Victor, 126n, 127n, 131,
132
Moss, Laurence S., 152n
Mundell, Robert, 35n, 326, 327n
Musgrave, Alan, 244

National Recovery Administration,
10–11
"Natural economic limit"
postulation of New View, 91,
117–18, 148, 366–67, 378
Near money/money distinctions,
87–110; adjustments of

imbalances between supply and demand, 122–23; asymmetrical asset preferences, 94–97; cash-balance interpretation of depression and, 12–15; example of claims on nonbank intermediaries, 90–94; excess demand for actual money, 88, 102–8; fallacies of composition and, 140–41; functional contrasts, 97–102; liquidity and money, 87–90; macroeconomic properties of demand deposits and currency, 126–29; transactions costs, 109–10

"Neutral" payments, 98–100

New Classical school, xiii–xiv, 237, 296–97

New Economic Policy (NEP) of 1971, 322–31

New Keynesianism, 283–86, 296, 298. *See also* Keynesian theory

New Keynesianism Economics (Mankiw and Romer, eds.), 283–84

Newlyn, W. T., 89–90, 98–99

New View of money and banking: cost-and-revenue analysis, difficulties for, 119–22; "natural economic limit" postulation of, 91, 117–18, 148, 366–67, 378; reserve requirements argument for bank distinctiveness, 123–26; vs. uniqueness of commercial banks' view, 90–94, 112–14, 149; unsatisfactory criticisms of, 114–15

Nixon, Richard, 74, 312, 316, 323–24, 329

Nixon administration, 312–15, 326

Nominal-GNP targeting, 273

Nominal vs. real money supply, 46–47

Nonbank intermediaries: claims on, vs. properties of medium of exchange, 90–94, 96–97; cost-and-revenue analysis and claims on, 122; "natural economic limit" postulation of New View and, 118; New View of money and banking and, 112–14; reserve drains of, vs. bank reserve drains, 115–17

O'Driscoll, Gerald P., Jr., 419

Oil price increases, 40, 42, 44

Okun, Arthur, 34, 36n, 51, 63n, 227n, 241n, 387, 409

Old Monetarism, 285–96

Oliver, Antonio Gómez, 42n

Olson, Mancur, Jr., 172n

O'Mahoney, David, 343n

"Optimum Quantity of Money, The" (Friedman), 263, 388

Organization of Petroleum Exporting Countries (OPEC), 44

Output: current, deficient demand for, 102, 103; response to monetary change, 169–78; unanticipated price inflation (UPI) theory and, 163–69

Overproduction, Say's law and, 4–6

Pablo, Juan Carlos de, 78–79

Paraguay, 72

Park, Y. S., 344n

Parkin, Michael, 343n

Parsons, Robert J., 113n

"Passive actions" fallacy, 48

Patinkin, Don, 6n, 11n, 88n, 120n, 139, 152–53, 166, 167n, 170, 181–82, 184n, 200, 204n, 254, 285, 422

Pazos, Felipe, 41n, 51, 52n, 70n, 82n

Peeters, Theo, 343n

Personal habits, assumption of stable money and, 35

Personal planning, inflation and, 39–40

Pesek, Boris P., 111n, 114, 130

Phelps, Edmund, 173n, 241n, 384n

Phillips, A. W. H., 175
Phillips, C. A., 152n
Phillips curve, 31, 56, 175
Pierce, Charles, 244
Pierce, David G., 128n
Pigou, A. C., 9n, 282, 287, 288
Pigou effect, 9–12, 39, 265–66
Plan for Reconstruction (Hutt), 209
Poincaré, Raymond, 44
Politics of inflation, 44–46
Popkin, Joel, 62–63
Popper, Karl R., 247n
Porter, Richard, 185, 189n
Portfolio-balancing demand for actual money, 94–95
Portfolio-transactions demand for actual money, 95
Poverty, 9
Price changes, 28
Price controls: arguments for and against, 328–31; imposition of, 73–75, 80–81, 314–15, 327–28; removal of, 72–73
Price expectations, 8
Price indexing, 369, 389–91; constant unit with, 146–47, 341–51, 369; in modified compensated dollar system, 389–91 (*see also* Real-GNP dollar); parasitism and, 157–58; problem of lags, 341–42
Price levels: analogy between price trends and, 52–58, 66; Austrian theory of the business cycle and, 229–30; in BFH system, 422–23; depression and, 10–11; in extreme inflation, 70; gradualism vs. quick fix approach to stabilization of, 76–84; imported inflation and, 40, 42–43; inflation and transmission of information by, 36–37; inflationary recession of 1969–70 and, 312–15; injection effects and (*see* Injection effects); interplay between individual and collective viewpoints and, 158–60; macroeconomic disequilibrium and, 394; in mild inflation, 70; momentum of increases and inflation, 43, 45, 58–69, 159–60; money supply increases and, 173–78; rational expectations/equilibrium always theory, 237–39, 241–42; real-GNP dollar and, 399; stickiness (*see* Price stickiness); unanticipated price inflation (UPI) theory, unemployment and, 164–69; wartime inflation and, 49–51
Price-setting practices, 35, 51, 54, 67, 70, 160, 161, 225–27, 394
Price stickiness: abolition of, consequences of, 409–10; analogy between levels and trends of prices and, 52–53; cash-balance interpretation of depression and, 7, 9–11, 17; defined, 408; early monetarist recognition of, 222–24; excess demand for money and, 102–4; interplay between individual and collective viewpoints and, 159–60; Keynes and, 248, 282–83, 409; logic of, 224–29, 408–9; rational-expectations theory and, 299–300; reconciliation with rational behavior, 169–73
Prinsep, C. R., 146n
Private money, 154–55, 352–58
Property rights, public-good aspects of, 161
Public Choice school, 285
Public-good aspects: of money, 154–55; of pricing, 161; of property rights, 161

"Quick Refresher Course in Macroeconomics" (Mankiw), 283

Rabin, Alan A., 150n, 217n, 238n, 407n

Radcliffe Committee Report of 1959, 87, 141n

Radford, R. A., 222n

Rational-expectations theory, 141, 156, 168, 235–50, 278, 297, 299–300

Rawls, John, 276

Real-bills doctrine, 47–48, 144–45, 308

Real-business-cycle theories, 296–97

Real estate investment, 38

Real-GNP dollar, 393–405; bank runs as pricing problem, 395–98; macroeconomic disequilibrium and, 394; monetary misalignment and, 395; parallels with other proposals, 398–400; redemption medium quantity, freezing of, 400–404; transition to, 404–5

Real vs. nominal money supply, 46–47

Recessions, 19, 20

Reflux, law of the, 147–48

Reserves, 26, 30; argument for bank distinctiveness and requirements for, 123–26; bank runs and, 395; bank vs. nonbank drains on, 115–17; excess, of banks, 119–20; free, 308–9; supply-and-demand doctrine of cash-balance determination and, 183–87

Reserves-targeting regime, 186–88

Reverse fallacies of composition, 145–47

Reynolds, Alan, 256

Riboud, Jacques, 343–44

Ricardo, David, 286, 296

Rinfret, Pierre, 323–24

Ritter, Lawrence S., 101–2

Rittershausen, Heinrich, 345n, 351n, 365

Roberston, Sir Dennis, 204n, 287

Rogers, James Harvey, 12n

Romer, David, 283–85

Roosa, Robert V., 321n

Röpke, Wilhelm, 17

Rothbard, Murray N., 256

Russia, 221–22

Salerno, Joseph T., 363n

Salin, Pascal, 44n, 343n

Samuelson, Paul, 258n

Santomero, Anthony M., 164n, 165n

Sargent, Thomas J., 246

Saving, Thomas R., 111n, 114–15, 130, 354n

Savings and loan associations, 90–92, 97, 110, 116–17

Say, Jean-Baptiste, 146n

Say's law, 4–6, 290

Scadding, John L., 179n, 193–95

Schacht, Dr., 44

Schelling, Thomas C., 55n, 172n

Schultz, Charles L., 228n, 239, 248, 284

Schumpeter, Joseph A., 124n, 135, 379, 422

Schwartz, Anna J., 19, 20, 125n, 221, 286, 421n

Scrope, G. Poulett, 223, 286, 342n

Seater, John J., 164n, 165n

Second Bank of the United States, 20

Seipel, Monsignor, 44

Selgin, George, 259, 274

Sennholz, Mary, 137n

Services, deficient demand for, 108

Shaw, David M., 128n

Shaw, Edward S., 90n, 93n, 94, 258n, 259n, 268, 415

Sheffrin, Steven M., 169n, 288, 409n

Shelby, Donald, 95n

Shiller, Robert J., 302

Shipov, A., 25n, 221, 222n

Shiskin, Julius, 24

Siegel, Barry N., 383n

Silk, Leonard, 25n, 323
Simler, N. J., 142n
Simons, Henry, 298n
Simpson, Thomas, 384
Smith, Paul F., 119n, 149n
Smithsonian Agreement of 1971, 331, 332, 334
Sociological explanations of inflation, 45
Solow, Robert, 236
Spain, 222
Spitäller, Erich, 164n
Sprinkel, Beryl W., 21n, 24
Stable unit of account, 277–79, 340–61; government money proposal, 340–42; interplay between individual and collective viewpoints and, 154–58; private money proposal, 154–55, 352–58; separate but actual units proposal, 351–52; separation of functions proposal, 342–51; single stable unit distinct from the medium of exchange proposal (see BFH system)
Stagflation, 58–60, 159–60, 219, 411
Stein, Jerome L., 63n
Stevens, Neil A., 325n
Stickiness of value of money. See Price stickiness
Stiglitz, Joseph E., 219, 228n, 246n, 284, 296–301
Stock-market investment, 38
Streissler, Erich, 45
Strongin, Steven, 407n
Structural unemployment, 15
Struthers, Alan, Jr., 141n
Sturc, Ernest, 81
Summers, L. H., 288, 409n
Supply-and-demand doctrine of money-stock determination, criticism of, 114–15, 179–95; Federal Reserve Bank of San Francisco Money Market model, 193–95; money and credit

confused, 182–84, 192–93; money-credit identity in Federal Reserve formulation of monetary policy, 185–89; money's distinctiveness as medium of exchange, 190–92; perverse changes in quantity of money under interest-rate targeting, 181–82
Supply of money. See Money supply
Suppression ("suppressed inflation"), 10
Sweden, 270
Switzerland, 72

Taxes: assumption of stable money and, 35; inflation and, 41, 45
Taylor, John B., 173n
Terbough, George, 298n
Theory of Justice, A (Rawls), 276
Thomas, Brinley, 270
Thompson, Fred A., 113n
Thorn, R. S., 259n
Thornton, Daniel L., 180n
Thornton, Henry, 47, 48n, 56, 144, 222, 286, 296
Thygesen, Niels, 343n
Timberlake, Richard H., Jr., 87n, 98n, 321n
Tobin, James, 27n, 30n, 90–91, 94, 96n, 111n, 113, 116–17, 119, 122n, 123n, 125, 143n, 148, 155, 180n, 237, 248, 264, 267, 282, 297, 299, 366–67, 378
Tooke, Thomas, 147
Torrens, Robert, 296
Torto, Raymond G., 183, 184n, 189
Tract on Monetary Reform (Keynes), 200
Transactions costs, 109–10
Tucker, Donald P., 202
Tullock, Gordon, 354n
Turkey, 81

Unanticipated price inflation (UPI) theory, 164–69

Unemployment, 8–9, 15–16, 31; inflation and, 50, 56–57, 62–63; Keynesian theory and, 200–201; macroeconomic disequilibrium and, 394; at natural rate, money supply increase and, 173–78; New Economic Policy (NEP) of 1971 and, 327–28; price controls and, 328–30; unanticipated price inflation and, 164–69

Union power, 61

Unit of account: fiat, 277, 337–40, 365, 366, 385, 411; stable (see Stable unit of account)

Vietnam War, 50, 310, 312

Viewpoints in monetary theory, 137–62; central points of macroeconomics and, 158–60; confusions of, 140–51; fallacies of composition, 140–45; illuminating interplay between, 151–58; individual-experiments and market-experiments, 139–40; need for distinction between, 137–38; other applications of distinctions between, 161–62; reverse fallacies of composition, 145–47

Viner, Jacob, 286, 296

Vining, Rutledge, 277n

Wage controls: arguments for and against, 328–31; imposition of, 73–75, 81, 314–15, 327–28; removal of, 72–73

Wage levels: analogy between wage trends and, 52–57, 66; depression and, 10–11; extreme inflation and, 70; interplay between individual and collective viewpoints and, 158–60; macroeconomic disequilibrium and, 394; in mild inflation, 35–36, 70; momentum of

increases and inflation, 43, 45, 58–69, 159–60; money supply increases and, 173–78; real-GNP dollar and, 399; stickiness (see Price stickiness); unanticipated price inflation (UPI) theory and, 164–68

Wage-setting practices, 35, 51, 54, 63, 67, 70, 160, 225–27, 394

Wainhouse, Charles, 233–34, 255

Wallace, Neil, 142n, 155n, 156n, 348n

Waller, James M., 87n

Wallich, Henry C., 180n

Walters, A. A., 327n

Warburton, Clark, xiv, 19–20, 25n, 68n, 199, 211, 215, 217, 218, 221, 285, 286, 298n, 411

Wartime inflation, 49–51

Weintraub, Robert, 383

Wenninger, John, 384

Wernette, John Philip, 199

"What Is New-Keynesian Economics?" (Gordon), 283

White, Lawrence H., 179n, 363n, 387n, 419n

Who-goes-first problem, 225, 228

"Why Are Prices Sticky?" (Blinder), 302

Wicksell, Knut, 94, 120, 218n, 256n, 276, 408n

Widespread indexing, 341–51, 369

Willes, Mark, 236, 242, 244

Williams, Aneurin, 342n, 358n

Wilson, James, 147

Wink, Robin, 302

Wolman, William, 326n

Wood, John H., 114n, 118n

Woolsey, William Warren, 411

World War II, 50, 307

Yellen, Janet, 409

Zanker, Alfred, 83–84

The typeface used for this book is New Baskerville, which is based on the types of English type founder and printer John Baskerville (1706–75). Baskerville is the quintessential "transitional" face: it retains the bracketed and obliqued serifs of "old-style" faces such as Caslon and Garamond, but in its increased lowercase height, lighter color, and enhanced contrast between thick and thin strokes, it presages "modern" faces.

This book is printed on paper that is acid-free and meets the requirements of the American National Standard for Permanence of Paper for Printed Library Materials, Z39.84-1984. ∞

Book design by Martin Lubin, New York, New York

Typesetting by Alexander Graphics, Inc., Indianapolis, Indiana

Printed and bound by Edwards Brothers, Inc., Ann Arbor, Michigan